The Climb

The Climb

CHRIS FROOME

with David Walsh

VIKING
an imprint of
PENGUIN BOOKS

VIKING

Published by the Penguin Group

Penguin Books Ltd, 80 Strand, London WC2R ORL, England

Penguin Group (USA) Inc., 375 Hudson Street, New York, New York 10014, USA

Penguin Group (Canada), 90 Eglinton Avenue East, Suite 700, Toronto, Ontario, Canada M4P 2Y3
(a division of Pearson Penguin Canada Inc.)

Penguin Ireland, 25 St Stephen's Green, Dublin 2, Ireland (a division of Penguin Books Ltd)

Penguin Group (Australia), 707 Collins Street, Melbourne, Victoria 3008, Australia
(a division of Pearson Australia Group Pty Ltd)

Penguin Books India Pvt Ltd, 11 Community Centre, Panchsheel Park, New Delhi – 110 017, India

Penguin Group (NZ), 67 Apollo Drive, Rosedale, Auckland 0632, New Zealand
(a division of Pearson New Zealand Ltd)

Penguin Books (South Africa) (Pty) Ltd, Block D, Rosebank Office Park,
181 Jan Smuts Avenue, Parktown North, Gauteng 2193, South Africa

Penguin Books Ltd, Registered Offices: 80 Strand, London WC2R ORL, England

www.penguin.com

First published 2014
001

Copyright © Chris Froome, 2014

Set in 12/14.75pt Bembo Book MT Std
Typeset by Jouve (UK), Milton Keynes
Printed in Great Britain by Clays Ltd, St Ives plc

A CIP catalogue record for this book is available from the British Library

HARDBACK ISBN: 978-0-241-00418-0
TRADE PAPERBACK ISBN: 978-0-241-00419-7

www.greenpenguin.co.uk

MIX
Paper from
responsible sources
FSC® C018179

Penguin Books is committed to a sustainable
future for our business, our readers and our planet.
This book is made from Forest Stewardship
Council™ certified paper.

'After climbing a great hill, one only finds that there are many more hills to climb.'

Nelson Mandela

To my teammates for their hard work and dedication, and for helping me achieve my dreams, and to Mum and Michelle for the endless supply of motivation.

Contents

PART ONE
Africa

We have come out of Mai-a-Ihii, leaving his tin house behind us. We have come down the Dagoretti road inhaling the blood scent from the market and from its four death-house abattoirs. I hold my breath as we pass a heap of rotting discarded carcasses. Sometimes in Dagoretti the blood runs down the sides of the road and into the drains. Today we are for the hills and the open road and we don't care.

We have skirted the Kibiku Forest, pedalled a right on to the Ngong road and down past the sad little Ngong Stadium, where the only facility is the grass that the cattle graze on. We have sped past the Kenya Power and Lighting Distribution Centre, which keeps us buying candles for the ambushes of darkness that are sprung on us by the power company. We have raced down to the Forest Line road and cut right past Ngong town, dodging the stray goat crossing the road and the colourfully painted *matatus* that grind to a halt at a moment's notice to collect or drop off their passengers. The chaos passes, and we're on to the open road and into the Ngong Hills.

One last ride before I die?

It will be in these hills, for sure. The canopy of blue sky barely above me, the world transforming itself from urban grime to rural safari below me. You can lift your hands up and away from your handlebar grips and stretch your arms skyward in triumph like a stage winner. Your hands will be breaking through the floor of heaven. One last ride before I die? Take me here.

He is Kikuyu and I am chasing him. As always. The land of the Kikuyu people runs out at an invisible seam and this is now Masai country. The Masai named the Ngong Hills. A giant was stumbling, as their legend would have it, from Kilimanjaro with his head in the clouds. He fell heavily and left the indent of his four knuckles in the earth. The Ngong Hills. These four summits. We are riding down the spine of them now, he and I, chasing each other over the giant's knuckles. I am sixteen. My head is never anywhere else but in the clouds. I dream of the great races. But first, I must catch him.

Twenty kilometres we race along this brown, arid, corrugated spine. The best views, where you can see the road snaking down for miles ahead of you, come at Point Lamwia where Karen Blixen, the famous author of *Out of Africa*, buried her lover Denys Finch Hatton. Lucky man. What a place to settle in for eternity. Salute. Then we are heading down into the Great Rift Valley.

For a while in the hills I thought I might get one over on him. I am mad for the climbs. He let me spin away once or twice but always he reeled me in.

Down. Down. The Magadi road has looped out of the green suburbs of Langata from near my old school, the Banda, but coming from Mai-a-Ihii we only join it down here past the bustling, street-side markets of Kiserian. We are on our plunge down into the Rift Valley. Lower and lower. Faster and faster. Past the busy town of Ongata Rongai. Onwards. The road ribbons and twists around the countryside, long straight stretches and big loops which will take us from two thousand metres and set us down on the Rift Valley plains at six hundred metres.

Downhill. No pain. Our calves will complain on the way home but, right now, this is fun. The addict's rush. We are the happy slaves of our own rhythm. We exist in our cadence.

We might see anything here now that the city is behind us. It's clear that we are in Masai territory. Passing through the village of Oltepesi, we stand out like a sore thumb among the local people wearing the traditional red *shúkà*. We ride on.

The road is nature's audition reel. Look! Waterbuck. If we're lucky we might see a leopard. Dik-diks, the small antelope found in these parts, bound out of sight into the thorny undergrowth. Warthogs and baboons. Eland, monochrome zebras and elegant giraffes.

People still claim to see the odd lion in this area. Not today. Apart from the dreadlocked one in front of me. Leone Nero they called him in Italy. Black Lion. I am chasing the Black Lion.

We pass ostriches with long legs no more muscular than my own.

If I point that out to Leone Nero and the boys they won't let me live it down. It's true though.

We are only cutting through this world, he and I. This is no Rift Valley tourist cruise. We are racers. I am chasing him. He is my prey. He is cackling like a hyena because he knows I will never catch him. I don't have it in my haunches. He has thousands of miles of roads and hills packed in there, all compressed into clenched muscle. Teasing me with his back wheel. Now you see it, *kijana*, now you don't.

I can't win, but he stays close enough to taunt me.

Down we go. It becomes stiller and it becomes hotter. The further into this dimple in the earth's skin we ride, the more it is like a furnace.

We will rest and laugh together when we get to the end. The end is the moonscape of Magadi with its salt-crusted shores and boiling soda lakes. There will be candy cotton pink clouds of startled flamingos. And my mother following an hour or two behind in the car will bring food to restore and recharge us before we turn back for home.

I know him. He will say, 'Put your bike into your mum's car and go with her. The long climb home is not for you, *kijana*.'

He knows me. Never.

We race on. There are two dangers: homicidal drivers and potholes. This is Africa. Do we worry? Never.

In fact, I have taken my helmet off. I shouldn't but the heat is my alibi. The helmet is tied round my handlebars, clipped on. He is not even dressed to race. He has a T-shirt and gym shorts on. And a pair of sneakers. I am in full bloody racing gear. He loves that.

People in cars stick their heads out of the windows. *Look at that skinny cyclist kid trying to catch up with that Rastafarian on a bike! Aw, God help him! Look!*

I'm thinking that I didn't pop him on the Ngong climbs but maybe I put some ache into his old legs. If I surprised him could I get away from him on the long downhill?

I make my moves and each time he responds. I get close enough so that he drafts me but when I press the gas he has already pulled away.

We hit a pitted stretch of road. Potholes and fissures and lumps. We hit it fast. If one slows then the other wins. We push hard. Then *pop!*, my helmet unclips as I hit one of the little speed bumps that wear and tear has made for the battered Magadi road. The helmet falls a few inches and catches my front wheel, sending it jolting sideways, towards him.

He rides straight over it. The helmet jams into his front wheel. The front wheel stops dead and the back wheel buck-jumps from the road. He says goodbye to his bike. He is launched down the road at over sixty kilometres per hour, flying like a missile with dreadlocks.

How far? He says fifty metres. I'm not so sure. That might have brought him into Tanzanian airspace. The flying isn't the thing anyway. The landing is the issue here on the downward grooves of the Magadi road.

He lands first on his elbows and his knees. The road seizes huge patches of his skin from the joints and from the front of his body. There is blood everywhere. His knees alone are a horror show. They look like the grafted-on asses of two young baboons.

I am scared and I feel guilty. Stupid. Sick. Any water I have left in my bottles I use to try to clean his wounds. I might as well try damming Lake Magadi with sticking plasters. He is calm but we are both sweating in the dead heat and I know that his sweat is running freely into his raw, vivid wounds.

We sit there on the side of the road for ten, twenty minutes. I apologize. He waves it away. Every time, he waves it away.

Maybe Mum will drive past and save us. Let it be.

We sit there and finally he stands up gingerly and gets back on his bike. A wounded John Wayne climbing back on to his horse.

This is too much.

'Stop. I can carry you on my bike. I can hold you.'

His laugh scolds.

'What are you now? An acrobat? Let's ride.'

Hours later Mum finds us in Magadi. Her son, the wading bird, and his mentor, the wounded lion.

She wants to drive us back to Nairobi straight away. He negotiates a compromise. We go to the hospital in Magadi. The soda lakes have given birth to a company town and the town has a hospital where they mummify him in bandages. We 'camp' for the night near the lake in a basic hotel.

In the morning he won't get into the car, so he and I saddle up. I have a hangover of such guilt that I swear I can actually feel some of his pain.

He rides hard though, the bandaged bastard. Hard up the long, long climb to Kikuyu and home. Hard enough to show me what it takes. Hard enough for me to forget the guilt and want to beat him again. He takes me on the hills. We do some sprints. He takes me on them too. He schools me. For hours he schools me.

We hit Mai-a-Ihii. We lift our bikes into his two-roomed tin hut on a corridor of two-roomed tin huts.

I should go home but he knows that I don't want to.

We sit and talk into the night about old races and racers.

'Tomorrow again?' David Kinjah says to me before he sleeps.

'Okay! Sure.'

Yes.

My name is Chris Froome. I am a professional cyclist. Before that I was a skinny *kijana* with big dreams.

Boyhood happened to me in a house just outside Nairobi, twenty kilometres south-west of the city, in a genteel suburb called Karen. The most famous resident Karen ever had was Karen Blixen and, although there are minor protestations that the suburb was named after a different Karen entirely, most people believe the place was named after the Danish woman who married her cousin, coming to Kenya to run a coffee plantation.

The homes around us were stately and elegant and secluded by means of long driveways and secure gates. In *Out of Africa*, Karen Blixen described the very land I grew up on as 'Africa distilled up through six thousand feet, like the strong and refined essence of a continent'. She was right about the land, but what was built on it, and those who live in the town, are very un-African.

Karen was once predominantly British but in the last couple of decades many Americans, Germans and Japanese have come to live there too. A few outliers from the emerging black middle class live in the town, but the place is primarily a colony of wealth, an enclave shielded from the sprawling city and its epic slums.

My earliest memories are from our big house in Karen called Windy Ridge. We had a pleasant, decent-sized home, and I had my own bedroom, as did my two brothers, Jonathan and Jeremy, who are seven and nine years older than me respectively. When they were fourteen my brothers were sent off to England to attend Rugby School. We were relatively well off, at least when I was young.

My mother, Jane Flatt, was born in Kenya in 1956 and raised in the highlands of Limuru. Her parents, my grandparents, Patrick and Patricia, had followed a similar path to Karen Blixen. They came here from Tetbury, England, early in the last century, drawn to the coffee plantations like filings to a magnet.

He was an archetypal character, my grandfather. The sort of grandfather you might see in films or read about in books. He won the war, or so he would have us believe. He had served in World War Two, and in Kenya he had fought for the British against the Mau Mau, a militant group made up of Kikuyu rebels.

He passed down funny stories that weren't really meant for kids. They were contraband, slipped to us from the adult world, and we loved them all the more for it. My favourite tale was about how Grandfather ended up eating his donkey in the jungle because he got so hungry. Some comrades found him there in the middle of nowhere. They were starving too and they all ended up tucking into the donkey. This upset Grandfather because his donkey had been his companion through the whole war. I was never quite sure what rank he held or what role he had played during that time, travelling with a donkey – probably not espionage.

Grandfather was an aficionado of hunting and fishing. He taught us both of these but duck hunting was his main bag. God knows what he was shooting with back then when he scoured the forests of Kenya with his donkey but it had left him deaf. He had a hearing aid and, poor man, my brothers and I (mainly my brothers, as I was timid) would have some fun at his expense. We would sit at the dinner table silently mouthing words to each other, making a great play of laughing heartily. Grandfather, excluded and frustrated by his impairment, would be frantically trying to tune in his hearing aid. It would be whistling with feedback as he tried to adjust it. Once he had turned it all the way up we would start talking at the top of our voices.

He would recoil as if our words were sudden gunfire.

'Stop shouting. No need for shouting.'

Growing up in Karen, we didn't have the usual activities or even the usual range of family pets. When I was six years old I remember crossing by my brother's snake enclosure, which was basically a waist-high pit covered with chicken wire, and I noticed that the back legs of my favourite pet bunny rabbit were hanging from the mouth of Jeremy's twelve-foot python. I had quite a few rabbits, but this was the one I had tamed, the one I could pick up and carry around with me. He was close to being my best friend. I would have known his hind legs anywhere but this was the last place I expected to see them. In fact, it was the last place that I would see them. Like most of our pets, he had a Swahili name but now he was just 'Lunch'. There he was, about to be digested. I knew he couldn't have found his own way into the snake pit. He must have been served up by my brother.

I got so angry with Jeremy that I picked up a wooden plank and started battering the snake enclosure. I managed to puncture holes in the chicken wire covering the cage. I wasn't a bad kid but I could throw a good tantrum if I didn't get my way or if somebody crossed me. Or if my favourite rabbit was used as snake fodder.

My brothers always did their best to knock that out of me. For my own good, of course – they were only ever cruel to be kind. They'd both give me a hard time in generous measures. We had some dog kennels, and when the dogs came into heat they would have to be put into cages to keep them away from each other. We also had a huge male turkey which my brothers would terrorize if I wasn't around to provide them with some fun. And then one day they found a way to combine the dog cages, the turkey and me into a new, ground-breaking form of entertainment.

We had air rifles and the boys would shoot at the turkey with the pellets that I fed my rabbits with. The pellets would fit comfortably into the barrel of an air rifle. So they'd sting the turkey with the pellets and make him angrier and angrier. One day that didn't provide enough amusement so Jeremy and Jono had to improvise. When the turkey was sufficiently demented with rage they caught him and put him into one of the dog cages. Then they caught me and put me in the dog cage with the lunatic turkey.

The ceilings were closed in and the cage door had a bolt that they jammed with a stick. The turkey and I were the same height, or maybe I was a little bigger, but that turkey could punch above its weight. I remember being absolutely petrified because he was so aggressive. He ducked his head down and came charging at me, his feathers puffed out in anger. I ended up huddled in the corner of the dog kennel with the turkey jumping and grabbing at me with its feet, whacking me with its wings and pecking at me all at the same time.

This was so funny for my brothers that they had to try it again and again. It was hysterical and they loved it. Only when I was in absolute floods of tears would they open the cage up and let me out. My sparring sessions with the turkey were usually two or three minutes long. Time enough for both of us. Victory inevitably fell to the feathered one in the red corner. Luckily my brothers never thought to feed me to the python for a laugh.

The turkey lived to be the fall guy in my own entertainment when Jeremy and Jono had gone back to school. The turkey stopped growing, while his partner from the dog cage didn't. No. I finally got big enough to traumatize the turkey myself. I would sneak up on him – *boo!* – then let him chase me. Repeat. Repeat again. Tease the turkey, let him chase, on and on. I thought that was a great game. Payback at last!

My father, Clive (or, as we all call him, Noz), grew up in England. He had been a good hockey player and had played internationally at Under-19 level but left it all to build a new life in Kenya. Noz started in the tourism trade, and soon established a successful company, Flamingo Tours, which specialized in beach holidays and safaris in Kenya, bringing people to the Masai Mara and to the perfect beaches and blue waters of the Kenyan coastline. Noz would organize the entire trip for holidaymakers, from start to finish.

Aside from the company and the house, we had some land: maybe ten acres, two or three paddocks and a very generous garden with a tennis court. As well as our menagerie of pets, we had Jersey cows. My mother ran a bit of a dairy on the property so we had a barn where all the feed would be kept for the cows, a milking area and stables. We had two *ayahs* (nannies), an *askari* (a night watchman) and a couple of *shamba* boys (gardeners) who helped out with the milking of the cows and the feeding of the livestock that we had on the property.

The Ngong racecourse is a feature of life in Karen and Noz kept racehorses, two at a time when I was quite young. The horses are a vanished memory as I was only three or four years old when they left, but the cows stayed and we had a bull too (no tease and chase with him). There were ducks, geese and chickens, and that turkey. We were comfortably well off, but our lives still had the wildness of Africa in them. Kenya was a magical place to grow up. Then suddenly it all ended.

I was five or six years old when my parents' marriage hit a reef and at the same time Noz lost control of the company.

The details are vague to me. Noz blamed the business setback on a very large loan that someone had taken out in the company's name without his knowledge. Money had been sifted away from the Flamingo accounts. Noz thought that it was being taken for an overseas branch but the money had just disappeared. It's blurry. My parents were divorcing at the same time, but the bank showed no sympathy when it came after the family to pay back the loan.

First they eyed up the house and the cars, and then came the bailiffs. They took furniture and anything they could from the house.

I have quite a vivid memory from that time. I had a little black bike that I would ride around our place and I was practically welded on to it. All day, every day, I would ride up and down our driveway and around our garden, pedalling backwards to apply the brake. There was a narrow dirt road that led to our drive, and I would be there raising dust until my mother summoned me for whatever meal was next. My brothers had gone off to school in England. Noz had already left by this time and moved in with his new girlfriend, Jenny, whom he later married. I was left to my own devices.

On this particular day I remember the gates being locked.

It was as if Mum knew what was coming. I don't know if it was the bailiffs or merely that Noz wanted to collect his possessions after the divorce, but I know that we had chained the gates because some people were coming to take our belongings from the house. It was a weekend and I was supposed to be going to a friend's birthday party up the road.

Outside the locked gates there was a big lorry, and people ready to do the lifting and shifting. My mother refused to let them in. There was a stand-off. I knew better than to whine about the birthday party. I recognized the man overseeing the operation as someone from Noz's company. I was the messenger boy in the negotiations, riding up and down on my bike, ferrying between the gate and my mum, relaying news of what was going on.

'Listen, open up,' said the man. 'Tell your mum we need to come in.'

I conveyed the message and my mum was very upset. She was crying. She threatened to call the police to intervene. I remember cycling down to the gate and saying gravely to the man, 'She's calling the police.'

'Okay,' he said finally, 'tell your mother that if she doesn't open up we're going to pull the gate off.'

And that's what they did. They attached strong ropes and big chains on to our gates and ripped them off their hinges.

My mother was a remarkable woman. As soon as they breached the broken gates she said to me, 'Right, don't worry about it. Get in the car.'

And we left. She took me to the party I'd been invited to.

'Don't worry about that,' she said again as we drove. 'We are fine. It's only "stuff". We'll go home and we'll sort it out. I'll sort it out.'

With Noz gone, we were on our own. Just Mum and me. Jeremy and Jono both continued with their schooling in England. When things started getting difficult in terms of finance, other members of the family stepped in to help with their education. By then Jonathan had finished at Rugby and was at university. Naturally, they have different memories of those times.

My immediate family may have been reduced to just me and my mum but, growing up, I was always really close to the *ayahs*. *Ayah* is a word used in Kenya for babysitter or nanny, and that's what we called them. We had two *ayahs*, Anna and Agnes. They were second mothers to me and it was Anna and Agnes who taught me to speak Swahili. They were both Wakambas, a large Kenyan tribe. They taught me to speak certain Wakamba words, but mainly we spoke Swahili.

Anna had a daughter called Grace. Grace was three years younger than me and I remember the two of us would often play after school. I'd be climbing trees, trying to set up a rope, slide or swing for us, and we would do all sorts of things together. Poor Grace. I would soon play the same kind of tricks on her that my brothers had on me. It must have been some sort of revenge. I'd terrorize her a bit but we were good friends. I gave her my bike when it was getting too small for me and taught her how to ride.

Apart from Karen, the other affluent area in Nairobi is Langata and I was sent to the Banda School on the Magadi road in Langata. It was a little piece of the British public school system set down in Kenya. The Banda School is set on thirty acres beside the Nairobi National Park. Twenty of those acres are playing fields. We had four rugby pitches, many hockey pitches, squash courts and a six-lane swimming pool. All very English, apart from the odd warthog escaping from the National Park and waddling across the pitches. Banda wasn't an all-white school; it was maybe seventy per cent white. It was quite expensive though and the other kids were all well off.

No matter how much some people might wish it to be otherwise, wealth or colour will never insulate you from the fact that you are surrounded by Africa. I remember one occasion when I was twelve years old in Banda and we were coming back from a school rugby game after playing up at Turi. We would always come back on the six-hour drive via Dagoretti with its abattoir, lines of hanging animal carcasses and bloody roads. We were on a school bus, just a bunch of pupils, one master and a driver. There was trouble in Dagoretti. The road was blocked and there was a riot in progress.

Our bus was trapped and there was traffic behind us and in front. There was nowhere for us to go. We had managed to get right to the front of the queue when the mob surrounded us. Suddenly people were shaking our bus backwards and forwards, an angry crowd rocking and banging the side of the bus.

I am back there. I am sitting in an aisle seat. The crowd doesn't break any windows but they're trying to push in the door, the main door, and our big rugby coach has wedged himself in on the stairs, pushing backwards against the door to stop anyone opening it. Then our driver's door is suddenly flung open. Someone pulls him out. He's a Kenyan guy from the Wakamba tribe, and this could be bad for him. As he is being dragged from the bus he pulls a weapon from underneath his seat. In Kenya we call it a *panga*, a machete kind of thing with a big wooden handle and an even bigger blade on it. One swing and you could do a lot of damage. We never even knew it was there. They pull him out, he instinctively grabs his *panga* and very quickly they let him go again.

He jumps back on the bus, turns round and has this huge grin on his face, really proud of the fact that he's scared them off. We kids, we love that the driver did that. We cheer and applaud and we are on our way.

At Banda I noticed one thing which puzzled me. Everyone seemed to have *ayahs* but hardly any of my friends could speak Swahili as well as I could. I always found that strange. Some of my friends couldn't put together two words of Swahili. I suppose it was a sign of how sheltered life could be in Karen or Langata.

'Wow,' I'd say, 'you've lived all your life here and you don't even speak . . .'

Anna and Agnes could not speak English so it was always natural to talk with them in Swahili. Other people had English-speaking *ayahs*, or ones with a bit of English, but in our house my mum spoke Swahili, as did Noz and my brothers. In my life now people find it unusual that I speak Swahili but growing up it was never a conscious thing, no one ever told me that I had to learn. It just came naturally. When I came home from school, for instance, I'd be straight down to the stables or hanging out with Mutheke, the *shamba* boy, helping with milking a cow or just chatting to him about life. We always spoke Swahili.

Anna and Agnes were always very protective of me when times were difficult, and sharing a language allowed them to speak softly to me sometimes about hard things.

Everything had gone bad very quickly for my parents, both professionally and personally. There were huge debts to be settled with the bank, and the house and our possessions didn't cover it. It is hard to imagine how Flamingo Tours sunk so rapidly. There were, at a guess, over a hundred employees, who were suddenly all out of work. Noz spent a couple of nights in prison. They took him in to ask about the accounts; I think they thought that he might have had the money salted away somewhere. There were no charges but the collapse of the company was big news at the time and affected many people.

Mum and Noz divorced while they were still living under the same roof. It was a tough period. My bedroom was closest to their room and before Noz moved out there were times when I would be woken up in the middle of the night to the sound of my mum yelling at him. I know that Noz would never have hit my mother but they would argue viciously. We had quite a few meals that descended into chaos. I remember a shepherd's pie dish being thrown at Noz once. And wine glasses. Things would flare up and Anna and Agnes would swoop in and take me away, leaving my parents to it.

At the time I didn't really understand much of it. I was angry with my mother because she was the one who did most of the screaming.

They were both having a hard time but, to my eyes, she was the one being emotional. Noz would always stay quiet. He isn't a confrontational man but I think he could stir her up just by saying very little. He wouldn't shout or get worked up and I think that made Mum even angrier.

For a while after they split Noz still lived in Kenya but in a different house. I would go and see him sometimes on weekends, or spend a week with him every now and then. It was always quite uncomfortable. I never really wanted my parents to see each other, and I always asked to be let out of the car a little bit further down the road when I was getting dropped off so that I could walk the rest of the way.

I knew that if they were together there was going to be some kind of confrontation.

For years afterwards I used to get this sick, sick feeling whenever people raised their voices. I can still remember that horrible churning sensation in my stomach any time I heard people shouting.

When I was seven years old Noz moved down to South Africa to start his life again. It must have been hard for him to do that. I know my mother always thought Noz had taken money from the company, but I can't believe that he had. When he moved to South Africa there were a few really tough years for him and my new stepmother, Jenny. He had nothing and had to start all over again. He lived with his mother at first, who had sold her property at an old-age village in order for them to buy a small place there. They started a new conference management business from scratch, running it from home for the first few years.

The day Noz left Kenya, my stepmother and I went to the airport with him. By the time we arrived I had fallen asleep in the back seat. He says that it was the one moment in his life when he actually cried – leaving Kenya, not wanting to wake me up and not knowing when he'd next see me. More than a year passed before we saw each other again.

After Noz left, my mother and I agreed that we wouldn't ever shout, or at least that she wouldn't shout at me if she was angry. If she did raise her voice I always got that memory back in my gut. The agreement was that if she was angry with me she would tell me she was angry with me. She would talk to me and tell me why she felt that way, but she was never allowed to shout at me.

If I am honest, when Noz left I was slightly relieved. This was life and we could get on with it now. There would be no more shouting. It wasn't easy. Mum didn't really have any qualifications and money was scarce. We stayed with my mother's parents for a while in the spare room of their house. We lived out our lives between Karen and Langata, and although most of the time the great yawning slums of Nairobi, places like Kibera, never concerned us, we had our own struggles.

Mum earned some money by house-sitting for people when they were away. Sometimes we would rent a modest cottage in the grounds of a bigger house. One of the places that we stayed in while we were house-sitting had a vast garden but it was completely overgrown. I spent ages with Grace cutting back the grass and making a cycling track through the garden so that we could ride our bikes around.

Mum needed a qualification and she decided to study physiotherapy. She would spend long hours interning at the Kenyatta and Kajiado public hospitals. And when she was home, it felt as though she spent all her free time studying for upcoming exams. I would sit for hours intently colouring in her workbooks, shading all the different muscle groups in different colours.

I learned how to amuse myself. Because of Mum's hours at the hospital I had to be dropped off at school very early each morning. School didn't start until half past seven but I would be there on my own at 6.00 a.m. every day. Mum would always pack me a bacon sandwich or a pot of yoghurt and fruit, and I would sit outside the classroom, on the step, and wait. After a while, the security guards started opening up the classroom earlier for me, so I could go in and sit at a desk and do my homework before school.

Academically, I wasn't great. I loved numbers and maths – they had a logical sequence that I could appreciate and enjoy. But I am dyslexic and a really slow reader. I would have to gaze at each word for a while, desperately hoping to recognize it. I dreaded having to read out in class. I couldn't do it fluidly, it would be, 'and – the – man – went – to – the –'

Because of the dyslexia I went to classes on Saturdays with a special needs teacher. I would try to work through exercises to improve my skills, but even then I found that I would read stuff painstakingly slowly and still not be able to remember a word of what I'd just read. The process of concentrating so hard used up all the available space in my brain. English and history, or anything that required a lot of reading, was difficult and I would struggle with the time limit in exams or class to read everything through.

My concentration span wasn't great either. I was a dedicated daydreamer. I would always be off in the clouds, thinking of whatever hobby I was fanatical about at the time. Butterflies were an early obsession. There was a famous butterfly collector not far down the road from me, a man called Steve Collins, who founded the Nairobi Butterfly Centre in Kenya. He got me into butterflies and I used to go along to his place and learn all that I could.

I used to love the detail of it. And the ritual. I would go off and catch a butterfly, and once it was dead and stiff, I would inject it with hot water to soften it again. Next, I would display it carefully on a board, knowing how to spread the wings properly and pin it securely. I would spend a lot of my time chasing butterflies and trying to find different varieties from all over Kenya whenever we travelled anywhere. If Mum and I took a trip I would take the net with me, down to the coast or to the Mara, wherever we were going.

I really enjoyed collecting, and I got to know most of the different names, the Latin ones, for the butterflies. The most rare and hardest to catch were the different types of Charaxinae, which I would lure into traps using rotting banana and mosquito netting. It was something I was passionate about. I've found that every time I go through a phase with a hobby or something I enjoy doing, that's all I want to do for a while. I get completely obsessed with things. That's how cycling would be for me. Still is. I'm lucky to have been able to turn an obsession into a career.

The butterflies lasted quite a while though, a couple of years at least. Cycling had always been part of life too and I had always had a bicycle, as far as I can remember. No matter where we moved, all those different houses with Mum, I would always get to know the maze of back roads and footpaths. Every single one. When we moved to a different house I was the pathfinder. It was an adventure for me to go out and explore the byways, learning all the back routes. I knew quickly how to get to places faster and which path was the most direct, or which road went where. These days I get lost sometimes on training rides – I've lost that gift.

I had the same little bike for a long time until I finally outgrew it. I then went through a stage of riding my mother's bicycle. I was the coolest kid in Nairobi. It was a big shopping bicycle with baskets on the front and back. I would ride it around, and although it was old-fashioned, the bike gave me my first taste of making a living from cycling when I went through a phase of being a kid entrepreneur. We were still living at Windy Ridge at the time, where we had a huge avocado tree that grew right on top of our barn. It was not one tree really, but two or three avocado trees that all came together in the one spot. I spent hours climbing up and gathering the avocados that were ripe. I would collect baskets full of them.

I couldn't stand avocados at the time. I would put them into the basket on the back of the bike and cycle up and down the streets at our end of Karen. I would ride up to people and ask them if they wanted to buy them. They were five shillings (35p) each or thereabouts – my pricing structure was fluid. Sometimes I would take my stock down to a small kiosk owner who sold the basics. It was just one guy in a wooden construction on the side of the road selling sweets, bread, milk and other staples. I would go to him and swap the avocados for sweets, or have him take the avocados on consignment for me. Some days when sales were good, and I was able to get a few notes together, I'd sneak them into my mum's purse.

My two brothers are accountants and as a kid I felt myself slipping towards that abyss. With Noz gone, I was often more conscious of our financial situation than a child should have been. There was a school car-pool and a few of the parents would share lift duties as the school was twenty minutes or more away, depending on traffic. On Fridays, the gang of us in the car would be allowed to stop for ice creams on the way home. If it ever fell on my mother's day to pick us up from school I would fret that she wouldn't be able to buy the ice creams and the other kids would find out that we were struggling. I really worried about that. I remember going into the shop with my friends and picking up the locally made ice cream because the fancy imported ice creams were six or seven times more expensive.

I would grab the local ones and offer them. 'Here we go, guys!'

And, being kids, they would all look at me and keep fishing in the fridge for the more expensive ones. I was in knots of dread. Mum always came up with the money but I can still feel the tension when I think of those afternoons when ice-cream time fell on my mother's turn to do the car run.

It's a quaint thing to say, but in Karen we made our own fun. There were good times, and my memories of those are still light and clear.

On a weekend, as soon as we had time to ourselves, one of my mother's favourite things was to go down to the Rift Valley. We would point the car south for forty-five minutes or an hour of driving away from Nairobi, open the door and step into another world. The Rift Valley is Masai land. The Masai are nomads, cattle drovers, but you can see how they worship this strange, arid, rocky terrain. It has an almost desert stillness, watched over by the extinct volcano Longonot.

When we got there we would take a dirt road off into the hills and the bush. Mimosa trees grew beside little rivers and the more we climbed and wandered, the more interesting the landscape around us became.

Mum loved the bush and the animals concealed there, the different sounds and the many different trees. As soon as I had sunburn, for instance, she would cover me in aloe, from the thick fleshy leaves of the little plants which thrive in arid places with low rainfall. She would break the leaves off and run the edges over my skin. Another discovery she showed me was the toothbrush tree, which has all sorts of beneficial properties and which people used for centuries as a natural toothbrush. The elephant pepper, whose fruit sticks upward out of the ground like so many red elephant trunks, was also a great find. I would play practical jokes on people that didn't know what it was, convincing them to chew it and laughing at the reaction as their mouth began to burn. Mum never tired of teaching me about the bush. She loved the nature of that place.

We would abandon the car and walk and walk and walk, often following tiny animal footprints and tracks. Finally we would find somewhere to stop and light a fire. We brought meat with us to cook on the fire and we would sit and eat and talk.

The bike became a part of it too. The road from Nairobi stretches out towards the Rift Valley and on down, down, to the great saline drink that is Lake Magadi, with its flamingos and its crust of salt, which in some places is thirty or forty metres thick.

It's a relatively quiet road, populated with big hills that roll all the way down to Magadi which rests at sea level. A descent of maybe 1,800 metres. Mum would put my bike in the back of the car and once we were out of the sprawl of Nairobi, leaving behind the traffic and the chaos, I would get on my bike and cycle down the long forever hill.

I loved it. The whirr of the wheels. The jolts of the road shooting up through the bike frame and through my body. The warm Kenyan air in my face and the road slipping under me as I chased the car through Masai country. Straight roads and steep drops. I'd pedal hard and get up to frightening speeds.

Those days, those places, those people, live with me always. Geography, maybe, is destiny.

3

Bikes were freedom. By the time I was twelve years old, I would often travel from Nairobi, where I lived with my mother, to South Africa, to see Noz, and on one visit I bought myself a mountain bike. It was bog standard really and came from a supermarket, but it had gears. I had never had a bike with gears before. I brought the bike back home with me to Kenya.

I loved that bike. I loved doing tricks and jumping with it, getting air under myself and my wheels. However, it wasn't long before all the jumping and all the landing caused the front fork to weaken. Kenyan roads are pitted like a face with acne scars and they are rough on bikes at the best of times. Some of the local bikes had springs above the forks to absorb shock. I had nothing but me and the handlebars above my fork, and it had bent all the way out. I had basically ruined the bike. My pride and joy.

I took the stricken bike down to the village market area. I wanted to find the local mechanics that operated on the bikes for the villagers. They could straighten my fork. Now, I was a white kid, the only white face in the village. This was before I had met Kinjah and before I had started racing. I was skinny and geeky, light years from the athlete that I was to become. My kind usually replaced their busted bikes with shiny new ones, from proper bike shops in Karen or Langata. I couldn't afford that so I pushed mine through the teeming market looking for my men. My supermarket bike wasn't too shabby for kids in the village but I was oblivious to anybody coveting my wheels.

I found the guys I was looking for. Mostly they mended punctures and fixed wheels and chains. I was their only white customer, a splintery little ghost with his supermarket bike. Big ears and a bike with gears, a great novelty to them.

We negotiated. They set to work. To their surprise I spent the next few hours just sitting there watching them as they welded pieces of metal on to the bike to reinforce the metal I had bent. I was fascinated. I loved watching them.

After that I would take my bike there as often as I could. I longed to have an excuse to bring it in for surgery. Kimani was the first guy I got to know. I don't think I can claim that I was his friend, but he saw me as the young *mzungu* (white man) who would pay to have his bike fixed, the kid who would try to negotiate the best price before work started. He tolerated me. I was a *mzungu* who wanted to pay the same price as a local. I'd say that amused him.

I didn't care. I was obsessed. I would sit there and observe, trying to learn from what they were doing. I liked it when Kimani or one of the mechanics worked on other bikes. It broadened my education. Bikes were almost another language, a form of expression. The parts worked together like the grammar of a perfect sentence. I wanted to master that tongue, to be able to parse a bike, to be part of their world.

It wasn't uncomfortable. They were into bicycles; I was into bicycles. That rubbed out much of the difference between us. I absorbed everything. They would talk about races, and I sponged up every word until my imagination was brimming. There was a race in Nairobi which they told me about called the Trust, sponsored by Trust Condoms. It sounded glamorous. I picked up on the idea and decided that I was going to start riding my bike in preparation for that. The Trust! Less jumping, more riding. I'd quiz them about the Trust because they were bigger and more knowing and they had ridden it before. I wanted to join them. I wanted to be like them.

But I wasn't them and I'd find myself in difficult situations down there sometimes. People might stop me and say, 'Right, give me your bike.'

I must have looked like a soft touch but with one bound I was always free.

'Why should I give you my bike?' I would reply. In Swahili.

So I was the skinny Swahili-speaking *mzungu* with the bike. They got used to me, eventually.

The legend of David Kinjah. First take.

He was an odd sight, David Kinjah, the sort of man you won't meet every day. A tall, dreadlocked Kenyan cyclist with a 100-watt grin, no sense of time and a generous soul married to a rebel heart. I remember the first time I ever saw him. I was at the Uvunbuzi Charity Ride with Mum. I was thirteen, on the road to fourteen.

This was my second event, having ridden the Trust race* a few months before. In Kenyan terms, it was a big event, maybe a hundred or so riders, including a few locals along on their sturdy Black Mambas (a roadster common in East Africa). I was on my Raleigh mountain bike. I even got a free T-shirt for my participation. Mum knew some amateur cyclists, predominantly white guys, in their forties and fifties. I went along with them for two or three rides. This was one of those days.

The riders in the Kenyan team jerseys and the road racers were so far ahead that I didn't see them at all during that ride.

Suddenly, though, in the steaming aftermath of the race, Kinjah was visible. Radiant and luminous in his bright Lycra kit, on his slender road bike. There were a few other guys with him. All of them were wearing Kenya national team kit. I could see that they were different. Made men. Serious bike people. Professionals. They looked like they were the centre of the world, masters of the universe.

The story goes that Mum went across to Kinjah and asked him quietly if he would teach me a little about bikes and cycling. I was hyperactive, with more energy than sense. She worried that one of my freewheeling adventures through life would end badly.

Kinjah said yes. He would.

I don't think Kinjah was pointed out to me in those terms, not as a cycling *ayah* or babysitter. More like, 'That guy is the captain of the Kenyan cycling team, you should have a chat with him.'

When I went over to talk to him, I said I was looking for a road bike, and asked if he knew of anything available at a low price. I

---

*I had only just managed to finish the Trust race, walking over the line. My mum, in her enthusiasm to support me, had driven into me with her car. I convinced her that, despite my injuries, I did not need to go to the hospital, as I was concerned that she might not be able to afford it.

secretly hoped he had an old bike I could use, but equipment was scarce, even for the captain of the national cycling team.

I remember him being so approachable and friendly, asking me questions. How long had I been riding? Which routes did I enjoy? I must have spoken to him for about ten minutes and at the end he said, 'Listen, you're not that far away from where I live – if you want to come up on a weekend, come for a ride.'

I took his phone number. I would be seeing him soon. And often.

I don't know what was said or what was planned for me between Kinjah and Mum, but from the moment I met Kinjah, learning the rules of the road or the best way to fix a puncture were things of secondary interest. I wanted to be like him. I wanted to spend so much time on the bike that my molecules and the bike's molecules became fused together. I wanted quads like a proper rider. Quads set like gleaming pistons beneath a slender torso and a narrow upper body. I wanted to sit on my bike and look as if I had been born for it. I wanted to race. And I wanted to win. I wanted a Kenya national team jersey. I wanted a road bike. I might even have considered dreadlocks.

I was both pupil and enchanted audience. Kinjah was fourteen years my senior. I loved hearing about the races he had gone to, the guys he had ridden with, and how he had ridden. The constant battles with the sprinters – 'dropping' them on the climbs before being caught again on the flat – these were epic thrillers to me. It was 2002 before I even saw the Tour de France on the television for myself. This world of Kinjah's, I could scarcely imagine anything beyond it.

Kinjah was a Commonwealth Games rider. Twice. He had once said goodbye to Kenya and left his village behind for a pro career in Italy. He was signed up with a small team called Index-Alexia Alluminio, which was a Trade 2 team at the time (the equivalent to Pro Continental, one level down from the top level at World Tour). They had some impressive riders on the roster. He spent the winter training with them, and on their training camp before their first race of the season Kinjah was killing everyone on the climbs. He was really showing them he was a climber cropped from the altitude of our beloved Ngong Hills. But come the first race, for some reason the sponsor decided to shut down the team. There was a free-for-all; everyone grabbed the bikes and the equipment, trying to compensate themselves however they could. Kinjah was left in Italy with no team, no support and no money.

The other half of Kinjah's life has been fixing bikes and tinkering with them. At the training camp he cleaned everyone's bikes for them. He was repairing the bikes and even showed the mechanics a few new tricks. So, after the team disintegrated, he got work building bikes in a factory for several months.

He stayed on for another six months, doing work out there, but eventually he was forced to come back with nothing. Not the triumph he had dreamed about, but at least he had been there. He had seized the day. He had followed his bliss. In Italy he was known as the Black Lion.

He came home with stories to Mai-a-Ihii, his tiny village some twenty kilometres outside Nairobi in the Kikuyu township.

Mum first took me to Mai-a-Ihii to visit Kinjah. With people, she was colour-blind and she passed that on to me. She wanted to have a look around. She somehow knew that this would become a second home for me.

Kinjah invited us in for a cup of tea. He made that sweet milky tea that Mum wasn't too fond of, black tea with cinnamon, milk and about twelve scoops of sugar. Very Kenyan.

At the time Kinjah's place was one big room partitioned in half. A sitting room on one side; a bed and a cooker and the bikes on the other. There was no electricity. Water came from a big round drum that held 100 litres. You opened the top and there was a jug to scoop water into a plastic basin. Water from the basin was for washing yourself with. That same water, with your dust and soap, was then used to wash your bike.

Going to the bathroom was another story. There was a line of small tin huts at the end of the alley closest to Kinjah's place with about four toilets in. You opened the door and there was a piece of concrete on the wall for stability, so that you wouldn't fall in. This was a good idea because there was no seat or structure, just a hole in the floor. He had a torch for guests to take along on these trips.

You sorted your own paper before you left. The open sewer smell was something it took a few trips to get used to.

Kinjah's place was an open house. He had a gang of cycling friends and disciples who came and went. He was a professor of cycling to the local kids and they formed a loose team known as the Safari Simbaz. They stayed with Kinjah when they needed to or wanted to, and went away when they had to.

There was nothing elaborate there and nothing threatening. Mum could sense the goodness in Kinjah and its hold over the others. No danger. As I was going backwards and forwards to Kinjah's place in the years afterwards she would always slip me a few hundred shillings (just over a pound) to cover communal supplies at the market as my contribution towards staying there.

That first day, full of sweet tea and proximity to a man who had raced in Italy, I just knew that every time I came to this place it would be a different adventure. I wouldn't know where we would be going. I wouldn't know who we would be going to see. Or what. I knew that sometimes they wouldn't even speak Swahili, let alone English. They'd fall into their own tongue and what was being said would just go straight over my head.

'Well?' he said as we got ready to leave.

'Count me in,' I said.

A legacy left to us by Flamingo Tours was a knowledge of all the camps that Noz had used for tourists and their safaris. The Masai Mara became a favourite place for Mum and me. Life had changed for us but that wasn't something we would complain about with the Masai.

'You lost your house? Well, they took our lands.'

The Masai are nomads who wander with their cattle but governments in Tanzania and Kenya have for a long time been trying to fence them in, cutting back on their historic homelands and making National Parks out of the world they used to travel through. The Masai are an interesting, welcoming people though, and on our trips to the Mara, Mum and I often encountered tribespeople who would stop and talk to us.

That's where Rocky and Shandy came from. One half-term break from school, when I was thirteen, I was with Mum in a camp in the Mara. There were a few other people staying there who Mum knew.

Some Masai came by claiming that a large python had eaten one of their goats. If we didn't go and collect the snake the Masai were going to kill it. Fortunately, the Masai had come to the right place. Mum had a big heart and I had a hankering for a snake.

Off we went with a large sack searching for the python that ate the goat. A couple of men from the camp came along too. A python that has eaten a goat will lose her girlish figure while metabolizing it, and won't be inclined to slither far in the open. The Masai had given us a rough idea where we might find the python and there, at the base of a bush, was a hole in which the python had set up its nest. The hole was just a short commute of ten minutes or so from the Masai *manyatta*, the village.

The python that had eaten the goat wasn't at home but it had given birth not long ago. There were hundreds of little pythons squirming about both outside and inside the hole. A few slithered away to hide but we were quick and we got at least a hundred into the sack. They may not have been happy about it but the Masai didn't like them. They would thank us in later life.

We took the baby pythons away in a car, off to a forest area, and released them there where there was more natural protection and fewer snacking opportunities for birds of prey, including secretary birds and tawny eagles, and mongooses. A few days later some of the other people from the camp caught the mother python and released her into the forest too. Meanwhile, I kept two of the baby snakes.

I brought them home and christened one of them Rocky and the other one Shandy. They were the cleverest names I could think of for two rock pythons. They were both a brown and black camouflage colour, but I could tell them apart because Rocky had dots on his eyes while Shandy had the dots lower down. This information didn't really fascinate Mum too much but she was happy for me to be happy. She never reminded me that I met Rocky and Shandy while their mum was away digesting an entire goat. Or that Rocky and Shandy might later acquire an appetite for skinny teenage boys.

Rocky and Shandy were each a foot long and their first home from home was in one of my brother's abandoned aquariums. They lived there to begin with on a carpet of newspaper, with a few rocks and some branches thrown in for good measure, but eventually we got somebody to build them their own place. This enclosure was a bit more roomy, being maybe five or six feet long, four feet wide and four feet high. It was a solid wooden construction with mesh on the top and one wall of glass at the front.

Their house was outside on the veranda, perched on a few rocks so it didn't lie on the ground or soak up water. We were living in Langata at the time in a cottage in the grounds of a much bigger house that we were house-sitting. The main residence had a large, well-kept garden with peacocks roaming around in it. I'm not sure if I ever thought of the complications involved if Rocky or Shandy escaped. It wouldn't have been a good thing for either of them to be found digesting a peacock.

We had our own piece of garden that was separate from the big house. Rocky and Shandy were pampered. I had a plastic cover which I slid over the mesh so that if it was raining they wouldn't get wet. I found some handsome pieces of driftwood in a dried-up river basin in the Ngong Hills while exploring with Mum and placed them in the cage so they could slither over them. They had a large water basin too. Pythons like water so they enjoyed swimming in it or just soaking in there. They had every amenity, and generally a better lifestyle than Mum and I had.

I liked to tell people, especially Kenyans, that Rocky and Shandy were free to slither about the house at night, then return to their cage in the morning. It was a complete lie, but I saw people listening with wide eyes, thinking, 'Wow, this boy has got snakes around his property.'

Pythons don't show affection or fetch sticks but there are compensations, particularly the novelty factor. Nobody I knew had two pythons. In fact, nobody I knew even had one python. When I went to the local supermarket I brought Rocky and Shandy with me. They weren't fully grown yet. But neither was I. The sight of us freaked some people out.

Rocky was my favourite. He was mellow and relaxed as pythons go, and I could hold him without any problems. Shandy was the opposite. He was moody and far harder to handle. Neither of them had much time for Mum. If they were in the house sitting with me on the couch and Mum came in, they didn't like it. They either smelled her fear or her cigarette scent and if she got within a couple of metres they lunged at her. Fortunately, they never came close to catching her and when Mum left the room they would settle down again. I don't know what it was about Mum they didn't like. Everybody else always thought she was great.

Not too long after the arrival of Rocky and Shandy, I went on holiday to South Africa to see Noz. Things had settled down for us all since Noz had left Kenya, although he was still struggling to build his new conference management business. I would travel to South Africa once a year or so to see him. I was amazed by the sprawling metropolis that is Johannesburg: shopping centres, movie theatres, arcades and sweet-shops. The trips were good but it was always great to get back too.

The days of going to the Banda School would soon be drawing to an end now I was thirteen, and there was no question of me following my brothers to Rugby School in England. Mum and Noz had put more thought into this than I had. One evening in Johannesburg, Noz, his partner, Jen, and I were out for something to eat at a small restaurant when Noz raised the subject. There was no beating around the bush.

'You're going to come to school here.'

There were tears. It might have been better if he had at least attempted to beat around the bush. Back in Nairobi, Mum was now working in a surgery. She had regular clients, we were getting by financially and I loved living in Kenya. The visits to Johannesburg were always enjoyable, and always a bit different, but home was home. This was the end of the world being presented to me in a snug restaurant. Leave everything you know. Leave Mum to her fate with Rocky and Shandy. And vice versa. Say goodbye to all your friends.

Generally, kids from the Banda School would move on to a secondary school on Langata road called Hillcrest and that's where most of my friends were heading. Only the really bright students or those with well-off parents would go to prestigious boarding schools in the UK. But these were the facts of life: an education at Hillcrest cost three or four times more than the equivalent experience would cost in South Africa. It was not a long menu of life choices that was being offered to me in the restaurant that night.

Noz's business was growing slowly, that was obvious. They were still running everything from home with just one telephone, and although there was income, it was not a Rugby School level of income. It was not even enough for Hillcrest.

This was all quite a shock but I would adapt and I would go to school in South Africa. It was not my choice because it was not a choice.

Mum had a dread. Well, two dreads. Me leaving, and Rocky and Shandy staying. When I moved down to South Africa, the two growing pythons would not be coming with me. I told her soothingly that Rocky and Shandy were low maintenance, really. If she could just throw them each a live rabbit every month they would be fine.

Rock pythons aren't for everyone, although they themselves aren't particularly choosy. In the Malindi district in Kenya a farm manager once stepped on a rock python and, having wrestled with the snake for an hour, was dragged up a tree. While hanging up there waiting to be squeezed to death and swallowed he managed to raise the alarm with his mobile phone. Villagers and police were able to free him. The snake was detained but escaped the following day.

Tip: if you get attacked by a twelve-foot python (the southern subspecies like Rocky and Shandy don't grow any bigger although other rock pythons can stretch to over twenty foot long) and it is trying to wrap itself around you, all you have to do is try to grab the head and hold the tail. Once you have those two in your hands you can start unwinding the snake in the opposite direction to how they are wrapping themselves around you. This was not the sort of handy hint I wanted to be leaving with my mum as I was heading off to secondary school.

I had been bitten on numerous occasions by Rocky and Shandy. As the primary carer I often had to check their mouths for dirt. This is a common problem with snakes, and the dirt can cause an infection in their lip. To prevent this, I used newspaper as a base in their cages, but I also had to pull their lip down from time to time and use a toothpick or a small stick to remove the offending grime. They wouldn't appreciate my dentistry at all. Rocky or Shandy would lunge and there would be a horrible ripping sound as they tore at my flesh. It was a powerful impact, and felt like somebody hitting me. When the snake pulled away I would hear more ripping and there would be blood flowing and a temporary tattoo of teeth marks. Thankfully, these bites were not poisonous, and they healed quickly.

By the time I was due to go to South Africa in May, when I was fourteen, Rocky and Shandy would have grown to around a metre in size. Not quite huge, but still large enough to enjoy eating live rats. I started them on mice. Locally bred. I built a little cage and bought a small family of white mice that came from a lab in Nairobi. I had three or four of them to start with, but in a couple of months this grew to twenty or thirty of them scurrying around.

The mice bred so quickly that I was able to feed Rocky and Shandy with a plentiful supply, but inevitably the snakes soon outgrew their modest diet. I could no longer even see the bulge in their stomachs after they had eaten a mouse. It was time to move on to rats. These weren't really an option for breeding at home so I ended up buying rat traps.

It's an interesting fact that snakes won't eat dead food. They are hygiene conscious like that. A dead rat would be deemed completely unacceptable from a bacterial and a freshness point of view, and for that reason Rocky and Shandy wouldn't be enticed by anything that had already been killed. Thanks but no thanks. So the rat traps had to be non-lethal. The poor rodent would head down a funnel and get stuck. I would then come along and release the rat into the python cage. It was particularly tricky if I disturbed Rocky or Shandy by getting up and leaving suddenly just after they had killed their dinner. If I was wanted on the phone or if my mum called me, they could go right off the rat if they hadn't started eating it yet. They would leave it there like a child refusing to eat its greens.

I liked to innovate though. The lengths involved in catching a rat meant that having one rejected by a disturbed python was extremely frustrating. As a solution, and drawn straight from the 'seemed like a good idea at the time' file, I experimented with putting the dead rats into the oven to heat them up again. I would then take the heated rat and dangle it annoyingly in front of Rocky and Shandy to make them agitated enough to lunge for it again. The number of times I got bitten doing that was considerable. On the other hand, who wanted to waste a rat that had taken a week to catch?

These were activities I loved as a thirteen-year-old boy. But they would be a lot to ask of my mother when I left home.

I came to understand my brother's abduction of my favourite rabbit. Jeremy had a python to feed, after all. At one stage during these nomadic years of Mum and me house-sitting between Karen and Langata, we had two empty houses. We stayed in a cottage while my grandparents occupied the main house. The cottage was opposite a kindergarten which had pet bunny rabbits as class pets.

You can sense what is coming. The bunnies couldn't. Some days when my school had finished and after all the kindergarten kids had gone home I would ride around there on my bike. Firstly, I liked doing tricks on their playground where they had ramps. Secondly, the kindergarten served as a sort of takeaway restaurant. When Rocky and Shandy were still small I dropped by the rabbit cage from time to time and took away one or two baby rabbits to bring home in my pocket.

As an adult, the guilt about that stays with me. Young children would arrive at class the next day and their little baby bunny rabbits would be gone. I did find it very hard feeding rabbits to Rocky and Shandy because the rabbits, especially when the snakes grabbed them and started the coiling process, let out a loud high-pitched squeal. I felt like intervening and stopping it. But the pythons had to be fed and it was my responsibility.

When I got to South Africa the life expectancy of the kindergarten bunnies in my neighbourhood would mysteriously shoot up. I was not sure how Mum would feed Rocky and Shandy, but I knew that she wouldn't be heading down to the kindergarten with two empty pockets.

4

A year before I was due to finish at Banda, Noz and I had spent a holiday visiting potential schools around South Africa. Mostly we looked at boarding schools. We had finally settled on St Andrew's in Bloemfontein.

It was tough. For a start, I arrived at a strange time. The English school system used in Kenya clashed with the South African school calendar so I arrived in Bloemfontein in the middle of the school year, and in the middle of winter. I felt as odd as a second left foot. More importantly, I was freezing, absolutely freezing. I had one duvet cover and one jumper. Everything was a shock to the system. I was so far out of my comfort zone that I became disoriented. The school was very strict, boys only and predominantly Afrikaans. It was enthusiastically Christian. We had chapel every morning and many of the pupils came from religious families. The overall feeling of the place seemed to be somewhere between a military academy and a monastery.

In our cupboards our clothes had to be folded in an extremely specific way, with sheets of smooth paper placed inside our shirt and then the shirt folded around the paper in a particular fashion. It made our shirts look perfect and unwrinkled, which was a clever trick, but not of huge interest to me as a teenage python keeper and trick cyclist. Everything had to be meticulous.

There were two people to a very small room, which was something of a culture shock. I was billeted with a boy called Clinton Foster. He was from Botswana, which I was pleased about because he was also not a South African. He had been there longer than me, having arrived at the right time of year, and he showed me the ropes.

Altogether, there were four of us outsiders: myself, Clinton, a guy called Mark Dunne from Zimbabwe and one other guy, another Zimbabwean. We were put into a special class to teach us Afrikaans, with the goal of being able to pass some exams in four or five years' time. Again, this was tough, but at least it was easy to find help in a school full of Afrikaans speakers.

Our maths teacher was an old Afrikaner who, to my amazement, couldn't speak more than a few sentences of English. I was being taught maths in Afrikaans and most of it was sailing over my head. Maths was still one of my favourite subjects; I had always been more at home with numbers than with words. One day in maths class the teacher was ranting on in furious Afrikaans and I was lost. I turned round to ask someone behind me what he had just said, but everyone was writing frantically and I was confused. The teacher looked round and saw me talking. He picked up one of the old wooden-backed dusters for the blackboard and hurled it straight for my head. He missed me by inches and hit the poor boy I had asked for help.

Some of the teachers were resourceful people. One of them had a cane which he had a nickname for. It was called Poopytoll. I didn't know what this meant, but presumably it was something imaginative about your bum being your 'poopy', and 'toll', as in paying the toll. I didn't know precisely; I didn't care much.

We were a small school, consisting of just a few hundred pupils, but every morning we would face the world wearing our blue ties and blazers and our wooden boater hats. It was Afrikaans with a dash of England.

The most difficult adjustment to make was the hard labour. We had dorm inspections twice a week, after school and on weekends. We were made to dress up in full regalia with the blazer, the hat and the tie. Then we each had to stand outside our door and wait for the axe to fall. There were rules. You couldn't just leave your bed with a duvet and a pillow on it. Sinner! You had to pack away the pillow and the duvet and replace them with a quilt that was immaculate and absolutely free of wrinkles. Wrinkles were an abomination before the Lord. We had to fold the corners in a special way into hospital corners – the edges were so sharp and pressed that you could cut your fingers on them. Obviously if we did bleed, we would have to hold our fingers out of the window. We then had to make a perfect V and tuck the quilt under nicely so that it looked ultra-neat. I had never done anything like this in my life. The prefects would walk into the room, look around and pull the bed out to check for dust. The dust could be anywhere, from the windows to the floor, but they would find it even though we had been mopping, sweeping and panicking. We weren't given much time to get the room ready, so the work would be frantic and our hearts would beat like crazy with fear. We were petrified by the prefects. They loved their work. They would go through our rooms forensically, snooping right into the corners, running their fingers along the skirting boards. Any brown stains or dust coming away on their fingers and we were in trouble.

The prefect tossed our room up anyway he wanted. He threw everything out of our cupboards, crinkled all the paper for the shirts and even turned our beds upside down. Then he would calmly walk out again.

'Right. Another inspection in half an hour. Get your stuff ready.'

To add to the pressure and intensity of the situation, I'd be standing outside my door praying that they wouldn't happen to stumble upon my secret stash of 'tuck' – my sweets, chocolates and biscuits that I'd brought back from my last visit home. At the bottom of my clothes cupboard, I would unscrew the floor panel and hide my bounty. Had the prefects discovered my hiding place, they would have 'confiscated' (and later devoured) the contents.

We youngsters also had to skivvy to clean the room of someone older. I did it for one of the prefects but there were two or three of us on rotation so we took turns.

If the dorms were messy or if we had been noisy after lights-out they would give us all hard labour. The prefects would take us out on a Saturday morning or a Sunday, depending on where the 'sport' was due to take place. A prefect once made us carry him outside on to the rugby field sitting on his couch, so that he could lounge there and watch. From his throne he would make us run and do press-ups, as well as these torture squats where we had to squat 90 degrees down until we were almost sitting. We had our hands out and we would crouch there holding the pose for maybe five minutes of agony. We were shaking but the prefect would still come along and whack our outstretched hands with a stick.

As we were only fourteen years of age, it wasn't hard to make us break down and start crying. A few of my overweight classmates couldn't perform the exercises at all, but if anyone stopped then the whole group would have to start again. That was the mentality.

It was awful, but the boys who weren't as fit became the enemy. If they collapsed in a drill, some of my other classmates would get up and just go for them. There was fighting and deep trauma for some of my friends. I was lucky that I was in good shape so I didn't attract too much attention.

Hard labour was the worst, but there were other things that they didn't tell us about in the prospectus. If we were ever late for anything, punishment would inevitably follow. Mostly they would make us stand in the quad or in front of the chapel on a weekend day from ten o'clock in the morning until four in the afternoon. Rain or shine, we would have to remain bolt upright and dead still, like figures in Pompeii. Living like this day-to-day was a struggle – but I was determined to survive.

Although Bloemfontein was tough and lonely, the experience taught me things. You are your own best resource when things are bad, and I had found my own ways of having fun. When Noz's business started to pick up I was bought a stunt bike which I took with me to Bloemfontein after about six months, by which point I had sussed out the lie of the land. Other kids had proper bicycles but the stunt bike was all that I needed. I could get pretty high on it and the forks wouldn't bend, no matter how hard I pounded them. I loved doing tricks, spinning it around and performing wheelies. It provided me with a world of my own to escape to. Racing would come later, but in Bloemfontein the bike served different needs. St Andrew's was a mixed school, made up of us boarders and the day boys who got paroled to go home every evening and on weekends. The bike became my passport to freedom because I could use it to visit my friends who were day boys. I would stay weekend afternoons at a friend's house and we would play computer games or watch television until I had to return for evening roll call.

We had our first ride together.

'You know,' he said to me afterwards, 'you look pretty good on a bike, a natural. You're obviously keen and you want to improve. Why don't you come training with us?'

I drank that in for the instant boost it gave me. A shot of pure enthusiasm.

'Really?'

Kinjah said I was a natural. He was a pro. It had to be true.

Later they would joke that my elbows were so wide when I rode that I looked as if I were about to start flapping my arms to take flight, but I didn't know that then. Cycling had me, hook, line and sinker.

And that's how it started. On the first few occasions Mum would drop me off at Kinjah's place and pick me up in the evening. Then we got to the point where he said, 'Why don't you just sleep here and we'll go and do the same thing tomorrow?'

Next, it got to the stage when Mum would call to collect me and I would turn to Kinjah and say, 'But we have that thing tomorrow that we can't miss . . .'

I'd throw him a look and he would say, 'Oh yeah. That thing.'

And Mum, not fooled at all, would read it and smile and say, 'Okay, okay.'

It went on like that. The first time we cycled together I was on school holidays home from South Africa and I went on two rides with Kinjah and the boys. After that it grew and grew until I was spending more and more time at his tin hut and with the team whenever I was home.

We had so much fun, riding out in the morning to visit one of Kinjah's family members and stopping there for lunch. We would meet the rest of the family, have some *ugali* and *sukuma wiki* for lunch and then turn round to ride home. Some rides would be up to 200 kilometres, which meant eight hours in the saddle with only one food stop in the middle. When we got back, the other side of Kinjah's life would take over – making bike repairs to earn a living. Local customers would bring in their bikes and he would often let us help, and teach us how to fix them.

This was an education, and a level of expertise far above anything I had known up until this point. Like at the market, where I had watched the local mechanics at work, Kinjah didn't have the kind of money available to pay for expensive repairs, and even if he had, it was unlikely that the local bike shop would have those parts available. He couldn't, for instance, just buy and fit a new derailleur. Instead, he would fashion pieces of metal himself and skilfully attach them to the bikes. Hey presto, it would work.

By the time I was sixteen years old, I had started training during term-time in South Africa too. I saved up for a set of rollers – a piece of indoor training equipment – for my room at school and I would spend hours on it. There were also shorter training rides that the school had come to tolerate me leaving the grounds for, and I would fit a longer ride in on a Saturday or Sunday, which normally lasted five or six hours.

When I went back to Kinjah, I could test out how much progress I had made by seeing where I ranked among the group. He had a great ability to judge exactly where you were at with your perform-ance levels and your capacity for suffering. He knew how to take you up to your absolute limits, and how to keep you there, but he would also show you that at any point he could 'drop' you, or leave you in his tracks.

Kinjah said that I was a good sufferer. Perhaps our hard labour in Bloemfontein had made men out of boys, stoics out of sufferers.

Shandy had never settled in quite like Rocky had. After I moved to St Andrew's he was still very aggressive, and a constant nuisance for my mother. The two snakes were also growing. Their latest caged enclosure had a small wooden structure built inside in the shape of an octagon, with a lid on the top and a narrow entrance at the front. This was their den within the cage if they wanted some darkness dur-ing the day; pythons like to hide away from everyone. However, they had got so big that only one could fit in the cramped den at a time. As they were snakes, there was no point in drawing up a timeshare rota.

While I was away from home, I knew that in order to clean the cage someone else would have to regularly risk their limbs to lift Rocky and Shandy out of the den. Anna, our *ayah* at the time, made her position clear. She wasn't touching any snakes. Ditto the gar-dener. So poor Mum was elected by default.

Before my departure I had tried to teach her a good way of evacuating the snakes.

'Mum, you just need to put a kitchen cloth over the python's head and then pick it up by the tail and they'll be fine. You'll be fine.'

I always did this if I was ever going to pick one up and I could see they were in a bad mood. A cloth over the head and they were immediately placid. It was a shame it didn't work on the prefects.

Anna's reservations were understandable, of course. One time in a house in Karen where we were staying, Rocky went missing. It was a house with thick vegetation and forest at the end of the garden. I thought he was out there somewhere. Three weeks had gone by since anyone had seen him, until one day Anna was in the house cooking a meal and my mother was the only other person home. There was a small sort of vent in the ceiling, a power outlet which had created a hole. I don't know how it came to be but Anna turned round and Rocky was hanging down into the kitchen, upside down, with his head precisely at eye level with her. She bumped straight into him. Anna's blood-curdling shrieks must have been heard in parts of northern Africa. My mother thought they were being burgled or kidnapped.

I was still at Banda at the time. Rocky was probably hungry or something. Neither Anna nor my mother asked if he was peckish. They closed all the doors and they stayed closed until I got home from school. I had to go inside, pick him up and put him back in his cage.

That should have been the end of Anna and my pythons but she actually had a moment of great heroism soon after this. Siafu ants are an African plague. You might be sleeping and they will march into a formation on your leg and in inexplicable unison they will all bite you at exactly the same time. The ants can get into your skin to the extent that many of the tribes use them for stitching wounds. They hold a siafu just above the wound and let it bite into the sundered flesh and then they break its body from the head and the pincers will still remain in the skin holding the wound together.

These ants got into Rocky and Shandy's cage in such numbers that the ants were going to kill them. The snakes were thrashing around inside, uncontrollable and incapable of getting the ants off themselves.

Anna screwed her courage to the sticking point. She threw a towel over the snakes, scooped them up and ran with them to the bathroom. Next, she dropped them into the bath, filled it up with water, and then began brushing the ants off the snakes. The snakes, unappreciative as ever, and in some pain, tried to attack Anna. It would have been far easier for her to turn a blind eye to them and pretend that she hadn't seen what was going on, but she didn't. She wasn't that kind of person. She knew how upset I would have been. They never appreciated it, but Rocky and Shandy really owed their cushy existence to the loving natures of Mum and Anna.

For Mum's sake, I let Shandy go free into the Nairobi National Park on the way to the airport at the end of a trip home for the school holidays. It was just Rocky at home now, and one python was far easier to manage, particularly as Rocky was quite a chilled guy for a snake. I think that secretly Mum kept him around because he reminded her of me. She would never admit that though.

By this time, Rocky was just over two metres long and as thick as an adult's arm. He ate chickens and fully grown rabbits. When I was at home I sometimes accidently left the cage open or left a bolt unlatched and he would find a way out. Or I might fall asleep holding him. When I woke up he would be nowhere to be seen, slithering off around the house somewhere. Rocky escaped a number of times, but if he was loose in the house I could usually find him quite quickly, lurking somewhere that was dark or covered. Usually . . .

'CHRISTOPHER!'

When she used my full name I knew it was trouble. Rocky had actually slipped into bed with Mum. He was lying right in front of her face where he could get the warmth of her bosom. She woke up eyeball to eyeball with Rocky.

'CHRISTOPHER! Get your bloody snake back in the bloody cage!'

It wasn't a good time to remind her of our deal about shouting. I couldn't help but laugh.

Mum was extremely tolerant. She put up with the snake and she enjoyed my endless struggles to be a good provider. When I was home I would set traps on the way down to the Ngong Hills. If we saw rats crossing a road we would stop for a moment and follow them with our eyes because they normally ran along particular trails. If we found a trail I would leave a trap there and come back the next day and look for it. Sometimes I would even catch elephant shrews, small rodents that jump in a similar way to kangaroos. The elephant part of their name comes from the length of their nose, which slightly resembles a miniature trunk. But there the likeness ended; they were tiny and wouldn't make much of a meal for a python.

In the end Rocky kept on growing until he was too big for the largest possible home-made enclosure, and when I was away at school my brother Jeremy went with my mother and released Rocky into the wild in a forest in a nearby National Reserve. It was a habitat that would have suited him well. By this stage he was too large for an eagle or a kite to bother him and far too big for my mother to wake up with.

Noz brought me to the bus station in Johannesburg and loaded me on to the bus to Bloemfontein. Half-term was over and it was back to the gulag. The bus was a jalopy and this was a long journey at the best of times. When we finally chugged into Bloemfontein the clock was crowding midnight. We were five hours late. The Free State was deep into winter and although I was better prepared than I was when I first experienced Bloemfontein's chill, here I was again, still freezing.

The school was several kilometres away. My stuff was in a large, heavy, old-fashioned trunk. I would need porters or Sherpas to tote it. The housemaster was supposed to have met me at the bus hours ago but there was no sign of him now. I looked for a payphone. Then I decided to arrange a hanging.

'Noz, it's me. I don't know what to do.'

'What's wrong?'

'I'm at the bus station in Bloemfontein. It's cold and I've been waiting more than an hour for the housemaster. I don't know what to do.'

'You just wait there, Chris.'

Noz got on the phone and gave a good piece of his mind to my Afrikaner housemaster, riot-act stuff. No quotes emerged but I could tell there had been a bollocking when the housemaster screeched into the station in his pyjamas. He was warmed only by his seething rage. He practically threw me and my trunk into the car. At the dormitory he physically dragged me in as if he were tossing a troublesome inmate into the prison cooler cell. He was rough in that muscular Afrikaner-meets-teacher way.

'If you ever go to your father again and tell him that I'm not doing this or that . . .'

Not long after that Noz came up to Bloemfontein and I told him what had happened.

'I'm not going to keep you here,' said Noz.

He went to see the headmaster and told him the story. The headmaster's heart didn't bleed too profusely when he heard about my woe. He didn't offer Noz the response that he wanted.

Noz said, 'Right, I'm taking him back to Johannesburg.'

And away we went. It was as simple as that.

The timing was good. The business was starting to grow and Noz could afford a better school for me now, called St John's.

This new place was more expensive, but even though I entered a boarding house, which wasn't cheap, the school still cost less than Hillcrest. I loved that Noz was just forty-five minutes' drive away and that I could go home most weekends.

St John's had the feel of five-star luxury. In the boarding house there were no doors on the rooms but each little cubicle had its own bed. It was one cubicle per person, which blew me away.

A matron showed us round the boarding house. There were duvets on all the beds and it looked so messy that I fell in love with the place straight away. There was a boy in there who had overslept and missed his breakfast. He was still in bed!

The matron said, 'Come on, Bradley, get out of your bed, you've got to go to school now. Put on some clothes and hurry up.'

My mouth was open. She made classes seem like an option. A lifestyle choice for Bradley. I knew then that I could live there and be happy and it made me feel better about Bloemfontein. Apart from having met a lot of good guys at St Andrew's, without going to that school I wouldn't have appreciated my new place so much.

First in St Andrew's and now in St John's, I wrote often to Mum. Maybe she noticed the changes in me. Butterflies, bunny rabbits, snakes and rodents no longer had anything to fear from me – they were too distant to remain as obsessions. I had even been a devoted collector of scorpions for a while but the gentle ambience of St John's didn't seem compatible with that.

The big news headline for me was that St John's had a cycling club. My stunt bike and my wheelies suddenly seemed like childish things to be put away. St John's viewed cycling as a cultural activity and every Friday afternoon there was a team ride for a couple of hours. Matt Beckett was in charge; he had these hugely chiselled legs that the rest of us would have killed for. Matt would become a lifetime friend.

On Fridays I rode along with the club on my old supermarket mountain bike. Most of the guys had proper road-racing bikes and I barely managed to keep up with the group but . . . I loved it.

Madly.

Deeply.

Completely.

Matt said that the Friday jaunts were in preparation for a race that we were all going to be in. I was part of that 'we'. My head was full of it. When I wasn't on the bike the muscles in my legs ached for the company of the pedals, for the pain of the hills and the sweet adrenaline of riding catch-up.

Officially, I was now in training for a race.

5

Growing up as virtually an only child, I found Kinjah's world to be a revelation.

We were cheek by jowl, together all day, every day, at his tin hut or out on the road. Kinjah saw me, I think, as this eager young skinny kid who was incredibly keen to learn. There were a few of us – me and some other local teenagers – and we would all end up sleeping head to toe in the one bed that was there. We would lie awake for ages some evenings, talking about Kinjah's time racing in Europe.

After seven or eight hours on the bikes earlier that day, the guys would be tired and dropping off to sleep, but I would lie awake even after Kinjah had gone quiet and imagine the world we had been talking about. Kinjah! He'd been racing in Italy. From this tin hut in Mai-a-Ihii, he had made it that far. There was no reason why I couldn't do the same.

While a lot of the kids I had grown up with had moved from the Banda School to Hillcrest, and were now getting into drinking and the nightlife of Nairobi, I was lying in a world they could never imagine and was perfectly content in this small tin hut. The sheets, which were more like heavy blankets, always had a strong musty smell. It wasn't an issue, just an observation, a scent that still comes back to me when I am thinking of those days.

I was a strange sight in the village. The only mzungu. People would ask Kinjah where he got me from, and did I even have parents. But they came to accept me. It took a while to be absorbed into the group within Kinjah's hut, for me to be able to really joke and talk with them, and for them to come out of their shells with me. We had to share some time and some history together first. We'd find a point where we had a little gag to share or something to recount. If you fell off your bike in front of one of the others, for example, and he had to brake not to run you over, you felt like you almost owed him

something for not flattening you. Things like that helped to disman-
tle the barriers.

There was banter between us all day long. They had nicknames for
each other and I had a few which I never fully understood, as they
were generally in Kikuyu. They were mainly along the lines of
'White Boy' or 'White Kid'. I was the *murungaru*, which means a sort
of gangly kid. There was constant teasing. If anyone did something
clumsy or silly, we would rag him all day about it. We spent long
rides teasing each other and laughing the whole way.

I imagine that initially the guys probably thought there was something in it for Kinjah, that my mum was paying him to coach me, or
something like that. That was never even discussed. Once we had
shared a few stories together, suffered on a few rides together, they
began to open up to me a bit more.

There was Njorge. That is a very Kenyan name. Njorge was one of
the younger adults, always up for anything. He was very happy and
smiley and was a decent rider, much better than me. All of them were
pretty much better than me. Njorge was one of the most open members of the group and easy to get to know. Then we had Njana, which
was a nickname. He was a bit mischievous and you could see that he
had the inclinations of an opportunist. Njana was very quick to find
people's faults and then to prey on them. I think if we had all gone
out drinking, he definitely would have been the ringleader, pushing
us to do silly things. I say that but I don't remember anyone in the
group ever drinking any alcohol; I never even saw a beer around the
house, it was just not part of the lifestyle. Njana quit riding at a fairly
early age and the guys who are still around give him grief nowadays
for being chubby.

Samson Gichuru was another one of the youngsters who started
out back then. He progressed well and would go a long way in cycling, becoming a good professional in Kenya and even spending a bit
of time with the UCI development team in South Africa.

George Ochieng was around at that time too. He was Kinjah's
training and racing partner for a number of years, but eventually
times got tough for him financially and he sold one of Kinjah's bikes
without Kinjah's permission. That was the end of their relationship.

Kamau was one of the more prominent riders who was always on the training rides and would lead the charge with Kinjah at the races. He was a quiet guy with a hard, chiselled face, but he was very likeable once you got to know him. He started off in life with close to nothing, but he would eventually have a proper house of his own not far from Kinjah's, with brick walls, electricity and water. He would also set up a *matatu* business in Nairobi.

I always enjoyed being in their company. I looked forward to those times immensely and thought that the longer I could stay there, the better it would be for me; all I wanted to do was ride my bike. If I was at home on my own, riding would be more difficult and far less fun.

Up to the age of seventeen I was definitely one of the weakest in the gang until some younger guys came along and I discovered that I was more capable than they were. That was good for me, and I realized that as time passed, and I came back a bit older and with a bit more experience, I could start pushing them all harder on the rides, particularly the climbs in the hills.

Before I started to improve, though, they were incredibly accommodating. The group would often cycle quite a bit faster than me, but at times they would give me a push or they would slow down so that I could stay with them, or ride in their slipstream. They would all be taking turns at the front, each acting as a windbreak temporarily so that the others could draft behind them, whereas I would be at the back barely hanging on, taking advantage of all of their hard work without reciprocating. But they never minded that. Close to home they would finally push on ahead and I would arrive back a good ten minutes after them.

Kinjah was terrible at time management. He would say, 'Okay, we're leaving at nine o'clock tomorrow,' so I would pitch up at eight. But he would be cooking something and then he would be talking. We would eventually leave the house at one o'clock. Naturally, we would be extremely late for whatever meeting or appointment we were travelling to, so we would be riding extra fast.

If Kinjah had no meetings or visits scheduled, we would be out all day. We would leave early in the morning, and then ride a good three or four hours before stopping for a meal somewhere, and then ride the same distance back. These were big, long days.

I say stop for a meal somewhere as if we were clicking our fingers for waiter service. We would stop at a place where we knew we could find food. It wouldn't be a restaurant as we all know it, but it would be somewhere where we could get a plate of *ugali*, the white pap. *Ugali* is maize flour cooked with water into a sort of doughy porridge. It is very popular in Africa and incredibly wholesome but also stodgy. We would have *ugali* and *sukuma wiki*, a kind of kale or spinach, or what Americans would call collard greens. Kenyans have a fantastic way of cooking and eating this which is really tasty and simple. We would break off a piece of the doughy *ugali* with our hands and eat it together with the *sukuma wiki* vegetables. There wasn't meat very often because that was generally quite expensive in Kenya and more difficult to procure. However, after a really heavy day of cycling, we would make an effort to source some protein. If we could find some beef to add to the *ugali* and *sukuma wiki*, we would make a stew with it.

One of my favourite meals was introduced to me by Kinjah. It consisted of avocados, which were plentiful, cocoa powder, which you could buy from the local kiosk shops, and a sprinkling of sugar. We would mash it all up and make a brown, creamy, chocolatey paste. After training, when we were low in sugars, we really enjoyed that.

On other days we would head off together to one of Kinjah's meetings in the Central Business District and we might end up stopping for a meal of chicken and chips from a local fast-food place. We would all push ourselves even harder on the road home to burn off the excess calories. Chicken and chips wasn't a normal meal for cyclists.

It was a Friday afternoon and I was riding home from St John's. I was fifteen years old. I hit the motorway on my bike. My backpack was filled with my schoolbooks and homework for the weekend, as well as some clothes. I swung into the fast lane and got behind a small *bakkie*. Sitting behind the slipstream, I was comfortably riding along at around 50 kilometres an hour. I was feeling great. Yes! I had finished school for the week. I was home for the weekend. I even had a race on Sunday. Life was –

He had a large, angry Afrikaner face perched on top of a large, stocky Afrikaner body. He virtually grabbed me by the scruff of the neck and dragged me across several lanes of traffic on his motorbike.

'*Kom hierso!*'

He was shouting in Afrikaans as he dragged me.

'*Kom hierso jou klein bliksem!*'

His big, volcanic face was close to mine. He had taken off his helmet.

I was busted.

On the weekends, if we were not racing at school, I usually went home to stay with Noz. He lived forty-five minutes away by car in Midrand, halfway between Pretoria and Johannesburg. The easiest way to get there, the way that we would drive to and from school, was on the motorway that connects the two cities. Motorways, it was pointed out to me now, were not for bicycles. The back roads to Midrand would get me there safely.

I had worked out, however, that Friday afternoon when it was time for me to go home was actually the best time to take a bicycle out on to the motorway. Traffic was generally bumper to bumper most of the way. The cars in the fast lane might reach speeds of 40 to 50 kilometres per hour, the sort of speed designed as an invitation to a young cyclist who was happy to tuck in behind a truck or car. It meant no traffic lights and a quick ride home. Until the police officer, who was now breathing fire into my face, had seemingly identified me as the biggest threat to the quality of life for God-fearing people in all of Johannesburg.

It had taken much persuasion to make Noz and the school see that cycling home and back to school would be in everybody's best interests, but most of all my own. With reservations they had both agreed.

I could understand their concerns. St John's was in Houghton, which is middle class and expensive. But Houghton borders Hillbrow and Yeoville, tough precincts closer to the central business district in Johannesburg. Hillbrow was once urban hip. Now it teemed with people who had fled the townships to a different sort of poverty. If you look at a picture of Johannesburg, Hillbrow is the area beneath the long slender tower which is a landmark of the city. The tower once had a revolving restaurant in it but now it serves as a geographical warning for those who do not dare risk the hinterland below.

Yeoville suffered a similar fate to Hillbrow in the nineties, transforming during just eight years of white flight from being an eighty-five per cent white district to ninety per cent black. The whites took their business with them. Banks redlined the area, denying loans to members of the black population, which meant they had to rent and couldn't buy.

Hillbrow and Yeoville were areas best avoided by kids on bicycles, but when I was heading home the quickest route was to cycle straight through them – quickly. I didn't want to puncture. Then there was the motorway issue.

'*Is jy fokken mal? Wat dink jy? Op die hoofweg? In die vinnige laan? IS. JY. FOKKEN. MAL?*'

I had no legal training but I knew the tack I must take here.

'I'm sorry. I don't understand Afrikaans.'

Mum had said to me once that if you ever got into trouble with the police you should never try to argue with them. It never worked as they would always use their power against you. The best thing to say would be 'I'm sorry' and then they couldn't carry on being angry with you. So, I was working the fool's pardon stratagem.

He switched to English but he was a little disarmed now.

'What are you doing on the motorway?'

I wanted to say something smart like 'doing the crossword' but I knew better.

'I'm really, really sorry, officer. I'm really sorry but I'm new to South Africa and I'm going to school now in Johannesburg. When my father brought me here first, he brought me here on this road and I don't know the way home on any other roads so I have to use this one.'

I hoped it sounded like my father was a Somalian pirate who had abducted me and brought me here for some reason to the posh school. I was not to blame for my foolishness.

'No, no, you can't do that. Follow me.'

He threatened to impound my bike. My most treasured posses-
sion.

'I'm taking your bike to the station. Your parents can come and
pick you up from there. Or you're not going home tonight.'

This was harder work. I had to increase the sob quotient in my
story.

'Please. My mum is in Kenya and my father is working. He can't
come and pick me up.'

He reprimanded me at length and made me follow him to the next
exit ramp, explaining to me the route home on the back roads which
I knew precisely, but I kept nodding gratefully as he explained every
twist and turn. I used the back road for about five kilometres and hit
the motorway again soon after that. For safety, I now rode even
closer to the car in front of me so I could stay ducked down behind it
and out of sight.

A couple of times back in Nairobi I joined old friends from the Banda
School for parties and nights out. Being teenagers, and fairly affluent,
my friends were drinking and smoking joints. With Kinjah and the
group I never insulted their intelligence by pretending to be what I
was not. I may not have been the wealthy kid they imagined me to
be, but at home and in St John's I still had a life of considerable privilege by comparison. I mentioned the nights out to Kinjah and he was
not at all impressed. I was surprised at how strict and stern he was
with me. That was not the way to go, he said. It definitely made an
impact with me. I realized I couldn't live fully in both worlds. I
would have to choose. Being a good sufferer on the bike, the choice
was easy.

With a role in each place, though, I learned a lot. Even about food.
With Kinjah and the boys, we had meals when we were hungry. If
we had eaten a substantial meal in the middle of the day we didn't
need to eat again. However, in Karen or Langata we had breakfast,
lunch and dinner, and those were set meal times. We had to attend
those meals regardless of the energy we had spent in between. It was
definitely a different take on the priorities of day-to-day living.

Kinjah's family had their own home and some land, which we in Kenya would call their *shamba*, a plot up in the highlands. I set off with the Safari Simbaz one morning through tea plantations and on a long ride up tarmac into the hills before heading off on a dirt road for a couple of hours. When we arrived at his family's place, Kinjah brought out the gifts that he had carried with him: an assortment of shirts he had collected from sponsored events. They were new, and would have been expensive, still in their packets. His family loved them.

At the *shamba* Kinjah's brother Dan took us away for a walk through the land to show us what they were growing. They had all kinds of vegetables. They'd live off what they were growing and sell anything extra to the local market in order to buy other foods that they couldn't cultivate themselves. They had a few acres in total. We walked for nearly twenty minutes around the *shamba* and Dan took us down a steep cliff where he told us of his plans to grow more crops.

The land there was fertile and green and very lush, with a small stream running at the bottom. After we walked back up we spent a couple of hours relaxing, sharing food with the family, before eventually heading home. It was a slice of Kenya that very few *mzungus* get to see.

When we left we were given a huge load of vegetables, which were very awkward to carry. I couldn't help thinking that surely we could buy these cheaply ourselves for about five shillings (less than 50p) from the local market near Kinjah's village, but now we were going to be carrying it all for a hundred kilometres. And there were hills all the way back to the village.

It was an unworthy thought after their hospitality and, more embarrassingly, the other guys wouldn't let me carry any of the vegetables myself. They took everything off me and loaded themselves up with about ten kilos each. Then, to my amazement, Kinjah and the group just exploded away on their bikes. They were burning up the dirt tracks, which were incredibly steep and tough. I thought to myself, 'Okay, I've got a real advantage here, I'm not carrying ten kilos of these wretched vegetables. I can get home first today.'

I could see them labouring and sweating but still I couldn't keep up. After an hour I could feel jelly legs coming on. I was mortified. Now they weren't just carrying the food, they were starting to take turns pushing me from behind on my bike up the steep climbs because I was lagging. Once we reached the main road I was content to cycle in their slipstream, and get sucked back to Kikuyu.

When we arrived back in the evening we didn't eat much at all. Just a few pieces of bread with avocado and some milky cinnamon tea before we were off to bed.

I used to wonder how I would ever get the body I needed to get to the world I wanted to end up in. Or whether *ugali* and the dirt roads would get me there. I knew I didn't have the muscles; Kinjah had explained to me that it would take years on the bike to develop them fully before I could really push on the pedals properly.

That became the long-term obsession. The goal. To develop the way Kinjah said I would, by doing these long rides and putting in the hours. Hour after hour after hour.

St John's was situated in a wondrous terracotta-coloured building in the middle of genteel Houghton. Nelson Mandela had a home nearby. On Fridays a group of schoolfriends and I would sweep out in a cavalcade of bikes down St David Road, on to Houghton Drive, and we were away.

We were highwaymen, kings of the road.

We rode from gladed Houghton to the wealthy oasis of Sandton and then back again. Johannesburg was notorious for many things and its homicidal traffic was one of them. We would hit the most densely trafficked roads in the city, Rivonia Road and Jan Smuts Road, where the cars and trucks would be gridlocked and irritable in both directions. In order to move at all we pedalled straight down the middle of the road. If a car door opened suddenly, one of us would get taken out instantly. If a newspaper hawker or a beggar dawdled in our path, there would be tears.

We were in the channel between the vein and the artery of Jo'burg traffic, racing each other. One of my friends would be on the inside of the cars while I would be on the outside, pedalling for my life to get past them. We saw fleeting faces of motorists, their eyes filled with alarm, pity and sometimes rage. Who were these wild, senseless kids on bikes speeding down the middle of Jan Smuts Road? Had it come to this?

For us, it was the best part of the week – pure exhilaration and freedom. I especially loved a stretch near the school, the hill on Munro Drive leading up to Elm Street. It was steep enough to make me yearn for bigger hills and proper mountains. That sinew of imagination linked all of us boys. This was fun but we knew there was a world of professional cycling out there that we were serious about. There was madness but there was love and dedication at the heart of it.

I had started getting a few results in the races we entered locally. We had changed housemasters and our new overseer, Allan Laing, was an enthusiastic cyclist himself. He was supportive and I also had an ally in Sister Davies, the school nurse, who headed up our cultural activities on a Friday afternoon. She and her husband were very keen cyclists themselves and they liked to enter the mass participation cycling events that were increasingly popular in South Africa. I occasionally saw the pair of them at the races and we huddled to compare times.

Sometimes the races would have a couple of thousand people riding. On weekends, poor Noz would have to wake up at 4.30 a.m. to get me there on time. He would have to drive me to the start line by 5.30 a.m. with the race commencing at 6.00. One morning, Noz drove me an hour and a half south at 4.00 a.m. to Vanderbijlpark. When we got there I realized I had forgotten my racing shoes. I didn't want to tell Noz I had forgotten them and considered trying to do the ride in my sandals. Noz, who was always supportive and interested in my racing, figured out my mistake quickly enough.

'Right, that's it. We're going home.'

He swung the car round, back towards Midrand. I learned not to forget my cycling shoes.

No matter how many people raced, I would have won the prize for being the most earnest. I wouldn't start in the early groups with the pros but I would race against the clock for the 100 kilometres, record all of my times and would try to better my personal best each week. I went along to more and more of these races all around Johannesburg.

I was still riding my old mountain bike but I had developed enough to be able to keep up with some of the racers. That was a short-term goal: keep up with the guys with the expensive, fast bikes. I still couldn't get close to the racing times of the professionals, but my fitness was improving.

Driving to the races every weekend, Noz and I spent hours together that we probably wouldn't have had if it wasn't for cycling. I think it was a challenge for both of us but it was fun. He was learning more and more about what I was doing, and he was proud of my results. Eventually I got the confidence to raise an important issue with him.

'Noz, I really need to get a road bike.'

We enquired, we saw the prices, and then we retreated for talks. Finally, we came up with a system. I would start by performing small jobs for him to earn some money. These ranged from washing the car, to a personal courier service on my bike, to admin work for his conference business.

Next, I was resourceful. School was like prohibition America and I saw an opening, supplying certain goods that were needed. With my growing reputation in the schoolyard as an obsessive cyclist who had influential allies in Allan Laing and Sister Davies, I had far more freedom to be outside the school than most other boarders did. Alcohol was in big demand. I would go out to the liquor stores and get bottles of vodka and brandy for the boys in my year and sell them at double the rate I had bought them. It was a tax to justify the risks for the mule. I could put cigarettes and other small items of contraband into the handlebars of the bike and bring those back too.

I was a teenage bootlegger. And so good at it that I even became a prefect at St John's without them getting wind of my extra trips to and from the school. I found work at a Johannesburg bicycle shop too, called Cycle Lab, in Fourways. I was paid by the hour and tried to work as many hours as my weekend would allow. Later, I even started instructing local spinning classes, taking back-to-back classes so that I could also make them a worthwhile training session for myself.

The money mounted up.

Eventually, I found a bike in the classifieds that was almost identical to the bike Matt Beckett, my buddy at the school cycling club, owned. It belonged to a man who had bought it to try to get fit and then hardly used it.

I thought I was getting a great deal. He wanted R10,000 for it, which was less than £1,000. It was sleek and so much faster than anything I had ever ridden before. Even though it was actually about three sizes too big for me (the frame was a 60-inch or perhaps even a 62-inch – today I ride a 56), I felt it was the right size for me at the time. I could grow into it.

After eight months of saving, it was mine.

It was Italian. A Colnago, with a blue and pink aluminium frame. It was a thing of beauty.

6

It's 5.00 a.m. It's dark. Dawn is still just a promise. The temperature is in the minus figures as I head towards the school sanatorium. I'm wearing my tracksuit and carrying a bag for my helmet. I'm shivering.

I saunter casually now, clearing my head in the fresh air. When I arrive I unlock my Colnago and go inside. I do the Clark Kent thing and materialize in my cycling gear.

Getting out of the school is easy in the dark. Getting back in, when things are busy, will be much harder, like a Colditz operation. I usually attempt re-entry during the breakfast-time rush. But the cold is turning me blue now. My hands grip the familiar curves of the Colnago handlebars. I hate the cold. Passionately. I am wearing thin school gloves. This is the only concession I make to common sense. The school gloves are warmer than my fingerless cycling ones. I think they are, anyway. There is no equipment capable of calibrating the difference in the coldness of my fingers when swaddled in school gloves as opposed to cycling gloves. I'm so numb that I simply can't imagine anything being colder. I ride out like this every winter morning, wearing only bib shorts and a short-sleeve top. No long-sleeve jerseys. No gilets. No arm or leg warmers. Occasionally, I put plastic bags on my hands before I put the woollen school gloves on over the top. Not big with the Eskimos, I imagine. They help me stay warmer for maybe sixty seconds.

I leave the school at 5.00 a.m. each day in this icy darkness. Matt leaves his home at the same time. He is a day boy; I board. I ride towards Matt's house; he rides towards the school. When we meet we spin off into the brightening morning for a full-tilt training ride. We are competitive with each other. It is kudos for me if we are closer to Matt's house than to the school when we meet in the morning. It is a small victory for him if we meet at any point nearer St John's. Sometimes I leave the school at ten to five just to play with his head.

The dark roads are empty and mysterious. The morning stillness is punctuated only by sudden birdcall and the odd *bakkie* ferrying labourers to their jobs, the men stoic and sleepy in their flat-backs, leaning into the angles of the hills so that we think they are about to tumble out.

As we ride, the air pushes against us and bumps us about. My lips are cracked from the cold. When you are on a bike the air has multiple personalities. I don't like descending into dips and hollows because all the cold air that has collected at the bottom freezes us even more as we pass through it. It's like being dipped in frost. Flashing over bridges or streams, the air is more robust, it shakes us down and roughs us up. I shiver and shudder down the slope of long dark hills. I descend in a blind fury because the act of pedalling gives me some warmth. Generally, if the sun is aiding and abetting me, I look for hills. Hills are an unrequited love early in the morning though. The air on the way down is unkind to me. Sometimes I even pull on my brakes just so that I have to pedal again to get going.

It's love though. Every ache and chill. Me and my Colnago and these hills. In love, everybody hurts. If you are serious about hills and bikes, it hurts.

Life made for a strange tapestry. The halls of St John's and the beloved chaos at Kinjah's were two of the bigger strands of my life as I left my childhood behind. With Kinjah and the guys, the bike was a staple of existence that tied us all together. In St John's, the bike was an instrument of subversion and escape. A minority interest.

In St John's there is one dominant faith. I enjoy rugby without being devout about it. The school is quite fundamentalist about the sport though. Rugby. Then cricket. If you don't play rugby, some form of observance is still compulsory. You go and watch from among the congregation while the school's first team plays at the weekends. You help with the rite that is the special school cheer or war cry. This isn't voluntary. It is like the draft. No dodging.

Matt and I were the two most ardent lobbyists for cycling. That placed us on the outside. We were not the cool kids, or even in the orbit of the popular crowd. We didn't run with the jocks or the big rugby players. My friends and I were a small and harmless subculture. We weren't nerds, nor were we troublemakers. We flew under the radar.

One day we fell in behind the headmaster as he was striding from one building to another. He had too much to do already without making time for a special meeting with the cycling posse. We urged him to understand the extraordinary time demands of cycling training. It had no beginning and no end.

'It would really help if we could be excused from coming to cheer for the rugby team, if we could have your special permission.'

'Gentlemen, I can't let people just come here and go off and do whatever they want. We have our school sports here. They take preference. That's how life is.'

However, life for a cyclist had become much easier since Allan Laing, our new housemaster, had joined. He turned a blind eye to me arriving in the middle of breakfast and sitting down at a crowded table, taking the spot to which a sympathetic friend had already carried down my morning meal. Runnels of sweat gave my game away but Allan was a cycling man and looked the other way.

Buying the gleaming Italian Colnago encouraged me to increase my commitment to a level befitting the bike's beauty. Matt and I both joined the local Super C Cycling Academy, named after the Super C energy sweet. This was the first time we were part of an official bike set-up.

The father of another junior schoolboy had finagled some sponsor money and an agreement to support the academy. I was very competitive with Matt at the time and he was already at the level I aspired to be. Matt had more of a natural build for a cyclist. He had huge quads and an impressively lean upper body. Take either end of him and you had the body of a genuine rider. I just had the skinny upper body. It came as a matching set with the rest of me. My relationship with cycling was like a detective with a puzzling case. I knew what I wanted to solve. It was just working out how that was the trouble.

The Super C Cycling Academy was a rudimentary set-up. We rode with youngsters from different backgrounds including a few

Afrikaans kids. We had enough riders to make an A team and a B team. We would go on to enter the national Junior Tour of South Africa for two years running. The race took place (and still does) in Ermelo in Mpumalanga. The Junior Tours gave us an annual serving of humility. It was more hard evidence for me of how far I had to go. Most of the stages were flat and by the finish we weren't even in the same postal district as the leaders. I would be dropped. Most of the team would be dropped. We would get nowhere and I would think of how much harder I needed to train.

I recognized that I had come into the sport relatively late, only starting to ride properly when I was thirteen, and that I had a lot of learning to do, and a lot of growing to do, before I could catch those front-runners. That was fine by me though: I knew I was in cycling for the long game.

We were still really just kids. I remember being absolutely intimidated waiting at the start line and looking across at some of the other guys who had giant quads and full beards. I hadn't even started shaving yet.

The team time-trial day, in particular, was the one stage where we got up out of bed nervous and then spent the day proving to ourselves that we had plenty to be nervous about. It was a day of trying to coordinate an effort between the six of us in the team when we didn't really know what we were doing, and didn't have access to any hard information that might cure our ignorance.

We were sappers coming out of the trenches and charging into no-man's-land. In a team time trial you ride together as a group against the clock, taking turns at the front of your mini-peloton in order for the rest of your teammates to draft in the slipstream behind, in theory. However, for us, one person would often cycle too hard and leave the rest of us behind. We lost most of our guys in the first few kilometres and were constantly dropping each other. Occasionally, somebody would decide to prove a point and drive hard until they fell off their bike with exhaustion.

I was one of the riders who always clung on until the bitter end. It was just dogged perversity, managing to endure the suffering. But I actually enjoyed those time-trial days much more than I did the road stages. There was more to do and I relished the unpredictable racing dynamic. There were certain skills to hone tactically but also a lot of pain to bear. I did whatever I could to survive, because pain had to equal learning.

Matt rode for a good few years but marginal pains killed him in the end. He didn't love it quite enough when cycling really started to hurt. He was sane that way. He simply decided that professional cycling was not for him. I, on the other hand, found some sort of solace in the suffering. More than that, I found that from the pain came satisfaction, from the suffering, joy. The older I got the more I liked being off on my own, pushing myself through the various stages of exhaustion for seven or eight hours at a stretch.

My school terms in South Africa left my mum on her own back in Nairobi. However, she had regular physio work at a clinic on the Ngong road and she was still in touch with Kinjah. In fact, it was more than that. She had practically become a member of the Safari Simbaz, acting as a soigneur, or carer, for the team; she would be on hand to offer any assistance, particularly during races or training rides. Kinjah had no back-up vehicles whenever he or the team raced, so Mum would drive behind as the support car, having bought plenty of bananas and water beforehand. She would do this even when I wasn't there.

She never told me the full extent of how involved she became and I only found out about what she had done for them many years later. She would often, for instance, drive up to Mai-a-Ihii with a car full of *posho*, a few pots of Cadbury's hot chocolate and some bags of sugar. *Posho* was used to make *ugali* for the team (it is the maize in powdered form) and the other ingredients were added to the boys' avocado paste. In this way, she looked after them, and they loved her for it.

Perhaps her involvement was a connection to me while I was away, but she saw too that life in Kinjah's hunkered hut, and out on the road, was about more than just the bikes. It was about opening up the world. For the Safari Simbaz, the hub of the world was Kinjah's house. Their individual journeys were the spokes that radiated outward.

Teaching a boy the discipline required for riding and training, as well as self-denial, put him on a road to the sort of self-fulfilment that he might never have dreamed about or have been able to achieve on his own. It gave him his first sense of possibility. The kids who buzzed in and out of Kinjah's hive, just like I did, would probably never get the chance to see the inside of a great university or go on to change the world. But they could work to be the best at something, and if not the best, they could get the best out of themselves. They could journey until they found the limits of what they were capable of, without the speed bumps of race or class. Mum saw that. She saw the enjoyment, the pride and the discipline; gifts that Kinjah gave away every day to us all.

I don't believe that Mum ever had dreams of seeing me grown up in a tie and bespoke suit, attached to a briefcase and a job that might make me a senior vice president some day. If she had, she never projected that vision on to me. From Rocky and Shandy, through to my obsession with bikes, she was happy to see me content so long as I was a decent person. She encouraged a sense of independence in my brothers and me, and the world and its infinite variety was something she loved and appreciated more than most people did.

She always enjoyed travelling out from the epicentre that was Karen, Langata and Nairobi. The Safari Simbaz races were partly an outlet for that, but I had left her without her fellow explorer for our adventures to the Rift Valley or the highlands. She loved the coast though. If Jeremy and Jono were home from England I would try to get back from South Africa, Mum would take time off work and we would head for the beaches of Diani, which fringes the Indian Ocean.

These trips were a bonus. When I was in South Africa I always returned to Kenya at least once a year, for the long summer holidays, but those days and nights were mainly given up to the bikes with Kinjah and the team. Generally, though, during most of my time in South Africa I managed to get back home more than once each calendar year. Paying for flights was a difficulty, of course. Noz could manage one return ticket for me in the year but a second trip was costly and I was expected to contribute.

It turned out that I was wearing the solution. In school in Johannesburg I had developed a habit that I still have. I had begun wearing kikoys, the very colourful type of sarong wrap garments which Ken-yan people wear, not so much in Nairobi but typically along the coast. In St John's my kikoys were the subject of some curiosity and even mild admiration. I was a walking advertisement for the clothes, which sadly weren't available in Johannesburg. The city needed a kikoy outfitter.

On a trip to Mombasa with Mum and my brothers I bought twenty to twenty-five kilos of the things. Kikoys in Mombasa sold for 200 shillings a go – about £1.50 per kikoy. Back in Johannesburg, to the discerning fashionistas of St John's, I sold them on for R100 each, about £7.00. I had to sell around a hundred of them to keep myself in airline tickets.

There was a hitch. Bringing so many kikoys back to Johannesburg meant not being able to carry very many of my own clothes with me. It was difficult enough flying my bike back and forth, so I ended up travelling just with bags full of merchandise and my bike.

There weren't enough pupils of taste in the boarding houses of St John's to buy the full consignment of kikoys but I persisted with my business plan. I dangled them before the staff who worked with Noz in the office. Some felt sorry for me, others seemed to genuinely like them. Either way, they paid up. There were a few local workers who thought they might look good in them too. Done.

I diversified the range, bringing in trousers and handbags made out of kikoy material. I went to a flea market in the Midrand shopping centre where they had an arts and crafts market and applied for a spot, setting myself up on a foldable table. After races on weekends I would head straight to my kikoy business. Some people loved the kikoys while others thought they were a bit kooky, but I mustered enough customers to sell three-quarters of the stock, covering my flights and a little bit extra for bike parts.

Having to save the money made me treasure our special trips to the coast even more. Mum looked forward to these excursions with her three sons – two accountants and the daydreamer – and my brothers and I enjoyed them because we didn't often get to spend much time together. Mum would always get me to go with her to the beach early in the morning, to do yoga with her. She would tell me how good yoga was for me. I was doubtful. I would look at the dawn sky maturing into morning and wait nervously for people we knew to begin passing us on the beach, who would steal furtive glances at me and Mum stretching by the surf, smirking as they went.

They might have mistaken my red face for sunrise but Mum never cared what people thought. If we were all in a beach bar or a cafe having some drinks or something to eat, and they piped up some music that she liked, she would get up and dance. Her three brave boys would be examining the cutlery as if they didn't know her. I think that just added to her enjoyment of those moments.

Mum dancing. Yoga on the beach in Diani. The boys. These things are stuck fast and fond in my memories of Africa.

Kinjah had set me believing that once I had developed physically, the mystery of how to be a full-time cyclist would be solved. I simply needed to keep training along the same lines. If I gave time to the bike, the bike would give the strength to my legs.

It was a healthy position to take. I couldn't force the muscles to grow. I needed to spin more. Kinjah always encouraged me to pedal at a high cadence, instead of grinding a heavy gear. By the time I was sixteen, I was riding the bike on a set of rollers in my room, as well as continuing to hit the cold, morning streets with Matt before dawn. I would often pretend to play squash (an approved school activity) with Matt in the late afternoon or early evening as the two of us headed off again for another training spin. I was still in constant contact with Kinjah, reporting to him on my progress and asking him more specific questions now about which gear was the best to use, and what my ideal cadence should be.

I watched the 2002 Tour de France with my mouth agape. It was the first Tour I ever saw. Ivan Basso and Lance Armstrong's duel in the mountains was like an epic dogfight between two World War One pilot barons. A residual of hero worship for Basso lingered with me until I came to learn the shady pharmaceutical secret of his success. You never get over that feeling of betrayal. Basso was my first and last hero of the peloton.

Sometime around then I met Robbie Nilsen. Robbie was a man

with fingers in several pies. A lawyer by trade, he had a passion for cycling and performance. He ran a junior cycling academy in Johannesburg called the Hi-Q Supercycling Academy (Hi-Q is a car servicing chain). Our meeting was timely. It was beginning to dawn on me that the typical South African fun race with a couple of thousand people involved wasn't going to be adequate preparation for a life on the lofty peaks of the Tour de France.

Kinjah and I were still exchanging ideas and training concepts but Robbie became part of the conversation too. We spent long afternoons together on weekends discussing practice ideas. I was coming to realize that the social aspects of the fun races I had been entering had trace elements that could be found again in the group training rides which we were now spending hours putting ourselves through every week. As harsh as it sounded, the group always tended towards the lowest common denominator. No matter the will or the intention, the capabilities and desires of the strongest rider in the group were normally tethered to the limitations of the weakest rider. The weakest guy may actually have been pouring all of himself into the road and the strongest guy may have felt like he was doing the same. But he wasn't. There would be some part of his inner self that he would never touch.

For these reasons, from then on I would be riding more on my own. It wasn't a hardship but I did miss the company of Matt, and the fun that I used to have back in the highlands above Mai-a-Ihii with Kinjah and the crew. Robbie and I developed a training system that began to make me feel stronger and lighter. I yearned to get better on the terms of a different continent; I wanted to be a rider of long epic races, not the flat short stories that we were enjoying in South Africa. I needed to be good after 200 kilometres; not explosive after that distance like a sprinter, but strong and powerful enough to finish in the main group. I needed bike habits like they had in Europe.

It became an obsession to me. I began doing these crazy rides. I would push the bike out the door, ride hard and try to maintain the same power output until I got back six hours later.

That was the sort of perversion that limited my choice of training partners, even if I'd wanted one. I wasn't able to train in a group any more, doing their five- or six-hour base training rides, coasting down hills and resting for enjoyable, but leisurely, coffee stops. I still had to ride the same kind of distances but at a pace that was consistent (and also progressively more uncomfortable) from start to finish. It obsessed me to the extent that I wouldn't even stop for water, thinking that if I stopped to fill up my bottles at a petrol station it would give my body time to recover. I wanted to train my body to recover and survive without breaking pace.

I attached a time-trial bottle cage underneath my saddle so that I could have two extra bottles stashed there. I had a small cooler bag attached to the front of my bike and I carried bottles in there too. I needed to have at least one bottle an hour, so I would carry up to six bottles on the bike at once. I would also take food with me and eat regularly while I was riding – but I would avoid having breakfast.

I managed to get a second-hand power meter, which became a really useful tool to train with. Robbie had done extensive reading about training according to power and power-to-weight ratios. I fed him my stats and we worked out what kind of numbers I should be aiming to maintain right through the five- or six-hour rides. We aimed for a power output of about 240 watts. For a teenager that's a bit grippy. Even years later at Team Sky that would be an effort. I would undertake those sessions three times a week and then on other rides in between I would take it easier or do shorter, sharper and more intense sessions. Some days I would do more climbing. Hills were no hardship. With the long sessions I would try to map out mostly flat courses for myself because it was easier to keep the power sustained. On a very lumpy course I would be pedalling like mad downhill to try to keep the power up, and then really relaxing on the uphill because the climb was hard already.

There I would be, somewhere outside the turmoil of Johannesburg, like a character from a comic strip streaking around the Gauteng province, with my legs in hell and my head in the clouds. The first ninety minutes would be quite bearable. After that the pain would start gnawing. My legs would put forward their case for a little freewheeling time on any slight downhill, just a small window to allow them to get a bit more sugar in the system. The brain had to win those arguments and keep the show rolling. Pushing and pushing.

By the end of the six hours the pain was a screaming presence. The last thirty minutes were the worst temptation but the best triumph. I had been doing this for five and a half hours. Maybe I could cruise home? Just take it down a notch? I had done the work and could feel the pain. Surely I had earned my parole? But my brain had to keep my body honest. The compartment that felt pleasure from suffering had to be the casting influence. Just do the last half-hour. Don't surrender having done so much. Then, miraculously, when I was so near the end, my body tripped the adrenaline switch and I had the strength for one last effort. Faster, faster, and no pain any more.

I look back at it now and I can see the madness, but I like that. It was necessary. It was purging and transformative. And in terms of my fundamental attitude to training, not much has changed.

For most of those rides I would head out from Midrand where I was staying with Noz and Jen. I had matriculated from St John's by this time, taking a sabbatical before university, and real life. I would hit the tarmac heading east. I would flash past stop signs where I should have been braking, or at least taking the precaution of glancing at the traffic. But I would go straight through, feeling bulletproof. The need to keep the power going would override all other considerations. I pored over maps like an ancient cartographer, devising routes full of left turns. Faced with an unhelpful red light, I could turn left without having to cross traffic. There was a triangular course that I devised which was perfect. All left turns and then straight back; east and west were the two ways that I would go. Left. Left. Left. Simple navigation.

They were big loads at that age but endurance is the winning hand. Robbie and I spoke about the science, and how we could help the circulation needed for the removal of toxins from my legs. Our theory was that the body had to develop an oxygen delivery system which would be more dynamic and fluid.

If we had only known it, this was precisely the work I would be doing at Team Sky years later. Tim Kerrison, the future Team Sky Head of Performance, and resident science boffin, would give a name to these rides: SAP rides, or SAP intervals. Sustained Aerobic Power. They are basically low-carb rides where we hit the road without having eaten breakfast but then start feeding within the first hour. We would be teaching the body to burn more fat as fuel, and we would email Tim with our power stats when we were done.

I look back in wonder now. The rides I was doing with Robbie were exactly the same. We didn't have a name for them, and we didn't even fully realize why we were doing it, but we knew it worked because I had responded well to it. We knew it was good before we knew what exactly it was.

Kinjah was an independent spirit. He taught me many things but there was one trait above all that he always shared, one standpoint. It was to never put up your hands and surrender to the real world. You might be outgunned and outnumbered but you never give up. Fight for the dream.

When I finished at St John's I knew that if surrender had to happen, it could wait. I would have to run out of road and have my back to a wall somewhere. University agreed to hang on for a year, but no more than that. I enrolled to study Economics at the University of Johannesburg. A couple of years on the lower slopes of academic life wouldn't kill me. I planned to spend as much time as possible tutoring myself (or torturing myself) in the saddle. With some balance, an academic degree could be earned without extinguishing the dream of becoming a professional cyclist.

To minimize the risk of abduction by an accountancy firm, I let my hair grow long and lank, wore bangles, dressed in hemp and kikoys and drove around in a rickety white VW Golf car with tinted silver windows. It was the sort of car that only a cyclist could love.

I was a student of cycling in one very specific and focused sense: I studied my own cycling and the ways to get better and stronger. With Robbie and with Kinjah I underwent the forensic analysis of every statistic and every ride. That was all. I wanted to be a professional rider in Europe, but I knew virtually nothing about what went on there, or how riders filled the eleven months when they weren't riding up and down France in the Tour.

I had started to enter more local races in Kenya and was granted a racing licence from the Kenyan Cycling Federation, whom Kinjah had introduced me to at the time. He was still on talking terms with the Federation back then, but I knew enough already from him about the antic failings of the organization, and how there would be no rope ladder thrown down to me by the men in blazers. The powers that be seemed very resistant to the notion that they should nurture the dreams of the country's best cyclists with funds and facilities.

I was also racing in South Africa. In the year I turned twenty I did twenty races for our Hi-Q Supercycling Academy, starting with the Berge en Dale Classic in Roodepoort, Johannesburg, in January 2005. From the start my cycling was decent but not awe-inspiring. I finished in the top half of the field after 105 kilometres of the Berge en Dale Classic. The pattern was set. In these races, where the distances were modest and the roads were flat, nobody was hurting. My party trick was my ability to suffer the longest when the going got tough, and these races weren't made for that.

Still, that year brought my first taste of the big time. In late August we travelled to Mauritius to compete in the Tour de Maurice. In the scheme of the cycling universe this wasn't a particularly important race. Nobody would gasp if they saw it on your list of achievements. But for me it was a milestone, my first time cycling overseas.

The Tour had a few modest riders who entered and a few small hills. On day two we raced to Curepipe. Not an especially long day but the road rose maybe 2,000 feet towards the extinct volcano of Trou aux Cerfs. It was enough for me, and I broke away from the main pack on the climb.

I won the stage.

That small glory was the stuff of short paragraphs on back pages, a minor entry in the record books. It was no game-changer but it encouraged me to believe that I could get into the game. Whatever I was doing, it was working.

When 2005 flipped over into 2006 the teenage years were gone and I had a modest achievement under my belt. I didn't know where the door to European racing was, but I was determined to continue fumbling about for it. Maybe 2006 would be even bigger.

It turned out to be a year in three acts.

All comedies.

7

2006 Act I: The Tour of Egypt

WHY DO YOU HATE US MR JULIUS MWANGI?

Despite the very publicized win at the selections to the 9th All African Games, the Mr Julius Mwangi alias 'Kamaliza' denied the Simbaz yet another chance to represent the country. David Kinjah, Davidson Kamau and Anthony Mutie who finished 1, 2, 3, respectively were termed as 'banned'. Kamaliza, as he is well known, said that he has banned them for misconduct, upon further investigations and meetings with the Kenya National Sports Council, he cannot give satisfactory evidence and reasons for this . . .

Kenyan cycling blog

Nairobi

At one time or another, each of us Safari Simbaz had fallen asleep in Kinjah's hut with the embers of conversation illuminating a common dream. It was a dream of riding our bikes in a tour in a foreign place, the world opening up to us in the way Kinjah had described when he had told us of his Italian days racing in Europe. In early February 2006, the dream began to take shape, or so we thought.

A gang of seven Safari Simbaz, including myself and Kinjah, cycled into Nairobi to the Egyptian embassy on Kingara Road. Standing outside in our cycling gear, we looked like athletic harlequins among the sensible diplomatic suits filing past. We were waiting on Julius Mwangi of the Kenyan Cycling Federation to honour us with his presence, and to sign the forms which would allow us to represent Kenya at the forthcoming Tour of Egypt. It was my first time representing the country as a professional rider, but it was an adventure for all of us and the first time we had been on tour together as the Safari Simbaz.

Earlier that day, we had briefly been allowed inside the embassy, only to be sent back outside again to have our visa photos taken elsewhere. This happened a number of times – back in, and then out again. Soon the whole day had passed sitting on the pavement, a day which we could have spent riding. This was far from ideal training preparation for the biggest race of our lives.

Most federations would take responsibility for the visa requirements of their national cycling team as a matter of course. The Kenyan Cycling Federation was different though. Mwangi, the chief poobah, was known everywhere as Kamaliza, which means finisher or someone who ends things. He ran a security firm of the same name, so I assumed the name didn't offend him. Nor did it entirely misrepresent his contribution.

From South Africa I had been sending my race results to his offices for some time. If Kamaliza or his cronies were impressed with me they had done a very fine job of disguising it. I wasn't sure that they knew I existed until Kinjah twisted their arms and got me included on the team for this trip to Egypt.

That is, if we ever got to Egypt. The embassy was closing in an hour and there was still no sign of our man. If we missed the day's deadline, we certainly wouldn't be racing past any pyramids. Finally, cool as a breeze, Mr Mwangi turned up at the last possible moment. He signed the forms. He had to really. He had put himself in charge of the entire trip. No team. No trip. He signed for all seven of us. Good of him to give us some of his time.

Cairo

A few days later we stepped out of Cairo airport. We decided that we needed a team photo to mark the momentous occasion. Gathering outside the terminal in a line, with our trollies and bikes held proudly in front of us, Julius Mwangi and the seven-man cycling team of Kenya. Happy as clams. I stood out, of course, like a sore, white thumb. We were all grinning and thrilled. It had been chaos getting here. It would most likely be chaos staying here. But for that moment, all was good with the world. Cheese.

All seven of us were Kinjah men from Mai-a-Ihii. Kamau was here. At that time he was working in a slaughterhouse in Kiserian. He got into cycling having ridden a *boda boda*, a bicycle taxi, in Nairobi for a while. He had great promise. Mischievous Njana was here too, and Michael.

I had transported my bike in a black, purpose-made bike case, which I had borrowed from a friend in South Africa. My fellow Safari Simbaz were fascinated by this padded container and had never seen one before. Rather than feeling proud of my expensive piece of kit, I suddenly felt like the white swell out among the people. 'What a *mzungu*! A case for his bike.' I knew this would take a while for me to live down and that I would be mercilessly teased; everyone else had covered their bikes in clear plastic wrapping and hoped for the best.

The good news was that we had arrived in one piece, which logistically was no small triumph. Nobody had missed the flight, our visas were stamped, and miraculously all of our bikes had arrived with us (we had all had visions of them ending up in Frankfurt or some other place halfway around the world). On the other side of the balance sheet, there were some less comforting things to consider. Julius Mwangi was our team manager, accompanied by a trinity of know-nothing bluffers from the Federation who would make up the rest of our support unit: a soigneur, a mechanic and a man with no designated task but whose presumed 'versatility' meant that he could fill in for any of the other know-nothings, without us riders noticing. Between the four of them they would need a long semester of tutoring just to learn how to change a back wheel. Not that they would be interested in that type of educational opportunity.

We suspected we knew the real reason why the Tour of Egypt had been graced with our presence. Coincidence or not, the peloton was mainly formed of African teams, representing the various nations or constituencies who would be present in the next elections for the African Cycling Federation. An invite here, we thought, assumed a vote in return for the Egyptian Federation. Elsewhere, there were two or three lower-echelon European teams in the race, including the Poles and the Slovenians, as well as a few other countries who were not known for their cycling prowess. The South African national team were the favourites by far.

Still, when we arrived at the accommodation the night before the race, we were smiling like lottery winners, raring to go for the biggest ride of our lives. The Tour of Egypt seemed to be reasonably well organized and there were elements that we associated with premier bike racing. There was a race book. There were clearly planned stages with a start and finish banner. A convoy of cars would follow the race. Somewhere in that convoy would be our support car containing our top-level support team. How excited we were just to be there.

We were given the Kenya national team kit: one pair of shorts and one shirt. One set of kit for the entire tour meant washing our own kit every evening. Washing it in the sink or shower in the undrinkable water, wrapping it up in towels and jumping on it, trying to force the moisture out, then hanging it up to dry for the next day. Despite these relative shortcomings, it still felt like we had arrived.

The Race

The first stage took us out and around the majestic deserts of Cairo. It was a short prologue, an individual time trial of 8 kilometres, to determine who would wear the leader's jersey. We had no issues. I was the only rider in the team with a time-trial bike and I managed a respectable 5th on the day.

For the next three stages over consecutive days the winds were a nuisance, blowing fiercely across the desert. The stages were mostly flat, which was disappointing for me, but at various points the crosswinds buffeted us, which made the racing tougher. Kamau had a bad crash when he was blown off course on to the side of the road on one of the few uphills. The bike canted him straight into a gutter. He lost minutes of time to the peloton, which meant there was no way back for him in his aim to finish highly in the final standings. In terms of competitiveness and the Safari Simbaz, it was just Kinjah and I who were left to compete for the General Classification for the second half of the tour. The rest of the guys were hanging in there, but looking up to us to produce the sort of result that we could brag about back in Kenya on our return. Kinjah and I were teasing each other in a master vs pupil sort of way.

The fourth day was a very long flat stage from one Egyptian town to another with mainly desert in between. Maybe 230 kilometres, the most exciting thing we would see all day were sand dunes. Otherwise it was just plain sand without the dunes.

Less than halfway through we were all barely surviving and trying to make the most of it. But it was harder than it needed to be. Unlike other teams, we spent much of our time, and precious energy, filling up our own water bottles. We each had two bottles for the race, and when we emptied them we had to drop back to the team car and pass them through the window to be replenished. Riders from other countries, meanwhile, equipped with an unlimited supply in the team's travelling cool box, would cavalierly throw away their bottles as soon as they had finished them.

It wasn't ideal but up until this point at least our system had worked. Suddenly, though, the car was nowhere to be seen. We took turns dropping back into the convoy but each time we would confirm each other's assessment of the situation – our support vehicle was gone. We dropped back again to ask other team managers if they had seen our car, but the answer was the same.

The sun was high and hot. Our bottles were now completely empty, and we were still expending every ounce of energy, pouring ourselves, mind and body, on to the road. We couldn't figure out what was going on, but the car wasn't the problem now. The problem was the stark fact that we were dehydrating in an Egyptian desert.

I dropped back from the peloton to the South African team vehicle. I had recognized the driver as Bart Harmse, a commissaire from a number of the South African races I had taken part in as a junior.

'Oom Bart, can I please get some bottles of water from you? Our support team has gone missing.'

I tried to make the request sound as reasonable and as respectful as I could, but the way Bart looked at me, his face said that this was one of the most half-assed things he had ever heard.

So half-assed that he took pity on us. I managed to get two or three bottles out of him and we shared them around the team as best we could. Still, there were seven of us, all thirsty and burning up. We were like a shipwrecked crew in a great ocean with the last canteen of water on the lifeboat long since drained. Except that, unlike a shipwrecked crew, we were all working manically, outputting as much wattage as we were humanly capable of. The water didn't last long between seven of us.

Poor Michael, it wasn't supposed to be like this for him. It certainly wasn't the dream. He was thirsty and struggling, and seemed to be pushing uphill in a place where there were no hills.

. Between us we tried to imagine that we were at home, that we were riding in our beloved Ngong Hills, swapping sharp insults and teases. We pretended for a while that we weren't toiling through this vacant desert. There was so much sand that it had lost its novelty. The road behind and ahead was endless and our water had been finished long ago.

We were all feeling it. When we looked at each other we could see the effects of this imposed drought. We were slowing and getting weaker. This was happening to us at different rates but Michael looked the worst. The shine had gone from his eyes and his grin had vanished. This was no ride through the hills. This was desperate.

I tried to imagine what was going through Michael's head. Above all, there would have been his pride. We were here together, riding this tour. It was another country and another chapter. When we returned home to Kenya, when we were back in Kinjah's place, we would tell stories of our big race adventure. The stories would be funny but with a spine of steel to them. This was the scenario: we all gave some and some gave all. The guy who wilted would be remembered, seized upon and turned into a figure of laughter.

Like the rest of us, Michael would never want to be remembered as the one who was dropped and left behind. No. He wouldn't want to be the first.

On the other hand, this was a just bike race. Bad things happened but usually nobody died. So why wait until he fell off his bike through dehydration or heat stroke? Why be a fool? How would the stories sound if he keeled over and got taken to hospital for a few days? Not good, either.

Something had gone wrong but it was out of our control. Broom wagons, those large buses to collect stragglers, followed races for exactly this reason. If things got too much, then we could get off our bikes and it would pick us up and take us home.

With these thoughts whirring in our minds, we pedalled on, each of us withdrawing into our own world of thirst and worry. I had an advantage here, probably. I like to suffer. I like it better when I know that the people around me are suffering too. For a year and a half I had been rehearsing this pain on the roads around Johannesburg. Nobody told me there would be days like this, but I trained for them. Just in case.

Eventually Michael's brain made a public service announcement to his body. This was too much. He was dehydrated, it was too hot, he had nothing.

He stopped, got off his bike and stood at the side of the road. I imagine he was half embarrassed and half relieved, waiting for the broom wagon to come. It would at least have bottles of water and air conditioning.

Michael's Tour of Egypt was over.

There was no broom wagon. Or if there was, it had driven past Michael and had left him standing on the side of the road in the desert.

He sat down by the roadside and didn't panic. A car coming from either direction would be visible from miles away. He would flag it down and hitch a ride. If they had no room they would have some water, surely.

No one came. Peering into the shimmering heat vapours coming up off the tar, it dawned on him that this road through the desert was a route that nobody used. The afternoon sun was focusing its heat right down on him now. Mad dogs and Englishmen, yes. Kenyan cyclists, no.

He sat and sat. Nothing. The wait went past the point of being funny; his life was ebbing away. He had to get out of the sun before he fainted. Or died. He actually had this thought: 'Right here in this desert, on my first ever tour race with the Safari Simbaz, this is where I will die.'

He started to dig. When he got past the surface heat, the sand there was cooler. He dug a trench and rolled himself inside, pulling the desert sand in on top of himself. His helmet was all that was protecting the top of his head, which was the only part of his body that stuck out from above the sand. In this hole it was cooler for a while but he knew that he had dug a provisional grave for himself.

By this point, he must have thought the rest of us had finished the stage. Surely we would look around, and go back to check on him? We must have realized by now that he hadn't been chauffeured to the finish. What would we do? Surely we would find the team car and drive back along the road? What if we couldn't find the team car? Suppose we assumed that he was okay? He might be somewhere with Julius Mwangi and the know-nothings?

Meanwhile, he lay there, dying in the desert.

After we finished the stage from hell, there was no sign of our team manager, Mwangi the Exterminator, and no sign of the car. There was also no sign of Michael.

The race organizers provided us with our keys for the hotel nearby and we checked into our rooms. We had been warned about not drinking the tap water there so our thirst stayed with us. Riding for Kenya and we had no water to drink at the end of a stage through a desert. It felt like madness. I walked to a local shop and bought a few five-litre drums of water and hauled them back for the guys.

There was still no sign of Michael. We thought he must have been having a time of it with Mr Mwangi and the 'support' team.

Finally Mr Mwangi pitched up later that evening. He had a big grin on his face and was showing us postcard photos of the pyramids and Mount Sinai. Mr Mwangi had been sightseeing up in Moses' footsteps, where he'd received the Ten Commandments.

We had two questions for Mr Mwangi. One. Had he really been off playing tourist all day while we were riding in the desert? Two. Did he happen to have Michael with him?

The eleventh commandment: Thou shalt not abandon your riders, Mr Mwangi.

We checked with the race organizers, but they had nothing to report back. No one had seen Michael, and no one was taking control of the situation, either.

When a cycling team functions as normal, the riders get up early in the morning, eat some breakfast and head off to their race. The clothes and belongings they will not use in the race are brought along behind them in the car with the support team. That gear usually arrives at the next hotel room before the day's racing finishes. However, that day one of the soigneurs from the Polish team had screwed up. He had collected all of the chargers for his team's radios and placed them in a bag for safekeeping. Then he had driven off and left the bag behind in the previous night's hotel.

In early evening, just as it was getting dark, the team had the option of continuing the race without radios for the remainder of the week, or sending the soigneur off to drive back through 235 kilometres of desert to collect the chargers. He would then have to drive the 235-kilometre return journey to get back in time to charge the radios so they would be ready for the next morning. Unlike in our own team, radios were the lifeline of a proper support unit, so the soigneur drove off into the dusk and the desert. He was an unhappy man. Although the road was empty and straight, it was time already for headlights, and the sheer monotony of the drive was a worry after a long day. He tried to keep cool and alert.

Odd. Was that a bike lying in the sand just there? It couldn't be. He pulled off the road and reversed. Holy shit. It was a bike resting on the vague border between road and desert. Maybe it had been left by one of the teams and somebody was supposed to come back along and retrieve it?

He stood there on the road looking down at the bike. What should he do? If he took it and the team came back to retrieve it, they could be there half the night searching around. But it seemed too weird to leave it behind.

Over there – what was that? He was sure he could see a helmet on the desert floor, lying on its own. He tried to figure it out in his mind: rider abandons, then leaves bike and helmet there for collection when he steps into the broom wagon. That would make sense. He walked over and picked the helmet up. Sweet mother . . . there was a head underneath it.

Michael had been lying in his little grave as darkness fell. The grim irony hadn't been lost on him. His last chance of being spotted was vanishing with the light. Yet the darkness was bringing a coolness to the desert. In his hole, his head tilted into the sand, he had fallen asleep. Empty.

He wasn't going to die from the heat. He was going to die from the cold and the sheer exhaustion.

But suddenly Polish hands were frantically scrabbling the sand off him, pulling him out of his grave. He was shredded with exhaustion and dehydrated to the point where standing up was a challenge. The Polish hands offered him water. Slow. Sensible. It flowed into him like life itself.

Welcome to the Tour of Egypt, Michael Nziani Muthai. Your Federation thanks you for your efforts.

We raced on until the end of the tour but Michael took the tourist option. He quite enjoyed travelling from hotel to hotel. Alive to give witness to the story of the week.

8

2006 Act II: The Commonwealth Games

This was the beginning. Of the end. The Commonwealth Games.

This felt far better than Egypt. It even smelled more like the big time. As riders we were staying in the athletes' village in Melbourne along with the rest of the Kenyan outfit in our country's quarters. There were six of us: Kinjah and me, Michael Nziani Muthai of the desert, Davidson Kamau, his brother Peter Kamau and Simon Nganga. We were pleasantly surprised to be treated like the rest of the Kenyan team, on par with far more high-profile athletes.

I enjoyed discovering who was who. We popped along to a couple of the track sessions. Watching Kenya, and being in the Kenyan stand when the team won a gold medal, was extremely special. There was an amazing atmosphere. I loved that Games spirit.

I had brought two bikes with me. I wanted to max out on the experience and to ride in both the road race competition and the time-trial competition.

If I was being truthful, my time-trial bike was a makeshift sort of thing, and definitely not an appliance of science. It at least had deep section wheels and aero bars. These provided a more aerodynamic position where my hands and forearms were lower, further forward and closer together to reduce drag. It all helped, but it was still the bare minimum. Kinjah had the same intention for the Games, to enter both races, and had come armed with the same equipment.

When we first arrived in Melbourne, Kinjah took me aside.

'Chris, it's a bit of a joke here at the moment.'

'What's new?'

'No. They want me to do the track events as well.'

Kenya had no competitor for any of the track events. Kinjah had tried to explain, to make them understand. He used short words. He. Could. Not. Ride. The. Track. It was a completely different discipline. Kenya didn't even have a single track in the whole country.

The argument was ongoing. Julius Mwangi and the Kenyan Federation felt that Kinjah was being disrespectful and rude. They assumed he wouldn't agree to do the events because he was too full of himself. They mustered all their expertise and explained the situation to him again and again: 'Listen, it's on a bicycle. You race on a bicycle. You need to race. So why can't you ride the track?'

Kinjah held firm and resisted. He wasn't going to humiliate himself in front of the world for Mr Mwangi's benefit.

'Listen to me, Chris. They also want us to ride the mountain bike race. There are three places. You, me and Davidson Kamau.'

It was easy to end that argument; I didn't have a mountain bike with me.

Kinjah relayed the bad news to Mr Mwangi and his organizers. They offered us a deal. If we agreed to ride the mountain bike race, they would provide us with three mountain bikes through the Commonwealth Games funding.

Kinjah and I both recognized the same patriotic opportunity; we were each going to get a free bike out of this. Kamau too. After the Games, we thought, we could send these mountain bikes back with Kinjah, so that other Safari Simbaz could use them. Kinjah was in charge of the budget and a deal was organized at a local cycling shop. He squeezed everything he could out of the poor shop owners. The bikes were decent and far more disposed for racing off-road than anything we had ever owned. Although they were not fitted with disc brakes, they were equipped with front suspension forks and they were much lighter than we were used to. The rear stay was made from carbon, which was elaborate enough for us. We were ready to go, or as ready as we could have been.

The mountain bike event that we had never planned to ride was coming two days after the time trial and three days before the road race.

The Time Trial

The next day I had a warm-up ride on the time-trial course along the beautiful beach route situated on the St Kilda Foreshore. Skirting the long sandy beach, I spotted some riders in their pristine English gear. Wow, they looked so professional. All wearing the same gear, skin-suits and aero helmets, and they were only warming up.

I made a mental note: borrow an aero helmet and pin the Kenyan gear on tight to make it look like a skinsuit.

When the morning of the time trial arrived they sent the African nations out first. In order of weakness. Christopher Clive Froome was listed to go first. Then Tumisang Taabe of Lesotho. Next, Rajendra Singh of Fiji. Also from Fiji, Percival Navbo didn't have a time-trial bike at all; he was on a standard road bike, and he got to ride closer to some of the genuine time trialists! It was nothing personal, but I knew that the purpose was to get us support acts out of the way first.

The time trial took us out on a fairly flat road along the coast. I would have preferred hills but my time-trial bike was quite heavy, it weighed over ten kilos, so the flat wasn't bad. The course was just over twenty kilometres each way. I recorded a time of 53 minutes 58 seconds.

The next rider didn't beat me. Or the next. Or the next. I knew nobody serious had started yet, but I realized that my time wasn't that bad, either. I was in the hot seat; I was the leader.

The hot seat isn't hot but it is literally a seat. It's at the finish line and the top three guys are taken there when they finish. When some-one beats the time of, say, the third guy then the third guy gets bumped off and the new guy takes his seat. If there is a new guy who beats everybody and comes in first, then the first and second move down the seats and the guy in seat number three leaves. After the fin-ish line they took me straight to the hot seat and I sat there in my cycling gear, having a drink. I had my first fifteen minutes of fame for a performance that wasn't even yet a result.

Somehow, I continued to be the top man for a very long time. There were about eighty riders in the field and forty-nine more had gone out before anybody beat my time.

All of my family saw me on TV. The broadcast kept on switching back to the hot seat and this young, skinny guy. Cyclingnews.com called me 'Chris Froome, time trial revelation'. I was sitting there in the hot seat when two managers from the English team first noticed me. Their names were Dave Brailsford and Shane Sutton.

'See what that kid has done?'

'Who?'

'That Kenyan kid. Wearing the sandals.'

'Doesn't look like a Kenyan.'

'Well, he is.'

I wound up 17th overall in a field of seventy-two riders but, thanks to spending over an hour sitting in the leader's chair, the result seemed to bestow more attention on me than a 17th-placed finisher had ever received before. Nathan O'Neill of Australia took gold. Kinjah was 31st.

Another member of the British Cycling management team spotted me later that day. His name was Doug Dailey. He made a mental note.

It had been a day to cherish for me.

Kinjah had endured enough. This was the Commonwealth Games, after all. When the media asked him about the Kenyan Cycling Federation he had replied that the organization did not run with the efficiency of a Swiss watch. One of his frustrations was that this was a competition on the world stage and we didn't even have any team kit. In the end we had been forced to purchase plain white and black jerseys ourselves and have the word KENYA laminated on to the backs.

Before my time trial we had all been called into a meeting in the Kenyan quarters in the village. The Kenyan Federation had been bullyragged in the media and they needed to express their hurt and displeasure. The meeting grew into a disciplinary hearing. Kinjah wasn't there, but he was in the dock.

The Kenyan officials were furious. Yes, they conceded that we had no kit, but drawing attention to that fact, as Kinjah had done, was a worse crime. Our team, who were all Kinjah's guys, were quiet and we kept our heads down. We were intimidated as this was a huge opportunity for all of us. At the Games here in Melbourne we were a long way away from the tin hut in a Kikuyu village outside Nairobi. The officials held all of the strong cards.

This was Kinjah though. In essence, he had brought us all here. So I decided to voice my opinion before Kinjah was completely hung out to dry.

They lined us up, and asked us one by one if there was anything we would like to contribute to the meeting. Too scared to say anything, everyone passed. I was the last one in the line. I didn't hold back. I said that it was clear what was going on, and that I could see they were trying to use this situation to destroy Kinjah. As soon as I had finished speaking, all of my teammates suddenly lit up like a fireworks display and began arguing passionately.

Kinjah was being set up. We were here to race. The meeting and the argument was not helping at all.

The Mountain Bike Race

The novelty of our new mountain bikes evaporated as soon as we visited the mountain biking circuit at Lysterfield Park, the day before we were due to race. When they had twisted our arms to ride the event we had asked ourselves, how bad could it be? We had grown up riding off-road so surely we could at least get around the course and finish? We could ride off on our bikes afterwards and chalk the day down to experience. But as soon as we saw the circuit, we knew exactly how bad it was. What had we got ourselves into?

The circuit was tight. We rode around our first practice lap through the dense forest and over worryingly large rocks. Suddenly Kinjah, Kamau and I screeched on our brakes at the top of what looked like an abyss. Surely there was no way we were going to ride off this? We looked at the sides and the barriers but they were all guiding us to the same conclusion: jump off the great rock, at speed. There had to be some kind of mistake.

We were still all looking around for an alternative route to descend when a group of other riders went steaming past. They flew straight off the edge and over the void. Kinjah and Kemau just stared at me. I stared back.

This was quite serious now, and the course was only beginning to unfold. After negotiating the jump as carefully as we could, and down several narrow descents, we made our way on to parts of the course that were elevated on planks of wood. These wooden sections were about the width of a garden path, but raised up off the ground above boulders and trees. It scared us out of our wits. If we fell off the planks, we knew the drop was big enough to ensure that we definitely wouldn't be competing in the road race three days later. We had never raced like this before in our lives.

It was going to be a three-hour race for us on a 6.4-kilometre circuit from hell. We would cycle around its perimeter eight times, and we knew that it would become scarier each time; the law of averages, as applied to chancers like us, meant that if we didn't fall off on the previous lap, we had a far greater probability of doing so on the next one.

We cursed Mr Mwangi for getting us into another fine mess.

I had heard that Burry Stander, a professional South African mountain biker, was in Melbourne. I knew he could help me in my predicament. Burry would later go on to become World Under-23 Cross-Country champion in 2009, and finish 5th at the London 2012 Olympics.* After a couple of sleepless nights I sought him out. I found Burry and Mannie Heymans, the Namibian mountain bike champion, in the athletes' village.

They took me through the course generously, even though we had some language difficulties; I didn't speak 'mountain bike'. This was the gist of it:

'Okay. Here's how you are going to mud-dive the swampy section. Got it? And this is how you are going to get through the rock garden full of death cookies [small rocks] and baby heads [slightly

---

* Tragically, six months after the 2012 Olympics, in January 2013, Burry was hit by a minibus in KwaZulu-Natal. He was dead at twenty-five which was a huge loss, particularly in South Africa where he was an idol to many and one of the best mountain bikers to come out of the country.

bigger rocks]. And now you have all these tricky bits. The whoop-
de-do's where you can sky. Be careful, no yard sale [a crash landing
that leaves a rider and his bike scattered all over the ground]. Land
badly and you could potato crisp your wheel [bend it slightly out of
shape] or taco it [I could guess]. Here's what gearing you should use.
Dude. No granny gears. This hill is a bit of a roid buffer [so steep
going down that your ass would come into contact with your rear
wheel]. And be careful in the wooded areas that a branch doesn't
clothesline you.'

Burry and Mannie were two very kind, open and confident guys.
I took that much from them. Most of the rest was lost in translation.
I thought to myself, 'Right, I'm definitely going to give this my best
shot. I'm fit. I've been training.' I knew I wasn't very good technically, but I was confident I could keep up.

It began badly and got worse.

Standing on the start line worrying meant that I didn't get into a
very good position. I was surrounded by hard-core mountain bikers,
who were all pressed up against me. When the gun went off I was still
trying to get my foot into my pedal. The riders bunched up just after
the first corner and I wound up quite far back. I thought to myself,
'Okay, just work your way through the field,' but it didn't work –
the other riders soon vanished into the distance and I was left chasing
in a cloud of dust.

At this point, when it was already too late, I remembered Burry
and Mannie's advice: it would be vital to push really hard in the first
kilometre, almost at full sprint, before the race got to the single-track
section. If I was stuck behind somebody when I reached there, I had
no chance of getting past.

I pushed myself to the limit for the first two laps, chasing as hard
as possible to hunt down the main pack. But I pushed too far and
crashed badly. I had let my growing confidence get the better of me
on the big drop-off, and ended up sprawled face first in the dirt. I
picked myself up and gave myself a talking-to.

'Chris, this is the Commonwealth Games. It's a joke that you're
even competing in this race at this level. Not only are you not going

to do well today, but you have a road race in three days. Accept that you are not a mountain biker; get through this. You've got yourself a mountain bike so just ride around. Gently.'

I had a brief but exciting tussle with the gold and silver medallists, Liam Killeen and Oli Beckingsale, two English guys. There was about an hour of racing left and I was surprised to find that anybody was still behind me. When I realized who they were – and that they were lapping me – I was a bit disappointed, but I moved off the track politely to let them past. A couple of other riders crashed out or stopped, so I ended up making up a few late positions, finishing 24th out of twenty-six finishers (three retired).

Kamau and I were listed as OVL (overlapped) in the final standings. So was Kinjah, but he had to be different. He had hustled himself into a good position at the start of the race and had ridden well for four laps where he stayed in the top ten or fifteen places. However, when he reached a point where he knew he couldn't maintain the same level, he jumped off the circuit. They put OVL after his name but his thinking was that he was a DNF (did not finish). No one passed him, so no one beat him. He loved analysing things differently to the rest of the world, so he was very proud and happy after the race, telling everybody that he was in the top ten or fifteen riders★ and that no one had overtaken him. He could have been a contender.

The Road Race

The road race took place on the 166-kilometre course around the botanical gardens in Melbourne. It was a long, lively race ridden in still, searing heat and it started very quickly. The course was twisty and the favourites were anxious to burn off the novices to ensure

---

★ As a good friend of Kinjah's, I should point out just how impressive a top-fifteen placing really was. The field wasn't quite the size of the Tour de France peloton. In fact, there were only twenty-nine riders. And I was one of those behind Kinjah! I didn't really count. Neither did our teammate Davidson Kamau, who finished 25th. Three of the others fell off their bikes and quit.

there would be no pile-ups at the corners. Kinjah went in an early breakaway and stayed at the front of the race.

Tensions lingered from the time-trial meeting and again Mr Mwangi and his sidekicks chose to pull another vanishing act. We had come round to the feed zone and they were nowhere to be seen. Early in the race a Scot named Duncan Urquhart had made a break. Kinjah was still in a group of four who had caught him and the group had stayed out ahead of the field for over an hour. This was a more than reasonable achievement for Kinjah, given the week he had undergone. What people watching on television wouldn't have noticed, however, was that every time he came to the feed zone he was attempting to recruit spectators to fill his bottles and to pass the team our food.

He had to slow down in the zone and point to where our officials had left our bottles and food before they had answered the call of tourism. He would point and shout with Doppler effect as he passed: 'Those are our bottles! Can somebody fill them? Please! And feed us!'

Eventually he managed to enlist a number of volunteers to look after us. They were some of the other Kenyan athletes who had already participated in their events who had come out to watch us race. To make matters worse, while he was still riding strongly Kinjah had dropped the first feed bag that he had been given and had lost his rhythm. He made his way back into the group of five, but the incident and the two hours of stress, recruitment and drought had extracted a toll.

Meanwhile, being in the front group of five and looking so distinctive meant that Kinjah had received a large amount of face time in the television coverage. In a bar or a cafe somewhere our brave officials must have spotted him and sensed that they were in danger of missing some reflected glory.

By the time we had reached the latter part of the race the rest of us had settled into a rhythm and were set into a routine of receiving our bottles from our newly recruited support crew. However, when we came round to the feed zone for the next lap we saw that our officials had finally arrived and were putting on a wonderful show for the cameras of tending to us conspicuously. Kinjah saw red. He grabbed bottles from other riders and tables and threw them at the Kenyan officials, screaming abuse at them. The crowd loved the 'Punch and Judy' show which erupted every time Kinjah came back round.

The casualty rate was high that day. Not only among the Kenyan officials. Two of the many non-finishers, partly due to the insufferable heat, included the English riders Ian Stannard and Geraint Thomas. I would come to know those names well in the years afterwards.

As the drama settled and the peloton went about its business, swallowing stragglers like a python digesting its prey, Kinjah and I were still performing well in the race. The rest of our teammates had dropped away; Kamau was the last of them to leave our Kenyan group.

I sat back in the peloton waiting, feeling reasonably comfortable, waiting for the final break in the race. I watched Mark Cavendish making his break for glory on behalf of the Isle of Man, but he was hauled in quickly. I waited and waited and finally I had a moment that was the highlight of my Commonwealth Games. It was nearing the end of the race, on the penultimate lap, and we had reached the hardest part of the course where there were climbs. Kinjah was now out of contention and I was the last Kenyan left with any hope in his pocket.

The peloton suddenly slowed up; it was the lull before the proverbial storm. We were on the flat but were fast approaching two tough climbs towards the end of the circuit. I thought, 'Well, I'm close to my limit here, and I think I'm going to get dropped, so I'm going to put in one last big effort. Why not?'

It worked extremely well. When the peloton slowed on the flat I burst ahead, hoping that I could stay out in front before the real contenders began driving hard, knowing that I wouldn't be able to follow them.

Here was another of these crazy Kenyans in their makeshift jerseys. Another lunatic from the unknown. They let me go. I got quite a decent gap before the climbs, I'd say I stretched it out to maybe 30 seconds.

The Aussies had been cycling tactically all day, and hung back to see if anybody else thought I might be a threat. It was Ryan Cox from the South African team, however, who really lit things up at that point. He broke away and came across to me. It was just the two of us up front. I sat on his wheel. The commentators ratcheted up the tension: 'Wow, here's one of the favourites, Ryan Cox, with a Kenyan, it looks like, but we've never seen him before.' I spent a bit of time in the breakaway with Ryan, until the peloton closed our show down. They came after us quickly, or rather, they came after Ryan; I just happened to be in the vicinity. I got passed on the final climbs as the Australians closed the race off. Matt Hayman won gold and Allan Davis got bronze. David George of South Africa squeezed into the silver medal spot.

I finished 25th, 5 minutes 15 seconds off the winner's time. Kinjah finished well that day, all things considered, placing 27th, at 10 minutes 32 seconds off the leader's result. He got cheered all the way home as word spread of the smiling, dreadlocked Kenyan who had raced half the day without even bread or water and took time to recruit feeders and bottle-fillers for himself and his teammates.

Kinjah gave a post-race interview, mowing down the Kenyan officials. We did the best race we could but again the Kenyan Cycling Federation had let us down. They weren't there to feed us.

The interview came over the PA system. I spotted an angry Mr Mwangi looking frantically around to see where Kinjah's voice was coming from. Kinjah and I grabbed our bikes and we made a swift exit to the athletes' village.

In the pits afterwards, the English guy with a Scouse accent, Doug Dailey, came by to say hello. He gave me his email address and I gave him mine. He said to keep in touch.

9

2006 Act III: World Championships in Salzburg

Full disclosure. While we were in Cairo for the Tour of Egypt, Mr Mwangi pulled me aside and asked for a favour. He needed me to help him on his computer to take care of some business, and had asked me to log in to the Kenyan Cycling Federation email, providing me with the username and password.

I thought it was odd that he had given me this information; he knew that I was a good friend of Kinjah's. Regardless of the peculiarity, I sat there and typed out the few emails he wanted done. They were administrative tasks to be sent to various people, and there was nothing of any significance. Mr Mwangi wasn't too confident of his written English, so I assumed he had found a good use for his spare *mzungu*. I made a mental note of the login details.

After Egypt and after Melbourne I had an idea.

I had already begun sending out my CV to cycling teams in Europe. A two-pager that I had typed up, which included all of my results from everywhere I had been racing in Africa, together with a few photos pasted on the side. I thought it looked great. In the back of my mind I was aware that European cycling teams were really only interested in seeing CVs which provided evidence of having raced in Europe. A few people got back to me and asked that very question. 'Have you done any races in Europe, sonny?'

I thought that if I did the Under-23 World Championships in September, in the city of Salzburg, which was definitely in Europe, it might be a giant step towards becoming a professional. Things were bad between the Kenyan Federation and the Safari Simbaz. Asking the Federation to enter me into the race and fund me to get there would be a waste of time. They knew I was on Kinjah's side.

So I sat down and logged on to the Federation email address. Posing as Julius Mwangi, I wrote a short letter to the UCI, informing them that I would like to enter Christopher Froome, one of my country's most promising Under-23 riders, into the World Championships at that grade in the autumn. Thank you.*

It is September and I am in Salzburg.

The entire Kenyan cycling team and officials. *C'est moi.*

I have a suitcase and two bikes in bike bags. I am like some weird refugee. I am an optimist though. I'm hoping there will be a courtesy car. I look for a sign welcoming me. The sign will be held by a driver, who will ask me if I had a nice trip and wonder where I would like him to drive me. He will insist on lifting my bikes on to the roof rack by himself.

There is no courtesy car. I am unattached.

There is a bed and breakfast. I booked it myself online. It is the cheapest bed and breakfast in Salzburg. Possibly because it is 7 kilometres outside of Salzburg.

It turns out that two bus rides will still leave me a kilometre away from my lodgings. I walk the last kilometre with my two bikes and suitcase, shuffling along. The perfect midpoint to an epic day which began yesterday with a (very) long-haul flight and stopovers.

That evening I made my way to the team managers' meeting. I had assembled my time-trial bike and commandeered a map. A storm introduced itself to the day. I tried to memorize the map before the rain took care of it but after a couple of minutes I couldn't even hold the map any more, let alone read it. It crumbled in the torrential rain and with a gust of wind it was gone. I was left with a wafer of paper between each thumb and index finger.

I found my way to the city using signposts but inevitably I got lost in the city centre. On the map, as far as I could remember, it all

---

* Mr Mwangi, I am sorry I impersonated you. To be fair, I did mention it all vaguely before I left, that time when I said that I had 'sorted something out'.

looked very simple. Now, there were so many roads with names that sounded vaguely familiar. I was lost.

I asked some slightly scared strangers about the venue for the meeting. It was to be held in a creaky old auditorium or a hall or a town centre or something – did this ring any bells? After asking what must have amounted to a good sampling of the citizenry, I was eventually pointed in the right direction. When I arrived at the location, I found the signs for the meeting, took a deep breath and walked into the auditorium. I had entered through the wrong door. I was not at the back as I had hoped to be. I had walked in at the front. A drowned rat. With his bike outside.

Everybody stopped what they were doing and looked up in horror. Then down at the rainwater that had fallen from my kit and was collecting in a tiny puddle around my cycling shoes.

The man who was making his presentation stopped the whole show and looked at me, aghast.

'This is a managers' meeting, only for the managers, not the riders. I am sorry.'

'I'm here for the managers' meeting, yes.'

'But –'

'I am a manager.'

He gave me a shrug, as if to say, 'I've seen everything now,' and asked me to sit down. The meeting was already half over. I was a bit disappointed that I didn't hear anything about the support vehicles. I was still expecting somebody to at least produce a box full of keys and to start to call out names: 'South Africa, Kenya, Lesotho . . . Please take your car keys.'

When they reached the end of the meeting they showed diagrams of where the support cars needed to be during the race. Rubbing it in, I felt.

Tony Harding was the South African manager in Salzburg. He had been quite instrumental in Robbie Hunter's professional career and I had seen him often at the races in Johannesburg. He came over with a big grin on his face and whacked me on the back of the head.

'What are you doing? Idiot!'

I told him my story. How Robbie Nilsen had helped me to train specifically for the time-trial event, doing lots of 20-minute blocks. And how Robbie had gone to Hi-Q, who had generously agreed to pay my airfares. I had instructed ten spinning classes a week to cover the rest of the costs, leading back-to-back classes so that I could treat them as training sessions, structuring the lessons around the intervals that Robbie had planned for me to do each day.

'Probably a bit hard on the corporate punters but that's life. It was hard on me too. Ever tried pretending to be warming down, pretending to be doing five minutes of very easy pedalling and looking relaxed and smiley and speaking accordingly while you are still actually pedalling like crazy? That is hard.

'Oh, and then I should tell you that I impersonated Julius Mwangi by email and I'm in a B&B so far out of town it might as well be in a different country.'

'Well,' said Tony Harding, more amused than impressed, 'you obviously want to be here.'

Then I got my big break. Daryl Impey, another young rider who went to St John's rival Jeppe High School in Johannesburg, was staying on his own in a twin room for the duration of the competition. Tony put my time-trial bike on his roof, drove me back to the B&B, and helped explain to the owners that I would be moving out before I had properly moved in. He then installed me at the South African team's hotel in Daryl's room.

It was a different world. Suddenly I was staying in a decent hotel with an organized team. I was driven everywhere. I was fed and watered. They even had a mechanic.

The mechanic had taken one look at my racing bike and said, 'Chris, you can't race on those tyres, they're old, they're falling apart.' He put these really smart tyres on my bike. First thing I did when I got home again was take them off my bike, so that I didn't damage them during training. I would keep them for a special race.

I could see that this team meant business. I absorbed their earnestness and filled my lungs with expectation.

The Time Trial

The time trial came first. It was actually one of the reasons why I time-trialled into Salzburg to the managers' meeting. Planning, management, strategy.

This race meant everything to me. I wanted to build on my previous hour in the hot seat in Melbourne, and the training that I had been doing with Robbie had made me appreciate the skillset required to put in a good ride. Hitting a high output of wattage and staying there was the pain that I had come to enjoy.

It dawned on me that I was at a world championship. I felt like I had partly shifted the earth off its axis to get myself there, and if I could make an impact now, it could change my life. If I could show the promise that was growing in my quads with every month of hard training, I thought I might finally get a shot at joining a European team.

As I waited for the countdown, in every sense of the phrase, I was on the starting ramp. It was my opportunity to seize the day, to shake the world. It was my moment, and I was ready.

There were riders on the roster who were being billed as the 'real deal'. People were already talking about them in terms of what they could achieve later in their careers at the Grand Tours. Their places in the landscape of the professional world seemed unquestionable. I, on the other hand, was a head-in-the-clouds kid who rode on his own outside Johannesburg, keeping left all the time. I was someone that even the cycling community in South Africa didn't take seriously. Maybe this adventure was too much, too soon?

I was more flustered than I should have been as I headed down the ramp. I had performed my warm-up on the turbo trainer and while on the starting ramp I was still trying to get my bike computer to reset. I needed to get it back to the zero setting before I started, but the countdown had already initiated. I was preoccupied as I pushed off down the ramp.

The first corner was 200 metres down the road. It was a 90-degree right-hand bend in front of a grand old building. The driveway was cordoned off by crash barriers covered in advertising, and there was a marshal standing on the bend peering down into a bunch of papers, which seemed to resemble a start list.

The building was situated on an intersection in such a way that when there was no racing you could drive up this road and head right or slip left at the edifice. They had left the slip without a crash barrier or advertising boarding because the race route wasn't going in that direction. We were clearly taking the right-hand bend on the bike. I knew that. But I was agitated and wasn't in the headspace that I needed to be in. When I approached the corner, still trying to pick up speed to make up the lost time spent worrying about resetting my bike computer, the unguarded slip to the left caught my eye. I was conscious of both the marshal and the turn, but when something attracted my attention to the left, my brain for just one-hundredth of a second decided to say, 'Hey, maybe we go left?' Subliminal. Then it issued a correction. 'No. We go right. You know it's right.'

I was wired though. I had already drifted to the left side of the road because my brain had raised the possibility of a left turn and I was now heading in a straight line towards the marshal, whose nose was still buried in his papers.

He was directly in my turning line. Yes, I had messed the corner up a little bit but I could still make it round easily. Only this guy was standing in the road. Did I swerve? Surely he was going to move out of the way, or he would jump back? He was standing on the road during the time trial, at a world championship. He must have been aware of riders coming down this way at high speeds?

I needed to keep my speed up. I hadn't started well and if I slowed down here I might have been a couple of seconds off my target before I had even taken the first bend.

I kept my line.

He didn't move.

We collided.

Or rather, he stood there and I hit him at speed. He hadn't even braced himself for the impact. My aero bars went straight into his chest. Poor man.

He went flying to my right, his feet up in the air, while I tumbled to the left. We both hit the ground. It was shown on television, and there was a photographer there, too, who caught everything. He captured the whole crash, frame by frame, as the marshal flew through the air with his papers.*

Behind me, as I got up, there was a large advertising sign. It said, 'Salzburg, Feel the Inspiration'.

I was devastated. After all my planning to get to the race, I couldn't believe that I was on the tar ten seconds into the race. I had gone from medal hopeful to comedy gold by the first bend.

But this was still the time trial. This was still Europe. I had nearly 40 kilometres left to show the cycling world my worth. I grabbed my bike as quickly as I could and got straight back into the race again. I didn't even check the marshal. Not so much as a 'sorry' or a 'how are you?' I almost bounced back up off the ground and was gone like the wind. It was over so quickly I could have fooled myself into thinking that the accident had never happened. I rode on. My brain calmed a bit. I thought that surely I couldn't have lost more than 15 or 20 seconds at the most? I had to get straight back into it. I reasoned that there was enough road ahead of me to claw back the time.

My intermediate placings were encouraging. After 10.1 kilometres the first split had me down in 52nd place. By the next intermediate check at 23.7 kilometres I was up to 40th. The time trial ended at 39.5 kilometres. I could tell myself that I had run out of road.

All things considered, I'd had a decent time trial. I had set off from the start trying to chase the power level that Robbie and I had calculated beforehand, something that I could sustain for the whole distance. Overall I came in 36th out of a field of over one hundred Under-23s from around the world.

There were some fine names racing that day. Dominique Cornu, the winner by 37 seconds, was one of them, a twenty-year-old Belgian rider who had already signed up for the professional Lotto team (sponsored by the Belgian lottery). Alexandr Pliuşchin was also there, a Moldovan prodigy who did not perform quite as well as expected and finished only two places in front of me. Edvald Boasson Hagen

---

* You can watch the crash on YouTube in a clip called 'Three worst time trials'.

from Norway, Rigoberto Urán from Colombia and the Brit Ian Stannard, all future Team Sky colleagues, finished further up the field ahead of me, in 5th, 23rd and 25th respectively, as did Mikhail Ignatiev, the Russian time-trialler, who placed 2nd. Tony Martin, the German who would later became the world time-trial champion, finished 18th.

I saw the marshal a few days later. He was bruised badly on his chest whereas I hadn't even drawn blood on my knees. The trauma for me was more about the shock of what had happened and knowing that everyone was watching. I felt like a red-faced kid again.

Although it clearly wasn't the European debut of my dreams I was quietly happy. I compared myself to the riders that I had beaten, many of whom were racing for the continental teams that I had emailed in the previous months.

That was an achievement for me, and a base to build on. I would go home and get busy with Google Translate and my schoolboy French to write to Italian and French teams, informing them of my news in language which would amuse and intrigue them: 'Hey, I beat your guys in the time trial.' No, I wouldn't quite say that, but I would have liked to.

It was after the time trial that the strangeness of being the entire Kenyan cycling team and management really struck me. There was nobody to talk to. I'd had a time trial which would be an internet comedy clip for ever. It was finished though. Over. There was no crowd to chat with. No management to debrief me.

Tony had organized a neutral service for me for the race, so that if I punctured I would get a spare. But neutral meant just that; the mechanics weren't there for moral support, or to mend my punctured psyche. I could have phoned a friend or family member but I decided not to. I persuaded myself that no one would want to receive a call from their boy who had ridden a time trial, on the biggest day of his life, and had managed to ride straight into a race marshal before the first bend. What was the right tone to take with information like that?

I went back to the hotel where the South African pros were

milling about in the lobby. These were big names in the cycling world that I lived in and men whom I respected and looked up to: Robbie Hunter, David George, Ryan Cox and Tiaan Kannemeyer. They had all been riding the pro-scene for a number of years. David George had been Lance Armstrong's teammate for a while at US Postal, whereas Robbie had already achieved a great deal, having won stages in the Vuelta a España and raced in the Tour de France.

When I walked in I hoped that they hadn't watched the race or at least hadn't heard about it. I tried to blend in and kept my head down as I passed through the lobby. A couple of them were sitting there, talking casually.

'How'd it go?' they asked as I passed.

Phew. They knew nothing.

'Ah, it went okay. Could have done a bit better, but yeah, it's all right. Came in 36th. No complaints.'

I kept walking, looking around frantically for the lift. Behind me I heard roars of laughter. The penny dropped. They knew. They hadn't watched the race but they had been alerted to the highlight, who was now walking through the lobby looking sheepish.

'What were you thinking?'

'What did you do?'

'How did you crash?'

'Did you have something against the marshal?'

They renamed me. I became Crash Froome. That name would stick with me for a good few years afterwards. Tony Harding, Robbie Hunter, Daryl Impey and the boys – I was Crash to them.

The Road Race

The road race was 177.2 kilometres of hard road, three days after the time trial.

A hilly course, there was a climb every lap, which would normally have favoured my strengths, but the inclines were really steep at points, more than ten to fifteen per cent. This meant that they were brutal and short, as opposed to long and gruelling – my speciality – and they were not effectively 'breaking' anybody over the course of a whole race. It was better, though, than a flat circuit and I felt proud to be in the front group approaching the close of the race.

It came to a sprint. A bunch of around fifty of us were left towards the finish, out of a field of two hundred. I was in there with Edvald Boasson Hagen, Mark Cavendish and Rigoberto Urán; riders I would never outsprint. I finished 45th in the lead bunch, 5 seconds behind the winner, Gerald Ciolek of Germany. The Germans had a strong team and had controlled the race well.

It wasn't a result that Europeans could relate to. In cycling, the judgement of European bosses was all that mattered. I knew that nobody would scan down the placings and say, 'Do you remember that kid who has been riding properly for a couple of years and who hustled and hassled to get here? Well, he raced on his own with no team and he came in ahead of riders like Dan Martin, Daryl Impey and Geraint Thomas. He might be worth a shot.'

I could say that I had finished in the lead pack at the World Championships. I could leave Salzburg feeling disappointed if I wanted to rummage for it or feeling much better about myself if I was realistic.

That was the end of my racing year. I stayed around for a few days to watch the professionals race on the same course that we had ridden. Paolo Bettini, a strong Italian rider, was the overall victor and I watched with awe as he attacked in his big chainring after 250 kilometres.

Even being in the big chainring was unnerving for me at that time. I had ridden the same race in the lowest gear possible, struggling to get up the viciously steep slopes. But there was a man who was riding against unimaginable resistance and he was sailing away from everyone else. There were 15 kilometres left and I watched him, thinking to myself, 'I've got a really long way to go to reach anywhere near that level.'

I flew back home to Africa encouraged, but realizing that my future lay elsewhere. The races in South Africa simply couldn't give me what Europe had to offer, or even what I might be good at.

The 2006 season was coming to an end, so I contacted the UCI again because I had heard that they had registered a mixed continental team for riders from developing countries. Based in Aigle, Switzerland, cyclists from a range of nationalities could train and compete in competitions wearing the UCI's blue and white kit. I continued to write to other teams too, telling them about my results at the World Championships, as well as my performance at the Tour de Maurice a month previously where I had repeated my feat from the previous year by winning the second stage, and then winning the third stage, too, before eventually going on to win the whole race for my first stage race victory. It wasn't as prestigious an event as famous French races such as Paris–Nice, but my palmarès was nevertheless starting to show respectable results.

The UCI came back to me. They said, 'Yes, let's give this a go. You're from Kenya, racing on a Kenyan licence. We'll give you a chance because Kenya is an underdeveloped cycling country.'

Underdeveloped? Man, they didn't know the half of it!

PART TWO

Europe

10

The big chainring. It was time to move on up.

If Kenyan cycling was underdeveloped, then I was a child of Kenyan cycling. I was twenty-one years old and had ridden once in Europe. My bike handling was poor, I was just a few years on from being the kid doing tricks and jumps in their backyard, and I had never steered a bike round a serious hairpin bend on the fast side of a mountain. The big chainring, also known as the real world of professional cycling, was still a dream.

I longed for Europe but I could feel the relentless peloton of time catching up with me. If I didn't get a move on, it would pass me.

When I had finished in the chasing bunch in Salzburg a rider called Peter Velits crossed the line somewhere close to me, but sufficiently ahead to be given 22nd place, instead of my 45th. Peter and I shared many traits. He was from Slovakia, which wasn't a traditional cycling country. He was a stage race rider who liked the climbs but time-trialled well, too. He also hadn't gone to Salzburg in 2006 to finish 22nd.

Peter had been a professional since 2004. He had finished 7th in the 2004 Tour of Egypt, although nobody from his team that year had been forced to bury themselves in the desert, while waiting for death. He had come 3rd in the Giro delle Regioni in 2005. I hadn't even heard of the Giro delle Regioni in 2005.

Peter had gone to Salzburg with far more realistic hopes than mine in 2006. The race was part of his professional calendar by then and this was his third attempt. In Salzburg he had time-trialled badly, finishing behind his twin brother, Martin, and behind me, even without the impediment of starting the day by crashing into a race steward. In the road race that 22nd place finish wasn't the stuff of his dreams. Indeed, he would come back and win the Under-23 Road Race at the World Championships the following year in Stuttgart.

Peter's name and story were well known to me by the time I got to Salzburg. Earlier, back in the spring of 2006, riding for the second tier Team Konica Minolta in South Africa, Peter had won the Giro del Capo, the much-missed annual stage race in the countryside around Cape Town. He was only three months older than I was, but he was light years ahead of where I needed to be.

That win in South Africa for his small and resilient home-based team was a bit of a coup for both Peter Velits and those riding with him. Despite the high-tech sponsor's name, Team Konica Minolta ran on the sort of budget that aspired to be called 'shoestring'. Yet it was a fine proving ground for African cyclists. The team specialized in producing buds and blossoms out of arid earth.

Having grabbed a few headlines through Peter Velits's win in Cape Town, the Team Konica Minolta roster was quickly hoovered up by wealthier teams. That's how it was and how it was supposed to be. You rode for a team like Konica Minolta on the way up. And perhaps on the way down.

Without the means to attract a new wave of Europeans, the team boss, John Robertson, opted to fill the gaps with home-grown talent for 2007. He pulled in Tiaan Kannemeyer and Jock Green and entered into negotiations with David George, the South African who had ridden with the US Postal Team alongside Lance Armstrong in 1999 and 2000. David had come home to win the Giro del Capo back to back in 2003 and 2004 with Team Barloworld, for whom Robertson had worked at the time.

I had known John Robertson for about a year, bumping into him regularly at races. In November at the end of the 2006 season John asked if we could have a chat. No strings attached but he had a team to fill. I had a sliver of credibility with some of the races under my belt and having been accepted into the UCI school. And my diary wasn't exactly full.

We met in Pretoria and got on well. I came away without any promises but filled with some hope as I went back to studying in Johannesburg. Unbeknownst to me, David George was still exploring his options as the deadlines for team rosters were looming. Finally, John Robertson opted to put my name down as the last on his list for the 2007 season. The line-up was eight South Africans and one Kenyan.

I was a shot in the dark for John.

If the other riders or the sponsors had asked to see my CV, he could have shown it to them on the back of a matchbox.

Starting in January 2007 I would be paid €300 a month for riding a bike. No more spinning classes. I would ride the Giro del Capo for the team in March and then head to Europe and the UCI school in Aigle, Switzerland, for three months or so until being reunited with Konica Minolta when they came to Europe in the early summer.

I didn't care about the threadbare CV.

For now, the country ahead was Lesotho. We arrived at Clarens near the border for Team Konica Minolta's early-season training camp.

I was a professional cyclist with professional colleagues. It is true that I turned up on our first day of training riding a bike which was by some distance too small for me, a bike kitted out with components that most of my teammates wouldn't consider suitable for a ride to the shops. I didn't care. I was a pro.

On the training camp, though, there were regular reminders that I was very much the newbie. I didn't have nearly as much experience as the other riders in terms of how things were done in a professional outfit. The guys would joke with me about my position on the bike: head down, elbows out. I didn't fit the slick, pro-cyclist mould. Plus there were the kikoys and the numerous bracelets and necklaces that adorned my body.

On the last day of training, John organized a tough ride for us – a good number of miles finishing on a stiff climb. I was keen but the older riders had a different idea. They decided that we shouldn't ride it flat out because this was only training after all. Instead, to keep John happy, we should simply make it appear as if we were riding at our limits.

This was awkward. John had told me before the ride that I would need to impress him to make the Giro del Capo selection. So I raised my issue with Jock Green and Tiaan Kannemeyer, the older guys on

the team, telling them that I really needed to do my best to show
John that I was good enough to make the cut. It was different being a
rookie.

Jock and Tiaan agreed to let me ride ahead as if I were 'attacking'
them. The caveat was that they told me to ride at about eighty per
cent of my maximum effort and they would keep a reasonable
distance.

When we got halfway up the climb, a couple of the sprinters
dropped off the back of the group, giving the impression that we
were going fast up at the front. This was my cue. I did a little acceleration, as if I were attacking, and it all seemed to be working
convincingly for about two minutes. Then John pulled up next to
me in the car, looked me up and down for a moment, and shouted,
'Chris, ride your fucking bike!'

There was no choice. I pushed as hard as I could for the last kilometre to the top. I felt really proud of myself when John came up to
me afterwards and said, 'Listen, if you can ride like that in the Giro,
you can win the fucking thing.'

I clung to Africa until the last moment. Not from sentiment, but
because I wanted to get as much training into my legs as I could
before I went to Europe. Maybe in Europe the six- or seven-hour
days that I felt I needed would be frowned upon. So I did the Giro del
Capo in early March for Konica Minolta (coming 6th overall and
winning the best young rider's jersey), and quickly went back to my
training routine.

Lesotho again.

The lowest spot you can find in Lesotho is 1,400 metres above sea
level, and eighty per cent of the country is at least 1,800 metres above
sea level. It is lumpy terrain. If the people had bikes they would produce climbers for export. As it is, Lesotho's national resources are
water and diamonds and in late 2006 in the Maluti Mountains they
eked the fifteenth-biggest diamond ever found out of the mine. It
was a white diamond that they called Lesotho Promise.

Much further down the other end of the world economic spectrum, my €300 a month meant that I was able to establish a basic

altitude-training camp for myself on the South African side of the border near Fouriesburg, just outside of Lesotho.

I went up there with a South African girl named Andrea I was seeing at the time. I think she expected some kind of a romantic getaway but she came up for the ten days of my home-made altitude camp and scarcely saw me.

I loved riding over the border with my passport in my pocket, ready to go up into the mountains, to leave all of my energy there and to return hours later.

Lesotho gave me a parting taste of real African soil. It is not a wealthy place and I needed to be careful of where I was riding. A white guy on a racing bike in the highlands was a rare sight. In fact, the bike alone would be a rare enough sighting for a Lesothan. I pushed myself hard up there. Sessions of five to seven hours doing huge miles with just one recovery day during the time that I was there. It was a strange feeling going from the familiar training routes around Johannesburg but my legs were ready. Even in Johannesburg I had been doing the same long hours most days, so these big days and big climbs were exactly what I had been getting ready for.

Life in Europe was due to start properly in Italy with the Giro delle Regioni, the annual six-stage road race for Under-23 riders. I arrived in Switzerland with just a couple of weeks to spare.

The UCI have had many bad ideas down through the years but the World Cycling Centre (WCC) on the land surrounding their headquarters at Aigle, in a crook of the Swiss Alps, was not one of them. For the first time I was part of a proper team set-up: bikes, kit, a room to ourselves, velodrome, gym and a canteen for all our meals.

After some days' training in Switzerland, there followed a trip to Belgium to compete in the curtain-raising Liège–Bastogne–Liège Espoirs race for Under-23s. This is the factory floor for European cycling – the long rides, the one-day classics, the short, sharp climbs, the shoulder-to-shoulder jostling, the narrow and rapid descents – where riders are made into racers.

I didn't like it much. I enjoy the first hint of elevation on a steep mountain, and if the mountain dwarfs us all, so much the better. I like stage races, those long wars of attrition. Who can suffer best? Who can suffer longest? These long hauls around the lowlands were never going to be my thing. I came 28th that day up in Liège, ahead of my UCI comrades but over a minute behind the winner, a rider called Grega Bole from Slovenia. It was a useful experience but I wanted to race in countries where the hills were mountains, and the climbs went on and on.

A few days later, in Italy for the Giro delle Regioni, a gang of us were in an SUV, heading to our hotel. It's like the start of a bad joke. A Frenchman is driving. Sebastien is small and compact and drives with compacted fury. The team around me are two Koreans, a Colombian, an Algerian, a Chinese guy and me, a Kenyan, often mistaken for a Brit despite never having been to Britain. Haijun Ma is the Chinese guy. We kid him all day about being too old for an Under-23 race. We demand to see his passport. He grins and says, 'Shhhhhh!'

Travelling together like this was still a novelty for our team. We tucked in behind the GB team car in front of us. The car was being driven by a ruddy-faced guy whom I would come to know as Rod Ellingworth. Somewhere in the car were Ian Stannard and Ben Swift, who were learning their trade at Rod's Italian academy. They are riding under the name 100% Me, an anti-doping initiative taken by David Brailsford at British Cycling.

100% Me was a very worthy and ground-breaking ethical statement but we were giddy and Sebastien was overexcited and aggressive and he drove our car right up Rod's tailpipe. Rod, as I know now, is sensible and solid, and always law-abiding. He was in no mood to engage with a *garçon* racer on this windy climb. But Sebastien decided to push his luck and when we got to a really dangerous stretch of road, a bad bend on a blind hairpin corner on the windswept mountain, he overtook at speed.

There were whoops in our car but I remember thinking that we were about to become a carful of dead foreigners if we met a vehicle coming the other way. I looked across at the driver of the GB car and I could see a black cloud of rage crossing his face. Rod rage.

We were unpacking the car at the hotel when Rod arrived in the car park having observed the speed limit and all the other rules of the road and driver etiquette along the way. He was furious with Sebastien. 'How dare you drive like that with youngsters in the car, you fool!' he shouted. For most of the guys on the UCI team this was a comedy and Sebastien was their champ for driving really fast when some people would have been afraid to drive at all. I remember looking at the red-headed Rod as he seethed and thinking, 'Wow, he's so angry that his face has gone the same the colour as his hair. His face and his hair are both really, really furious.'

Day one of the Regioni was a standard affair, a circuit race followed by the predictable bunch finish. My main problem was staying in contact with the bike and with the road. At one point I even rode at speed into the driveway of a private house, coming to a halt just before I hit the garage. John Robertson, who was there with the South African Under-23 team, said later that his main memory of the day was frequent reports including the words 'Chris' and 'Crash' on the race radio. There were three riders called Chris in the race that day, but it didn't take long for John to figure out that this series of unfortunate events was happening to the same Chris.

I had journeyed from Africa to Aigle with not much more in my account than potential. The roads I had worked on alone or with Kinjah and with Robbie had never offered the challenges that you find in the Alps, or any other self-respecting European mountain range. I had an odd flappy-bird style of riding, poor handling skills and, despite my training methods and eternal diet, still needed to lose at least a couple of kilos. On top of those handicaps came my lack of experience, which might have been considered harmlessly eccentric if it hadn't been so annoying for other riders. When I had the strength in my legs to push on at a critical moment in the race, I was invariably starting from too far back and would try to overtake by weaving through the middle of the peloton where the traffic was most dense. Curses would follow me through the congestion.

My descending was also terrible. I wasn't scared of falling off or of the speed of the downhill, but it might have been better if I had been. I would take risks, trying to go faster than everyone else on the corners, and although I had the *cojones* I lacked the bike-handling skills, a combination that led to a lot of crashes. Rod Ellingworth would later say that his riders spoke of how much space I was given on the descents. No one wanted to be too close. I could understand that.

I was suffering from a basic misconception. I know now that most of the brake work on a descent is done on the front wheel. Back then I reckoned that on a downhill the front brake would catapult me over the handlebars. The long, mostly straight descents in Kenya were no preparation for the winding roads of Europe. But as Rod would also say later, his riders also mentioned that I was pretty good going uphill.

I invested my hopes in the second stage, the first of the two mountaintop finishes. This stage was a loop around Città Sant'Angelo, a medieval town near Pescara. There were some decent climbs, including a good 6- or 7-kilometre ascent to the finish.

There were attacks all day. Under-23 races are filled with riders who have a desperate need to make a name for themselves. If you don't succeed as an Under-23, it's unlikely you'll get the chance to do so afterwards. I hung in going up the final climb and as my legs felt good I rolled the dice and took a chance. I pulled away from the bunch in the company of a Russian rider, Anton Reshetnikov, and the Slovenian Grega Bole, whose back I had watched cross the finish line first in Belgium the previous week.

At a kilometre from the top we were clear of the pack behind us. Belgium hadn't been my sort of terrain but this was.

Bole was on my wheel. I was sucking him along up the hill and I could tell from his quickening breaths that he was panicking. If he lost touch with me the peloton might swallow him up and then he would finish with nothing to show for his efforts. He wasn't in a position of strength but he decided to negotiate:

'Don't drop me, don't drop me. You can have the stage but don't drop me.'

I had been in Italy in this dream world of professional cycling for only two weeks. This must be what the guys do, I thought. They cut deals. I have the power and I don't need to start making enemies; I know I'm stronger. He can stay on my wheel and get his 2nd place.

We toiled round the last hairpin and the finish lay ahead of us, one last uphill straight. At this point in big races the small caravan of vehicles in front of the leaders vanishes, leaving the riders with nothing but clear road. With 100 metres to go, the cars and the motorbikes veered off to the right. I turned up the power and followed the vehicles.

Grega Bole rode straight on towards the finish line. I chased the vehicles. I chased the . . . uh oh.

By the time I realized my mistake and did a quick U-turn, the best I could do was claim 2nd place. As he watched me disappear down that side road, Grega forgot about our deal, though I couldn't blame anyone but myself.

Still, the good definitely outweighed the bad that day. People were aware of how strong I'd been on the climb and I was startled to realize how comfortable I'd felt. I was losing too much time on the descents so a good overall GC (General Classification) result wasn't going to happen that week. But while you can coach technical problems out of a rider, you can never turn a non-climber into someone who can win mountaintop finishes. I was pleased with how I had performed on the climbs and, overall, I was pleased with the way the week was panning out.

In any stage race the road gives and the road takes away. The third stage was the longest and by the time we got to Cignolo I had come off on another couple of descents and surrendered over a minute in time through poor handling.

Stage four was better and passed without major incident and then we were into serious climbing territory again. We were heading out from the quaint spa town of Chianciano Terme and finishing on Montepulciano, racing through 149 kilometres of rolling Tuscan hills.

Again, there were attacks all day. With 20 kilometres to go I was feeling strong and made a play of my own. I was followed by Cyril Gautier of France, Christoff Van Heerden of South Africa, the Australian Cameron Meyer, Claudio Apolo of Portugal and two Belgians, Tim Vermeersch and Detlef Moerman.

I don't remember if it occurred to me how strange it was for a kid with the air of the Ngong Hills still in his lungs to be riding through

Tuscany with French and Belgian riders by his side. If I entertained that thought, it was briefly. With 3 kilometres to go, Moerman and Meyer made a break of their own. Myself and Gautier chased them down.

On and on up the climb we went. The stage was going to fall to me or to the Frenchman. The pack were behind us but I felt strong and sensed they wouldn't have enough left for both the chase and the aftermath. With about a kilometre and a half to go, at the spot they call Porta al Prato, I kicked on. I felt comfortable again and the gap stretched. Gautier kept in touch like a relative who knew that if I died he would inherit the stage. With the finish in the Piazza Grande in sight, I emptied the tank.

A stage win. UCI code KEN 19850520 – this was the first Kenyan code to appear at the very top of a stage classification in a professional European race. The first ever. The world didn't shake but there were decent riders on the mountain that day, including Rui Costa, Bauke Mollema, Ben Swift and Ian Stannard. Years later, people would say that I came from nowhere, but on this day I felt that little corner of Tuscany was somewhere.

Rod Ellingworth had his base not too far away at Quarrata. Rod watched me win and made a mental note.

Two meetings from that week stand out for me. Luca Scinto, a guy from Tuscany who was quite well known in Italian cycling, was there at the Regioni with an Under-23 feeder team. He grabbed me at the finish line one day and had someone translate the words of seduction. He wanted me to come to his team the next year. I was flattered. But when I relayed the story to a friend who'd spent some time racing in Italy, their response was not what I had expected: he was a controversial character. As it turned out, in 2013 two of his riders tested positive in the Giro.

The other meeting was with Rod. On the night of that fifth stage I didn't waste any time, and with my stage win fresh in Rod's memory I looked for his name on the room roster stuck to the lobby wall, and went and knocked on his door. He was there with the 100% Me team.

It would be interesting to ask Rod exactly what we said to each other because I don't quite remember. He knew who I was by then, which was a start, and I know I would have told him that I wanted to get to Europe on a more full-time basis. I imagine he mentioned to me about racing under a British as opposed to a Kenyan licence.

It was a constructive talk which had no firm conclusions but at the end Rod said to me, 'Listen, you've got talent and you're heading in the right direction. Keep it up.'

Doug Dailey had been keeping an eye on me since the Commonwealth Games in Melbourne and now Rod Ellingworth was, too. Their attention encouraged me.

I had only been in Europe for a few weeks but this was what I had come for: big days in the mountains and a few mentions in key dispatches.

Réalisant mon espoir, as the old Talking Heads song says.

11

One day I was learning to paddle in the still and familiar waters of Johannesburg. The next I was shooting the rapids down mountains with magical names. In professional cycling the speed of events picks you up and carries you along. You look up from the road and from the race and there is a strange new landscape rolling past on either side of you.

Breathe it in and ride on.

I was dividing my time in 2007 between Aigle in Switzerland and the Team Konica Minolta house in Tielt in Belgium, though there wasn't a lot of time to be divided. John Robertson was keen on us entering the classics and criteriums in the Low Countries, but I tried them and didn't like them. Or they didn't like me. The bends and the accelerations and the short cobbled climbs suited some. For a boy raised in Nairobi, far above the sea, I might have had a chance in the south of France but the grey north was not going to be my *terrain de prédilection*. So the guys would head off and race and I would spend the day training, looking for climbs, doing my own thing.

After Italy, the Tour of Japan was the next decent stage race of the season. In my head I drew a ring around any stage race we entered. These were for me, my proving ground and my shop window. Japan was seven stages starting in late May. We began in Osaka on my twenty-second birthday. A year earlier I had been back in Johannesburg and the thought of being paid to spend a week racing in Japan was about as far away as Japan itself.

I grew into the race and on the penultimate of the seven stages I got my chance. The stage, 128.5 kilometres beginning in the Shujenzi Stadium in Tokyo, took us out around a circuit corrugated with stiff climbs. There were so many climbs that I couldn't have designed the stage better myself.

I went with the first break. There were ten, eleven, twelve of us, but I felt strong. We chipped out a solid lead, but the relentless climbs took their toll on my breakaway companions. The peloton started reeling us back in, and morale and speed were diminishing quickly. With two laps and over 30 kilometres to go, I attacked the break. These were the scenarios that Robbie and I had in mind when I used to hold my power output as high as possible, for as long as possible, around Johannesburg. No crashes today, no rookie errors. I felt in control. I won by about 50 seconds. The stage put me 6th on GC behind an Italian, three Kazakhs and another Italian.

I was still 6th after the race finished in front of big crowds the next day.

I rode for Kenya that summer in the All Africa Games. Daryl Impey won gold in the road race; I took the bronze for Kenya, finishing between two Eritreans. I rode Mi-Août en Bretagne, a modest four-day stage race in north-west France, and won. The GP Tell in Switzerland went well, especially on the mountain stage, the fourth, from Chur to Arosa. A big Alpine climb. I finished 2nd behind a serious climber, Mathias Frank, nearly catching him on the long haul to the summit finish.

Like many smaller teams, Team Konica Minolta offered its riders the chance to develop. I could feel through 2007 that I was doing that. I made rookie errors but I knew that the more rookie errors a rider made, the longer he would be a rookie. I tried to learn something every time.

Not everything was perfect, of course. John wanted me to ride the Tour of Britain in September but I thought the race was too flat. I would have preferred the Tour de l'Avenir, which was a more suitable race, and an event renowned for young riders announcing their talent. A young Greg LeMond won L'Avenir by more than 10 minutes, and from that moment people believed he would go on to win the Tour de France. I thought if I could do something in L'Avenir, European teams would be paying attention. But being in Britain was important to John Robertson.

By then, though, I was getting enough nibbles of interest from bigger teams that I felt I would be able to secure a contract for the following year.

I remember getting a call out of the blue from Robbie Hunter. How he had got my number, I'm not sure, but he left me a message saying, 'Hi, Chris, Robbie here. Can I give you a call sometime to have a chat about your plans for next year?'

To paraphrase the line from *Jerry Maguire*, he had me at 'hi'. Robbie was a guy whom we African riders always looked up to. The most successful cyclist in South Africa, he had ridden the Tour de France several times. Daryl is crowding him for the title these days, but at the time of that phone call, Robbie was the most successful road cyclist that South Africa had ever produced. He got there on his own will, no academy or anything. He fought to get where he had to go. He was the model. And Robbie Hunter wanted to talk about my plans!

I took the hard negotiating position that whatever his plans were for me, they were my plans too.

Robbie was with Barloworld, a team with a strong South African flavour. Barloworld had received a wild-card entry to the 2007 Tour de France and done well, taking two stages and the polka-dot King of the Mountains jersey. Mauricio Soler won stage nine and the jersey. Robbie won stage eleven and finished 2nd in the competition for the green points jersey for best sprinter.

Those of us on the lower rungs of the ladder were surprised and impressed.

Off the road, the Tour of Britain worked out well for me. Barloworld were there and I spoke with Robbie about their plans and my plans. Once I spoke with Barloworld I had my heart set on joining. I didn't even explore the other options that were floating around.

Robbie wrapped our talk up with an invitation. 'Come to the Worlds in Stuttgart in a few weeks' time. We'll have the contract ready for you to sign. We'll sign you up for 2008.'

Stuttgart. I came. I raced. I was conquered by my own fatigue. I had been pushing harder and harder since that meeting with John Robertson in Pretoria in 2006. Now, at the World Championships, I didn't hit anybody at the start but time-trialled worse than I had in Salzburg. I found a shard of energy at some stage in the road race but finished 21st, a good way behind Peter Velits.

Signing my name to a contract was the only exertion I was fit for.

There were no fireworks or marching bands when I showed up in Stuttgart. Claudio Corti, the Barloworld team boss, asked the team soigneur, Mario Pafundi, to see to me. Mario is now with Team Sky, but back then he was to keep an eye out for a tall Kenyan kid who was coming to the team bus, as instructed, to sign a contract.

I went along at the appointed time and stood outside the team bus obediently. Knocking on the door or sticking my head in seemed too cheeky. I waited for somebody to emerge for the meet and greet; I had never met Mario before. Meanwhile, he was a couple of yards away scanning the crowd, looking for what he thought a tall Kenyan kid should look like.

Time passed. In Mario's part of Italy they're not familiar with *mzungus*, so I stood outside the Barloworld bus for a long time before the penny dropped. Eventually I was fetched inside. The contract was signed.

It was minimum fare. I don't think it even met the UCI standards. The money was in the region of €22,500 a year. As a neo-pro the UCI rules state that the minimum duration should be two years.

Inside, I was offered a one-year deal. They ignored the two-year rule.

So did I.

I'd told myself that I could be up there with these guys. I took my one year at minimum and prepared to grab the big brass ring. Secretly it was my intention to make the Barloworld Tour de France team.

T. I.E. my friend, T. I.E.

This is Europe.

Mid April 2008: I rode yesterday. This morning I am in France but yesterday I was in Holland. Racing. I raced more than 200 kilometres of an event I've already forgotten the name of. Me and Félix

Cárdenas, the Colombian climber. The sponsors needed a presence there. Cárdenas pulled a short straw. So did I.

We rode. We finished. We did our jobs. Then they put us in a car for five hours and dropped us at a hotel 80 kilometres north of Paris, near Amiens. At 2.00 a.m. That's the first lance they stick in your romantic thought bubble about Paris–Roubaix, the Queen of the Classics. It doesn't start in Paris. Not since the revolutionary spring of 1968.

Cárdenas and I weren't sharing a room. That would make sense. I went to my room where another rider was already sleeping. I am meek, too meek for Paris–Roubaix perhaps, too meek to switch on the light. I fumbled around for a while. Found the bathroom, found the bed, found some sleep.

In Holland yesterday, after about 150 kilometres, we hit the infamous baby heads. The pavé is what they call those narrow stretches of cobblestoned farm paths. The cobbles are as big as melons. Or baby heads. A very long time ago it was somebody's idea of fun to make cyclists ride over these things. Maybe riders were upholstered differently then. Maybe fun was different then.

We hit the pavé and the bikes did the shake, rattle and roll that people had come out to see. The pavé was a one-way system, so the highway bottlenecked drastically when we hit the cobbles. All around the riders become erratic as their tyres found purchase and then slipped on the smooth, damp stones. Keeping the rubber on the road and our craniums off the cobbles was all any of us cared about.

The marriage of the rider and the bike hits a literal rough patch on these lumps. The bike doesn't want to know you any more. It spits out the water bottles that haven't been taped in. It jolts and jounces and makes noises it has never made before. The bike wants to throw you off like a stallion bucking a rodeo cowboy. You grip the steel of the handlebars, hold on for your life, squeeze until your knuckles are frost white. You would die this way rather than take your hand away for a second to squeeze a brake.

And you have to ride aggressively if you want to survive. Very aggressively if you want to win. You don't simply have to subdue the violent uprising of your bike, you have to beat those around you at

Kenya, where it all began. [Photo credit: Michelle Cound]

The Safari Simbaz – back with David Kinjah's team in the tin hut where I learned to ride as a boy. [Photo credit: Michelle Cound]

Mum never tired of teaching me about the bush and the animals that lived there. She told me about the different sounds and all of the different trees.

Boy racer – on my bike on holiday in La Péniche, France.

The Masai Mara became a favourite place of mine.

My grandfather taught my brothers and me to fish and hunt.

Without Mum's encouragement to follow my dreams,
I would probably have never got to the Tour de France.

First take – the race where I met David Kinjah, aged thirteen.

David Kinjah and I having lunch together during one of our epic training rides.

The Black Lion: my first cycling mentor, David Kinjah.

Nobody I knew even had one pet python. I had two: Rocky and Shandy.

Having a laugh with my mates in Africa.

Matt Beckett, a lifetime friend.

Hippie – when I had hair.

With my brothers Jeremy and Jono, our *ayah*, Anna, and her daughter Grace.

Me with game rangers at the Masai Mara nature reserve, 2004.

the same time. To win without risk is to win without glory, Eddy Merckx once said. Belgians love cobbles★.

When riders hit the pavé, the peloton gets compressed, then shattered and scattered. If somebody falls or rides too gingerly, you can't get past them. The line ahead gets away from you. There are distractions. Tyres give way with a hiss of surrender. Spokes buckle and wheels bend like surrealist art installations. Bikes, even support motorcycles, just slew off the road.

In Holland yesterday we clung to our bikes as the cobbles sped past below us. The organizers had erected a line of yellow plastic tape along the route to keep us on the course. On the other side of the tape was a nice smooth cycle path. Concrete and flat and inviting.

I had a revolutionary idea. Those who love cycling on baby heads could feel free to do so. Who was I to judge them? I like concrete though. So I ducked under the tape and rode along on the concrete bike path. Cry freedom, brothers.

Soon I was passing up through the peloton – well, parallel to it. I was bellowing at the odd farming family who had come here to watch: 'Guys, can you please move out of the way!' I felt great. The hard stares from the mud-stained faces of the other riders burned holes in my back. I felt even better. 'How is that pavé working out for you fellows?'

Of course, pretty soon a commissaire arrived alongside as if he were chasing a three-alarm fire. He had his car window down and he was blowing a whistle. Multi-tasking. No man in history ever looked so excited to be blowing a whistle.

My new friend was very agitated to see a bike on the bike path and not on the cobbles.

'No, you're finished. You're out of the race. You're disqualified. Stop! Stop! Stop!'

★ In some parts of America they actually call these big pieces of rock Belgian Blocks. They ended up in America having been used as ballast in ocean-going ships. When the ballast was swapped for cargo the Belgian Blocks were put to the same use as in the lands of northern Europe. They made hard-wearing, bumpy roads with them.

It was like a psychopath you had briefly dated telling you that it was all over. It is a shame but it was good while it lasted. Basically, phew!

Listen, mister commissaire, it's not you. It's me.

I put my hands up in the air.

'Okay! I'm stopping!'

I dropped back and said to the team car that the commissaire had told me I had to stop. Their eyes narrowed. I thought about suggesting that maybe he didn't like Africans but the eyes within the team car kept looking at me.

The Italian mechanic cut the silence with a razor grin.

'Well, what did you do?'

'I was just riding on the path.'

'Ha! You've got a lot to learn, Chreees! A lot to learn.'

I had been in Europe since January. Arriving in Italy at that time of year, I was assaulted by the cold.

The team gofer, a guy called Romano, picked me up at Milan Malpensa. He had Daryl Impey and Mario in the car with him and together we drove the motorway. You picture olive groves and sunshine. This was just autostrada and industrial premises and snow.

I had one thought: We train where? This may not be for me.

Romano spoke Italian. So I thought. Rapid, staccato sentences. I couldn't catch any of it. Romano is missing a finger, he's got a bit of a stump there on one of his hands. He's from Bergamo and actually speaks Bergamesque, which is a Lombard dialect and only barely related to Italian. It sounds like somebody trying to speak excitedly with a potato in their mouth.

I remember Romano driving quite fast on the autostrada, talking with his hands, gesticulating all the time to get his points across to Mario beside him up front. He was so loud I assumed they were having an argument. I was mesmerized by the missing finger.

It was a new and strange world.

We drove to Adro in Brescia, which was where the team had the *magazzino*, or warehouse. Claudio Corti's house was over the *magazzino*. The team bus was there too, along with all of the bikes and equipment.

There was nothing special at all about it and, again, no mountains in sight. I was expecting mountains. The Italy I remembered from the Regioni was all Tuscan villages and nice climbs.

We ate, Corti and some mechanics and the gang of us from the car.

I'd been warned by the older guys about the etiquette of eating in Italy. Salad first. Then a plate of pasta or rice, followed by a plate of meat or chicken or fish. You don't just go and pile everything you want on to a plate. So I just sat there watching what everyone else was doing before getting up to serve myself.

I'd lived in Karen, in Kinjah's, in South Africa, in Switzerland and in Belgium over the previous few years. And yet I had never felt so foreign. I was way beyond the borders of my comfort zone.

We were a small squad, just nineteen of us: six Italians, two Brits (Geraint Thomas and Stephen Cummings), one Austrian, one Portuguese, three South Africans, one Swiss, two Colombians, one Spaniard, one Australian and one Kenyan.

Daryl Impey, John-Lee Augustyn and myself were coming in as neo-pros. Robbie Hunter had been there a year or two. Mauricio Soler, the Colombian climber who had made such an impression on the Tour de France, was there. Enrico Gasparotto was the Italian national champion at the time. Paolo Longo Borghini, Giampaolo Cheula and Francesco Bellotti were the main Italians. Corti had his son Marco starting off in the team as well.

Geraint Thomas and Steve Cummings spent most of their time down in Tuscany, so we seldom saw them. Corti wanted the rest of us living close to the service course for training, but seeing as the two Brits lived in Tuscany, I took it that this wasn't an iron-clad rule.

I shared an apartment for three weeks with John-Lee Augustyn and then struck out on my own. I didn't want to live in Adro with everybody, including the team boss, right on top of me. My girl-friend, Andrea, was coming over from South Africa later in the year to follow a career in modelling. We had met while I was at university in Johannesburg, and living together was going to be a serious step. I found us a place in Chiari, 15 kilometres south of Adro, but on the main rail line to Milan where she hoped to work.

It meant that to train I had to ride up the road to Adro and then keep going north for the same distance again to get to the mountains and the lakes near Sarnico. A 60-kilometre extra tariff on the training day. I liked that.

Chiari was bigger than Adro. It had supermarkets, a rail station, canals and a nice piazza. All the benefits of space and being able to do my own thing.

Mostly I trained alone. I already knew that the social aspect of a big group ride can sometimes seduce riders into training at a lower intensity. I dipped into the company every now and then but mostly I stuck to my seven-hour rides, punishing myself as much as I could. The others called me a training fundamentalist. I didn't argue.

I loved the mountains around Lake Iseo. Flying through mountain tunnels and little villages. Music thrumming on the iPod. Dreams of the Tour in my head. The work pattern remained the same but the rides were tougher than in Johannesburg. Find the threshold and hold it there for as long as possible, twenty minutes or more. Long intervals. Again and again. And again.

The place I found was the upper floor of a two-level house. It had one main bedroom, one smaller bedroom and a kitchen-cum-lounge area. The landlord asked for a very reasonable rent, I think about €600 a month, and I was happy to go with that. It was more expensive than sharing with the guys in Adro but the word was that in Adro, Claudio Corti knew every move you made. I wasn't so keen on that.

I remember there was considerable fuss about signing the contract for the place once I had agreed to rent. I didn't have a resident's card and, as the landlord wasn't used to foreigners renting, Italy's bureaucratic maze turned what should have been simple into something deeply complex. Eventually, we got it done.

I settled in, and started to learn Italian. Most language students buy tapes and listen, but I printed out common Italian words, cut them up and taped them to my handlebars every day.

The guy who lived downstairs, also a Romano by name, lived with his mother, Sante. She was an absolute angel, always asking how I was, and even though we couldn't really speak we would sit there and trade a few words every day. When I first arrived it was just before Easter, which the Italians call Pasqua, and everyone was getting together for a big meal on Easter Sunday. Romano and his family asked me to join them for their gathering. I went straight into their family meal for Easter, a huge spread of Italian food and hospitality. There were little parcels of pasta, ravioli, cannelloni, the works. I remember thinking I was going to have to do seven hours' hard training to work it all off. And then they broke open the Easter eggs.

Paris–Roubaix

Saturday in Holland. Sunday in France.

It is five minutes before 11.00 a.m. on Sunday now, 13 April 2008. We mill around in the Place Charles de Gaulle in Compiègne. There are 198 of us. All clean for now. The locals smile at us as if we were farm boys waiting in line to go off to the trenches. They've seen real war in these *villes* though. This is their fun, conceived in 1896.

Welcome to the Hell of the North. Paris–Roubaix.

The posters for this year's race show a rider coming towards the camera with a big apocalyptic sky above him and a long straight of pavé beneath him. '*La Dure Des Dures*' is the slogan, 'The Hardest of the Hard'. When they ran this race for the first time it took the German Josef Fischer 9 hours and 17 minutes to ride the 280 kilometres from Paris to Roubaix. For some reason (perhaps the thrill of seeing a German suffer) they decided to hold the race again and again after that.

All this history is new to me.

Cobbles and more cobbles is the forecast. Expect widespread cobbles after Arenberg. The clear sky itself is a small mercy. Nothing more. The roads are a little damp from yesterday's showers but heavy rain is what gives the Hell of the North its most lasting flavour. Sean Kelly, an old warrior of these rides, once said that a Paris–Roubaix without rain is not a Paris–Roubaix. I can live with that. I'll take the dry, bland version any day. Yesterday's drizzle will keep down the dust we might have been swallowing today.

When I woke up this morning I didn't feel like a professional cyclist. I felt hungover. The race and the travel yesterday subtracted something from me. I'm not sure what is gone or what remains. My insides felt like they had spent time in a blender. My hands were sore from gripping the handlebars on the pavé. I asked some of the guys this morning, 'What do we do for our hands? We're riding Paris–Roubaix today, what do you guys do?' I'm asking because the gloves don't seem to offer sufficient cushioning against the expected battering.

Every rider had his own theory. I was sorry I had asked. One guy tut-tutted. He didn't use gloves. The more padding between the glove and the handlebars, the greater the friction generated. The greater the friction, the greater the chafing, and so on until the chafing causes sparks which cause bike and rider to burst into flames.

Other contributors had come up with varieties of home-made padding and strapping which they would put underneath their gloves. Simple.

I thought that sounded good. It made more sense. I taped my hands before getting on the bus. I felt like a boxer. On the bus as we drove here I looked down at my hands again and again. Like a boxer, except I wasn't just going into the ring. I was going into war.

Off we go. All 198 of us. We know that many of us won't finish. That's the point. Attrition and suffering.

I have learned a couple of things about these sorts of races since coming to Europe. One. I don't like them as much as I like stage races and mountains. Two. The meek shall inherit the broom wagon. So, if there is a breakaway, go with it. If there is a gap, barrel into it. The stretches of cobble aren't quite the hell they are made out to be, but you need to position well before you hit them. If somebody wants to pass you, make his life hard, very hard. Today I shall not be meek. My flappy-bird wide-elbows style will keep me near the front of the group for when we hit the pavé in the second half of the race. That's the plan.

The legends of Paris–Roubaix just add to the allure. Two years ago George Hincapie was gripping his handlebars so hard over the cobbles that they came away in his hands – literally detached from the bike. As a metaphor for the race, Hincapie holding his useless handlebars as the bike skittered about the pavé is perfect.

They abandoned the race for obvious reasons during World War One and Two but started back even before it was reasonable to do so.

The 'Hell of the North' tag came from a report by two journalists sent out to recce the course in 1919. The war had claimed the lives of two men who had been winners of four previous editions of Paris–Roubaix: three to Octave Lapize and one to François Faber. The journalists, Victor Breyer and Eugène Christophe, drove the course. Breyer described 'shell pieces one after the other with no gaps, outlines of trenches, barbed wire cut into one thousand pieces . . . nothing but desolation. The shattered trees looked vaguely like skeletons, the paths had collapsed and been potholed or torn away by shells . . . here, this really is the hell of the north.'

Recce duly done, they resumed with the organization of the race immediately.

Next time around they didn't even wait for the Second World War to finish. In 1944 a French rider, Jean Robic, fell and cracked his skull on the famous cobbles. The legends and the stories kept coming though. Fausto Coppi won in 1950 after chasing down two escapees from the pack then taking an orange from his pocket and eating it as he encouraged his two rivals to head off again. He would catch them up, he said. And he did. Coppi rode the last 100 kilometres all alone.

Two years later, though, in maybe the most famous race of them all, Coppi's genius just couldn't shake Rik Van Steenbergen. The two entered the velodrome in a state of exhaustion and Coppi lost Paris–Roubaix in a sprint to the line. Van Steenbergen was, of course, Belgian.

The history of crashes and wounds is just as long. In 1998 Johan Museeuw crashed in Arenberg and his wounded leg became gangrenous so quickly that he almost lost it. He came back to win the race another couple of times. Museeuw was Belgian too.

Bernard Hinault once described this race as bullshit and a con. He won the thing in 1981 though. That was a day when he fell seven times and ran over a small dog. At one point he ended up having to put his bike on his shoulders so he could run past a commissaire's vehicle. His dues paid, he competed once more, but never did Paris–Roubaix again after 1982.

If Hinault could ride through the baby heads and the bullshit, so can I. So must I. It's a rite of passage. An observance. A pilgrimage that every rider should do at least once. I love suffering and this is the place of high suffering. This race, one of the five monuments of the classic season, is also part of the soul of European cycling.

When today ends, in the old velodrome in Roubaix, there is a communal shower block with cubicles that reach shoulder high, and each cubicle bears a plaque with the name of a previous winner. We are told by men with shaking heads that this time, for the first time ever, the water will be hot. They tell us this despising our modern-day softness.

On the road there are breaks from early on. Nothing serious. Nobody panicking. One group goes but by the time they get to the pavé at Vertain they are among us again. Still, even the first pavé sectors do some serious damage to our numbers. It isn't hell though. You can figure it out. Today, at least, the race doesn't live down to its name.

I get one puncture early on but recover quickly. I try and try for about 100 kilometres to follow team orders: 'Get into a break.' Two or three of us have been told to do this for the first half of the race. There are no really serious breaks, though, until three guys get away from us a short while before we reach Troisvilles. They go but I am not a part of it. I miss the break. Now it's a different game. I've already spent a lot of energy trying to get into the breakaways and I've missed the serious one. I've just got to survive as long as I can.

For nearly 100 kilometres there are no cobbles at all, then just a few patches, at Quiévy, at Quérénaing and more at Haveluy. From Arenberg to Roubaix, however, it's lumps and bumps as often as not. Most of the 50 kilometres or so of pavé lie between here and Roubaix.

It takes the race over 160 kilometres to reach Trouée d'Arenberg. Paris–Roubaix didn't always come along this route, but when they discovered a long-forgotten stretch of pavé in the forest here, they decided this was too good to miss. This is where the cobbles cease to be a novelty. The difficult patches of cobbles on Paris–Roubaix are rated like hotels and three stretches are of five-star difficulty. This is the first of those three and the most eerie. The pavé is three metres wide, fringed by grass, and then there is a sheer wall of birches and cypresses, towering so high that it feels like twilight in early afternoon.

The stones here have been in the ground since Napoleonic times. There were mines under this forest too, but they have gone now. Arenberg, according to the wisdom of the elders, is not where you win Paris–Roubaix but certainly where you can lose it.

Not for me though. By the time we get there I have already lost the race.

On the way to Arenberg, the three riders out front are still hanging tough like desperados, ahead of the posse of about sixty chasers. From Haveluy, the last cobbles before Arenberg, the pace increases. Two kilometres before Arenberg, there are inevitable casualties. A big crash. Bikes and bodies are scattered everywhere. And this is where my race effectively finishes.

I am not far behind our team leader, Baden Cooke, a tough Aussie with a talent for sprinting. Baden gets a puncture. I am nearest, so I sacrifice my back wheel to him and wait for the support car as he speeds off. A small thing.

I feel okay, I've done something pretty useful today. I was right there when the lead man punctured so I gave him my wheel. At this stage there were only two or three of us left on the road anyway. Robbie Hunter had packed it in on the first cobbled section and got into the car. He wasn't feeling up to it today and he said he wasn't going to suffer for nothing. Inwardly, I smiled. Suffering for nothing – so many times I've thought that's exactly what I do.

By the time the car comes, Baden has joined up with a group of about thirty riders who will come out of Arenberg in pursuit of the three leaders. My hands are battered from gripping the handlebars but I decide that I might as well go after the group.

As luck would have it, Daryl Impey rides past just as I am getting going again. Daryl got dropped on the last pavé section. I am intent on getting back to the race though. My war isn't over.

Daryl is surprised. 'The race is gone, Froomey. Don't worry about it. There'll be other days, mate.'

'No. I want to catch them.'

So off I hare after the group, leaving Daryl behind shaking his head at me. Not for the first time.

The race comes on to another stretch of cobbles and having waited for our team car I now find myself behind a line of support cars. The group is on the far side of the cars. I think to myself that maybe I can use the cars to move up again and I start making my way through the convoy. All of a sudden there is a screeching of brakes and a car shudders to a halt just in front of me.

I am not even holding my handlebars by this point. I am perching on the saddle and resting my arms on top of the bars, trying to guide them as opposed to holding them with my hands, which are extremely tender and sensitive. There is no feeling left in my hands. Pain from gripping the bars through all the vibrations has surrendered to numbness from the cold. With my hands largely redundant, I don't even attempt to brake. I ride at speed straight into the back of one of the commissaire cars.

Another day; another commissaire.

'Hello again!'

I tumble over the side of the boot, sliding off the car and rolling on to the grass. I look out on to the cobbles and see that I have damaged the front wheel of the bike pretty badly. I have to wait for the team car once more and change the front wheel. By the time that is done I will be too far back.

Of course, before the team car arrives Daryl Impey comes upon the scene again. He finds the young sapper whom he last saw speeding back to the action now lying on the grass with a madly bent front wheel in his hand. He explodes with laughter and shakes his head again. I realize – again – that I've still got a lot to learn.

The car comes but Daryl and I must ride on for another 20 kilometres. There is no choice; the car is full. Of 198 starters only 115 riders will finish the race and *all* the cars are full.

We ride through the Arenberg Forest and I remember thinking

that even a Belgian couldn't love the cobbles in this tree tunnel. They are large and really uneven – almost designed to do you damage. The Friends of Paris–Roubaix love and preserve this stretch for that very reason. It is treacherous. The top riders hate and avoid this place for the same reason. No summer contender wants to catch a gangrenous leg on Napoleonic cobbles in April.

Daryl and I push on through another couple of pavé sections. The feeling of being two soldiers making our way home after the war is hard to avoid – this landscape is so evocative, so unchanged. Eventually we get to the second feed zone where our soigneurs, surely with space in the car, are waiting.

Our soigneur that weekend was a temp whom the team had hired for the day. He had brought his friends along in his car. What sort of a soigneur would fill his car with friends on a workday among the pavés of northern France? A Belgian sort.

Our Belgian soigneur looks at me and Daryl, tattered and mud-splashed veterans of Paris–Roubaix by now. He shrugs his shoulders, gets back into the car and leaves.

We sit there asking each other the same question: 'Well, what now, genius?'

A couple of graduates from two of the posher schools in Johannesburg, sitting by the side of the road in France. We respect this race but by now we don't really want to ride another 60 kilometres of it. There are still a lot more cobbles and the stuff underneath my gloves, the taping which made me feel like a boxer this morning, has wadded and grown dirty and chafed my hands raw. By the end, when it was just the two of us chugging along, even though I had been trying to steer the bike with my elbows on the cobbles, the jostling which the bike was taking was causing my forearms to get all bruised too. Paris–Roubaix, I've had enough, thanks.

Finally the sweep vehicle comes into sight, the broom wagon, with a trailer on the back to throw the bikes into. We throw ourselves into a couple of seats on the bus amidst the brotherhood of the wasted. Two *mzungus*, a long way from home.

Strangely, I didn't dislike the day. I was sorry it ended. I liked the way that it was a fight for position before the pavé. On the cobbles themselves there was pain but it was almost like a time trial. You got in your line and you just rode it.

And the pain and suffering? A pleasure.

I remember sending Robbie Nilsen an excited email afterwards saying that Paris–Roubaix was just like the intervals we used to do at home. An interval every time you hit the pavé, a 20-minute threshold effort over the cobbles.

It was a taste of European cycling like nothing else.

Oh, and Paris–Roubaix 2008 was won by Tom Boonen. A Belgian. What did you expect!

April 2008. Another week in the life.
   20 April: Amstel Gold Classic. Finish 139th.
   23 April: La Flèche Wallonne. Finish 115th.
   27 April: Liège–Bastogne–Liège, La Doyenne ('The Oldest').
   Today. Finish 84th. Shattered.

I'm 160 kilometres into the Liège, wondering what all the fuss is about.

Then we ride down a hill and turn right. Suddenly there is a race on. I'm not in it.

Three times this week, in the Amstel, in the Flèche and now in Liège, my objective has been to get in the first key breakaway. In all three of them that just seems impossible. I ride the narrow roads. I get battered by the crosswinds. I get to the front when nobody cares about who is at the front.

I know next to nothing about these races or how they unravel. I hardly know who is who. As an amateur, I dipped into the Tour de France on television. Otherwise I have lived in my own little world of training and nutrition. Paris–Roubaix was a revelation. This is a week of three revelations.

When the race starts, through those early miles, I cover the waterfront and go with all those little moves. In the phoney war I am a phoney hero. I cling like a limpet to breaks that go nowhere.

A rule of thumb: you wouldn't want to be a part of any break that I am a part of.

When a real break opens up, I can't get back to the front.

Again and again I have been spat all the way to the back of the bunch. I try to move up but riders seem to close in around me wordlessly and I just get spat out again.

The roads are skinny and crowded. I find it really difficult to be anywhere at the front of the bunch when I have to be. This war for position, it's something you don't really see when you are watching a race on TV. It's like being in a washing machine. You go up the middle. Guys come up on either side. You get thrown backwards until you are so far behind that you try to go up the outside yourself.

That works and you get to the front. Then they come round you and spit you out the back again.

No respect. Not yet.

This afternoon after 160 kilometres I never see the front of the race again.

Afterwards, I ask Robbie Hunter about this: 'How do I stay in the race until the race starts?'

He looks at me like a disappointed father. 'There's no secret. You have to fight.' He says it in quite an aggressive way. 'You're not in fucking Kansas now, Dorothy. You have got to fight.'

'Fine.'

For the next few weeks I am always looking for Robbie Hunter. Tracking him and following him. Sticking to him. Shoving people off his wheel if I have to. No backing off. Earning position. Seizing respect.

Try to move me off that wheel if you want. I'll be asking you, what's your fucking problem? I'll be taking elbows, giving elbows, come what may. It's not me, but it has to be me. I'll be there. You'll be testing me. I'll be testing you.

Learning the rules of Fight Club.

12

Nobody was happier than I was to see the back end of April.

My secret plan to winch myself into the Tour de France field had taken a few serious knocks as we chased around northern Europe.

That was okay. It had been a long shot in the first place but I had needed the idea in my head on those seven-hour training rides with no company except the techno coming through the iPod. Dreams are what keep us all fuelled. I had always dreamed of a blinding sunburst of breakthrough but instead I was looking at a watery dawn.

In Barloworld I knew my place. The April calendar didn't suit me but there was no point in crying about it. We were a small team and I was the rookie. This was what I had signed up for. So I kept quiet, learned what I could and did what I was told. And I knew that the month of May would be better.

I was still learning Italian. Claudio Corti had only a little more English than I had Italian, so we didn't interact too much.

His thoughts and wishes were transmitted to me through Robbie Hunter or his PA, Francesca. Living down in Chiari alone (Andrea wouldn't arrive until late summer) kept me out of harm's way. When the team needed me for a race, Romano would drive down to collect me.

Otherwise I worked alone and I worked hard.

Life in Chiari was enjoyable to the extent that there was actually a life in Chiari. Since leaving school the idea of home had taken on many different guises: Johannesburg, Aigle, Tielt, Chiari. I'd laid my head down in each of those places but home was probably still Mum's place back in Nairobi.

One day I thought about it and realized I hadn't been home since the Christmas of 2005. Andrea had come to stay with us for a while and we had gone up to the Mara like in the old days. And then I went back to the fast side of life.

I kept in touch with Africa as much as I could, sending reports, questions and stories back to Robbie and to Kinjah. The path to Chiari and to Europe had been laid down by those two key influences. Now that I was here I was surprised by how much they had taught me – and also by how much there was still to learn.

Those rides with Kinjah and the Safari Simbaz had mined out a huge well of enthusiasm and passion in me. The sense of fun and the pure thrill of riding is something that can get lost when you start doing it for money. Kinjah's joy stayed with me though and still does.

Robbie's ground-breaking theories on training were the foundation for what was being built. His ideas were still serving me and I was conscious that I was doing things differently to the other professionals around me. So many times now I follow Tim Kerrison's training programme at Team Sky and think, 'This is what Robbie had me doing years ago.'

What had to be learned though was the determination to keep pushing hard even when the thrill was gone. I had to develop the hardness of a drill bit to drive through the field when necessary. And my bike-handling technique needed constant work and tampering. Robbie and I talked about these things through emails and the occasional call.

Although I hadn't been home in so long, I knew Mum was still willing me up every hill and through every field. She was pleased to see me doing something I loved and something I seemed to be good at. For a long time she had taken Kinjah's word that I had some talent. And whenever I talked about cycling, she recognized my passion and said, no matter what, I was to follow it. Thank you, Mum.

In her own way she had given me as much of a foundation to build on as Kinjah and Robbie had.

With Mum I don't remember ever being told, 'You can't do that,' or 'These are the rules.' She didn't believe that rules existed merely to be followed. 'Do it if you want to,' she'd say, 'and you can find out for yourself what it's like, what the cost is.'

I really loved that philosophy. I still do. She made me think about how stupid it would be to do certain things, about how actions would hurt other people or hurt myself or betray the things I believed in. It was a sensible philosophy. Obeying rules just because they are rules isn't the same as having your own moral compass. Mum knew that character is what you do when nobody is watching.

Mum instilled a sense of responsibility and good morals in me that I live by to this day, and I know that diverting from these would be a betrayal of her. Cheating would not be an option for me.

I never felt rebellious. I never felt that breaking rules just for the sake of it would be a rite of passage or something to emphasize my individuality.

I remember one incident in particular that reflects Mum's philosophy. She happened upon one of my older brothers attempting to smoke a cigarette. He was trying to hide it but she said to him, 'Hey, come on then, let's have a smoke.' And she pulled one out of her own pack and made him smoke it in front of her. He just coughed all the way through it until he got nauseous. He never wanted to smoke again.

And we never wanted Mum to smoke again either. That was another story.

From Europe I would speak to her over the phone. I'd try to call her every other weekend if I could, though more often than not we communicated through emails.

It was only the previous year, when I rode the Giro del Capo and then the Regioni for Konica Minolta, that she seemed to appreciate for the first time that I could actually be a professional.

It was funny. She would support me in that indiscriminate way that mums have. I couldn't detect any difference in tone between the 'Wow, well done!' she would send to me if I'd done something in a race that meant nothing in South Africa or the 'Wow, well done!' she would send if I had placed well in a serious race. She gave the same support, no matter what. And I think she did know the difference.

After I left Kenya and then left Africa, she stayed in touch with Kinjah, and continued to be an integral part of the whole effort with the Safari Simbaz.

My cousin, Sarah Penfold, had moved back to Kenya. Sarah was a photographer, and on weekends she and Mum would drive behind the Simbaz wherever they were racing. Sarah would take photos and help Mum with the food and the water for the riders.

Mum became an avid supporter of cycling and continued to be a great friend to Kinjah and the boys. She would still arrive with baskets of food for them, and as her appreciation of things grew, she became very, very angry about the Federation and how it wasn't supporting these riders.

She grew extremely passionate about the whole thing. Not only because of what Kinjah had done for me, but because she saw something in the purity of cycling that appealed to her. She loved adventure and being out in the world, and cycling was opening up those things to so many kids.

She knew what was important and what mattered in the cycling world and that wasn't big races or big money. It was the sense of who you were that you carried with you. The possibilities. I think when she said 'well done' it referred to more than just finishing places or winnings.

Even though I wasn't home often, her growing passion for cycling and her constant encouragement diminished the distance.

April had been significant for another reason apart from the frustration of the classics. I became a British rider just before riding La Flèche Wallone. The trail which had started with Doug Dailey back in Melbourne and continued through contact with Rod Ellingworth had led to this. I swapped my Kenyan licence for a British one.

My feelings are complex and maybe impossible for somebody from a less complicated background to understand. I know people who feel they are from Yorkshire and Britain; from Merseyside and Britain; from the Isle of Man and Britain; and so on. Well, we were raised in Kenya feeling that we were of Britain. My brothers were sent to England when they were old enough. We lived in Karen, which was a little piece of England. We ate Sunday roasts with Yorkshire puddings. We had pythons not ferrets, scorpions not corgis, but there was a duality in us. We were from a tribe of interlopers, a line which had come to Kenya, whereas true Kenyans had sprung from the soil. Our relationship to Kenyan earth was different. Our people had come to make a living from that earth. The Masai and the other tribes had a more spiritual tie to the land. We were on it. They were of it.

Still, we loved Kenya. Always will. But given the failings of the

Kenyan Cycling Federation – not just failings but vindictiveness – it never felt like a betrayal to explore the other part of the Froome family identity. I wasn't a product of Kenyan cycling. I was a product of Kinjah cycling. And Jane Froome cycling. And Robbie Nilsen cycling. Mr Mwangi and his blazers did nothing for any of these people and were in a constant state of war with Kinjah. There are people running Kenyan cycling who carry grudges until their shoulders bleed.

Naturally, the process was made more difficult than it needed to be. The first step was the surrender of my Kenyan passport. The Kenyan authorities wouldn't accept it as they didn't have the documentation for such a procedure. A receipt, in other words. So I created a document. I drew up an affidavit at a lawyer's office and went to the Kenyan embassy in Pretoria, gave them my passport and asked them to sign the affidavit confirming the transaction.

Done.

After that it should have been blue skies. If both countries are agreeable to a transfer in these circumstances the process is usually quick and smooth. So long as Kenya didn't object I could be travelling, pending selection, to Beijing for the 2008 Olympics. Kenya objected.

The process passed from my hands and people at higher pay grades began negotiating with each other. I got on with riding.

The Vuelta a Asturias began in the city of Oviedo on 3 May. For me this was an opportunity to demonstrate to Barloworld that I was a better rider than I appeared to be while slogging around the Ardennes.

Stages. Mountains. Time trials. I was hungry.

Things started well. Day two contained two stages: a regular road ride out of Gijón in the morning, and a time trial of 17 kilometres in the afternoon. Samuel Sánchez González won the time trial and went on to win the gold medal in the road race in the Beijing Olympics later that year. I finished 5th in the time trial, 26 seconds off the top.

Then two days later on stage four from Pravia to the mountaintop finish at Santuario del Acebo, a stage I would have ring-fenced as full of possibility, I blew up. I was 26 minutes off the top this time. It was sickeningly disappointing.

The team divided into two after that, some going to the Giro in Italy, the others to the Tour de Picardie.

I went to Italy. Not to the Giro but back to Chiari to train.

Corti, the old pragmatist, had told everybody in the team that they were on the long list for the Tour de France. I still trained hard and said the right things if asked, but my hopes were slender.

It was around this time that my brother Jeremy got in touch. He had been working in Dublin for a while but had decided to pack it in and move back to Kenya. The first thing he had to deal with back at home was bad news. Mum had cancer. The doctors said it was cancer of the bone marrow.

Mum had always smoked and we had always hated it. My brothers, Jeremy and Jono, and myself grew up giving her a hard time about it. She smoked about twenty a day, cutting down to ten a day if people badgered her enough about it, but always going back to her pack-a-day habit.

To be honest, we were horrible to her about it. We'd hide her cigarettes when we were away somewhere, and we knew that she couldn't get to a shop. Or we'd put little firecrackers into her cigarettes. We'd tip out some of the tobacco from the end so she'd sit there and light these things and they would explode cartoonishly right in her face. Mum would be left with the filter dangling from her mouth. Sometimes we'd break the little firecracker open and pour the gun powder in there, so that when she lit the cigarette the whole thing would start fizzing up. It was mean, but she understood what we were trying to say. We desperately wanted her to quit and perhaps there was too much of the stiff upper lip in us for us to express that in any other way.

She tried. For our sake. She never smoked in the house and never smoked in the car. She'd always get away from us to smoke. We respected that, and we knew that she genuinely did have a hard time stopping. She tried all the patches, all the chewing gums and whatever remedies were going.

News like that swings into your day like a well-aimed sledgehammer. Things had been looking up for Mum. She had a couple of relationships after Noz left. She was involved with Kinjah, the boys and the weekend races. Her job was going well, and with all her sons in Europe, she had been doing some work on an American army base in Iraq.

If we worried about Mum it was because she was in Iraq, even though the base was in a safe area. The job gave her a shot at some tax-free earning for a few months. She could come back from a three- or four-month stint doing massage or physio with soldiers and have a large cheque to cash.

Despite our concerns, she was determined that she would not become a burden on her sons. She was reaching retirement age and, having been a homemaker for most of her life, she had minimal savings.

My goal was to be able to buy Mum a house near Nairobi, where she could live and set up a physio practice. Since leaving Windy Ridge, she had never stayed anywhere for more than a year or two, and I wanted somewhere for her to settle down. It was one of the driving forces in the back of my mind, if ever I needed the motivation to push that much harder. I was determined to be successful enough to make this happen.

She came back early from this latest tour to Iraq because she was feeling ill. She went into hospital in Nairobi for tests and the news was bad.

Jeremy told me they were looking at doing a bone marrow transplant but in the interim she had developed quite a bad lung infection which turned into pneumonia. She was coughing really badly. All that would have to be dealt with first.

There is an agony of indecision at times like that. Should you go home and maybe complicate the process of her getting stronger, by your presence? Mum would worry that we were worried. Seeing us gather in Nairobi would alarm her. Yet, if she was really bad, I wanted to go back.

In the end, we decided that there was likely to be a long road ahead with the transplants and her recovery, and that Jeremy would need relief or help at some stage. In early June I went with the team to the Euskal Bizikleta, a stage race in the Basque country. That year, 2008, was the last year that the Euskal was staged.

It was a short affair. Three days and three stages. I rode the first two days in mediocre form, finishing 51st on stage one and 80th the next day. That evening I remember having a long talk with Jeremy. Mum was still in hospital. She was struggling with the infection, but the doctors had her on antibiotics and were keeping a close eye on her. When the infection was cleared out, they still wanted to look at the possibility of doing the transplant.

Mum was quite ill but she was fine for now.

The next morning, about 11.30 or so, not long before the start of the stage, we were all kitted up and had put the radios on. We were ready to go to sign on when Robbie Hunter came to speak to me.

'Listen, if you need to go home just say. Don't mess around. You don't have to be here.'

I was moved by Robbie's words. I explained that Mum seemed to be all right – in a battle, but doing okay. If things got worse Jeremy would tell me.

Half an hour later my phone rang. Jeremy.

'Bro, I'm really, really sorry. There's nothing we can do. She's gone.'

Mum was fifty-eight. She had suffered a cardiac arrest related to the chest infection. They brought her round once, but she arrested again not long after.

And that was it.

I couldn't breathe. My lungs closed up.

I remember standing outside the team bus, so angry and so distraught. I hit the side of the bus with my fist. I sat down on the ground behind the bus, talking to my brother.

When we finished talking, I got on the bus. The team looked up at me with a single set of eyes as I walked on. My tears told them everything. They were around me and then they were gone.

Robbie said to me, 'Just sit down, take your numbers off, take your kit off. You're going home.'

It was a really long bus journey back to the hotel. I sobbed all the way. Gianni, the bus driver, kept on looking at me in the rear-view mirror and shaking his head in sympathy.

The only flight to be had was the next morning. I don't remember the details of getting home. I was taken to an airport and after a number of transfers ended up in Nairobi. I can't recall where I flew. I just remember getting back to Kenya and being with my brothers. Jono had flown straight from London. I was the last of us to arrive.

There are hard moments and soft moments in my memory from those weeks at home.

We shared our memories and told stories about the trips we had taken together. I had my own recollections of the times when just Mum and I lived together, and how she loved all the possibilities in life and nature. She took such pleasure in sharing those things. The three of us grew up with our maker's mark on us. Mum had always been colour-blind when it came to race, completely so, and we all took that from her. And we all, even my two accountant brothers, took some of her openness to life.

So many stories. Sarah recalled a shouting incident between Mum and Julius Mwangi at a race. Kinjah and the boys and Mum and Sarah had turned up for a race and Mwangi had barred them, as they had no licences. Kinjah pointed out that Mwangi had refused to issue the licences. Mum flipped and told Mwangi he had no right to behave the way he did. He was taken aback. He shouted back at her, 'What's your problem?' and told her she shouldn't get involved with the politics, it was nothing to do with her, she should get in her car and go back home. At which point Sarah, who is quite petite, whacked Mwangi with a camera bag or something.

That tickled me a bit. Still does.

Me, my brothers, Sarah and a few others from Mum's life – that was the farewell group.

Seeing her body before the cremation was a tough blow.

Together, we went into the room where they had prepared her body and dressed her. We all said a few words.

Jono had been really fantastic. As the oldest brother, he'd taken charge of the family and had sorted out most of the logistics and arrangements, along with all the legal stuff that needed to happen for us to take over the estate, which was basically an envelope with the cash that Mum had earned on her last trip to Iraq. There were some shares, too. Not much; she wasn't a material girl. When she had money she gave it away or lent it to people knowing it would probably never come back. Much of the work she did, she did for free. She could never turn anybody away.

After a couple of days we took Mum to a local crematorium. I found it hard but something about it would have pleased Mum. It was basically a tin roof with open sides, like a warehouse with no walls, and a big fireplace in the middle.

We brought my mum's coffin through, unloaded it and put it on top of the open fireplace. We all took a burning branch and lit the fire, watching the flames slowly gather momentum. It was hard to stomach, in that the coffin disintegrated quite quickly and then the body was just there burning. I don't know how long it was that way. I stopped looking.

I hadn't prepared mentally for this. I hadn't expected the really pungent smell of burning flesh, I guess. At least a week had passed since Mum's death. My memories of that day at the crematorium are about how harsh and brutal it was compared to the sanitized version of death that other parts of the world have become used to.

I had imagined flowers, soothing music and togetherness. This was raw. I cried my eyes out.

Afterwards we all sat together. Around this warehouse there was grass and a wall. It was Sunday and there must have been a Sunday school in session somewhere nearby. As we sat, the African hymns just came to us in the air. It was a beautiful coincidence that Mum would have loved, our grief mingling with this lovely high-pitched singing.

Very emotional. Very African.

When it was time to go we gathered some of Mum's ashes. One thing we maybe didn't need to know was that they had to keep stoking the fire to make sure that the bigger bones would burn. They need a higher heat. Again this was raw, but in Africa that's how death is. There are no sugar coatings.

A few days later, we held a memorial service at the St Francis Church in Karen. The church was overflowing with people whose lives had been touched by Mum, many of whom I'd never met. It was moving and emotional, and the memories still bring me to tears.

I stayed in Kenya for perhaps another two weeks. There was no bike, no training. It was good to be with my brothers and to go through the process of our grief together, before separating again.

I remember thinking at one stage, 'Wow, I haven't even touched a bike now for probably a week or two.' I was still pretty emotional and not in a very good place, but that amount of time away from the bike would have been a record.

Then one day Claudio Corti called me from Italy.

'Froome, how are you doing?'

'Okay, Claudio. I haven't really been training or anything, but I'm with the family and we've had a good time together. Thank you.'

'Froome, do you want to go to the Tour?'

I just went quiet. I didn't know what to say. I didn't give him an answer other than silence.

'Froome, you do the Tour. Okay? Bye.'

I put the phone down, went back to my brothers and told them that the team wanted me to do the Tour de France. More silence and shock.

The talk, when it started, came down to what Mum would have wanted. What she would have said. My brothers knew. I did too, but I wanted them to tell me.

'Why stop living your life?' she would've asked. 'Don't mourn. Don't be miserable.'

Jono had said this to us a couple of days before the crematorium. We were all in tears and Jono had said, 'Listen, she'll be looking at us and telling us not to be ridiculous. She'll be saying, "Get over yourselves. Don't sit there crying for me. That's not living. Living is making the most of life. Celebrating it. No wasted moments."'

Jono and Jeremy said those things to me again and I knew they were right.

As it happened, it hardly mattered. While we were mulling these things over, a press release went out in Europe. I was named in the team for the Tour starting two weeks later in Brest.

Three years later, Jono, Jeremy and I went down to the coast, to Diani, south of Mombasa, where Mum used to come and had so often brought us. We went out on a boat to just beyond the reef. There, we scattered her ashes. It was beautiful and graceful and we brought many flowers too.

We had thought we might scatter her ashes on the Rift Valley, but when we thought of Diani and the ocean, it just seemed more appropriate for Mum.

Life is strange and often funny.

Sometime later Jono found a note on Mum's computer. It was her will. She left us her possessions, such as they were, and asked us to scatter her ashes in the ocean at Diani.

The four of us, my brothers, myself and Mum, shared a last smile with each other.

13

2008: The Tour de France

Three days of the Tour de France. Please make it stop.

Merciless. Helter-skelter. A war zone. A long daily grapple for survival.

Three days in and I was 168th in a field of 178. At least one of those guys behind me was an injured teammate.

This bipolar peloton was in a different mood than I had ever seen it in my limited experience, rolling with a shocking, wicked momentum once it got past the daily pleasantries of the neutral zone.

I was out at sea and completely out of my depth. Whatever happened to those leisurely picture-postcard rides through fields of sunflowers? This was faster than any race I'd done before.

Could I just have the old dream back, please?

Three days and already my ambitions had been whittled down to merely getting through it. Hang in there and get to Paris. I wanted to finish the Tour and to have that experience. Any other fanciful notions had been purged. Despite my shiny new British racing licence I was still being written up as the first Kenyan to ride the Tour de France – okay. If I could be the first Kenyan to finish it, that would be enough – better than enough.

They say that all good things take time and that all the crap gets delivered by same-day express. They're right. It started badly. Day one was Brest to Plumelec. We had only 10 kilometres or so to go when our team leader, Mauricio Soler, crashed. He had broken his left wrist on the Giro earlier in the year and he damaged it again now before any of us had crossed a finish line. It was the right wrist, too. He also ripped a hole in his shorts and in the flesh on his leg, high on his left thigh.

Soler was our leader and the hero in the mountains a year previously. He had earned our loyalty. There was nothing for it but for

Félix Cárdenas, Giampaolo Cheula and myself to wait for Mauricio and to attempt to nurse him back to the group. Mauricio was shaky. He almost took himself out on a barrier a couple of kilometres further down the road but we survived.

Giampaolo and I finished stage one 4 minutes and 4 seconds adrift. 'Happy' days.

I wanted to finish for myself. For Mum. For the past and for the future. But already I felt lost. The race was being decided somewhere up ahead of me every day. Most riders get a recce of the key stages in the weeks and months before the Tour. I just had a map. I rode blind into the valley of death and rode blind up the climb that led out of it.

In June I had travelled to Africa to grieve. I took at least two weeks' sabbatical from the bike, and when I got the news from Corti, I went out for two long runs and found out the hard way that runners use different muscle groups to cyclists. I ached in places I had forgotten existed.

When I flew back to Italy I went straight out on the bike for six hours. I rode six hours every day for six days in a row. No recovery days. Then I joined the team up in Brittany for the hullaballoo of Le Grand Départ, which was as underwhelming as the weather was overcast. For the last couple of days in Brittany we were restricted to two-hour training sessions. My body needed more.

The peloton hit the road carrying forty-three of us who had never ridden the Tour before. I wondered how the other forty-two had spent the previous month.

Stage two. More of the same. Not waving but drowning. Soler was wounded and there was nothing we could do for him after a while except leave him to his agony. Both of his wrists were bandaged up now. He came in last on the day, over 7 forlorn minutes behind everybody else. I lost another 2 minutes or so. Again, the race and the main group all finished ahead of me, and I only crossed the line when the drama was over.

Next day, on the third stage, we lit out from the walled town of Saint-Malo on the road to Nantes. The rain came at us with frequent ambushes. We would think we had seen the last of it each time the skies teased us with a show of blue. Then the deluge would resume.

We rode through a forest. The water seemed to have gathered in the leaves above to fall on us in engorged droplets. And the winds never settled on their plan. Most of the time they hit us sideways. Cross-winds leave you with few defences and nothing splits a field quicker. I found myself yo-yoing from the back of the peloton into the convoy of support cars and back out. The vehicles offered some protection from the wind but amidst the cars was not where you wanted to be.

It was not a bad day for the team though. Up at the front, Paolo Longo Borghini was part of a small break which built a good lead and kept it. He finished 4th. Robbie Hunter was 12th. I was almost 5 minutes behind but people told me that my race would start the following day with the individual time trial.

I wanted to believe them. I wanted a small taste of whatever Paolo and Robbie were having.

We were a platoon of nine carrying the hopes of Team Barloworld through this twenty-one stage counterclockwise yomp around France. Me, a mongrel with a Kenyan flag on my dossard and a British passport in my bag. Two Colombians, Félix Cárdenas and our leader Soler, both skinny like saplings, as if bred for climbing. Baden Cooke, the sprinting Aussie. Two South Africans, Robbie Hunter and John-Lee Augustyn. Two Italians, Paolo Longo Borghini and Giampaolo Cheula. And one Spaniard, Moisés Dueñas.

We were not a close bunch. That's how it is in pro teams. Language, experience, seniority and different schedules mean we generally have just a superficial relationship with each other. I was friendly with the two South Africans, of course, but with, say, Moisés Dueñas or the Colombians I had little more than a nodding relationship unless we needed to communicate during a stage.

I roomed with Giampaolo Cheula, one of the Italian riders. He was a tough fellow: squat with blond hair and a blond moustache. He finished the Tour the previous year and had been with Barloworld since 2005. That gave him some seniority and he didn't mind letting me know about it. But it wasn't just me. I think John-Lee Augustyn and Daryl Impey also felt that Giampaolo liked to give us a bit of a hard time. Probably because we were all neo-pros or because our backgrounds and our accents didn't fit the picture of the typical European professional.

Earlier in the season, back in the Vuelta a Asturias, I was fussing with the mechanics late one evening getting the bike right for an individual time trial the following day. Giampaolo, who had a 'neo-pros should be seen and not heard' attitude, couldn't help but give a thin smile and ask me, 'Well, Chreees, what thing will you do tomorrow on this special bike of yours?'

As it happened, the time trial went very well. I came 5th. I didn't say anything but the next day I thought to myself, 'There you go, Giampaolo. See?'

He wasn't a bad guy. He was once given all the tough flunky jobs and I'm sure he just felt a responsibility to preserve the pecking order that he came up through. It was fair enough.

Ah. Stage four. They told me that my race would begin here on a cheekily short time trial at Cholet. The stage was a shade under 30 kilometres – a bit too abbreviated for any real suffering, or so I thought.

Soler came down to breakfast with the results of an X-ray, which revealed a broken bone in his right hand. His left hand was still so sore that he was finding it hard to apply the front brakes. The poor man was getting a worse reputation for crashing than I had, but he said he would do the time trial anyway.

It was a race of three parts: headwinds starting out, crosswinds in the middle and a tailwind pushing you the last 10 kilometres home.

Soler finished close to the bottom of the pile, fresh evidence that the Tour was breaking him day by day.

For me, it turned out that the wisdom of the crowd was correct. The first good day arrived. There were no worldwide headlines but some encouragement dripping slow. I finished 33rd, which was the best of Team Barloworld, and 6th in the young riders' category behind guys like Vincenzo Nibali and Andy Schleck. I felt like I was just coming into my strength when the finishing line loomed.

Giampaolo, my room-mate, came in 118th. It wasn't my place to offer consolation or advice to an elder though.

The next morning brought the longest stage of the Tour, a 232-kilometre ride to Châteauroux. It was long and flat and Mauricio Soler's heartbreak came to an end. He crashed in the neutral zone and gave up the ghost. We rolled on, knowing that the day was a play with the drama all packed into the final act. It was a stage loaded for the sprinters, and Mark Cavendish won the battle.

I was far behind, hanging in there and thinking of the mountains.

We had a couple of transition stages to go, and then another long flat stage on the Saturday before we would get to stage nine, and go up where the air was rare.

Until then I would be watching from a seat near the back.

When we hit the mountains I felt at home. Not at home like a guy banking on a stage win, or even at home like a rider rolling all day with the front group. I just had a little surge of confidence. Any ambitions for GC were gone in the first couple of days, but that was okay. I'd made it this far in what would prove to be an accident-prone team – accident prone or disaster prone, take your pick. Now I could test myself.

I'm neither superstitious nor religious, but for me, of all people, to escape the various calamities raining down on Team Barloworld for those three weeks of the Tour meant that maybe somebody was looking down on me, giving me a steer when she wasn't enjoying the flora and fauna of France. Getting to the mountains was the first suggestion of that.

Stage nine ran from Toulouse to Bagnères-de-Bigorre, taking us into the high Pyrenees. Riding out of Toulouse, there was a static of excitement buzzing through parts of the peloton. Everyone has their talents and when the Tour route is announced each rider can see the days where he might thrive more than others, and the days where he might toil harder than most.

This was a day that we mountain goats had been looking forward to. Four category-four climbs as appetizers. Then a category three and finally two category-one mountains, Col de Peyresourde followed by Col d'Aspin and a roll down the other side of the mountain to the finish.

I wasn't in the front group all day long astounding the race commentators but neither was I back in the society of the gruppetto, in the blurry ranks of the indistinct and undistinguished.

I did have a brief shining moment as the stage leader on the road though.

At the bottom of the Col d'Aspin the group I was in must have been about forty or fifty strong. We were maybe 5 kilometres up the climb and I remember being towards the back of the group feeling relatively comfortable. 'I'm in the group,' I thought. 'We are on the climb. I won't be picked off here.'

I looked across and saw David Millar, the Scottish rider, a couple of yards away. My knowledge of the pros was limited but David Millar, though never a climber, was still a big deal to me. He was in difficulty. He was on the tip of his saddle, really squeezing out any energy that he had left.

It was strange but that put some iron in my soul. I remember the feeling that seeing David Millar struggling gave me, and the energy that shot through me. If he was suffering and I was feeling just about okay, then that had to be a pretty good sign.

'All right,' I said to myself, 'if David Millar is about to go out the back pretty soon now, there must be others around here that will be going with him. Time to get out of here.' I started moving up through the group maybe two-thirds of the way up the climb.

The Col d'Aspin isn't a legendary Tour de France ascent but it is one long haul. I got to the front of the group probably two or three minutes later.

I was in the front tip of the leading group as we ascended but knew that I wasn't likely to be with them when we came down the far side. 'So what the heck,' I thought. I attacked.

I remember thinking that I was going quite fast. 'I'm not going to rip the field apart but I'm going to do this for a few more minutes. I'll blow out of the picture soon enough but I want to have my moment in front while I can.' I never got more than 20 metres in front. And my lead hardly lasted more than a minute.

What happened next was that the Italian Riccardo Riccò came flying past me as if I were standing still at the side of the road posing for an oil painting. He was on his big chainring, no doubt, out of the saddle. He just burned past and went sprinting off. By now I couldn't even turn the pedals any more. I looked at Riccò's disappearing form and thought that I had never seen such talent.

People said that evening that Riccò's explosive burst had reminded them of Marco Pantani, one of the best climbers of his era, although his career was filled with doping allegations. They were still saying that a week later.

I got back into the bunch and was duly dropped just as they were cresting in the last 500 metres of the climb. I rolled over the finish line in 51st place, second best of the team after Moisés Dueñas.

'Okay,' I thought. 'These are my mountains. Game on.'

Wrong. Next day, stage ten, I came home 120th, 33 minutes behind Leonardo Piepoli. Col de Tourmalet nearly broke me and my lesson for the week was to respect the course. But there was lots still to learn as we paused for the first rest day of the Tour. The tutorials were just beginning.

Oh my God. Had he murdered Cárdenas?

Félix Cárdenas, the Colombian rider, had been rooming with Moisés Dueñas, the quiet Spaniard who sat just across and in front of me on the bus as we went to and from the race each day.

We had come out from breakfast downstairs to find the hotel lobby full of French police. Reporters were being kept out. Everybody else was being kept in. This was the Hôtel le Rex in the middle of Tarbres; it was not a normal morning. Chris Fischer, the Barloworld company rep on the Tour, told us to stop rubbernecking and to head to our rooms. We got up to the sixth floor and there were police there too.

We went to our rooms and left our doors open. There was activity around room 604.

The next thing I saw was Moisés Dueñas being led away by the police. He was 19th in GC, our breakout success of the Tour, and he was being frogmarched out of the place. Claudio Corti and Massimiliano Mantovani, the team doctor, were accompanying him to the police station.

You have to worry about the quiet guys. Had he killed poor Cárdenas in some mad row about leaving the cap off the toothpaste?

It wasn't too long before somebody mentioned the word 'doping'.

I was stunned. More stunned than if Cárdenas had been butchered. Looking back, I am stunned by my naivety. He was our GC hope. I couldn't believe it could happen. Of course, I knew that professional cycling had a massive, long-term infection that it was struggling to get rid of. Manuel Beltrán, another Spaniard, had already been thrown out of the Tour, having tested positive on stage one. Yet I never imagined that a symptom would be so local. Our team? This guy? He seemed like such a nice man, very quiet but always friendly, and always with the hint of a smile on his face.

It was shattering.

Dueñas had returned a positive test after the time trial back at Cholet. EPO. As soon as that was announced the police turned up to search his cases and raid his room. The word came quickly that they had found a private pharmacy in there.

We left soon after to ride stage eleven. I was distracted, mad, disappointed, betrayed, confused – all or any of those things at any given time.

The more I thought about it, the more angry I got. I remember feeling that this guy had cheated us all. He had got in there and trespassed all over my dreams. He was ruining the sport I had always wanted to be a part of. I had come to this Tour, to this life as a pro, with my warped vision that it had cleaned up, that the past was the past, that the big doping/cheating scene was an abandoned and sealed mineshaft.

Now this. This wasn't the sport I had thought I was getting myself into.

I knew enough about the team to know that this wasn't an organized operation. It wasn't done through the team. Dueñas had been freelancing, taking a risk at our expense, and that struck me as incredibly selfish. We all had our journeys and our backstories about getting to this level. It wasn't easy for any of us but he had put all of our careers at risk. Barloworld were already speaking about how this was going to have huge repercussions in terms of their sponsorship. Who could blame them?

Our team was in jeopardy, our careers were in jeopardy and, if this continued, our sport was in jeopardy. Again.

People wanted to interview us, not about cycling but about Moisés Dueñas and doping.

For Barloworld, things got worse when we set out on the road. The team was in a bunch when we came to a situation where we had to cross a very narrow bridge at the same time as the road turned, descending from the Col de Larrieu.

I wasn't involved but Cárdenas and Paolo Longo Borghini got their handlebars wrapped around each other's while they were squeezing over the bridge. They took each other out and Borghini got flung into a small ravine. Robbie Hunter came down too, but he was okay to continue. Cárdenas hurt his ankle and had a bad, deep cut on his knee and ripped a muscle in his thigh, but he rode on for a while. Borghini broke his collarbone and abandoned immediately. They were both taken to the hospital by the end of the day.

The crash was fate's gift to conspiracy theorists – one Barloworld rider arrested after breakfast, another couple having to withdraw a few hours later. Nobody wanted to hear about X-rays and scans and freak accidents.

Finally, Robbie Hunter got very angry with a journalist who asked him if it wasn't just a bit too suspicious. Robbie went for him and told him where to shove his microphone. I thought, 'Good luck to the next guy who wants to ask Robbie that question.'

To infinity and beyond. That seemed to be the route of the Tour de France 2008. Nine of us started in the Barloworld platoon and by stage twelve there were just five of us left.

Then Baden Cooke came down heavily off his bike halfway to Narbonne. He rode on for a while but had to abandon, so we lost another one.

Baden wasn't the big news of the day though. He was just a footnote. They busted Riccardo Riccò in the morning. He had tested positive for a sophisticated new variant of EPO back on the individual time trial in Cholet. Just like Moisés Dueñas. The difference was that Riccò had made a ham-fisted attempt to escape the testers after the stage but had got stuck in traffic.

Journalists and fans had nicknamed Riccò The Cobra because of the way he struck so suddenly on days when he was in the mood. Luckily, genuine reptiles aren't litigious.

None of his teammates in the Saunier Duval team turned up for the start in the morning. We heard later that the Tour organizers had sacked Leonardo Piepoli as well as Riccò after being dissatisfied with his answers about doping. Piepoli (one) and Riccò (two) had won three of the Tour's first ten stages between them. If Riccò showed the audacity of dope with his lunatic charge past me up the mountain, Piepoli had been just as odd. This was the Tour de France 2008. Piepoli was born in 1971. Stage ten in the Pyrenees was his first ever stage win on the Tour.

Piepoli and Riccò stole three stages from good riders. By the end of the year we would know that Bernhard Kohl, King of the Mountains and 3rd overall, had been cheating us also. So too had Stefan Schumacher, who took both individual time trials on the Tour.

Riccò got a twenty-month ban. A couple of years later he was banned again. Twelve years this time. The Cobra was taken to hospital having become seriously ill after giving himself a blood transfusion with 25-day-old blood.

We were a forlorn quartet in the evenings back in the hotel: me, Giampaolo Cheula, Robbie Hunter and John-Lee Augustyn. We made jokes about the space we had on the bus and why we were still sharing rooms but the atmosphere was heavy with worry. Would we have pro careers after this mess? What would happen next? Would any of us get to Paris?

What happened next would wait until stage sixteen, just when we had begun to relax.

Before then, we knew we weren't blessed, but maybe we weren't cursed, after all. Although stage fifteen over the border in Italy had been a bad one for me – I spent too much of it in the gruppetto – I was still alive and it had been a few days since one of the team had last left the race.

We were in the mountains again. Stage sixteen was an attractively lumpy Alpine stage with two massive out-of-category climbs. First the Col de la Lombarde and then the Cime de la Bonette-Restefond or La Bonette. We would descend down the other side and into the tiny hamlet of Jausiers for the finish.

I was going okay. John-Lee was having a great day. On the way up

La Bonette, John-Lee was part of a lead group of nine. Barring disaster, the stage was going to go to one of the nine. Near the top they rode over a narrow ledge high on the mountain and John-Lee decided to make a move. He upped the pace and went for it. If he didn't get the stage he would still get some mountain points at the top and a slice of televised glory. It was the highest point of the 2008 Tour.

It worked. John-Lee stole a small lead. He hit the top first. The descent from La Bonette is incredible, just shale and escarpment to your left as you ride hell for leather. John-Lee was fearless though as he led this mad scatter down the mountain towards the finish.

Next thing, the road veered right, but John-Lee didn't. He misjudged the turn, riding over a bank of mud like a mountain biker doing a trick and landing quickly. Then he fell down the side of the mountain.

He slid thirty or forty metres down scree and shale before he managed to stop his own momentum.

Above him, on the road, two of the motorbikes from the convoy pulled in. One motorbike man scrambled down the shale towards where John-Lee was lying. Like a wounded animal, John-Lee came to life in a panic. He began crawling back up the scrabble on his hands and knees, climbing on pure adrenaline. When he got to the top, another motorcyclist leaned down and took his hand and pulled him up on to the roadside.

There is some madness in us all, I swear. John-Lee could have died just there. But that was far from his thoughts. Instead, he remembered his bike. He immediately started pointing down the slope at it, where it had continued the descent for some time after he had stopped his own fall.

'What about my bike?'

The original rescuer had made it back to the top. He shrugged his shoulders at John-Lee. The second motorcyclist did the same. You could almost hear them say, 'You have got to be joking, man.'

John-Lee had to wait until the team car arrived with a spare bike.

He got his fifteen seconds on TV though. Still, he wasn't happy.

By the time John-Lee went down the mountain I had settled into my survival strategy.

On the mountain stages, and in the second half of the race in general, I was attempting to ride one day fast, where I could punish myself as much as possible and try to be in the front of the race or the breakaway at the most important points, then the next day my aim would be to get to the finish by expending as little energy as possible. I would ride this day lagging back in the common room that was the gruppetto, even though I could probably go faster on the climbs.

The day John-Lee came off I was going easy in order to save my body for what was to come, which was my first trip up Alpe d'Huez.

It was a massive stage, involving 210 kilometres over three out-of-category climbs: Galibier, Croix de Fer and Alpe d'Huez.

The peaks got lower in that order – Galibier being the highest – but the cumulative suffering made the day more interesting the later it got.

Galibier is an epic adventure; a long, hard mountain. A four-man break instigated by Stefan Schumacher reached the top first but I was comfortable in the group which followed them as we crested the peak of the lunar-landscaped mountain and headed down towards Col du Télégraphe and on to the small town of Saint-Jean-de-Maurienne.

Next was the Croix de Fer. Jens Voigt was doing an incredible pull for his Saxo Bank teammate Carlos Sastre. Jens was known as a rouleur, or a good racer on the flat, but this day he was riding at an absolutely phenomenal pace and I was hanging on at the back of the group, just pushing it as hard as I could.

This was my day and I was in a bullish mood. I held my ground, fending off a few French riders who came up beside me and who expected me to yield to somebody more worthy, or more French. They dropped back, cursing my name, as I waved off the suggestion of food.

I rode for a kilometre or two on the wheel of the double Vuelta a España champion Denis Menchov, who was weakening. His troubles attracted the cameras and I got into the shots – 'Who's that following Denis Menchov?'

Jens took us up and up. I think he was pulling for three-quarters of the ascent of Croix de Fer, before he just peeled off and literally stopped pedalling. Job done.

I was hugely impressed. I remember thinking, 'Well, now he's out of the race, he's out of the stage today. Alpe d'Huez has to be as tough as they say, if even Jens has given up.'

As he was dropping back he was beside me for a few moments. He looked across.

'You must eat,' he said. 'Think about feeding your legs.'

He was right. I had made a mistake and had only one energy gel left in my pocket, and all of Alpe d'Huez ahead of me. It was a compliment that he had taken the trouble to notice and to care. Jens was saying, 'Look, you've done well to get this far, but now you need to eat something because I know what is ahead of you, and you don't.'

Less than 2 kilometres later I dropped back to the car and took his advice.

Corti looked at me with a smile. Of course I needed gels and food.

I came home in 31st spot, which left me 88th in GC out of a field of 150 survivors.

It wasn't a headline result for me but it was an indication that I could get there. I just needed a bit more experience. I was growing into the Tour. I definitely felt the second half of the Tour was better for me than the first half had been, when I was still trying to retrieve my lost fitness.

For the first time I was confident that I would get to Paris.

The team was hugely supportive. Claudio Corti, Chris Fisher and even Alberto Volpi, the hard-to-please directeur sportif, all said encouraging things. 'You just need time and experience,' they told me.

Paris. Four of us rode into the Champs-Élysées. Although we were a subplot, and our presence was no distraction from the pomp of the day, I took a spin at the front on one of the eight circuits which took us up the main street. The crowds, the city, the school-is-out giddiness, it all blew me away.

Reasons to be Cheerful

1. Survival.
2. The mountains.

3. The second individual time trial of the Tour. This took place the day before Paris, and it was longer than the previous one – a full twist. Schumacher won again but I came in 16th, just behind Jens Voigt. Today, if I subtract the names of the guys ahead of me who I now know to have doped, I feel even more pleased than I did then.

4. Final reckoning. My position was 84th out of the 145 who finished the race, which made me the best of the four Barloworld boys who made it to Paris.

It was done. We went out and had dinner and cocktails with the sponsors on the Bateau Mouche, up and down the river, living large for a night.

My brothers, Jono and Jeremy, had followed me to France and showed up at different stages. Jeremy arrived on one of the mountain stages, on a day when I had decided to stay with the gruppetto and save myself for a more promising tomorrow. Unfortunately, Jeremy wasn't in on my plan.

I was riding as slowly as I dared when I heard Jeremy's voice from the side of the road.

'Go on, Chris. You can do it.'

'Oh no,' I thought. 'I can go faster, but I can't tell Jeremy that.'

He'd been waiting by the side of the road, looking for his brother. Now here I was in the final group.

'Go, bro!'

I was mortified. I tried to communicate with my eyes and eyebrows that I could go faster, but not today. I wanted to shout, 'Come back tomorrow! I'll be pushing harder.'

We went around a switchback and were going so slow now in the laughing gas gang that Jeremy had made it to the next bend ahead of us.

'Hey, bro! There you are again. Keep it going.'

It was the same for the next bend, and for the one after.

'Don't give up, bro!'

'Great to see you, Jeremy,' I thought, 'but this is embarrassing.'

Robbie Nilsen came over to France too, and brought a mutual friend, Gavin Cocks. Gavin was responsible for a lot of the money and a lot of the heart behind the Hi-Q Academy back in South Africa.

When I was about eighteen years old and still in St John's I did a race in the high country around Lesotho. Noz came with me. The race wasn't long, less than 100 kilometres, but the attraction was the three huge mountain passes, each about 20 kilometres long, which we would ride over.

In my enthusiasm I went out too hard and a kid of about fifteen or sixteen years old took me on and beat me. His name was Edwin Cocks.

Edwin loved his bike. He gave the hours to it and I knew that we would be following similar paths.

Not too long afterwards, Gavin, Edwin's dad, came home from work one day and found Edwin hanging from a door handle with a belt around his neck. Edwin had been having a hard time in a romantic relationship and for three years Gavin and his family lived with the thought that Edwin had taken his own life. Then some friends of Edwin's approached Gavin with something to tell him, something they should have told him a long time ago. Edwin had been playing a game which they all played at school. The idea was basically to suffocate each other and to give each other some sort of natural 'high' by just passing out for a few seconds and then releasing the choke. They labelled it the choking game and Edwin had tried it alone. It had gone wrong.

Gavin now actively travels around the country giving presentations at schools and talking about how dangerous it is. I know that when he looks at me, Edwin is in his thoughts. It must be incredibly hard for him, but he has a huge heart. He and Robbie have given the joy of cycling to so many other kids in the years since Edwin's death. Without the Hi-Q Academy, I for one wouldn't have developed the way I did, so I owe much to him.

My first Tour is forever sandwiched between memories of Mum and of Edwin. I'm proud that I finished.

I never rode alone.

14

Early 2009: Tour Méditerranéen

We had been looking forward to this. After a successful time trial earlier in the week, and having worked hard to get our team leader, Mauricio Soler, up to 3rd place in the standings, we were now in contention going into the final day of racing, which would send us up Mont Faron, overlooking Toulon. It was not a bad effort for a team on the verge of extinction, but if we wanted to win, this was the day to put in a performance. The race was most likely going to be decided on the big mountain.

There was a huge fight just to get into the climb and everyone scrambled for position. I remember thinking that this was nuts. I couldn't believe how fast we were going at the bottom, considering that we hadn't even got to the ascent yet.

Very quickly, however, a pattern started to emerge, with riders pulling and calling 'gruppetto'. In other words, they would do their work, take their turn and then form a group and head up the mountain at their own easy pace.

There were about thirty of us left after a couple of minutes of the long haul, with maybe 10 kilometres remaining. We had gone up the first little rise and then the road flattened out for a way and there was a lull. We were all looking around to check who was still with us when Mauricio Soler suddenly took off. *Swoosh*. He went for it and attacked.

'Good luck to him,' I thought. He was obviously feeling good. The rest of us, meanwhile, continued to watch each other. Nobody wanted to get on the front just yet.

It suited me. I just had to stay on the wheels of those chasing Mauricio. All of the teams had crumbled and there were different-coloured jerseys speckled all over the mountain. In front, we were just a group of individuals by now, responsible only for ourselves.

We were all happy to let Mauricio go but then a rider from the Cofidis team attacked. I had no idea who he was but I went with him because he looked like he meant business. I sped up and got on to his wheel.

He turned out to be David Moncoutié, who was quite an established climber and a very interesting man. He had come 13th on his third Tour de France in 2002. Higher if you subtract the dopers ahead of him (five riders who finished in positions above have since either served bans or admitted to doping). One thing that everybody agreed upon was that he, Moncoutié, was never a doper.

I later heard that he had turned down big contracts at various teams who wanted him as a team leader because he didn't want to ride GC. He wanted to ride races his own way and target certain stages. In this way, he stayed with Cofidis his whole career. He was into homeopathy, vegetarianism, breaking early on mountain stages or hanging with the gruppetto if not. He dealt with doping by racing for and against himself, getting the most out of his own talents.

I have huge respect for David Moncoutié now, but that day I didn't really know who he was. He just looked like a good bet to follow up the mountain. Mauricio was up the road so I sat on Moncoutié's wheel. He never once asked me to try to come through or to take a pull. If he had asked I would have told him that I was fine where I was. 'My man is up front. You can take me to him, Tonto.'

Instead, he just glanced back a couple of times to check I was still there.

I liked my odds. Moncoutié was a big guy and he was riding well but surely he wasn't going to last too long up there doing all the work?

Still, it felt like he was going fast. With every kilometre we went up he seemed to be gaining a kilometre per hour in speed. Little sprouts of worry began to form in my brain. This shouldn't have been happening.

With 3 kilometres to go, my legs felt like they were tweeting my brain: *This guy is going too fast for you, sucker.*

Suddenly, Mauricio was in our sights a few hundred metres in front of us; it was the first time we had seen him for quite a while. The road behind looked empty. I could sense that Mauricio was starting to die a little. He had to be. His back was getting nearer to us and I was tiring too. But this guy in the Cofidis gear was just getting stronger. I stayed sitting on his wheel thinking that this wasn't going quite as well as I had imagined it would. He was not blowing up.

Mauricio never looked back at us and Moncoutié kept pounding away on the pedals in front of me, never out of the saddle, never relenting from the huge pace. We got within 100 metres of Mauricio, going round switchbacks with a kilometre to go, when I realized that the only way Moncoutié was going to fade now was if I threw him off the mountain. That wouldn't get me signed up with another team for next year, at least not with a French team.

We didn't have radios on, so I leaned round the side of Moncoutié, shouting up the mountain like a put-upon mother calling her son in for dinner.

'MAURICIO! MAURICIO!'

Finally, Mauricio looked back and saw us. He had thought he was clear and could go easy. Now at least he knew we were coming, but ominously his speed did not change.

With 800 metres to go we passed Mauricio. I gave him a push to get him in on Moncoutié's wheel, hoping that Mauricio had more left in his legs than I had. Neither of us is a sprinter but this Cofidis guy who had dragged me up the mountain, he surely couldn't be a sprinter either?

The road flattened out. Maybe he would ease up here and leave the door ajar? Go on, Mauricio. He didn't. With 100 metres to go, Moncoutié blew us away. Mauricio finished 2nd. I was 3rd.

On the team bus afterwards I sat down and began telling it from the mountain.

'I don't know who that Cofidis rider was but for quite a big guy, he could climb so well and –'

Robbie Hunter guffawed.

'Chris, did you really not know who that Cofidis rider was? Seriously?'

After that I always looked out for Moncoutié in the races. This was the guy who would be in the breakaway on a climbing day, when the

GC riders had let a big group get away from them that didn't have any contenders in it. This was the guy I wanted to be with to get to the finish.

He would choose the right kind of moves because he was older and knew how the races worked. 'Look and learn, *kijana*,' I thought. 'Look and learn.'

I was in Johannesburg at the end of 2008, just as the year was sliding into 2009. It was time for a term report to my old friend Matt Beckett, to catch him up on my news.

I told him that I had committed to Barloworld for another year and even had an agent now, a man called Alex Carera. Alex had received some interest from the Lotto team, and had something on the table, although I felt like I still owed Barloworld as they had put me in the Tour.

'Are you on the big money yet?' Matt asked.

'I went up from 22,500 to 30,000 euro. So yeah, crazy.'

'Maybe you could get work packing bags at a supermarket, double your money and buy a yacht,' he replied sarcastically.

I mentioned that the Kenyan Olympic Committee had dragged their feet on releasing me to get my British cycling licence until it was too late to go to the Beijing Games.

Matt asked if I was sad or upset.

I was. I felt sad because it was so petty and because they had nobody going there to represent Kenya anyway. Also, the road race course – and this was rare for the Games – was long and lumpy, which meant that it might have been perfect for me. Finally, I was sad because poor old Kinjah would be putting up with all of this rubbish long after I would.

Matt wanted to know about the other thing, that thing everybody was asking about: doping.

There's an unspoken rule, isn't there? Call it a code among professional athletes. It was like *Fight Club* again. In the same way that the first rule of Fight Club is no talking about Fight Club, the first rule of professional sports is no talking about doping. No matter what you have seen or what you have heard, you say nothing. If a doping story breaks, you are always surprised. You never heard anything, you never saw anything and nobody ever spoke about it. 'My, oh my, this is a shock.'

It was different among friends.

'What's the story, *bwana*?' Matt asked.

He knew about the Tour bust, but the whole world seemed to know about that one. Matt wanted inside juice.

'Does the dark side have a gravitational pull?'

He knew that as Moses of the Hemp I was probably too naive to even sense it but surely there was something I might know?

I told him about Fanny.

I liked Fanny, or Christian Pfannberger to give him his full name. Fanny is Austrian and typical of the Austrians I've met – so blunt that they make Germans look diplomatic. I enjoyed his company though.

I roomed with him for a one-day race late during the previous season and he had made me laugh. He was complaining about his head being sore because he had been drinking too much over the summer. Apparently it was the right time for the wine in Austria or something and Fanny did his bit as a patriot and drank plentifully. Now he had come to the race and he was saying that his head was hurting because he hadn't had a drink in a few days.

Earlier in the season, in the spring of 2008, Fanny had set the world on fire. He made top ten in each of the three big Ardennes classics:

Amstel Gold – 6th.

La Flèche Wallonne – 9th.

Liège–Bastogne–Liège – 5th.

That was impressive work. But there were cryptic things that he liked to say. 'It doesn't matter what the muscles look like,' he'd tell me, 'it's what's in the muscles that counts.'

Daryl, John-Lee and myself, being the neo-pros in the bunch, discussed our suspicions. We knew that Fanny had form. He had served a two-year doping ban a couple of years before he joined Barloworld so there was certainly the whiff of dark-side sulphur about him.

One of the things he would commonly ask us was, 'Have you been tested at home?'

He wanted to know when they would come – was it in the

morning or in the evening? And would they do urine *and* blood or just urine?

It felt like he was trying to work out any sort of pattern that the testers might be following.

We all liked Fanny and maybe it was just his robust Austrian way, but we always found that side of him to be strange. After the Tour bust knocked some of the innocence out of us we found his behaviour more worrying.

And yet . . . he asked these questions to guys he hardly knew. Surely he was too bright to do it again after a two-year ban? And he drank wine. If he was still doping surely he would be more sober? Or more cloak and dagger, at least? He was good company and a funny man. He couldn't be another one putting all of our careers in jeopardy, could he? Or could this all be far worse than we thought?

Fanny was moving on to ride with the Katusha team in 2009. We were sorry to see him go, but there was some relief among us too.

'That was some scary shit, Matt. Finding out during the Tour that other guys might still be doing it.'

'Yeah, but think of it this way. You've only been a professional for a year and a half, or two years. You've already been able to achieve top-ten results and top-five results in some of the Spanish races. If you are competing against guys who are doping then either it's not helping them that much, or you have serious talent. You should be encouraged.'

Matt was right. I was encouraged, but angry too. I trained harder.

Barloworld had given us just twelve months' worth of further lease on the dream. We had only one more season together, so for 2009 we would be 'Team Dead Men Walking'.

The news of the end being in sight was announced at our training camp in January in Tuscany. When they came out and told us it felt like we were being given months to live. Then all of our bikes were stolen in the middle of the night. My room was the closest to the bike storeroom. I heard noises early in the morning and thought it was unusual for the mechanics to be working already but went back to sleep. I woke up properly a few hours later at about eight o'clock and everyone was standing about scratching their heads and looking around. Thirty bikes had disappeared overnight.

Andrea had arrived in Italy before the Tour de France and was soon to depart again. Neither her career nor our relationship had ignited in Lombardy. It's tough living with a cyclist. I had one day at home after the Tour before leaving again to race in Holland for a week, which is just how it goes.

Cycling was changing too. We had biological passports now. It was a novelty to be a part of it, to have to log on and tell the computer where you would be at any given time. If you left the house you had to say exactly where you would be going, even if it was the supermarket or the shop round the corner.

I literally put down every movement and I was fascinated by the process. If I went shopping for half an hour, somebody would know. If I took a walk, the same thing. One evening, Andrea and I went out for a meal in Sarnico. It was a rare occurrence for us to go out like that, but I logged in as usual, putting down the name of the restaurant and that I was going to be there from seven o'clock till ten thirty.

I was sitting with Andrea and our food had just arrived when I got a phone call.

'Chris Froome? We're here to test you, we're standing at the restaurant reception.'

I was blown away. It worked.

'I'm just going to pee into a beaker, dear. Back soon.'

Of course, I didn't really know how we would proceed, given that we were in a restaurant. We got a few funny looks until I asked one of the waiters, who gave a shrug as if he were used to this and waved us to a quieter and more private area of the restaurant which wasn't being used.

We sat at a table there, filled out the paperwork and then I went to the bathroom for the urine sample. Next, I sat in a dark corner to do the blood.

It was an odd introduction to the new era. I don't know what I would have told Fanny if he had still been around to quiz me.

★

Early in the summer of 2009 I was riding the Giro d'Italia, another Grand Tour. Over the first few days I performed a new trick: riding and puking at the same time.

Barloworld's view of me for a while was expressed with a mix of encouragement and concern. Claudio Corti would take me aside on occasions for one-on-one chats. During the 2008 Tour, after the day I went with Menchov on Alpe d'Huez, we had one that I recall clearly. He offered me advice to dial it down a bit sometimes.

'We know you are strong,' he said. 'You don't have to show us by attacking, attacking, attacking. You don't have to prove anything to us.'

I understood his point, but he didn't get mine. I felt that if I attacked earlier in races I could be at the front for a while. I wanted to get my piece in there because I knew that when the big guys made their moves in earnest, I would be dropped. I didn't see why I should wait around for that. Maybe it would get me a better GC position but I wanted to try lots of situations and learn from them. I was stubborn about wanting to do it my way whereas Claudio thought it was more a matter of me having an itchy trigger finger. He wanted me to just stay calm.

But here I was, getting sick, and it was because I insisted on doing things my way. It started as soon as I got up, when I ran into John-Lee at the hotel.

'John-Lee, I'm feeling bad. I don't know how I'm going to make it through the day. Seriously.'

I told him what I thought the problem was, but he just smiled and patted me on the back.

'Keep it quiet, my friend. No need to be telling everybody.'

I knew what he meant. What I carried about in my suitcase was worrying to Claudio and company. I was dabbling with different things that might help extract the best out of myself, and had spent some time with a Scottish friend of mine the winter beforehand, a guy called Patrick Leckie. He was incredibly bright and a straight-A student, but disguised it well. You could speak to Patrick and decide that he might be a little bit slow, but I had known him since school and knew different.

Patrick wasn't bad athletically but sport wasn't really what got him out of bed in the morning. He had been on a trip to India and then done some community work with monks in Thailand. I think that sort of life would have interested me if the bike hadn't claimed me as its own.

Patrick came back from his travels and he was a hundred per cent vegan – the whole nine yards. I went to see him at St Andrews in Scotland and spent a few days with him, sleeping on his floor.

I loved the trip and remember Patrick telling me about all the amino acids and nutrients that your body can get from eating sprouting vegetables. When a vegetable begins sprouting it has an extremely high content of amino acids, which are good for recovery and energy. It was just a cornerstone of basic healthy living for Patrick, and he convinced me that I needed to have at least three handfuls a day of these things.

So I bought into it. Soon I was mixing them with porridge in the morning or with muesli, and throwing sproutings in with whatever I was eating.

I had started a miniature gardening allotment in my suitcase and every evening I would take the little transparent trays out and rinse them, before stacking them on a windowsill where they could grow. I would rotate the trays so that the new vegetables would be at the bottom, the three-day-old ones would be the next level up, followed by the six-day-old vegetables, and so on.

I would be swapping them around as the races went on. The crops were mung beans, alfalfa shoots and quinoa. I mainly grew mung beans, which were little green beans that I would pour water over after a few days. I would then wait, and after a few days more they would already be several centimetres long. They grew rapidly.

To the Italians, this was all blasphemy, even offensive. They would set about eating their pasta in the morning, whereas I would be there with these strange shoots that had been growing in my suitcase, scattering them on my breakfast cereal. It worried Corti, in particular.

'Please, you really need to do things the way that we've done them in the past. They've worked for us. We know how to eat before a race and you don't need to eat these things.'

I would nod, but I kept cultivating and would eat the harvest in secret after that.

During the Giro, though, I was sick and it was my fault. I had grown some quinoa but had put too much water on it. It had started fermenting, or hadn't grown properly, and it started to go slightly fizzy.

I ate a whole bowl of it in the morning, thinking to myself that it didn't really taste very nice, but I ate them regardless. I put it down as a credit in the 'sufferings' account. Quinoa is used as a substitute in South America for rice and it is supposed to have many health benefits for your body. Normally you should cook it but I had been sprouting the seeds and eating them raw and now I could taste the mistake as I chewed. After eating a whole bowl of the stuff I felt very sick.

My stomach rose up against me and every time I threw up I could see the little quinoa grains, and the fermented taste would come back to haunt me. It was one of the longest stages of the Giro – or at least it felt that way.

2009 was the year of treading water. Barloworld had been granted wild-card entries to the Tour de France for the two previous years but weren't going to make the cut for a third time in a row – bad results, a doping scandal and imminent extinction had taken care of that.

Although we raced in the Giro, we hadn't really done enough racing beforehand to make a success of it.

I was now living out in Nesso, a village on Lake Como. I had a small house in fine isolation about 15 kilometres from Como itself on the winding road around the lake. It should have been perfect but in March I came down with a cold that I couldn't shake for a fortnight. I was off the bike for a couple of weeks because I knew that if I even pushed the bike out the door I would weaken myself and make things worse. I had to sit it out to get better, which left me behind for the season.

During the Giro, even when I wasn't sick, I had struggled. I hated the stages where we went up into the snow; I had never felt so cold in my life. Stage seven is still in my bones. It was a freezing cold day, or a *freddo*, as the Italians say. We came down from the heights of the Maloja Pass, which was a mad descent, and I was so numb and so miserable that I couldn't change gears or brake properly. It should have been a good day for me but I came in 120th.

I was overweight and unfit. When I was sick I lost form and conditioning and let my eating go off track. I raced the Giro at 71 kilos. Back then I would normally race at 69 to 70 kilos. These days I ride at 66 kilos.

I also found that it was a very strange and far more unpredictable style of racing. In the middle of the stage, when everyone would be riding hard and the leading team were controlling on the front, all of a sudden four guys would attack, even though there was a breakaway in front. It was different to every other race I had done.

The best day was stage fourteen, although it may also have been the worst day.

I asked the mechanics before going out for extra gears but the feeling was that I was merely making a fuss. Most people would have been running a compact and a 27 for those kinds of gradients, which were really steep. I remember that the day before the stage I went to the mechanics and said I was aiming to get in the breakaway the following day, and for that I would need really light gears to get up the climb. But their attitude was macho-dismissive and they said that 25 would be 'fine' as a climbing gear. 'What do you want more than a 25 for? You should be embarrassed even for asking! You'll be fine on what we give you.'

I wasn't really able to argue and I was slightly intimidated. But this was another lesson – I should have fought harder. When it came to the key moment in the race, I literally couldn't turn the gear when I needed to.

Up the last climb, the Aussie Simon Gerrans and I had the stage between us. The road kept going up, and getting steeper as it did. I felt strong, but I sensed that Gerrans did too. In the end, I broke first. My legs seized up and Gerrans pushed on. I was struggling and a group of four other riders eventually picked me off on the last kilometre, so that I finished 6th.

The gears farrago actually ended as an embarrassment to us all. In an attempt to diminish the gradient I began riding zigzags up the hill, pushing over and back across the road. As I got to the sides to turn, people in the crowds were pushing me to try to get me up because I was almost coming to a standstill. Naturally, the papers got pictures of this fun.

Unfortunately, when the Barloworld team car reached the same point on the hill, it too broke down and the same crowd were photographed pushing it up the slope. The next day there were two photos in the press: one of me being pushed up the stage, and another of the car. The caption read something like: 'Hill 2 Barloworld 0'.

It was no wonder we didn't have a sponsor to save us for the following season.

Despite all of this, I finished 36th overall in the Giro, which wasn't a bad result, but still disappointing.

The year lagged by.

I was British now and competed in the National Road Race championships in Wales late in June.

A few times on the Giro I had ended up riding close to Bradley Wiggins, the former Olympic track rider, and in Wales on the Iron Mountain, as the most celebrated climb was called, it was Bradley Wiggins and me who were left to summit the top of the climb together.

We had a lead of a minute on the chasing group as we went into the laps of the finishing circuit. The group started chewing into our lead quickly enough and I looked across at Bradley. Then I looked at the shrinking margin and made a break for it. Bradley got swallowed up whereas I stayed out on the front for longer. Only on the final stretch did Kristian House, Daniel Lloyd and Pete Kennaugh go past me. I settled for 4th but it was a good day of racing and the welcome from the crowd was warm.

After Wales I had nothing substantial on the road ahead. My body didn't have anything substantial left in it either. I was often feeling poorly and having to take time off the bike, which sucked away my spirits.

When I watched the Tour de France on television, I kept an eye on Bradley Wiggins. I was interested in his approach – he was lively and lithe in the saddle and he time-trialled well and competed decently in the mountains. I felt our strengths were similar.

Wiggins was carrying no extra weight. I knew that if you wanted to ride clean, your diet and nutrition are huge issues and I was always exploring that side of cycling. I had been training for a long time without breakfast but race days were different. You couldn't go out to race without food inside you. That seemed logical. But on race days I never felt the same hair-trigger lightness that I did when I was training. I watched Bradley, wondering how I would forge the gap.

The silver lining was that I had a team for the following year. David Brailsford, who seemed to have been Yoda to Bradley Wiggins's Luke Skywalker in the track days, was starting a road-racing team with a British flavour.

Most of the staff who would form the backroom support for this new team had been involved with the British set-up at the 2008 Worlds in Varese. I had known some of them beforehand but that week put me firmly in their minds and I was comfortable with them. The riders Steve Cummings and Geraint Thomas from Barloworld were talking to Sky at the same time. It was an easy decision and though the line-up wasn't announced until December, I knew from about April onwards where I would be racing in 2010.

The summer petered out without leaving any marks on me, although two small things close to the end made me happy to be moving on.

In September I raced the World Championships for GB in Mendrisio, Switzerland. I brought my Barloworld Bianchi time-trial bike and the GB mechanics simply cracked up when they saw it.

'You actually race on this thing?'

'What's wrong with it?'

The mechanic put pressure on the bottom bracket with his foot to show me how flexible the bike was. The whole thing moved and flexed.

'So?'

'So that's what happens when you stand up on the bike and

whenever you get out of the saddle. Basically, when you put the power through the pedals it's being lost in that flexion; instead of being transferred into a forward direction, it's becoming a sideways movement on the bottom bracket.'

I made a mental note. *Don't stand up. Stay seated.*

He wasn't finished.

'And your gears!'

'What about them?'

'They're a bit of a joke. Half Shimano and the other half Campagnolo? Sort of a nine-speed chain with a ten-speed cassette. To be honest, your whole bike is a joke – the cables you're using are the wrong cable housing and you've got brake housing on the gear shifters. We'll re-strip it for you.'

They did, and I came in 18th. It was still nothing to write home about. I was three spots ahead of Brad, but that didn't mean much as he had suffered a mechanical and ditched his bike midway through his time trial.

I was disappointed with the diagnosis on the bikes that we had been using at Barloworld. Then, at around the same time, I had to compete in a race about a hundred kilometres from my house on Lake Como.

I got a lift down with somebody but I wasn't feeling too good; I'd been sick again and I really just wanted to shut down the year to sort out my health. I wanted to get ready for 2010 and a new start.

It was a hilly one-day race, and I had completed about three-quarters of the course when I pulled out. It was a lost cause. I had been dropped and I didn't feel great. The race was being run on laps so I just pulled in to the team bus when I came around to it on the circuit. Instead of going back with the team to the hotel and returning home the next day, I put my backpack on and got ready to ride the 100 kilometres home myself.

As I was leaving, Alberto Volpi, the director, stopped me and told me that I needed to get myself together. Volpi basically accused me of pulling out of the race on purpose because I knew I had a 100-kilometre ride to get home.

It was a pointless, silly sort of argument. I said, 'Listen, I was dropped. It wasn't because I didn't want to be here, I'm just not in good form and I couldn't be at the front of the race any longer. It's a hard circuit and I don't feel well. I need to get home and I don't have a car. This is how I'm going to get back now.'

I finally arrived back at my place at about 10.00 p.m. after doing the long ride. I was still annoyed.

Our last race together as teammates with Barloworld was in October. It was a one-day race in Italy, and one of the smaller events, with only seven of us there to ride. We didn't really have a leader for the race, and we felt like we were mainly there to make up the numbers.

The night before the race, we had a final dinner together. It was a chance to swap some old war stories and to say goodbye, and the guys decided to order a bottle of wine between the seven of us. The waitress came over to uncork it and we nodded as if we knew something about wine. She was ready to pour the glasses when Volpi walked over from another table and seized the bottle.

'No', he said sternly. 'Tomorrow there is a race.'

He walked off, and with him went the wine and all of the sentimentality in the room. That was Barloworld, over and done with.

That story of the wine reminds me of Fanny. The following month Christian Pfannberger got a life-long ban having tested positive riding for the Katusha team. He had enjoyed another good spring in the Ardennes. In 2010 he became the first athlete to be named in the Austrian National Anti-Doping Agency's investigation of athletes allegedly involved with illegal blood-doping with a company called HumanPlasma.

We liked him – we really did. But we were young and naive and learning.

15

GOALS SET BEFORE THE START OF
THE 2009 SEASON

Medium-long-term goals (next 2–3 years)

Minimize difference between performance on good form and
bad form – more consistent and predictable performances.
Ride the Tour again and focus 110 per cent on that.
Medal in CW Games TT in March 2010.
Look realistically for first Tour stage win in 2011 (mountaintop
finish).

Long-term goals (next 3–5 years)

Reach top 5 in the Tour.

General goals

Develop mentality to keep focusing on next goal and keep
improving. Assess mistakes and learn. More discipline in
everything I do. Stop letting others influence my riding
negatively – be my own leader!
Learn more about my body as far as diet is concerned.
Challenge the conventional system.
No idols as they only test positive – only aim to beat them.

(*Memo sent by me to Rod Ellingworth.*)

Rod Ellingworth. I can still see his outraged face looming behind the
wheel that day when a car full of cycling hoodlums from the UCI
school sped past him on a hairpin bend high on a mountain.

Now he was my coach.

Contact with Rod was constant and always useful, but an email that I sent to him before the start of the 2009 season sticks in my mind. I had written down a list of goals with a five-year plan with my aims as a cyclist. I'm surprised now at my presumption. Back then, Rod probably was too. I planned for an increasing number of podium finishes over the five years that would follow, and an improvement in consistency.

We had been working together for three months and Rod was still having to explain the basic facts of cycling life to me. My blissful ignorance of the pro world wasn't charming him at all and would have to end. He told me that we could not forget about the off-the-bike work, and everything that we did when I wasn't riding. He said 'we', although he meant me. He talked about my day-to-day organization around the team, and of how I needed to understand the 'where' and the 'when' if I was told to be somewhere. This was essential.

Another thing was my cycling knowledge. Every day I needed to be watching races and reading cycling results to help me move forward tactically; I was still very poor in this department. Despite all of this, Rod said there was an outside chance of me riding the Tour de France that year.

I am sure, looking back, that this sentence was the only one which properly registered with me. 'Really?' I thought. 'Great.'

Rod continued. Other areas to work on included my climbing ability, how to cope with crosswind sections, how to improve my position in the peloton, how to get on the wheel in front faster and my general vision in the peloton of where my teammates were. He wanted me to have a better strategic understanding of what the team needed, using the riders around me to find out, and the team radio more often to get the information I needed. He told me not to be scared of asking simple questions.

He was right. I still saw myself as 'kikoy and sandals' type of guy, a serene presence in the dog-eat-dog world of cycling. I was very quiet within the team and grateful that people at Sky were interested in a man who grew sproutings in his suitcase. I certainly wouldn't have been one for suggesting anything over the race radio.

I realized that I was about to become a well-chewed bone if I didn't shape up. *Kijana*, welcome to Team Sky.

There are certain catchphrases and accessories which are lightning rods for criticism of Team Sky. Many people seem to hate the 'aggregate of marginal gains', for instance. And the bus. Some day a large finger will point down from the clouds and issue a bolt of lightning which will destroy our vehicle in a flash. And lo, a godly celestial voice will boom out, 'How's that for marginal gains?'

I suppose it all depends on whether you are on the inside of the bus looking out, or on the outside looking in.

Stepping on to the Team Sky bus was like being upgraded on an aeroplane. You went from the cramp of economy to the sinful indulgence of first class. You didn't feel guilty; you just felt that this was the way it should be for everybody, that nothing was too good for the working man.

There are nine riders in a race, so there are nine reclining seats with all the clip-ins for our MacBooks, a reading stand and a plug point right next to the seats so that we can charge all of our devices. There is also a holder for our drinks, and a big sound system. The bus alone was something to write home about.

The faces of those who would be on the bus were launched at a grand affair at Millbank in London in early January. Dave Brailsford had apparently sat down with some journalists three years previously outside a bar in Bourg-en-Bresse during the Tour de France and mused openly about starting a British Pro Tour Team. They believed him then and this was the proof. Dave is a guy you believe. He radiates energy. I believed him when he came looking for me because his record already said more than enough. He had hauled the British track cycling team to a couple of gold medals at the Athens Olympics in 2004, four golds at the Worlds a year later, a crazy rush of nine golds at the 2008 Worlds and then seven golds at the Beijing Games.

There was something about all the energy and all the talk of innovation and detail that was irresistible. I signed a two-year deal on €100,000 a year. This was not a fortune in cycling terms, but I figured that this would be my finishing school as a professional.

By the time we got to Millbank, twenty-five other riders had heard the siren song including my old teammate John-Lee Augustyn. We were a British team with underlying flavours: eight Brits, three Aussies, three Italians, three Norwegians, two Frenchmen, a Canadian, a Spaniard, a Belgian, a Finn, a Swede, a Kiwi and John-Lee the South African.

When the media wanted interviews it was Bradley Wiggins, 4th in the previous year's Tour de France with Team Garmin, and Edvald Boasson Hagen (Edvald had won four of the eight stages of the 2009 Tour of Britain) whom they buzzed around, like bees ready for the pollen of hype. Bradley and Edvald were the marquee potential. When journalists recalled Bourg-en-Bresse and Dave Brailsford's thinking-aloud session, they remembered his belief that a British Tour de France winner could be produced by a British team within five years of the team being created. At Millbank, with Bradley having been aggressively recruited, they could see that future. It didn't have sideburns yet but it soon would have.

We were duly launched and then went off to Valencia to train. Our enthusiasm was an advantage in itself. There were no old lags insisting on things being done the way they always had been done. However, in the broader world of cycling there was an undercurrent of resentment. The Hollywood-style launch, the money, the aggressive recruitment and the Jaguar team cars, while all of the other teams had more regular makes, annoyed some people. There were smaller touches too, such as the thin blue line down the spine of our jerseys and its representation of the slender border between winning and losing. As 2010 got rolling, these petty grievances preyed on the minds of others much more than they bothered us.

We were in good hands. Take the bus as a metaphor for the rest of the set-up. I had received help before, from Kinjah and Robbie especially, but I had never had a coach before, someone like Rod who was calling me on almost a daily basis to catch up on training or talk about what we were going to be doing tomorrow or the day after or for the rest of the week. It was day-to-day contact.

My career had always been a walk on high wire. I had always felt alone out there and not too far away from the slip that would deliver me to the pavement again. Now there was this safety net, this web all around me telling me how to stay on the wire and spreading a safety net in case I tumbled.

There were simple things, such as the soigneurs. Or carers, as Team Sky calls them (something else that gets up the noses of the old school like pepper spray). At Barloworld the majority of the soigneurs were former cyclists in their sixties. They gave massages and grumbled about how it was better back in the day. There were only two young soigneurs in the Barloworld team: Mario Pafundi, who is now at Sky, and Hanlie Perry, who is now at British Cycling. They were more representative of Dave Brailsford's carers: young, incredibly hard-working and attentive to all our needs.

As for coaching, at Barloworld nobody had ever really called. I had found that quite strange, expecting somebody to check up on me every day. A pro cyclist has a mountain of work in front of him always, and a circus of distractions elsewhere. Barloworld had just sort of said, 'Okay, see you at the next race, kid.' Nobody ever checked to see if I was on the mountain or at the circus. The assumption was basic: 'You have turned pro so put on your big-boy Lycra shorts and keep doing what you have to do, and whatever the hell it was that got you here.' After the races we would get some token advice from Volpi or Corti: 'Now you need to do a bit more long training.' It was as vague and as general as that.

Micro coaching and long-term planning wasn't a marginal change. It was massive.

To me it is a big challenge to the legacy of the mass-doping era. I believe the prevalence of cheating and the fatalistic belief that 'everybody' was doing it retarded the progress of clean science in cycling training. You see it in the recidivist guys like Riccardo Riccò. Even though they've been caught before there was no way they could contemplate racing clean. It wasn't an option for them because they believed first that everybody was doping, and second that no matter how intelligently or how long they trained, they couldn't beat a doper without doping themselves.

Many people still believe that. To train hard and to train

scientifically, to be skinny and to be innovative? That can't possibly be enough. You must be doing something on top of that. The proof?

'Don't know. You just must be.'

Things have changed. In the culture of the peloton they have changed. I was training in Tenerife in 2012 when the Cannondale team were staying up there too. One of their riders, Ivan Basso, approached me. He had been suspended for two years after Operation Puerto in 2006, a doping investigation that had involved some of the world's most famous cyclists. He wanted to ask me a few questions about what training I was now doing and what I was eating after the races. He asked the same of my teammate Richie Porte. He even asked Richie about our protein recovery drink, and how he might be able to get some for himself.

He listened intently to everything that we said and I was happy that he came to us. He wouldn't have asked if he believed we were doping. He would have believed that he had the answers already.

It was like talking to a neo-pro. His journey had taken him full circle and he was welcome to the information. I think Ivan Basso believed (and I think he was right) that he was coming back to a peloton that wasn't dirty in the majority. It was not pristine clean, and probably never will be, but in terms of the peloton's culture, we have passed the tipping point.

Back in 2010, in terms of detail, I was finding more and more that Sky was at the other end of the spectrum compared to my experience at Barloworld. They were obsessive, which was the way I liked it. The team nutritionist, Nigel Mitchell, knew every morsel of food that passed through our lips. And why. On the Barloworld bus we commonly had packets of biscuits, Italian biscotti, in the cupboards. We would arrive, hungry after a long journey, and demolish a packet between two or three of us. Compare this to the Team Sky bus, where the closest thing to junk food you could find would be a fruit yoghurt.

The list of those small, good things, which are different about Team Sky, is endless. And yet 2010 was not a good year for me in terms of results; there was no lift-off.

It culminated when I went to the Giro d'Italia in May, which is the best I can say: I was there. In racing terms, I got my head kicked in, bought the T-shirt and came home.

I hated that. I had come to believe that I had some genuine potential. A serious team had signed me on as a future star; they would drill down in the right places and the great gusher of my potential would be untapped. They had offered the people and the equipment to shape me into a real climber and GC contender.

However, by the time we got to the Giro that view would seem to have changed. Or they had never had the view at all. I had become the guy whose job it was to get on the front and start pulling on the flat days. That wasn't my strength, but it became my role.

Through the previous spring I had been the odd-job guy that the team were calling on for hard labour. Maybe that was why I had been signed, after all – for being quiet and uncomplaining. I thought to myself, 'Blessed are the meek for early in the race they shall inherit the front of the peloton.'

My highlights of the season were few and far between.

2010: A Brief History (pre-Giro)

January

THE TOUR DOWN UNDER

The days were long and flat and hot. I liked the weather, but nothing else was my cup of Earl Grey. The race was suited to leading out sprinters and pulling on epic flat stages. I finished 76th.

I was still innocent in the ways of the pros. One day I was going back for bottles or for someone's feed bag during the race. I was very happy with how I was going and content to carry out this extra errand. The bunch was quite strung out and I was coming back from the very front where I had been working hard. I was drifting backwards through the field and Sean Yates, our sporting director for Team Sky, was at the front of the motor convoy in the car, waiting for me. And waiting. I was happily coming back slowly but I hadn't stopped pedalling; I was just letting myself be carried back through the group. Sean was getting impatient although it wasn't really registering with me. Suddenly he was shouting in the radio.

'Froomey! Where are you? Put your effing brakes on and stop!'

My new team turned out to be first-rate Sean Yates impersonators. All week long I heard it. 'Froomey! Where are you? Put your effing brakes on!'

February

TOUR DU HAUT VAR

Two days of good climbs corresponded to my best result of the season so far: 9th overall.

GRAN PREMIO DELL'INSUBRIA-LUGANO

A snappy title with a snappy finish. I crashed out.

March

VUELTA A MURCIA

No mountaintop finishes and only a short time trial. I found myself asking, 'Why am I here?' I finished 55th.

VOLTA A CATALUNYA

Two good days of riding and then I was as weak as a kitten. I finished 72nd.

April

A volcano erupted in Iceland, cancelling all flights.

I took this personally.

I had been trying to organize my life off the bike as per Rod's guidance. We were travelling north to the three Ardennes Classics (the Amstel, La Flèche Wallone and the Liège–Bastogne–Liège). I assumed that as the first race was on a Sunday we would be travelling up on the Friday at the earliest. So I didn't read the email. As it turned out, the team flew up on Wednesday without my knowledge and I missed the flight. Then the volcano erupted and it wasn't just a case of being on the next flight. I felt bad for Rod and drove to the Ardennes all the way from Tuscany, realizing that Europe was far longer than it looked on maps.

AMSTEL

After such a long journey, another disappointing placing: 76th.

LA FLÈCHE WALLONNE

I died on the Mur de Huy hill, or at least I was dead for the eleven minutes that I lost there. I came in 119th. Afterwards, an environmental splinter group tried to sue me for littering after I threw away a drink bottle during the race.

LIÈGE–BASTOGNE–LIÈGE

I was sick and I didn't tell anybody, finishing 3rd from last, or 138th, if you want to look at it like that. I made a note to the Ardennes: 'Goodbye, I never liked you anyway.'

TOUR DE ROMANDIE

I felt sick and weak again, this time on the time trial. I rode straight on at a right-hand turn near the finish line and ended up in a flower bed, crocked. It was the end of my Tour de Romandie.

I would like to say that apart from the sicknesses, the crashes and the bad results, I was happy. Except that I wasn't. I seemed to be in a catch-22 with the team. I wasn't feeling one hundred per cent or even ninety per cent most days and they were giving me the job of going in the early breakaways. I would spend a lot of energy trying to do that, but if I ever got into the breakaway, I knew that it meant being dropped when we got to the mountains. If I didn't reach the breakaway, I knew I didn't have the strength at that time to do as well in the mountains as I felt I could have done, even if everything was all right. So I looked bad on the flat and bad in the mountains. I had the best care and coaching I had ever received, but I felt inexplicably weak.

2010: The Giro d'Italia

The race started in Amsterdam on 8 May with a time trial. Bradley burned the place up whereas I was as limp as a dishcloth. On the second day, though, Bradley was taken down in a huge crash. Although we got him back to the race, another even bigger crash with 7 kilometres left held us up. He lost 37 seconds through the chaos.

Day three brought even more chaos. But it was a better kind, if you liked that sort of thing: evil crosswinds, a long-haul stage and a scattered field. My job was to lead out for Greg Henderson, the Kiwi sprinter, so that he could have a crack at winning the stage, and so that Brad could get some GC time back. With 10 kilometres to go, riders from other teams were surprised to swing round a tight corner and find most of Team Sky lying on the ground. We had crashed. Most of our bikes suffered damage and Brad lost 4 minutes. Greg didn't get to the ball. He had the strutting confidence common to most sprinters and was seldom happy, especially not now.

The mountains were days away but already I felt hollowed out. Stage four was a team time trial, which was something I should have been good at. Unfortunately, after I had done a number of solid pulls on the front, I was one of three Sky riders to get detached before the end.

Team Sky have an aggressive race philosophy. The team happily assumes responsibility for controlling a race, and if that means sticking four or five of us out at the front for three hours, then that is what we will do. If other teams can keep up with us, that is good for them. If not, it is still good for us. Either way, though, it is a hard gig as a rider. You don't get many days swinging the lead with the gruppetto. In the Giro I would race up to 200 kilometres on the front of the peloton, swapping off with maybe three or four other guys.

I limped on. I remember a couple of days of bad rain when the dust of early summer turned to a porridge of mud. On the lowest point of the revolution when pressing the pedal down our feet would dip into water and the cold started to insinuate itself into our feet and then on up through our bodies. When racing there is only one thing I hate worse than the cold, and that is the cold stiffened by rain.

On stage seven I was 7 minutes behind Cadel Evans. The mountains were waiting for us the next day. Maybe I would feel happier in their arms?

Steve Cummings and I had to chase down a breakaway group the next day, then hang back and pull Brad into contention. The last climb was up a mountain hidden in a soup of fog. We got Brad into a good position and although he lost a little time, he moved up from 26th to 23rd in the GC. Steve and I collapsed with the effort. Steve lost 5 minutes and I lost 12 in the closing kilometres. It was a decent day of work but my right knee was causing me pain. There was a sharp, stabbing sensation just above my knee, with a bruise forming in that area. In the mountains it was especially bad and I knew there was something seriously wrong; it was really hurting.

Every time I pushed down on the pedal on that side, the pain shot through. I tried to compensate by using my left leg more, but then that leg began to get very tired.

I started getting physio strapping every day in an effort to support it. On the flat stages that worked okay, but on the climbs, where I was putting more pressure through my knees, was when I really felt it.

So, I was in trouble in the mountains and having to do big pulls on the flat. Those days pulling on the front are tough for any rider, and although I remember thinking that if Brad won or if Greg took a sprint stage I would feel part of the glory, neither eventuality happened. The job, though, means you keep doing your long pulls. You ride on with hope in your heart and pain in your body.

I rode on until stage nineteen. Not all of the days were bad but I was bothered in the long term by a lack of direction in where I was heading as a rider, and in the short term by the nagging pain of my injury. My knee felt as if there were something pulling inside at the tendon.

I was also still learning the politics of the peloton on Grand Tours and I was naive and unsophisticated about reading the race. On stage eleven, for instance, we rode in monsoon conditions. Brad and three others from the team got into the right group after just 20 kilometres of the 262-kilometre stage. I, meanwhile, got into the wrong group, so that whereas Brad picked up 12 minutes on the leaders, I lost

46 minutes in the gruppetto from hell. I was the lowest-ranked Sky rider on GC that evening. An Aussie rookie named Richie Porte ended up in the *maglia rosa* of race leader when the rain stopped.

On stage nineteen out of Brescia to Aprica my knee howled at me all day. There were three big climbs on the stage and the last one was Mortirolo.

Mortirolo fights you – it is brutal and relentlessly steep all the way up with just a few stingy gaps for recovery. On the climb just before Mortirolo, I had dropped off the front of the race and gone to the gruppetto but as we were riding along I noticed that Greg Henderson was off his bike. It was lying on the side of the road because he had gone into the bushes to go to the loo. His stomach was bad that day.

I waited for Greg and the two of us rode to the top of the climb together. I thought to myself, 'Okay, the two of us will work together to get back to the gruppetto now.' It was raining again and I struggled for a moment to get my rain jacket on. Then Greg suddenly shot off down the slope and left me there. I couldn't believe it.

A few members of the team had a go at him for that afterwards. Despite my waiting for him just moments before, he had left me on the descent to push on alone. He had managed to get behind a passing team car in the next valley and had rejoined the gruppetto, so now I was the very last rider on the road.

When I reached the Mortirolo I could feel that I wasn't going to be riding anywhere quickly. I rode the first 3 or 4 kilometres mostly pedalling with one leg, and I was all alone, well behind the gruppetto.

The team car radioed at that point, and said that the gruppetto was 17 minutes in front. I knew that was the end for me. The suffering seemed foolhardy and unprofessional, and it was time to call it a day, or cost myself the season. I radioed back to our directeur sportif, Steven de Jongh.

'I'm done here. Finished. I need to stop.'

The message from the car was, 'Okay, just keep going at your own pace, don't do any more damage to your knee. Gemma, one of the soigneurs, is up on top of Mortirolo, giving feed bags out to the riders. You can get in the car with him.'

There was a commissaire vehicle close to me and an Italian policeman on a motorbike. The team car was up with the gruppetto making sure that everybody had their rain jackets and the commissaire vehicle drove on up ahead too but kept coming back down to check on me.

I remember fans on the side of the road really trying to push me on. They were shouting, '*Grinta, grinta!*' which means gumption or dig in. But sadly all I was thinking was, 'If only they knew that I'm just heading for my lift at the top.' There was no point in encouraging me.

The policeman kept looking across. I was grinding so slowly that he would stop his motorbike every couple of metres and put his feet on the ground. He knew I was done. After he had looked across a few times I spoke to him in Italian.

'I'm going to stop on the top of the climb.'

'Okay, do you want to hold on?' He indicated for me where to hold on. 'I'll take you up.'

I didn't want to do it.

I didn't want to disappoint the fans that were cheering me on with such heart, so I pushed on for another 2 kilometres.

He asked me again, smiling sympathetically. Clearly his patience was wearing thin at the speed I was riding up the climb, and I was starting to feel guilty about keeping him there.

I held on for barely 10 seconds. We went round just one hairpin bend only to find the commissaire car waiting round the corner. The doors opened and they leapt out and ran over to me.

'Stop! Stop! Stop! *Disqualificado!*'

They made a huge drama of taking a large pair of scissors and cutting my number off my back. A camera crew from the Italian station Rai happened to be with them to film my disqualification. Rai were competitors of Sky Italia, and seemed to be enjoying the moment.

I initially didn't think much of it as in my mind I had already retired and was focused on getting to Gemma at the summit. The sound of me clipping back into my pedals quickly drew the attention of the commissaire holding the scissors.

'No, no, no! You can't ride any further.'

I asked if they were going to give me a lift to the top but they told me there was no space in their car. We stood for a good few minutes

arguing about how I was going to get to the top before they conceded that I was allowed to ride on, after all, but only because they
had cut my numbers off.

It was just another 2 or 3 kilometres to the summit, but it took me
half an hour. The policeman was still nearby but, having been scolded
for taking a lift, I knew better than to hold on again.

Finally, I reached Gemma at the top. After I climbed into the car I ate
some food, put on some warm clothes and we drove back to the team
hotel. However, when I arrived back it wasn't over. I was inundated
with press enquiries about being disqualified for holding on to the
motorbike.

It was typical of my luck that season, but I was beyond caring
really. What nags long term is the show-trial element – I was
demobbed on the mountain with the cameras rolling. That, and years
of people who haven't got the faintest idea of what actually happened deciding that somebody who would take a pull up a mountain
would definitely dope and betray his sport.

I knew the truth. And I knew that I didn't have to get on the bike
any more that week. I was going to put my knee up and rest for a
while. It was time to regroup.

Back in the peloton, Brad's Giro d'Italia had fallen apart that day as
well. He had lost 37 minutes. Meanwhile, our teammate Greg still
hadn't won any sprints during the race, unless we counted his breakaway from me, when he found his strength on the descent.

There was a 'back to the drawing board' mood about the entire
team.

In that first year I felt that Team Sky was too corporate. We had
our spreadsheets, our pie charts, our plans and our targets from day
one, and part of the sense of control had been to make the year unfold
exactly as it had been planned.

But after the Giro I definitely got an inkling that things were
unfolding very quickly for us, too quickly perhaps. The season was
getting to the business part at a galloping pace. Suddenly the Tour de
France loomed and we didn't seem flexible enough to deal with it. As
a team we believed that if we paid our customary homage to the god
of small details everything would work out in the end.

Dave summed it up well afterwards: we spent too much time worrying about the peas and no time considering the steak.

There was certainly a lot of planning and preparation that had been done around Brad. He had been doing recces of all the Tour routes but I don't think there had been much structure put in place in terms of assembling a Tour group and of training and racing together as a team. There was lots of time spent Brad-building but little time spent team-building.

I remember talking to Steve Cummings some time after the Giro and not long before the Tour. Steve had his doubts. He was knackered and felt that the Giro had been for him, as it had been for me and Brad and every other member of the team, a far harder experience than we had anticipated. It knocked us about. Steve said he had put on something like four kilos in weight after recuperating from the Giro, and now they wanted him to go into the Tour and do the same job but even better. Why?

Because that was the plan. And we had to stick to our plan.

I took a few weeks off after the Giro. I hadn't made the cut for the Tour so I nursed the wounded knee and tended the wounded pride. The Giro experience had deflated me.

Noz had flown to Italy during the Giro and even though I stayed with the team until the end of the race, I saw plenty of him during the days after I had abandoned. He then came to stay with me for a while. We visited Rome together for a few days and enjoyed each other's company before we went back to Tuscany.

At some stage while Noz was still around I took a quick trip to Manchester in the hope of addressing my knee problem.

I felt that my position on the bike was quite a big problem. We had changed my posture earlier in the season and I seemed to be battling with that. I felt as if I were a little bit too high on the saddle, which was putting an extra strain on my knees.

This was where I was paying the price for being an unusual specimen within the cycling world. Riders who had entered the professional scene in their teens would have had their riding posture and position sorted out early in their careers. I was aware from numerous jokes that I looked 'kinda funny' in terms of style, but I had never had a professional come up to me and say, 'Your position should be like this.'

I had always simply got on a bike and ridden in a way that felt natural to me. Maybe I was right. Maybe I was a chiropractor's worst nightmare. I didn't know.

When somebody finally took me through the posture and position work, I was keen to listen. It was Phil Burt and Matt Parker from British Cycling who analysed me initially. They had come over from the track team. Matt is a performance analyst and Phil is a physio. I was happy to receive their professional opinions.

Now, I'm not sure if it was their track background (they had not worked with climbers before) or my unorthodox riding style but I think we made a fractional, honest mistake when we were first doing the bio-racer set-ups. That process involves capturing the bike's measurements and putting them into a computer to calculate all of the required angles for your knees and your body. Then a decision is made on what is optimum in terms of height and position.

From the start I had a feeling that I was a little too high in my saddle but it was all so marginal that I assumed I would get used to it. I didn't.

Meanwhile, back in Manchester on the flying trip, I had an MRI scan on my knee, which showed that it was inflamed but had no lasting damage. I told them that it felt as though I was having to stretch to reach the bottom of my pedal stroke and this was putting additional pressure through the saddle. Matt and Phil were open to the idea of slightly lowering the saddle. I had done a lot of reading up on positioning by then and had read that climbers should typically be a bit further back behind the bottom bracket so that they can use the leverage to get up the climbs. Flat riders would typically be a little further forward where they can be on the tip of their saddle and pedal over the bottom bracket, a bit like time trialling.

I went back to Tuscany to recuperate and then experimented.

I lowered my saddle from about 81.5 centimetres down to about 80.5 centimetres, so around 1 centimetre lower. I tried that for a week and then I moved it back up again.

The comparison was interesting. When the saddle was higher both before and during the Giro I had been getting bad saddle sores. With the saddle lowered these stopped straight away, and only returned when I raised the saddle again a week later. It was just an extra bit of pressure. Even now, if somebody puts a new saddle on my bike and it is a millimetre too high I feel it straight away.

The impact on my knee was just as obvious. The pain I was getting along the side of my knee and on the top of my knee came from having to stretch further than I normally did. When I lowered the saddle it stopped.

(Also, with the high saddle I'd get constant saddle sores on my undercarriage. I had this fluorescent yellow chamois in my shorts and at the end of many a long stage, I could see exactly where the sores had burst. Not much fun.)

The trial and error worked. I moved further and lower back on my bike and have ridden that way ever since. It's actually an extraordinarily low position for someone of my height, and my inseam, but that's just where it feels most comfortable.

The happier the undercarriage, the better the rider. Who said that? Merckx? Coppi?

Later that year I watched the Tour on TV, and then rode the British Nationals, followed by the Commonwealth Games in Delhi. I had one or two other adventures but generally I let 2010 slink away to its own unmarked grave.

I don't visit there very often.

Postscript: The Odd Couple

While 2010 faded away, I would always have Greg Henderson.

After it was established that I was quiet and easy-going, it was decided that Greg would be my room-mate. Blessed are the meek for they shall also inherit the Kiwi.

I remember being in rooms with Greg quite often. I knew he had strong opinions and a way of expressing them that didn't need amplification. The other riders would see me in his company and wink at me knowingly: 'Enjoy!'

Greg was a bit of a strange one. Even for a Kiwi. He would perch on his bed in his boxer shorts and headband, and sit there playing the harmonica. He always brought a little harmonica with him wherever we travelled. I wasn't about to complain about his dress sense; I was sitting there wearing a traditional Kenyan skirt.

His musical talents were a different matter. A music lover is someone who can play the harmonica but chooses not to. Greg was the opposite: he couldn't play the harmonica but did so anyway. I would put my earphones on and watch something on my laptop to drown out the noise.

That was how we spent most of our evenings.

We didn't talk much, even though Greg would talk a lot himself. He had very strong opinions and was quite intense, so he would get worked up about things and always had an axe to grind. CJ Sutton was the other sprinter on the team, and Greg would spend hours deconstructing CJ. I would be listening and nodding: 'Yep. Yep. Sure. Interesting.'

I did feel sorry for him in a sense. He was a little bit of a loner and didn't seem to have any close bonds with anyone on the team. I didn't think he was necessarily a bad guy, but just slightly socially inept. I think he would say the same about me.

Like me, Greg didn't make the Tour de France team that year. He was left out in the end in favour of Michael Barry. Dave explained that if a team was going for the yellow jersey, it had to put all its eggs in one basket, which was Brad. The lesson of the Giro seemed to have been that there was a lot of energy spent on riding for Greg and CJ which had produced no stage wins and left Brad exposed. Dividing resources had diluted the effort.

After the Giro, not putting me in the Tour team had been an easy decision. However, Greg had enjoyed a more successful start to life in the team and excluding him was a tougher decision.

That August we did the Eneco Tour, a predominantly flat race in Belgium, which was one suited to the punchy riders. Edvald was doing really well in the race, as it was made for him, but Greg had already won a stage. It was the last night before the final time trial, when Greg decided that he wasn't going to do anything much the next day and thought he would have a few drinks.

He came back into the room at around 1.00 a.m. and got on the phone to his wife. He was complaining about an argument he'd had with someone downstairs.

'Ah, I'm gonna kill 'im,' Greg was saying.

This was 1.00 a.m. I had been asleep for a couple of hours already and the time trial was a far bigger deal for me. I wasn't the champion of serenity at that moment and turned the lights on.

'Greg? Just leave it, man. Please. Just turn off your phone and go to sleep. Sort it out in the morning, whatever the problem is.'

At 7.00 a.m. Steven de Jongh came to our room.

'Greg, pack your bags, you're out of here, you're going home. You're not starting the race today.'

Apparently Greg had been down in the bar, and at some stage somebody had urinated on the front door. The owner of the hotel was there, who also happened to be a special guest of the race, and possibly even a sponsor, so not someone we should have been upsetting. And there had been an argument not over the urine but the mop. Who was going to mop it up? Greg got involved and offered typically strong opinions in his robust way.

It was not only that, but Greg had also been winding up the mechanics and other staff by telling them they would soon be out of a job, because he had heard they weren't going to get their contracts renewed.

I don't know the details but, fairly or unfairly, they sent Greg home anyway. I don't think he quite fitted into the Sky model. He just didn't tick all the boxes for Dave and the guys, even though that year I think he was our most successful rider.

If only he could have played guitar.

16

After hours in the last-chance saloon, downtown Kraków.

It was early August 2011 and somewhere Bradley Wiggins was recuperating from the broken collarbone he had suffered during the Tour de France. Team Sky were fretting about him as saving the season hinged on Brad's health.

Meanwhile, I was in Poland: flat, unforgiving Poland. The Tour of Poland had just ended and I had finished 85th on GC – not exactly knighthood territory.

The team were flying out the next morning but my flight home was later in the day for some reason. I had worked hard all week on a predominantly flat course only to end up buried on the foot slopes of the GC.

That night I did something I had pretty much never done before – I went out on the town. The race finished in Kraków and I painted the town red. Well, sort of salmon-coloured; I was new to the game.

I switched off from it all. I'd put so much into the year: the races, the training, the weight loss, the Biltricide, the altitude work and the life lessons. But now people were avoiding my eye and I felt like a dead man walking. Sometime in the next few weeks the hints would start falling, and then the chat.

Obviously, Chris, we have to make changes . . . regenerate the team . . . we appreciate everything you have done . . . we wish you . . . whatever you do . . .

I had never done anything after races, or in between, for that matter. The candle in my life had only ever burned at one end and I scarcely existed off the bike. However, on this night in Kraków my friend Adam Blythe, the British rider, was hitting the town. For once, I got on his wheel and went with him. We met up with a few other riders, including Tom Boonen, the king of the cobbles, as well as a couple more Belgian guys.

You've been a good guy to work with, you will be missed here . . . I think you've made friends . . . unfortunately you've had some bad luck . . . some illness . . .

Now I was feeling good. We had a fine dinner and went on to a club afterwards. This was new territory for me but all I remember is a lot of fun. We were dancing like fools, drinking like fish (well, not like fish, but like cyclists on a night out), telling jokes, trading stories and laughing a lot. We were blowing off half a season's worth of worry and stress.

We are all under pressure . . . let me just say this was the hardest decision . . . the best of luck in whatever you choose to do . . . you gave it a shot, Chris, you really did . . .

Shot. Yeah. That was one thing that stood out in Kraków that night: one euro for a shot of vodka. If you're in the valley of despair and can't see the road back, don't head to the bars in Monaco. You would need a mortgage to buy a round of drinks. Fly to Kraków instead. Even with the airfare you would come out ahead.

It was getting bright when I got back to the hotel, and due to some administrative quirk, probably my own doing, I was staying in a different hotel to the other guys. At least I had no room-mate to worry about.

I was drunk. Not completely drunk . . . just, you know, happily so, happily so . . . happily what? I didn't know. I just thought, 'What the hell, we'll always have, um, Kraków drunk.' Happily so.

I lay on the bed, looking up at the ceiling, content for now: I had gone a whole night without thinking about my career. I was relieved that nobody had asked me with grave concern about how it was going with me and Team Sky, and whether it was terminal, or how long I had left.

If they had asked I would have said the only thing I could say:

'Well, it's not *going*. I'll definitely have to rethink things in the next week. Rethink everything. We won't be having a reunion like this in Kraków next year.'

That would have killed the atmosphere nicely.

So, Chris, this is goodbye . . . hopefully we can meet somewhere down the road . . . I'd like you to keep this chamois as a memento of your time

here . . . yes the saddle sores . . . I knew you would enjoy that. You know
where the door is.

My seasons had a bad habit. They would slouch off in late summer to
die quietly somewhere in the shade: 2010, 2009, 2008, 2007 – those
years all died young.

In 2007, I had gone to the World Championships in Stuttgart
intending not to do anything more vigorous than sign a contract
with Barloworld. I raced but my heart wasn't in it and I had rolled
around the roads thinking of home; I wasn't in good form and I was
quite tired by the end. The year was done.

After the race I was sitting in the airport waiting for my flight. I was
going to Zurich and from Zurich onwards to Johannesburg. In the
boarding area I spotted a guy in a seat facing me. He was lean and
trim – the cut of a cyclist – and he also looked familiar. There weren't
many professionals at that stage who I would have felt confident about
recognizing, but this man I knew. I had watched the documentary
Overcoming, about a year in the life of Team CSC, and he had featured
heavily, along with Bjarne Riis, Carlos Sastre and the rest of the riders.
I glanced down at his feet, and he had a sports bag with his name on it.

It was definitely him: Bobby Julich.

He was interesting to me for a number of reasons. Firstly, he was
a late starter like me and in the early nineties he had trained alone
hoping for a pro career to come along. When he finally did get picked
up by a team, again like me, he had shown that he was not just a good
time trialist but as a rider had more than one string to his bow. He
had later finished 3rd in the infamous 1998 Tour that was marred by
doping, crashed in the individual time trial the next year, but then
never seemed to take it on to the level that people had expected of
him, even though they talked him up as the new Greg LeMond.

He had started in the Motorola team, joining a group that already
had Lance Armstrong in its ranks. When Bobby Julich crashed out of
the 1999 Tour, Armstrong was on the cusp of his long, dark domin-
ation of the Tour and became the only American rider that mattered.
There wasn't any love lost between Bobby and Armstrong.

I knew Bobby Julich's story so I said, 'Hi,' and introduced myself. I remember being blown away by how open and approachable he was; he was just very easy to talk to. He wasn't some remote cycling god demanding reverence, but a good guy who seemed genuinely interested in what I was doing. Stuttgart had been the final race of his career. He had just retired and although I'm sure he had some big matters, like the rest of his life, on his mind, he asked me what I was doing there. I told him that I had just signed on as a professional with Barloworld.

He might have said, 'Good luck to you with that, sonny, the team's barely professional even if you intend to be.' He didn't though. He wished me all the best and gave me a few bits of advice.

Bobby became technical director for his old team Saxo Bank after that for two years, before quitting in 2010 to move to Sky. Late in the same year, as my season was looking for a tree to die under, I was told that I would be working with Bobby Julich in 2011, instead of with Rod, whose Tuscan classroom was getting too crowded.

I was fascinated by the karma. Our paths had crossed by chance the day after Bobby had ended his long pro career and I had signed up for what I had hoped would be my long career. Now Bobby would take up the job of putting the paddles to my chest and shocking me back to professional life.

I wondered if he had been quietly looking out for my results in the years since we had met.

No, actually, he hadn't.

Bobby cheerfully told me later that he even had to google my name when he was told by Sky that he would be coaching me – I clearly didn't make big first impressions.

When I reminded him of the brief encounter at the airport he recovered well though. He said that he remembered me as being very keen and enthusiastic and that I had really been picking his brain. He told me he reckoned it was going to be fun to work together. I felt like a Labrador.

I told Bobby I was going to move to Monaco.

'You're not a millionaire, are you?'

'No. But I'm going to do it anyway.'

If it was enthusiasm Bobby was looking for, he had found it.

★

I needed to change. Quickly. I was riding at a decent speed through the back door of the last-chance saloon. On the way out, that is. I had one year left of a professional contract which might be my last. I was earning €100,000 in that year, which was not exactly enough to retire on, and hardly enough to live on if I moved to Monaco. I decided to gamble.

Whatever ability or talent I possessed was getting lost in translation from training to races. I kept all my training data, and every page told its own story.

An SRM power meter file from April 2010, for instance, pre-Giro, showed that I was doing a lot of what I called 'over-under' intervals. Robbie Nilsen and I had come up with the name and structure for these, which involved taking my power to above my lactate threshold and keeping it there.

The intervals were all pretty consistent. For 3 minutes at a time I would go over my threshold, which meant pain. There would be 1 minute of recovery in between, but this wasn't complete recovery – it was at a level that would allow the burn to subside ever so slightly.

Nowadays, it has become one of the intervals that we do most often with the team when we're getting close to peak fitness, but that April I was doing the over-under at a very high-power output all of the time. And although I was producing these impressive numbers alone, I would never reach anything close to them in competition.

In my race results from 2010, nothing really stood out. Comparing my training with my racing was like looking at the stats of two different cyclists.

I needed to be better. If 2011 went poorly then I would be all out of chances. The footnotes of professional cycling are filled with the one-line obituaries of careers that lasted a year or two – short stories with different beginnings, but all with the same end: 'He had promise, he never fulfilled it, and they cut him loose.' 'All he ever wanted was to be a pro cyclist, but he couldn't cut it, so he came home.'

I didn't want to be one of those guys.

Team Sky was the standard bearer for marginal gains and attention to detail but inevitably there was a hierarchy. Twenty-six riders don't all get the same attention. The guys who would deliver stages, who would win classics or contend in Grand Tours were not expendable and Team Sky was in a constant process of honing and perfecting them.

The domestiques, however, who would help them, were more of a batch lot. If one of them wasn't functioning you would rattle him about a bit to see why. If nothing changed, then you unplugged him and gave his €100,000 to some guy who *would* function.

That was life. Everybody is equal but some are more equal. In that corporate context Team Sky would do its best for me, but delivering performances was what counted. It was up to me to produce.

The move to Monaco would be a huge change for me, sorting out a lot of my life off the bike. And although Bobby Julich had probably been given a lot of the team's waifs and strays to work on, he suited me. Rod had taught me many invaluable things, refining much of the work Robbie and I had done over the years in South Africa, but Bobby had a long career as a professional and somehow being able to tap into that experience became a vital resource for me. He could tell how I was feeling before I had even expressed it.

Italy could be so chaotic that it wasn't a great place for somebody with my administrative skills to be living in. Often I would go away for a week of racing and come home to find the electricity was off. A missing comma or a stray apostrophe in the detailed instructions to the bank would have stopped the payments to the electricity company.

I'd spend a week with no lights and no fridge.

I would have to make at least one visit to the council, one visit to the electricity company and one visit to the bank. I would write letters struggling with the Italian words relating to bureaucracy. Just as I was setting off for the next race a week later, the lights would come back on.

Another complication was that if you were not a resident, you couldn't register a car in your name, get the internet at your home, or even, in theory, rent a home. My life off the bike was disorganized at the best of times but Italy wasn't helping. I loved the country but we were a bad marriage.

I had managed to buy an off-road motorbike with big suspension, knobbly tyres and a great guttural roar through the friend-of-a-friend's-cousin sort of thing, and I would ride it through the mountains, exploring Tuscany on the odd day off.

One hot day in the late summer of 2010, another season fading into disappointment, I got on the motorbike wearing a helmet, T-shirt and shorts and rode the four and a half hours from Tuscany to Monaco to meet an estate agent.

You can imagine what the Monaco estate agent thought of this guy in his T-shirt and shorts. She showed me three or four apartments and in the end I chose the cheapest, which was a room, or, as the estate agent called it, a studio apartment.

I went back to South Africa over the winter and stayed with my good friend Matt Beckett in a cottage on his parents' property. I trained very hard, with my sessions starting at 6.30 a.m. and going for six or seven hours. Some days Matt would come out on a scooter to motor pace me for hours at a time in order to simulate that feeling of being in a race. I got myself ready, Skyped Bobby a lot, discussed what I was doing and fed off his encouragement.

In January 2011, after I had returned to Europe, the team travelled to Mallorca to train. The first race of the year would be the Tour of Murcia in Spain, in early March. Not long before that, I settled up everything with the landlord in Tuscany and left. Bobby had said that the trauma of moving house could cost me a chunk of the season. He didn't know me well then. I owned just a bed and some drawers and the move took place on a recovery day. A friend of the landlord packed my things into a truck and drove my belongings and me to Monaco. I was training as normal the following morning, just in a different country.

Rod had often talked of sorting out my life off the bike. Ironically, the move away from Rod was a big part of that. I had internet in my home now instead of having to find Tuscan cafes where I had sat slowly sipping on a pot of green tea while using their Wi-Fi. I could now Skype family and friends. There wasn't an alpine range of red tape to climb through every month. I could go to a race and lock the door and come back to find everything still working.

Yes, it cost a fortune, but it was a better life. I was more balanced and more focused. I also discovered what had been eating me and my potential up: parasitic worms.

Looking back, my tweets through 2010 are an odd mix of defiant optimism shot through with chips of worry. There are several references to getting sick, followed up by grand proclamations that all ailments and bad times were soon to be a thing of the past.

In truth, I didn't know what was going on. I was the domestique who lived on his own and did things on his own, which was good and fine if I was producing. But I couldn't afford to be the domestique who also complained constantly of not feeling too good.

Or maybe I should have complained more – at least I might have discovered the cause more quickly.

Before and after the Commonwealth Games in Delhi in October 2010 I found my way back to Africa. The season had fizzled out and I was drawn home. I spent a couple of weeks in South Africa before going to Delhi. Afterwards I made my way to Kenya to spend some time with Jeremy, who had relocated home and was by then working in a gold mine (as an accountant, that is). His life had progressed but personally I felt as if I were working in a coal mine, with a knife and fork.

In Kenya I was called on for the usual UCI biological passport tests. I never mind those tests; they are no intrusion at all compared to the benefit to the sport. And I had good reason to be grateful for them. I was sick of being sick, tired of being tired, and it was the extra nudge I needed to seek medical help. The labs where I could have the tests done for my biological passport were adjacent to the offices of Dr Charles Chunge, a tropical disease specialist in Nairobi. Jeremy knew of my ailments over the previous year, and had recommended that Dr Chunge check me over. Jeremy had recently been treated for bilharzia by the doctor and had suffered similar symptoms.

Dr Chunge listened as I told him about my recurring pattern of illness and fatigue, and ordered a full blood-screening to check for anything out of the ordinary.

The UCI was looking for things which might have enhanced my

performance, whereas Dr Chunge was looking for something that might be sabotaging it.

He came back to me within an hour.

'Chris, you're riddled with bilharzia, just like your brother.'

Gulp.

Quick, Batman. To the Wikipedia.

Bilharzia is a disease caused by parasitic worms of the Schistosoma type. It may infect the urinary tract or intestines. Symptoms may include: abdominal pains, diarrhoea, bloody stool, or blood in the urine. In those who have been infected a long time, liver damage, kidney failure, infertility, or bladder cancer may occur. In children it may cause poor growth and difficulty learning.

The disease is spread by contact with water that contains the parasites. These parasites are released from freshwater snails that have been infected. The disease is especially common among children in developing countries as they are more likely to play in infected water. Other high risk groups include farmers, fishermen, and people using infected water for their daily chores. Diagnosis is by finding the eggs of the parasite in a person's urine or stool. It can also be confirmed by finding antibodies against the disease in the blood.

In other words, on a trip home I had come in contact with infected water. It was hard to say exactly on which trip that was as they were annual post-season events and bilharzia can remain dormant for years. Where, is also a mystery; it could have been while fishing, or mountain biking through stagnant water – the possibilities are endless in Kenya where over twenty per cent of the population is infected. Somewhere along the way these tiny snails had issued their larvae that had pierced my skin, got into my system, transformed themselves into tiny flatworms and had set up a community inside me, feeding off my body. They were literally dining on my blood.

In Europe, bilharzia is virtually unheard of, so every time I had complained of illness or abnormal fatigue, doctors assumed from the symptoms that I had glandular fever or mononucleosis, as Americans call it. Not knowing to look for bilharzia, they hadn't found bilharzia.

Bilharzia had found me, though.

The definition of the parasite, like many medical definitions, sounds scarier than the reality. If you subtract the uncomfortable knowledge of having a parasite living inside you, what remains is a reality that many people live with from day to day in rural Africa. Sometimes it is detected, often it isn't.

Unfortunately, for an endurance athlete, life is spent running the system down and then recovering. The bilharzia caused me to feel extraordinarily tired at times and left me open to colds and infections. It was debilitating enough to hinder my career but not bad enough to set alarm bells ringing. The team saw the inconsistency and saw it as a part of me. With help from those worms, it was.

The parasite gets into your system and penetrates your organs. The more time it has to colonize, the more difficult it is to get rid of, and it feeds off red blood cells, which for a bike rider is a nightmare.

If you are lucky, and catch it early enough through a screening, one dose of treatment should work. If not, you are into a war of attrition, nuking the parasites every six months, until finally you win and they're banished.

In November 2010 I had my first dose of Biltricide, whereby I swallowed the large white pills and hoped for the best. The side effects are like an exaggeration of what Biltricide sets out to cure. For the best part of a week I was pretty wiped out as the stuff flooded my system and went to war. After a couple of days, though, I was thinking about getting back on the bike. There would be another blood test and maybe another dose of Biltricide in around six months down the road.

For now, though, I had a new year, a new home and a new coach, as well as a matching number of challenges:

1. Learn the tactics of race riding.
2. Improve technically.
3. Wipe out the worms.

I got lucky.

I found the worms and I found Bobby Julich. The worms had been eating my potential and Bobby saw and believed in my potential.

When I first started working with Bobby, he sent me out on some tough training rides to push me to my limits and determine what I was capable of. He was amazed with what he saw and went straight to Rod with his findings. Same old, same old – the sorrowful mystery of Chris Froome.

My training files belonged to a guy who should have been on the podium at the Tour de France, whereas my race results belonged to a guy who should have been on the couch watching the Tour de France. It made no sense. Bobby thought my power meter had to have been incorrectly calibrated. Rod knew the story as he had been watching me for longer than Bobby had.

'No, the data is spot on. That's Froomey.'

So it began. Bobby set about enacting my finishing school and I had some structure in my life now. Surely it had to translate into my racing?

The first change would be less tinkering and experimenting on my own. I had always been fiddling with diet, equipment and bike set-up. Even worse, I had experimented randomly with training, pushing myself way beyond my limits just to see how far I could go. I enjoyed the suffering because I thought it would help. But it depleted my energy levels on long races and that in turn ate my confidence.

Secondly, Bobby was frank about things. I didn't know how to race. My heroic charges when people were least expecting them gave me a couple of minutes in the spotlight but didn't produce results. Bobby set about teaching me how I could get the right watts out at the right time. Videos, race reports and stats – I learned to study them all differently. I learned that the key parts of the race were when people were holding back, and the highlights were when everybody was going flat out.

Thirdly, my style and technique needed to be sanded and polished. So I began doing Pilates and started to respect rest a little more. I became the parasite, feeding on Bobby's racing experience.

I was still going towards the back door but I had a hand on the brake and my feet on the ground, fighting the momentum of the exit. For the first time in a long while I felt excited about the road ahead.

A typical morning conversation with Bobby went along the lines of:

'Okay, we need to put in a good effort today, so keep the intervals at this level here.'

'Can't I do them at a higher level?'

Bobby wanted me to back off. I always wanted to train harder. Usually we compromised.

The Tour of Murcia came and went. Over three days there were no highlights for me other than a top twenty in the individual time trial on the last day. Back in the Sky offices in Manchester I knew that nobody was sitting bolt upright wondering what was happening.

The Volta a Catalunya was better. Not that much better, but I had one of those days when I felt all the parts coming together. It happened during stage five when four of us broke away and stayed ahead for most of the day. We were never going to get away with it, and when the gap was big enough so that it made one of our number, Francesco Masciarelli, the race leader on the road, the big guns duly hauled us back in time for the sprint finish.

But I was learning about using my energy at the right times, and whether it was that or the bilharzia, or both, my strength seemed more evenly spread out over the week in Catalunya. On the last two stages I finished in the main group.

On to the Vuelta a Castilla y León. I beat Alberto Contador, a Tour de France winner, on a mountain finish on stage three and then came in the top ten in the time trial. I finished 14th overall, only about a minute and a half down on the winner. Today, some people still say that I had never done anything before my results during the 2011 Vuelta a España, but I've always smiled at that opinion. Were these insignificant results? Not to me.

Still, I admit, there were no congratulatory telegrams from Manchester, but I hoped that somebody was noticing. Bobby was offering favourable assessments and I began to daydream about getting another contract.

I was a replacement rider for the Tour de Romandie. I can't recall who pulled out but I got a late summons. I'm sure they had erected special crash barriers around the flower beds of local residents when they heard I was coming, but fortunately I managed not to lay myself out amidst the blossoms this time.

I climbed well. There were a couple of big category-one climbs on stage one and I finished 8th. The next day was lumpy and I crossed the line just 2 seconds off the guy who won the stage. More importantly for me, and for the team, was that I was turning in good performances. I was doing my pulls and being effective in the mountains; I was earning my corn.

I took a few days off after Romandie, struggling with a chest infection. It was the sort of thing I had hoped would be banished along with the worms, but fortunately my recent performances (and whatever Bobby and Rod were saying now about my potential) had been enough encouragement for Dave Brailsford to take a gamble on me. At the Tour of California I would be team leader and our designated GC rider.

The team consisted of Kurt-Asle Arvesen, Alex Dowsett, Mathew Hayman, my old mate Greg Henderson, Jeremy Hunt, Ian Stannard, Ben Swift and myself – not a bad group at all. As a bonus, I would get to room with Greg again, so it was harmonicas and kikoys all round.

Stage one at Lake Tahoe was designed for me. They had front-loaded the race with climbs and there were good hauls up hills with great names such as Spooner Junction, Brockway Summit and Emerald Bay. Bobby had a house close to Lake Tahoe and we did some training rides up there to take a look at the route.

However, the day before the race the weather moved in and it snowed heavily. The organizers still wanted the race to go ahead but we would be starting on the lake shore and riding straight up into the mountains all day. We were standing on the start line, kitted up and ready to go, and I remember being so heavily wrapped up that only my eyes were showing; I had a beanie on and a balaclava covering my nose and mouth. I never remember being that cold before or since, and although I'm stoical about all sorts of pain, I hate the cold.

I'd had about three or four shots of espresso in the camper van before braving the outside, when the organizers told us that the race had been called off.

It was a big relief, but by now we were already on our bikes, buzzing on caffeine, and we had to get to the next hotel. I don't recall whose idea it was that we should ride as far as we could towards our hotel, with the option of jumping into the camper van if it got really bad. I don't recall it, so I don't know where to direct my bitterness.

We did about half an hour on icy, sleety roads, and then it started raining hard too. It was freezing, and despite heavy winds and more snow, we just kept going.

Only the Team Sky riders had opted for this madness. We were the only ones out there like dogs in the rain. Marginal gains? I don't think so!

After an hour I got into the camper van, with snow all over my face. I was shivering and numb beyond pain although I knew that the pain would come when the numbness lifted. I had to dry off as best as I could with towels and then wait until we reached the hotel.

The race was a big deal to me. It would be the first time, and maybe the last time, that the team would ride for me. I went to the sauna in the hotel with a couple of the guys to sweat out whatever hadn't been sweated out on our failed attempt at a training ride through the blizzard.

I had come to California confident and looking forward to it, but after the disaster of the snow-and-sauna day I had a cough that started small but grew. I told Bobby that I wasn't feeling quite right; Bobby told me I would be fine. 'Training has been good,' he said. And he was right. I planned to reproduce those numbers on the mountains stages in California.

The race went okay at first. I took some antibiotics and got through the first couple of stages, which were made for sprinters. We won them both – Ben Swift one day and then Greg the next. All was good and I was 33rd on GC, just 10 seconds off the race leader's jersey, which Greg wore.

The next day was a summit finish on Sierra Road and my kind of stage. I finished 2 minutes 53 seconds behind the stage winner, and was now nearly 3 minutes behind on GC, even though I had moved up to 17th place.

'Oh well,' I thought. We had finished that evening in the town of Modesto. The American poet Robert Frost was born just about an hour up the road in San Francisco. He famously wrote about the woods being lovely, dark and deep, and how he has promises to keep, and miles to go, before he sleeps. So did I. Frost also said that what he had learned about life could be summed up in three words: 'It goes on.'

So do stage races. I was bruised but the race went on, and I kept on.

I felt no better but hung in there. I did a poor time trial on stage six, where I got it wrong tactically. Although I had known there was a time trial coming I had spent the previous day riding about 200 kilometres in a breakaway. I time-trialled 1 minute 39 seconds off the winner but stayed 17th on GC, which sounded a lot better than it was, as the Tour of California was the week after the Giro and many of the top riders were either tired or away.

I had hoped for better.

On stage seven, the ride to Mount Baldy promised more. The stage started with a tough climb only 10 kilometres into the race, and the plan was for me to go into the breakaway on that first climb. It wasn't a top-secret strategy – everyone knew there was going to be a breakaway of the really strong guys who were trying to climb the GC ladder. That was the breakaway to be in.

The breakaway formed without me. Swifty, a gentleman and self-less rider, worked like a dog to pull me across the gap. I had the luxury of sitting on his wheel, and once there he peeled off and dropped back to the bunch, job done.

The pace was rattling with 3 kilometres left to the top of the climb and everybody was pushing it. I stayed in the break but I was on my limit just to be there, and I knew that I wasn't going to do any damage. We were approaching the summit when I realized that I was not going to be able to stay with them at all.

I was blown off. Soon the peloton came and swallowed me. Ben and the rest of my teammates tried to pretend it wasn't an issue, but I could feel their disappointment, and all the more acutely because I'd been in their position so many times before.

Before I knew it, I was slipping back through the peloton. GC leader? I couldn't even stay in the peloton! I tried really hard to hang in there, and to save some face. But I couldn't.

I ended up in the gruppetto. And soon I was barely hanging on to their tails. Over the top of a climb, I was just managing to stay with them and I knew that if I dropped off them I would be out of the race entirely.

I think that day was one of the hardest days I've ever had on a bike. I remember fighting to be with the gruppetto, hanging on with my fingernails. Mentally, it was such a knock for me. I came in 118th of 126 finishers and lost 32 minutes. I wrote in my race diary that night: 'Felt okay before the race and went in the break up the first climb but blew my tits off, couldn't even get into the peloton and ended up in the gruppetto 30 minutes down.'

There was nothing else to be said.

A year previously Team Sky had chosen me for the Giro. This year I hadn't made that cut but I had been given this chance to be the GC leader in California. The guys had worked for me as well as I could have wished, but I had failed. I had been given my chance and had blown it.

I didn't feel myself but I could imagine that evening some people in Manchester taking calls or going online: 'Thirty-two minutes. That's Froomey for you.'

After California I knew I wasn't a realistic choice for the Tour de France and I was back to being anxious over whether I would get a contract for the following season. The Tour de Suisse might have helped. Its nine stages began in Lugano in mid June with an individual time trial on day one and day nine.

I time-trialled well on both of those stages, but in between, my graph was basically the story of my life: good rides recognized only by those who read the small print, contrasted with bad rides that screamed for attention and could be picked up on another continent.

I was 11th in the prologue and decent in the mountains the following day when Mauricio Soler, my old crash-prone colleague from Barloworld, took the win.

And then on stage three I lost 10 minutes, dropping from 9th on GC to 30th. It was just my good fortune that Dave Brailsford, noting my respectable results on the first two days, flew out to be in the team car for day three when I attacked much too soon and rode like a novice. He saw me drop like a stone from the lead group. 'Well, that's Froomey, isn't it?'

With that, my confidence flew out the window. Though it was a bad day, I'll never forget how my teammate Dario Cioni nursed me through the stage. He was so strong that day but he stayed with me, encouraged me in that calm way of his, and without him, 10 minutes would have been 15.

But I had no energy and over the next few stages I slowly dropped down the GC. I knew that riding a good overall position was no longer on the cards, so I looked for opportunities to get a stage result in the days to come.

I was offered some perspective when Mauricio Soler came off his bike on stage six at high speed. He hit a spectator and then a solid fence, head first. He suffered a fractured skull, a cerebral oedema and other injuries. They placed him in an induced coma that night, and although he recovered, he never raced again.

Over the last three days I began to feel more comfortable. I finished 9th on the time trial on the final day and left Switzerland wishing that the race had another ten days to run.

For the Tour de France, I opted not to sit and watch it on TV and depress myself. It goes on, I thought to myself again, and there was still one last shot at redemption – Bobby and I regrouped and he pointed me towards the Vuelta a España.

I kept my head down, focused on my training and watched everything that I ate.

I rode up into the mountains every day, occasionally with Bobby in tow on a scooter, overseeing some of the more specific intervals he had set for me.

I rolled straight on to the Tour of Poland. I was feeling good physically now, and had lost some weight (I was down five kilos for the summer). Although I felt strong, I couldn't help noticing that there weren't any Polish Alps.

The team didn't seem to be using me right here.

But I had no choices – I hadn't earned choices. The team wanted me to go in all the early breakaways and be the go-to guy on flat stages. I would end up sitting on the front for long pulls, doing hard labour. Later, I would miss out on the key breakaways.

I kept quiet, and did my job, but I couldn't help feeling that this wasn't for me.

I remember speaking to Bobby at the end of the Tour of Poland. He was frank.

'Listen, Chris, it's going to be difficult to get you into the Vuelta. There are other guys that they want to take, but I'm trying to convince them to put you in. It's between you and Lars Petter Nordhaug.'

Lars Petter was in his contract year too. He'd ridden the Giro earlier in the year, whereas I hadn't.

I spoke to Alex Carera, my agent, and it was a back-to-the-wall talk.

'Alex, I don't know if I'm going to get into the Vuelta. We need to start talking to teams now to see what my options are. Worst-case scenario, we can use those offers to try and set a benchmark for Sky, in case they want to decrease the salary I am on.'

At this point I was thinking that the decrease in salary might be my best possible option. Any time Alex called Dave Brailsford to talk about my future, Alex was hearing a lot of 'hmmmmms'

and some 'umming'

and a bit of 'ahhing'.

Alex wanted to play hardball but Dave didn't want to play anything. The best I was hoping for was that they would cut my wage to €60,000 or €70,000 a year and keep me as a cheap and cheerful adornment so that I would get another shot at proving myself. Surely they looked at the training numbers uploaded to them every day? Surely they could see something in me? On my good days, I was doing what barely anybody else in the team could do. On my bad days, unfortunately, the same could be said. I could still live in Monaco on €65,000. Well, just about.

Later, Alex would show me texts he had been getting from Dave. Things were worse than I'd thought: '*What has Chris done all year? He's done nothing,*' and '*We don't know if we're going to keep Chris.*'

At the end of the day, I was a commodity and this was the

corporate world. If you're not performing, or if you don't deliver, they're going to cut you and move on, without looking back. *Adios*.

I saw it with other guys on the team. Guys who I thought were pretty good riders and really good teammates would get cut from teams all the time. 2011 wasn't going particularly well for the team in general and there was a rumour that there would be a lot of bloodletting before 2012.

It is quite cut-throat in that sense. In the cocoon of the bus and the hotel there is this manufactured feeling of 'We're all friends, and we're all in this together, we are almost a family,' that kind of thing. But there is a very thin line, probably a blue one, between becoming a made guy in the family and being kicked out of the family.

Lars Petter finished 16th on the Tour of Poland. I came 85th. It's true – sometimes you don't need a weatherman to tell you which way the wind is going to blow.

I got home the Monday evening after Poland, a little delicate from the night before. I had a short recovery ride, just an easy hour to get some air into my lungs. The next day Bobby called, with bad news I assumed.

'Chris, you're going to the Vuelta. Lars Petter has gotten ill. He's in bed with a bad flu and he's on antibiotics now. They're not going to take a chance with him so they're taking you instead. You're in.'

It was that close. Scarily close. But Bobby and I started making new plans, big plans: Vuelta plans.

17

2011: *Vuelta a España*

Stage One: Another Fine Mess

The pre-race plan was distributed.

'Objective: GC with Bradley. TTT is an important kick-off for the team. Kurt and Ian will take care of Bradley and his positioning on the easier days. Dario and Thomas will give Brad protection on all the mountain finishes and will help Bradley with his positioning. Xabier, Morris and Froome will do their best to survive as long as possible and will fetch bottles etc. Then in the sprint stages, CJ is our sprinter.'

Okay – I certainly wasn't coming in as the high-mountains domestique that I'd hoped to be. I was going to have to work extra hard; I wasn't going to neglect my bottle duties but I decided I was going to be there in the mountains when Bradley needed me. I had to be.

Away we went, tilting at windmills. Brad was Don Quixote and in my head I was his Sancho Panza, at least when we were in the mountains, which were my red-ringed days of heavy work. We were rooming together, which was interesting because we are not a good mix. Brad is shy and reserved with people and I am much the same, which means we don't bring the best out of each other. Actually, we don't bring anything out of each other. It was a quiet room and, as Sancho Panza tells the Don, a closed mouth catches no flies.

It was especially quiet on the evening of the first day after the time trial which, if I'm being frank about it, we messed up.

Bobby J had been in charge. Team time trials are all about the group dynamic. Your time is taken from the fifth man home in a team of nine so you have to stay together for as long as you can and at least five have to be together at the finish. The guy doing a pull on the front has to maintain a certain speed and as soon as it drops, he moves aside to let the next guy through.

Bobby was nervous, but we all were, and maybe we overthought it. This was beachfront, Benidorm, during heatwave time, and we had our time-trial suits and helmets on as we did about three laps of the circuit at around eighty to ninety per cent beforehand, working out who would pull and where. We were just making ourselves tired.

The course started off up a climb of about 3 kilometres, which made it quite tricky. We didn't want to drop any guys too early but CJ Sutton is a sprinter and Stannard is a big lad. If they lost contact on the climb, they could struggle to finish inside the time limit. We needed to keep them with us, so that they would be able to do some big pulls after the climb.

The greater danger is the one you don't expect. Just a kilometre in, Kurt-Asle Arvesen and Xabier Zandio overlapped wheels and crashed. We lost Kurt, and Xabier was held up and fell behind, so we had a split. We rode conservatively, hoping the others would come back to us.

On the descent we let Brad, our best time trialler, pull us on his own so that he could pick his own lines and wouldn't have to peel off while navigating one of the four roundabouts before joining the beach road. In retrospect, that wasn't the best thing to do – it was too conservative. On a descent you can make up a lot of time if you are interchanging the lead because it's really easy for the guys on the wheels and quite hard for the guy on the front taking all the wind. As strong as Brad was, his leading the entire descent didn't help our time. We got to the bottom and felt we really had to dig in deep. We did and immediately lost a couple more guys off the back.

With 5 kilometres to go there was a communications mix-up. We were on the flat now, passing through a town and riding a full-out time trial. CJ, our sprinter, had sat up as his race was done. At the same time, Xabier, who had pulled himself back to the rest of us, had done a big turn on the front and then sat up, which left just four of us. This spelt disaster and the radio had to tell Xabier the bad news: 'You have to get back on, Xabier. *Vamos!*'

He did a huge effort to get back on but by the finish our pace line was breaking up all over the place. We finished 20th of twenty-two teams, 42 seconds off the winning time. Footon, who were a second behind us, and Andalucia, who were even further back, were the only teams with worse times.

It was just one bad day. Nobody said much afterwards and we put on brave faces – we had lost 42 seconds but over three weeks that shouldn't matter too much on the GC.

We hurt though for Bobby, who had put a lot into this, and for Brad, who had come back from his broken collarbone to try to salvage something from the season.

One other thing that I recall from around this period was that I had been looking at videos of time trials. I had said to Bobby that I didn't feel my racing position was aggressive enough – I felt comfortable but too high up on the front and was taking too much wind.

Bobby said, 'Okay, let's give it a go,' and we literally took two whole spacers out of the handlebar, dropping it by about a centimetre and a half. This was a huge difference and it felt fantastic. It felt fast and it felt like, without compromising the power, I had adopted a position that was far more aggressive and that my back was flat.

I am a man of constant marginal gains.

Stage Two: Fuhgeddaboudit

We talked together on the bus in the morning.

Dave B said, 'Yesterday is yesterday, so forget about it, the real race starts today. Forty-two seconds in the mountains is nothing, don't worry about it. Get on with the race now.'

I nodded.

I needed to impress the team here. In my mind I wanted it to be like one of the stages back in Murcia where I had been the last guy with Brad over all the mountains. That was the job I wanted to do again; to show them I could be useful up there. A high-mountains domestique was what I wanted to be – for now.

Alex had told me that Jonathan Vaughters at Garmin had been on to him wondering about my availability for next year. So there was a worst-case fall back if I needed one but I had a chance here to persuade Dave to keep me at Team Sky, even if it was for less money.

Riding as an under-23 for the Hi-Q Supercycling Academy, based in Johannesburg.

2006 was a year in three acts. Above, Act I: the Tour of Egypt. With our trollies and bikes held proudly in front of us, Kinjah and I gathered with the Simbaz at Cairo airport, along with our manager, Julius Mwangi (*second from right*), as the seven-man cycling team of Kenya.

Act II: the Commonwealth Games, Melbourne. Me racing for Kenya in the mountain bike competition, which we had never planned to ride. It began badly and got worse.

Warming up for the time trial at the Commonwealth Games. I wound up 17th overall in a field of seventy-two riders, but spent over an hour sitting in the leader's chair after recording the fastest early time. Two managers from the English team first noticed me. Their names were Dave Brailsford and Shane Sutton.

Act III: Under-23 World Championships in Salzburg. After 'borrowing' the email address of the Kenyan Cycling Federation to enter myself into the race, my time trial started disastrously when I crashed into a marshal just 200 metres into the course. [Photo credit: Roberto Bettini]

Riding for Team Konica Minolta in 2007. Despite the high-tech sponsor's name, the South African team still ran on a shoestring budget.

In 2007 I rode for the UCI development team, a mixed continental team made up of riders from developing countries based in Aigle, Switzerland.

In 2008 I swapped my Kenyan licence for a British one. I know people who feel they are from Yorkshire and Britain; from Merseyside and Britain; from the Isle of Man and Britain; and so on. Well, I was raised in Kenya feeling that I was of Britain.

Me with my second cycling mentor, Robbie Nilsen. I first met Robbie through the Hi-Q Supercycling Academy, but he has continued to offer me advice and help me train throughout my career. We didn't know it at the time, but much of our training back then was precisely the same work that we would be

The red dirt jersey – training in Kenya in 2010 after joining Team Sky.

I could reschedule the daydreams. I could survive. 'It goes on.' There would be other days and if I did well here maybe I could go to the Tour the next year as a high-class equipiér. If I got a chance, maybe then I could go for a stage myself, and do the sort of thing that David Moncoutié would do – get in the early breakaways that survive to the mountaintop finishes. Not being a GC rider, I would not be a threat to anyone and would stay under the radar. They would let me go and then one of those days I would win a stage.

That would be enough.

For now though I was the ninth man on the team. I knew Thomas Löfkvist was intending to be the last man with Brad in the mountains. I would do what I was told to do. I thought the heat was going to be a factor: Thomas grew up in Scandinavia and I grew up in Africa. But maybe I was clutching at straws.

Since breaking his collarbone, this was Brad's first day of real racing. He would be riding gingerly so I needed to mind him. There would be a sprint at the end so I also needed to see if I could get CJ into position.

Once we started, the racing was on the flat and there were crosswinds so the job was just to protect Brad. Kurt was captain on the road and he called the pulls according to the tactics we had laid out that morning on the bus. I could do a long pull if needed. They certainly weren't saving me for later – they weren't sure where I would be later.

The plan was simple and it worked. We had a good day and kept Brad buoyant in the GC. CJ timed his sprint perfectly and won the stage.

Yesterday? Hey, fuhgeddaboudit. It's a bike race. It goes on.

Stage Three: Hurt Locker

Tougher than we thought – days with lesser-category mountains sometimes turn out that way. Some people hung back waiting for the big climbs, while others wanted to make a point. The heat also hurt us, although we were not alone – the sun seemed to mess with my SRM power meter, which meant that mine read four degrees at one point.

We had lined up proceedings for Brad going up the final category-three climb. Thomas Löfkvist had done a long pull on the earlier slopes then pulled off. I felt like I might blow a kilometre from the top but I looked around and everybody else also seemed to be struggling. Good. I endure pain better if everybody is suffering; you draw morale from wherever you find it.

I led Brad over the line in the lead group: I was 12th, he was 13th on the same time. Mission accomplished.

We did well and in my mind I had proved a point in my private mission to show I could be Brad's main man when the going got tough. I hung in there till the end.

Tomorrow was the Sierra Nevada.

Stage Four: Starsky and Hutch

The first uphill finish to the Sierra Nevada was to take place in the afternoon: 2,112 metres in height, 39-degree heat, with 23 kilometres of ascending. One long haul.

We followed the wheels and a group of forty broke off as we approached the mountain. With 7 kilometres to go there was a minor breakaway but I stayed close to Brad – we were becoming a duo.

Daniel Moreno and Chris Anker Sørenson had gone away in the break a little bit earlier, and they stayed away. For me it was the first mountaintop finish where I alone had been with Brad. I had stayed with him and been on the front at times to keep things under control, but, most significantly, I was now the only guy left with him.

We finished together in the bunch behind Moreno, Sørenson and Daniel Martin. I was still on duty right to the end.

I got some words of praise; in my own mind I was being promoted to the job of last guy with Brad.

The adrenaline, the excitement and the buzz – it was all running through me for hours afterwards.

Stage Five: Darkness, My Old Friend

We slept the night before at the hotel up in the Sierra Nevada. A lot of people come here to do altitude training, where the land is barren and dark volcanic earth is all around. I didn't sleep very well.

I felt terrible most of the day and any effort to move up in the peloton hurt. At one point I dropped back to the team car to collect bottles and ice and then pushed back up hard through the peloton with them. I took nine bottles: seven in my jersey and two on the bike – one for each rider.

Over the last 50 kilometres I seemed to feel comparatively better. This is a theme I notice. When I'm going well, the start of the stage seems to be the hardest part. I struggle to shake that sluggish feeling but towards the end of the race, particularly in the last 50 kilometres of a 217-kilometre stage, I'm starting to feel good again. I've flushed my legs from the hurt of the day before.

I felt very much at ease as we went up the last category-two climb. The final kick to the end was sharp and steep, less than a couple of kilometres up a pavé road to the finish. I stayed with Brad, helping to close any gaps opening up in front of him in the mad scramble up the harsh gradient to the finish line.

At the finish Brad nodded in my direction, a hint of a thin smile. It meant 'thank you', but that's about as chatty as we got. In the room when we turned out the lights at night we said, 'Goodnight now.' In the morning when we got up we said, 'Morning.'

That was it, really. No hostility, just long minutes of silence.

From the beginning – and I did find this a little bit odd – we wouldn't talk about the race much. Any discussion we did have felt slightly strange. I remember going to talk to some of my teammates about it, saying, 'It's really weird in the room with Brad – if I say anything, he'll just say "yeah" or something in agreement, and that will be the end of it, there won't be any further discussion.'

Stage Six: The Hangover

This was the hardest day so far. I was sore from start to finish and badly positioned for most of the stage. I knew in future I would have to be further forward when it got lined out like it did.

Sometimes when the peloton was strung out and I was near the back of the line, Steven de Jongh's voice would crackle on the radio:

'Chris, you are too far back now, you need to move up.'

My legs were okay over the last climb, a category two, but the peloton started splitting on the downhill, which put us in the red again to close it. Although the stage wasn't a mountaintop finish, it was a long 200-kilometre haul in the heat, and the Sierra Nevada and the sleepless night on top of it were catching up with me now. Two days after a really big effort is usually when I pay the price. That day was no exception.

Brad and I finished in the group 23 seconds behind Peter Sagan, the stage winner.

We lost Kurt-Asle Arvesen. He had a bad crash the previous day after colliding with a spectator at high speed. Today his body was spent and bandages and dressings could only do so much to plug the seeping energy from his skinless limbs. CJ wasn't feeling great either. And tomorrow looked like it was going to be dull.

Stage Seven: The Cure

I woke up feeling much, much better. There was a relaxed start from the peloton too, which helped. The race kicked off towards the end in the crosswinds, but it was only 25 kilometres and there were no major dramas apart from a messy crash in the final stretch that we luckily avoided. It was a good day all round.

This meant there was no change in the GC positions for Brad and me: I was 21st and Brad was 22nd. It had turned out to be a nice recovery day before tomorrow's trek from San Lorenzo de El Escorial, which promised to be a tough day of climbing.

Stage Eight: Crash Froome, the Return

I was using the compact osymetric chainrings for the stage, which meant that no SRM stats other than my heart rate and speed would be recorded. I would need the lighter gears when the gradients reached close to twenty per cent later on.

There was a crash halfway through the stage, but we didn't escape it this time. There were winds again and the bunch was all crammed up on the left. Someone in front of me braked too hard, or I hadn't reacted quickly enough, and I went into their back wheel and subsequently off the side of the road. There was a small drop which sent me tumbling off into a ditch of brown desert-like sand. After a soft landing I rolled on to some prickly shrubbery but my ego hurt more than anything, as I had to clamber back up and rejoin the race.

I tried to hold something back during the stage, and not to go too deep while maintaining position in the front group. Bobby's lessons were getting through to me. Even in the final shakedown I stayed close to Brad, and when it kicked off I rolled at his tempo to the line. We didn't go too far into the red, which meant another good day. There would be higher mountains tomorrow.

Stage Nine: Szrekkie for Ever After

A massive day! I punctured on the run-up to the final climb, just as the race was hotting up. When I changed the wheel the new one had the magnet attached at a different point so I had no speed-readings on the final climb.

If you're missing the speed, you're missing the distance too. That is not so crippling an issue on the last climb as when it happens earlier in the day, but still it made me edgy. I just don't like not having all the data.

Luckily after my puncture the peloton had started gradually up the climb so it was not the usual helter-skelter I had expected. As the climb ascended, so too did the tempo until we met the crosswinds with 4 or 5 kilometres to go.

We hit a ribbon of flatness on La Covatilla, which was a relief after climbing for so long but the reprieve was only for about a kilometre and a half. Then there would be a 3-kilometre hustle to the finish. By now the front group had whittled to twenty and Brad and I moved near the front. We were the only Sky riders up there.

I could feel a really strong wind from the right, and when nobody wanted to take responsibility for working, the opportune moment presented itself.

'This is it,' I thought. 'I'm not just going to pull normally and wait for someone to attack. I'm going to pull with everything I have. Let's go.'

The wind from the right meant that everyone was riding over on the left-hand side of the road, trying to get some shelter from the guy just to their right. That created a diagonal line, or a diagonal echelon. The guys on the edge of the road were almost in a line behind each other, coming close to riding off the edge.

The guy at the front, who was me, was in a tough position but I exploited the hand I had. I moved just two feet from the edge of the left side of the road. That space of two feet offered shelter to one rider only: Brad. His front wheel was side by side with my back wheel and nobody could get shelter from Brad as there was no room. They would have to ride directly behind him. It was a perfect cross-wind scenario and I pushed really hard. I squeezed the watts higher, up over my threshold.

Depending on what I have ridden beforehand, I know I can push for half an hour on a mountain at, or at least close to, my threshold. Behind Brad, the field disintegrated.

When we got to where the road climbed up again and I had pulled for the flat section, I knew my job was done. There was no one left apart from four guys, including Brad. I pulled off, expecting the four to rush past me, continuing their battle for the summit. But no – they seemed to slow down, showing no sign of wanting to maintain the tempo. They almost seemed to have stopped and were just looking at each other. I realized they must all be pretty tired because no one was taking it up.

So I pushed on again, back to those four guys. As I got to the rear wheel of the fourth rider, Brad took it up, and got on the front. The wind was still coming from the right but now we were going uphill again. Brad put it right in the gutter. I don't think he knew that I was back on; he'd seen me pull off and I had done my turn. Now I was clinging on to 5th.

I wasn't thinking about the GC. I had done a great job today and this was bonus territory; I wasn't completely spent. I wanted to get back to Brad to be able to say to him, 'Well, let's ride again a bit more like we just did,' but Brad had taken it up. He was in time-trial mode, going hard, and I was now pinned to the back on the edge of the road, trying to steal any sliver of shelter from the rider in front of me, but there was not much shelter to be had.

Getting to the last kilometre, the metal barriers appeared at the edge of the road. I saw the first barrier at the last second and pulled out, just missing it. I pushed to get back on the wheel ahead of me again, turning myself inside out with effort, my shoulders almost touching the hoods of my handlebars. And then, boom! It was sprint time. Daniel Martin won the sprint, Bauke Mollema was 2nd and Juanjo Cobo was 3rd. Brad and I were 4th and 5th. Race leader Joaquim Rodríguez, meanwhile, finished 50 seconds off.

Brad and I moved up to 13th and 14th in the GC and that night I knew things had changed. This was probably the best day Team Sky had experienced since we hit the mountains. I got it right in the crosswinds and we blew the field to pieces.

Steven de Jongh, our race director, came and patted me on the back.

'Where did that come from, Froomester? Great ride, man.'

He told me that I had basically put Bradley back in the race and that my pull on the front blew away the contenders like seed heads off a dandelion.

I had matched my training numbers and added some grown-up thinking on the road.

At last.

I went to see Stefan Szrek, the Belgian soigneur who was giving me post-race massages over the three weeks. As I walked in the door I could see it on Szrekkie's face: his beaming smile that said, 'Good job'. He didn't need words. He was just shaking his head, smiling and laughing. I grinned back at him.

I always have a good chat with Szrekkie whenever I am on his table. He sticks on the latest music he has downloaded, usually house or trance, and massages me while he is half dancing with a big grin on his face. He's great company: he speaks English with a very Flemish accent and sometimes he'll stick his Flemish words into the middle of a sentence just to keep you guessing.

For those three weeks I had him all to myself, which meant I didn't have to queue for a massage. However, as he was the only soigneur with just one rider to massage, he had other jobs to do. These included doing everybody's laundry and being responsible for matters at the finish line, such as giving us our recovery drinks and producing clothes for anybody who needed to go to the podium. He would also escort riders to the changing camper or go to anti-doping with them. This was the stress of Szrekkie's life as far as the Vuelta went, and it kept him in a state of constant panic.

I thought I had problems?

Stage Ten: The Pain Mutiny

Time-trial day: 47 pounding kilometres around lovely Salamanca. Or Bradley's playground, as Steven de Jongh said.

The plan for the day was clear. Brad would be going flat out and the stage would be between him, Tony Martin and Fabian Cancellara. The rest of us would fight for scraps. Well, I would. In a nod to my new status within the team, I was allowed to go flat out too, whereas everybody else would be riding within themselves. It was time trial today, and a rest day tomorrow. The team could recharge the batteries.

When we went out to look at the time-trial course I took head-phones and music along with me. I listened to the beats and focused on the route, concluding that I really liked the look of it. It wasn't pan-flat but rolling, which was perfect for me.

Brad and I were using osymetric chainrings. When you start off with them it feels a bit odd. It isn't a circle that your pedal strokes are forming any more but more oval-shaped. However, after one long ride the new movement seems very natural.

I enjoy the feeling when I stand up on the pedals; it feels like I can really push and that the power coming out would get me up any mountain. For me it feels right, and more natural than pedalling in perfect circles with every revolution of the pedals. Other people say there is no difference: no logic to that feeling, and no science – that it's a mechanical placebo. Well, it works for me.

I think there is particularly more to gain on the osymetric

Stage seventeen, Vuelta a España, 2011. I hadn't won the Vuelta, but I had won a stage in a Grand Tour – my first win as a professional. I had just been in the greatest mountaintop finish I am ever likely to experience. Just to have been part of it – blow by blow – had been to know the best of our beautiful sport. I had beaten Juanjo Cobo, the hometown hero also known as the Bison, by one second.
[Photo Credit: PA Images]

On the Champs-Élysées after the 2012 Tour de France. I finished second on GC, 3 minutes and 21 seconds behind my Sky teammate Bradley Wiggins. [Photo credit: Michelle Cound]

chainring when the road is going uphill. The angles seem better and you can feel more of a difference as you pedal. You give a little extra force on the uphill, and then on the downhills you ease up more than you normally would. That's the way I've always liked to ride, anyway.

So the course felt right in that sense. And Bobby was always good on time trials. He would speak in terms of letting a carpet unroll. You are unrolling it. It starts off big and as it unrolls it gets faster and faster, right to the end. That's how I needed to think of my effort and my energy – the carpet. I needed to get it going, get it going, to build up the momentum. As it is getting smaller and smaller, it is getting faster and faster. When it's completed unrolled, that's when my race is done.

I do the same with my gearing. I start off possibly pushing with a heavier gear but keeping the power up there and as I tire towards the end I make it easier for myself using the lighter gears. I always imagine this concept of the carpet rolling out.

Years ago in my South African days, Robbie had come up with some time-trialling rules. Typically I would go out too hard and then die. So we decided that for the first ten per cent of any time trial (say it was 40 kilometres, well then, for the first 4 kilometres) I would go at below my threshold. I would basically make an effort to go easier than I should be going so as not to put myself in the red too early.

Today, for the first 3 or 4 kilometres of the time trial, I was looking at my power meter and making sure that I was saving some energy, which is hard to do with all the adrenaline and excitement. On days like this, when I am full of confidence and desire, I run the danger of going flat out too early. I won't realize the mistake until ten minutes in when I feel barbecued.

I felt I was holding a little back but the SRM was confusing. It had to be wrong. My body thought I was not going hard enough and my head thought I was maybe losing time. After about 2 or 3 minutes of this internal debate I put an end to it.

'Okay, I'm not going to look at the meter any more. It's not reading correctly today. I haven't calibrated it right.'

I continued riding and hit a heavier gear. The carpet started unrolling. It was at a good lick and I was riding on feeling and instinct now in my new lower flat-back position. *Go.*

Brad came off the ramp 4 minutes after I did. By all accounts he looked as if he had been shot out of a rocket launcher. At the first intermediate checkpoint after 13.3 kilometres of road he was 1 second ahead of Tony Martin, who had set the landmark time for the day, 55 minutes and 54 seconds. My own time was 25 seconds off Martin's pace at that point.

By the 30-kilometre time check though, Brad was feeling the pain. He was now 19 seconds behind Tony Martin; meanwhile, I was 1 second behind Brad and getting stronger.

Not long after the second time check, however, I could feel the tiredness invading me. Suddenly I wanted the comfort of my power meter again. I looked down and could see I was hurting. Aha, maybe it was right now – it had fixed itself!

My brain will tell me anything in times like this.

I was going to try to hold but I was feeling rough. Everything was screaming at me now to slow down. *Just a little bit. Slow down.* I would try to hold these numbers though to keep the average.

Marcus Ljungqvist, our director sportif, was now in my ear on the radio. There were no details, just encouragement: 'Great ride, Froomey. Keep it going, Froomey. That's it, you're smoking this TT. Brilliant. Very good.'

I had a couple of energy gels tucked up my shorts and took them. The sweetness gave me a quick shot of revival but after a while my legs were talking treason again. I could hear them. *You can start to ease off now, boss. You have done the work. You really have. You are almost there. Just ease a little. It won't hurt you. Go on. You have done it. You are spent. You need to take it easy. Everybody is impressed by what you have done. Listen to Marcus. 'Great ride,' he says. You can relax a little bit now. No need to beat yourself up any more.*

Then the counter-argument came blaring from my brain. *Shut up! Rubbish! Time trials are won or lost by seconds. A game of inches. Legs, you should know that by now. Every second we can get, we keep clawing at it. There's not a chance I'm going to let you slow down. We need to get a contract.*

I got back up to speed again. Then I saw the numbers dipping. No. No. Fight. Fight. Back up again.

Coming in through the cobbled streets back into Salamanca, I could see the town in the distance full of big buildings which looked welcoming as I got closer. There is a charm about the town and I love the place, I really do. All the more so because coming through now I knew that this was the end. I got out of the saddle and pushed a bit harder. Down in the saddle again and now the finish line was in sight through an old archway. Yes. Over the finish line into a courtyard.

I was hollow; as empty as I could be. All of me was out there on the road but I knew that it was a really good time. I was right: it came up as 2nd behind Tony Martin, who had been around a minute faster than me. Now I had to sit and wait for a lot of other guys to come through.

Tony Martin. I didn't count Tony Martin. This was his playground as well as Bradley's, but Tony wouldn't challenge on the GC. Looking at the GC, I thought, 'Okay, I am the second-best time trialist at the moment. I am very happy with that. We will see who does what from here on.'

I sat with Szrekkie for a few seconds at the finish. He put a towel around me and handed me a bottle as I sat there on the top tube of the bike, just waiting. Every couple of minutes he laughed with approval and patted me on the back. 'Well done, boy, *grot verdomme*.' I started to feel nervous. Around me people were talking about Brad's time and there were flashes of his progress after the second check. I heard the figures. Hold on, that time was down on mine.

Okay. I struggled to get to the end. Maybe Brad would make the time up there? As he was coming closer I was making the calculations in my head. I saw it suddenly – Brad wasn't going to do a better time than me. I almost felt scared. This was going to upset people; this wasn't the plan. And as I knew all too well, in this team we lived and died by the plan. Now I had gone and beaten Brad. It was as if I had coldly dropped him on a mountain pass, and this could be seen as a sin, instead of a good thing.

I was quite worried and turned to Szrekkie. The look on his face said it all: 'Ooh, you're in trouble now!'

He gave a half-sheepish sort of laugh, which was not reassuring.

As Brad came over the line, Szrekkie disappeared to go and catch him and sort him out. I looked around.

This might not be so good. It could cause problems. This was not the position I wanted to be in.

One of the chaperones from the race organizers ambled over to me and said that I had to go on the podium.

I looked at him blankly. Why would I have to go to the podium? I hadn't won the stage. Maybe I was the most aggressive rider or had I won some gimmicky award?

'No,' he replied. 'You are the leader of the race. Leader of GC. You've got the red jersey.'

Wow.

This was a lot to take in. It was like I had been zoomed out from where I was to this new place. I was scared, happy and trying to make sense of it. It was dawning on me now that I would be the leader if Brad didn't do it. He was in front of me at the start of the day, but not any more. I had seen the other GC contenders' times.

I was ten days into a Grand Tour, it was a rest day tomorrow and I was leading the race. This could not be happening: I was the leader of a Grand Tour! I would have the jersey for one day at least, which was more than I could have ever hoped for from this race.

Did this mean I might be able to get a contract?

That was all I had been thinking about in the last 7 or 8 kilometres on the long stretch of road where I could see the tar and Salamanca in the distance. All the time when I was really hurting, really struggling to find it in me to keep maintaining that kind of speed, I was thinking of the telephone calls with Alex and Bobby. I thought of Bobby asking about my contract and Alex telling me again and again that Sky just didn't want to say anything.

After this, would they want to keep me? I remember looking at Salamanca and thinking that today I could make sure they gave me a contract. I was not slowing down; I wanted an answer. I wanted to make up their minds for them with the time trial. That really drove me over the last few kilometres.

I had to stay around afterwards for the podium stuff, and tried to remind myself that this might never happen again. I should just be happy and enjoy it.

For some reason they pulled Bradley into the changing-room van too, where the podium riders get dressed into a set of clean kit. 'Why am I here?' he asked. He was getting quite grumpy about it and I didn't blame him. Why had he been pulled in here? He continued to ask but no answers came and the chaperone looked confused as I gazed across from where I was sitting in the van. I was embarrassed really. What could I say? If truth be told, I was still a bit scared. I just wanted a contract.

They eventually said to Brad, 'Okay, you don't need to be here. Just Chris.'

Sensitive. Thanks.

I held my breath, wondering what would happen now. Brad turned to me and said something friendly and approving: 'Good ride. Well done.'

And he walked out.

I breathed a sigh of relief.

Next in my mind was what the bosses would say. Brad had given me a couple of nice words but what would Dave make of it? What would Shane Sutton, Brad's coach, have to add? This was a migraine for them.

I did the podium ceremony, feeling that I just had to smile and make the most of it. I was in the leader's jersey, after all! But at the same time I felt very awkward and out of place. I was apprehensive about what was to come.

When I talked to Alex later I wouldn't be Cuba Gooding Jr and he wouldn't be Tom Cruise. Show me the money? No, I wasn't that sure of myself. More like, this should get me a contract? Shouldn't it?

18

2011: *Vuelta a España, Continued*

Day of Rest

I awoke in the morning from uneasy dreams and found myself transformed in my bed. Yesterday I was a bargain-basement domestique
having a good week; today I was a commodity. Forty-seven kilometres changed my life.

We were having a rest day and our team was scattered like fur-
loughed soldiers about the amazing hotel which was actually a castle,
a real castle. It was very old and we were the only team staying in the
lovely setting. We were impressed.

Alex Carera, my agent, was arriving to meet me. It certainly was
an old-world place to be speaking of new-world things like contracts
and cash but it had to be done. We sat in the courtyard and talked,
where I knew we would be seen.

I could sense that yesterday had caused some unease in the team.
'It's still all about Brad,' Shane Sutton had said to the media. I hadn't
said anything different and told the microphones I was really happy
to be in this position, and that I had never expected it, but that we
were all here to work for Brad. I went straight for the party line – the
safe option.

I hadn't spoken to Dave Brailsford or the guys at that level. I hadn't
even spoken to Brad.

We went out for a recovery ride in the afternoon and my teammates chatted quietly to me. Dario was very enthusiastic. He said
how proud he was to be with me, to be on a team where now we
were leading a Grand Tour and defending the jersey. He had taken a
lot of happiness from it. He had been there and had seen me struggling in Castilla y León and Catalunya. On a bad day at the Tour de

Suisse, he took care of me. He was one guy who saw I had talent but it wasn't quite showing. I trusted his views.

I asked Dario what he thought. Did he reckon I could keep this up for three weeks now that I had done it for ten days? Or had I hit my limit and was a bad day looming just around the corner? In an ideal world, could I go all the way?

He just looked at me. 'Why not? Three weeks. You just have to do ten days again and then you are finished. You do a criterium on the last day and that's it. You have done it now once already. Do it again. Don't see it as twenty-one days. Look at it as ten days. Start again tomorrow.'

That's so Dario. Pragmatic, simple, solid.

I was wary of being the man who goes into hospital with a terminal disease and comes out cured but moaning about the bland hospital food and the thin mattresses. I knew that when I came to Spain I would have been happy just to leave with a contract, any contract. After the last ten days, though, I was starting to think I was worth more. All that potential wasn't counterfeit. My belief that I was suited in temperament and genetics to being a Grand Tour rider seemed to be spot on.

In the short term we had eleven stages left. Brad had struggled yesterday and I had been with him in the mountains doing most of the pulling. I led the race on GC. I didn't expect, and couldn't expect, the team to cancel their bets on Brad but I thought it would be smart if they hedged their risk by having two protected riders for the rest of the Vuelta, and to let the best man win. That seemed like good tactics – good for me but also good for the team. That couldn't come from me, though; it would have to come from the management.

It didn't happen. In Team Sky we get many things right but the plan is still the plan is still the plan. Especially if it involves Brad, who has so much more history and friendship with the top table. I understood that.

I was still there as a teammate, to do the domestique role that the team had asked me to do. I was still relying on the team for a contract and I didn't want to upset people in the moment when I had at last delivered a notable performance. I wanted to show them I was a team player but I also wanted that recognized; I wanted for the team to simply say to me that although this was a position nobody had expected, on the long flat hauls I shouldn't be doing the heavy lifting any more as Brad and I should be recharging and waiting for the mountains. Ultimately, I wanted them to tell me that if it got to the endgame and I had a better chance of winning the Vuelta than Brad had, then I should go for it.

I knew they were holding their breath, though. They were thinking, 'This is just Chris Froome's career in microcosm. We've had the brilliant, but something will happen to dull the light. Stand by for his Tour de Suisse day, his Tour of California day, or his "landing in a front garden" day. It has happened before and it will happen again. It's just a matter of time.'

I understood that too.

But I was different now. One of the secrets of the last ten days had been that I didn't turn myself inside out looking for a result one day and then die a death the next. I was in the Vuelta and riding with the sole objective of being the best teammate possible for Brad; any urge to attack had been out of my mind. I had endured long, hard days but I hadn't had the chance to empty myself to that level; there had been none of my crazy, hell-for-leather attacks. I was always riding at Brad's pace in the climbs and I had learned from that. And what I didn't tell Dave, or anyone, was that riding at the front, just pacing Brad, was easier than the way I used to ride.

Something else that had been troubling me came to a head on that rest day. The last day or two I had been suffering from a bad rash and the previous night had been the worst. Brad and I had exchanged our usual 'goodnight' as the lights were flicked off and he fell asleep. I couldn't sleep at all, after all the excitement, and then I started to feel the red, welted bands around my legs. These were where my skin had been in contact with the rubberized cuff grips that stopped my shorts riding up.

I already had the red jersey but now, in a matching colour, were large continents of this itchy, angry rash around my body. If I scratched at them they would get worse and spread; if I didn't scratch, I would lose my mind. I had been wearing physio tape during the time trial to support my back and now there was a rash anywhere the tape had been. I had worn bandages on my knees, and there was a rash there too. It must have been the mixture of heat and moisture, I reckoned, as I recalled that for the last ten days we had been pouring water over ourselves as much as possible.

I finally dozed off but at about 3.00 a.m. I woke up scratching myself on my legs, my torso, my back and my waist – basically anywhere that had experienced continuous friction. It was crazy and I was bleeding from the demented scratching. Creeping out of bed, I found my phone and looked up the doctor's room.

The doctor was Geert Leinders.*

I knocked on his door and woke him up.

'Look at this.'

'Ooooh!' His eyes opened very wide.

He was very sympathetic for a man woken at 3.00 a.m.

'That is a problem.'

He got me some cream and I lathered it on to myself, hoping to calm the rash. I went back to bed and fell asleep straight away, thankful that the morning would bring nothing more pressing than a rest day.

In the morning, though, I started sniffling a bit. The health forecast was for a cold, or another chest infection, either of which would be devastating coming so soon after I had taken another dose of Biltricide following the Tour de Suisse. I told the doc how I was feeling; that I was a bit run down, and that I had a nasal snuffle and a snotty nose. 'Okay,' he said, 'as a precaution we had better put you in a room on your own. We don't want you passing anything around the team.'

So I was packed into a room on my own with my nasal sprays and my creams.

I felt sort of bad. Myself and Brad never really bridged that gulf of mannerly silence and now I was bailing out. On the other hand, at

---

* As I would later discover, my rash wasn't contagious, and neither was Dr Leinders's controversial past with the Dutch Rabobank team, about which I knew nothing.

least I was not holding my breath any more waiting for Brad to say something or bracing myself to say something that would engage him. I felt much more relaxed. I could answer phone calls, which there were plenty of, without feeling that every word was being digested right next to me. Things were a lot easier. I could speak freely about my contracts and about how plans and matters were within the team.

I'm sure Brad felt the same.

Looking back, I would love to have had Brad's impression of all this because as a team we were in a weird situation. But he never really speaks much within the team. It's as if he has his circle of people around him all the time who muffle our idea of him. By the time he comes back from races and gets through speaking to the directeur sportif, to Dave, to Shane Sutton and to his soigneur, I reckon he is all talked out. He doesn't contribute that much at the table or when we're all on the bus together.

He can make everybody laugh, though, which goes some way towards making up for this lack of connection. He has a particular talent for doing impersonations. In the team the guys reckon it is a defence mechanism, shielding him from his own reserve. Either way, he is very funny.

He does an impression of me with a really hivvy Sith Ifricin iccint. It's almost too much but that's what good impersonators do. It does make it very funny and I enjoy his humour a lot. He could be mean and bullying with the impressions but he isn't. They are just entertaining.

We get a couple of pairs of Oakley sunglasses given to us about twice a year. I have a child's delight in being handed classy sunglasses for free and it is still a novelty. One day I asked innocently if the bus had an alarm on it, because I usually leave my Oakleys on the bus overnight. Brad twigged that, and he killed me on it:

'*We cin survive without the 800k bus, think you, ifficer, but whit about my Oakleys? Are your min looking for them? Do you nid a discription? An artist's skitch? I cin't bileev this is hippinining . . .*'

He does a pretty good Dave Brailsford too. He picks up on all of

Dave's little motivational speaker phrases and runs them together like a slightly demented version of Dave:

'*The three Ps of our culture and of our team: Professionalism. Performance. And, ehm . . . Whatever. The two Ps of our culture and the W.*'

Our favourite is his take-off of our press officer, Brian Nygaard. Poor Brian really likes his wine; it is a passion for him. Wine and fireworks – Brian's face would light up when talking about fireworks. Brad took the fireworks theme, while playing the press officer, and all with a Danish accent:

'*A press conference is like a firework display: first you have the silence, anticipation. The small flares go up, you answer them, but then it kicks off and explosions are going off all over, it's chaos in there! Left, right, the one you never expected, then before you know what just happened, it's over. Time for a glass of Brunello to take the edge off . . .*'

We love the impressions but I think sometimes we all wish that Brad would give us more of an impression of himself. There is something else behind the impressions and the gruff geezer cloak but we never get to see it.

Alex and I sat in the courtyard and tried to speculate about what the team were thinking.

Shane Sutton had pulled me aside on the way to my room earlier in the day. He said to me, 'Listen, about your contract. Don't worry about it – we've got your best interests at heart. We didn't want you to stress about it in this period, and that's why we haven't responded. We want you to focus on the race. Of course your value will go up, but don't worry about that; we will sort you out. Just get this race done, and don't have all these people in your ear. You will get lots of offers now but don't pay any attention to it. We'll look after you.'

I wasn't sure why Brad's coach was telling me this. I told Alex I had been told not to worry, and that the team would look after me.

Alex took out his phone and scrolled down to show me his texts from Dave again.

'*What has Chris done?*' read the message. '*Nothing.*' Etc., etc.

'Does this sound like somebody who believes in you and wants to keep you as one of the top riders?' Alex said.

Nothing? Nothing! I was insulted. I had worked my arse off all year and Dave had the daily uploads of my stats to prove it. I had worked so hard just to be there in all of those other races for other riders. True, I hadn't backed these results up on overall GC, but I took it easy in time trials so I could work for the other riders the following day and I had shown good results on stages. Apart from one night in Kraków, I had lived like a puritan and trained like a martyr. Nothing?

Alex said that the best thing we could do now that I had UCI points for having been a leader was to carry on with the GC challenge: 'Just stay up there. When you have UCI points, teams will pay for you – points translate into contracts. I need those points to get you the best deal.'

Alex said that if it was okay with me, he would be putting out a press story the next day saying that I was speaking to other teams but that I had not made a decision yet for next year. He would tell people Team Sky hadn't given me an answer.

This was fine by me – it was the truth.

I had been on the phone a lot to Noz and my brothers, explaining the situation to them, and they had each said the same thing – their belief in me was total, and no matter which way it went from here on in the race, I would do well regardless.

I didn't have to sign anything immediately. If I slipped off the GC I would still have been in the leader's jersey for a stage, and my value would have increased. I had been in the top five a couple of times in other races and I would be okay. If I could see it through, then I would be worth a lot more.

I would have to gamble on myself again but it was fair enough and I wanted to get to the end of the race. If I blew up, my value would plummet from where it was now as I sat in the courtyard. If I did well, it would cost Team Sky a lot more than I would accept at this point.

Seriously, though, did our bus have an alarm? That day Oakley gave me a pair of red sunglasses to mark the occasion of me being in the red jersey. What happened if the bus got raided in the middle of the night and those Oakleys were on board?

Stage Eleven: Back in the Chain Gang

The words Alex planted with the media came up as a harvest – he had twelve expressions of interest from other teams. However, there was no word from Team Sky apart from Dave telling me hurriedly that this wasn't an issue, and that they would keep me. I was grateful, of course, but I didn't want to sit down to discuss with them how much they would pay to keep me *after* those other twelve teams had gone away.

I had been wearing the same pair of race shoes for the past ten days of racing. They had a flamboyant splash of red on them, and nobody had noticed till that morning. Bobby J sent me a message: *'Red Shoes? You had this planned from Day One, didn't you!!'*

That morning we all went to Steven de Jongh's room for a team meeting. It was our first debrief since the time trial and I left feeling disheartened. The meeting started with a general congratulations.

'Fantastic, you have first and third on GC at the moment. Chris? Amazing! Storming ride. Don't know where that came from but you are now in the leader's jersey. Well done.'

Everyone had a little laugh. Me too. Good.

'Now to today's stage. We have these climbs on this route. We want the team to ride on the front as expected. At the climb, Xabie, do your pull, and then Thomas, Dario, Morris and then Froomey and finally Brad.'

I didn't speak up. I remember just pausing for a second and thinking, wait, would it be the other way round – Brad then Froomey?

No?

Okay. I was here for Brad. This was Team Sky. This was how things were done and this was the deal. Although I was in the leader's jersey, nothing had changed. We had the plan. Sancho Panza should have been careful about what he wished for.

I was a bit disappointed though. Somebody could have come up to me before the meeting and said that this was their position: they were thrilled with my performance, they would be putting this much on the table to keep me because they saw my future going in this way, but for now, though, they had more faith and more of an investment in Bradley. I wouldn't have minded if they had asked me to continue doing the same job as I had been doing. But if there was a chance I might win the race, I wanted them to be happy about that. If anything happened to Brad . . .

This was surely where the team wanted to be? We were leading the Grand Tour and it hadn't been a fluke. I was in the red jersey because I had climbed well and done a good time trial.

The possibilities weren't explored or talked about. Or, at least, not with me. It was a reminder that I was just there to work for Brad for as long as possible, even though I thought that we could have had a little bit of flexibility. I was leading the race, after all, and the chance to continue leading it would have been good. So why not play with both cards, keep them both alive and then go with the one most likely to deliver victory?

The meeting just stressed the team's position: it was still about Brad.

There was nothing I could do, so I got into race mode again and my mood picked up. Going to sign on for the race in the morning I felt a new sort of energy – I was the race leader and people were looking at me differently now that I had the red jersey. It was a really good feeling and lifted me a bit; it reminded me that the jersey meant more than contracts and money.

Noz had flown over to Spain. He had planned the trip a while beforehand but it made me smile inside knowing he would see me in the red jersey that morning. He gave me a big hug when I stepped off the team bus and we had a quick chat before I went to sign on for the start.

As I was rolling through the first miles of the day's stage while fangless breakaways hissed and faded, other riders stopped by and said nice things:

'Wow!'

'Well done.'

'Congratulations.'

'Impressive.'

That was a great lift. A lot of the guys who weren't English speakers gave me kind compliments too:

'*Muy bien, Chris!*'

'*Impressionante!*'

'*A topé!*'

A couple of riders even said that for a domestique to be wearing the leader's jersey spread some hope and pride around the rank and file. They talked about how it had happened: working in the mountains for Brad, followed by a good time trial – the domestique's dream script.

I felt boosted by all these words from other teams and riders. The peloton can be a hard place and these guys didn't need to say anything to me, but they had made a point of it. That had never happened to me before.

Meanwhile, the plan that we had for the race was to pace things in a certain way coming up to the last climb. Xabie was to start off the climb, next Thomas and then Dario would go as long as possible until I was to lead Brad into the final effort.

We came up to the foot of the last climb, known as Estación de Montaña Manzaneda. Xabie got us on to the climb but then Thomas, for some unknown reason – because there was no breakaway that was really dangerous, and nobody in front who was a threat to us – did an enormous pull at the bottom of the climb. We went very deep into our reserves for a good 3 or 4 kilometres and the effect was that Dario was dropped and Thomas, who had done his pull, swung off. Xabie hung in there but the distorted look on his face said that he was not going to be able to do much of the pacemaking. He took a short spin on the front before fading.

Our teammates were supposed to be the mountain guys but we had burned them off before we were even halfway up. It was just Brad and me left in a group of thirty or forty now, with more than 10 kilometres to go to the finish. What happened to the team tactics?

I was in the leader's jersey, but as I was riding for Brad it was still my responsibility to control the bunch and ride on the front. I was looking about me. Shit. What now? Other riders were starting to jump around, making attacks. Something needed to happen. Somebody needed to get to the front in order to start controlling this.

Steven wasn't giving the orders on the radio so I turned to Brad and asked him.

'Okay, what do we do now that we have no teammates left?'

He just looked at me and sort of motioned me forward. *You go ahead.*

He was basically saying, 'Ride tempo, a steady tempo. Don't do too much, don't hurt yourself, but you need to control the race.'

So I got on to the front and rode up the climb at an even pace for about 3 or 4 kilometres until we reached a section which flattened out again. There, for 10 minutes or so, we had level riding, a little downhill even. There were forty guys who were all sitting on my wheel now, Brad included. We turned left and started the last part of the climb, which was maybe another 3 kilometres, and then the attacks started happening – real attacks. I had nothing in the tank; I could keep the same steady pace but I couldn't follow the surges and the other guys were really going for it now. I was hollow and Brad was gone too.

I felt so deflated watching the riders accelerating around me, knowing that I couldn't respond. I had spent my energy getting them here while some of them had been freewheeling or at least conserving their energy. Twenty-four hours. Everything had changed, and nothing had changed.

One guy left behind with me was Carlos Sastre, a Saxo Bank teammate of Juanjo Cobo. I was a little way back from him when he looked over his shoulder. Seeing that it was me, in the leader's jersey, he subtly eased up enough for me to get on to his wheel. Then he continued pulling. He could see I was in trouble and it was a generous, simple thing for him to do. Carlos is a Tour de France winner, who had no need to help me, so it was pure class. He had better legs than me at that stage and although he could just have pulled away and left me there to get to the finish line alone, he was saying, 'Look, kiddo, sit on my wheel and we will get to the finish together.'

He rode at a speed I could just about handle and I didn't need to say a word to him. The pace was comfortable enough for me to hang on and to limit my losses; Carlos saved me as much as 30 seconds. I got to the line 27 seconds behind Brad and Juanjo Cobo. David Moncoutié, the old fox, picked off the stage.

I went to Brad to congratulate him – he was taking my red jersey to bed with him for the night. Then I went to Carlos to thank him. '*De nada*,' he said. *It's nothing, no problem.*

I filled in my race diary that evening: 'In the leader's jersey, hard day but we had the privilege of riding on the front. I felt super today. Really well recovered after the rest day, also no bloating or holding of fluids.' I hadn't encountered that sluggish feeling I had experienced previously quite often. It was overall a positive day in my eyes: 'I stayed on the front and controlled the race until a little over 2 kilometres from the top where it all kicked off. I tried to limit my losses as much as possible. Brad the new race leader.'

Steven de Jongh had told the media: 'Hats off to Chris. He was in the lead but nothing changed with the position of Brad, of course. He is our leader and he still was after the time trial. Chris was a hundred per cent happy with that and he did an amazing ride. Bradley will thank him for that, I'm sure.'

And, in fairness, he did thank me.

All was back to normal. Now I could go back to being the domestique in the mountains, which was the plan from the beginning. Well, my plan from the beginning.

And the plan is the plan is the plan, after all.

19

2011: *Vuelta a España, Closing Stages*

Stage Fourteen: Rocky Mountain High

We wore black armbands today. A year before on the Vuelta we lost our soigneur Txema González. He was a beloved figure and is still missed, and he would have loved this day because we did our best climbing performance so far.

Nothing much had happened on stages twelve and thirteen. During the latter, Thomas, Xabie and I had fended off a series of attacks on the Puerto de Ancares ascent. Vincenzo Nibali took a 6-second time bonus in an intermediate sprint, jumping above me into 2nd place, just 1 second ahead. Brad and I finished the stages together.

Today, on stage fourteen, we were relatively fresh, and the last climb of the day was an epic: La Farrapona. It started with more crosswinds and Brad and I pulled the same stunt as earlier in the week. He was on my wheel coming up the last mountain and we waited till about 6 kilometres to go. I got on the front with Brad still on my wheel and we pushed on for a couple of kilometres to get rid of a few guys. It worked well. We lost Nibali and Fredrik Kessiakoff and then got down to just a few diehards: Brad, myself, Mollema, Menchov and Cobo.

There had been a break up the road all day but there were no key players in it. Rein Taaramäe, the Estonian, was in there, who would scoop the prize, as was David de la Fuente, who was Cobo's teammate, although he had to drop back to work for Cobo.

While we were shedding Nibali and company, Brad was saying, 'Easy, easy, slow down.' I knew he was on his limit so I sat up higher to make a better slipstream to pull him along a bit more easily, thinking maybe this would help him. I was a little ignorant as to the urgency of what he was saying. We were going the same pace but it would have been better for him if he had been sheltered even more.

I felt good and told him, 'Just a little bit longer.' I was not going to go at this speed till the end but we just needed to get rid of a few more guys and then I would ease up. I went hard for a couple more minutes and then backed off, telling Brad that now I would take him to the finish. Nice and steady.

He wasn't comfortable with that last acceleration. I knew I needed to slow because he wanted me to but at the same time I felt we had to push on for a bit longer to do the real damage. Over these yards our relationship was evolving wordlessly.

When I did slow down, riding at a steady pace with just a few left in the group, Brad asked me to get him to the '1 kilometre to go' mark.

'What the hell are you talking about? One kilometre to go? I'm going to take you all the way, sucker!'

Well, no. What I actually said was: 'No worries. I feel fine. I'm slowing for you. Don't worry about me. I'll take you all the way.'

Cobo had gone early to catch the front group and we had let him go, while De la Fuente dropped off the back of our group. Cobo wasn't really on the radar as a big contender so we let him chase the stage.

There were four of us in the group now. With that previous acceleration on the front we had gotten rid of pretty much everyone that mattered.

As we rode I was thinking about Brad. He didn't quite get where I was today. He thought I had done my effort and now I was blowing, but the only reason I had stopped was because he was asking me to go easy. I knew that I could take him all the way.

There were a couple of points where I was going steadily for the last couple of kilometres where he pulled around me and put himself on the front. This was unnecessary. He didn't need to, but maybe he wanted to do some dog work and contribute to his jersey.

The four of us – Brad and I, Mollema and Menchov – finished together.

I was hit by a revelation as we crossed the line. I had pulled really hard in the crosswind earlier and I knew now that if I had saved that effort for climbing on the steep part of the mountain I could have dropped people. I could even have dropped Brad but I worked to leave him enough space to be sheltered from the wind. That was the job, but the transfusion of self-confidence I got from this realization was massive.

I knew now I was controlling the guys around me on these climbs. The penny had dropped. I watched the stage online that evening and studied how people struggled to get on to the acceleration that I did, which thinned out the group into one line. Somebody would sit up, which caused a gap, and that was it – they were out the back, destroyed.

Brad was in red, 7 seconds in front of me and 36 seconds in front of Bauke Mollema. But I had felt quite good all day; I had ridden within myself. This self-confidence was a new thing.

Stage Fifteen: Changing of the Guard

Alto de L'Angliru is a 12.3-kilometre climb. That statistic is the most straightforward thing about it. Otherwise it is a mountain that just beats you up all day long. I think David Millar once made a statement about how ridiculous it is; that it shouldn't even be in a bicycle race. He was right. It is just too steep, with lots of insane gradients and one sheer climb that is so extreme you can never get a rhythm. But Angliru is known for this; Angliru is very, very hard.

At the team meeting we decided on everything as normal, all the way. We were still leading and I was riding shotgun with Brad. I was a high-mountains domestique at last and the team would get me and Brad to the last climb. I wasn't going back to the car for bottles any more now, which was one of the perks of my promotion.

About a kilometre up Angliru, once again it was only Brad and me left from the team.

The other riders around us were trigger happy and it was Carlos Sastre who attacked first. He was joined by Igor Antón, who overtook him, and then Cobo launched himself into an attack on Antón. He accelerated and was gone. This Cobo was becoming a problem.

I thought to myself, 'I am here with Brad. Stay calm.' It didn't even cross my mind to chase after Cobo; I knew I would have to claw him back at a tempo that suited Brad. I felt good – I would pull us up this climb and we would catch Cobo. I was ready for this. The mountain didn't necessarily play to my strengths; I had never ridden anything this steep, with these staccato efforts. I would have preferred longer and less sharp vertical climbs. But I'm sure we all would have done.

It took us 44 minutes to get up the mountain.

I didn't have a power meter on because it doesn't work with the smaller compact chainring. This meant no power stats, but from the beginning I started a tempo and I wanted to keep it very uniform. I paced myself. This mountain gives you no recovery. Angliru just goes and goes all the way. A little bit of flat here and there, but then it gets steeper and steeper, harder and harder.

Cobo had disappeared and I was on the front of our remaining group riding hard. Kilometre after kilometre, it got pared to fewer and fewer riders on my wheel. Finally it was just Brad, Menchov (again) and Wouter Poels, a guy from the Vacansoleil-DCM team.

We couldn't hear much on the radio because of all the spectators shouting and a bad signal. We couldn't see Cobo either – he had gone and he had kept going.

'On and on,' I thought. 'Pace it steady. No accelerations. Keep a rhythm and get up the hill. Get Brad up.'

We must have been 3 kilometres from the top now and every pedal stroke hurt. The cadence was down in the forties per minute, and even the high thirties. 'One stroke at a time,' I kept thinking. 'Grind it out.' There were birth pains in my legs now as they issued every stroke; each one a torture. I was feeling terrible and maybe doing seven kilometres an hour at the most. It was like riding through a sea of treacle and even people on the hill seemed to be walking faster than we were riding. The TV motorbike in front was wobbling because it was going so slowly. Eventually it toppled over and we had to ride round it. We were hurting so much we didn't even see the funny side.

I had been on the front for 8 or 9 kilometres now, for half an hour.

Maybe I was just slowing Brad down, I thought. Maybe I should move over and let Brad go ahead now if he had something.

There had been little communication between us on the way up. A few times he had said, 'Steady,' or had asked to go easier and I had eased off slightly. But now I was at a point where the climbing was really steep and cruel and I was struggling. It was like riding up a big wall and it was beating me. We were not going very fast and I was spent from pulling.

It was no longer best for Brad to have me on the front and I moved over to the left, even though there was very little room due to the lunatic crowds. Brad grinded past. I tried to come back in on his wheel. There had been some mistake, surely? It felt like we had dropped from maybe eight kilometres an hour to six kilometres an hour. I could see now that he was labouring and puffing worse than I was. He was going slower in front than he was behind.

Was he going to stop?

Both of us were battling with our gears – the wrong gears – and the seconds passed slowly. It was still really hard and felt like the energy was being pulled out of us and down some great sucking drain in the mountain. It was like we were doing heavy gym torture in the middle of a long race, on a hot day. Still, we shouldn't be ped-alling this slowly. We couldn't be. It was too much pain for too little gain. We rode at Brad's pace and I realized that we had definitely been going a little quicker when I was on the front. With this new, deflated tempo, I had reclaimed some energy. For maybe 30 seconds we had ridden at an agonizingly slow pace but I needed to get back on the front. I had more to give. I could take us back to a dizzy eight kilo-metres an hour!

Now, though, I couldn't get past Brad; the crowd wouldn't leave enough space for two bike riders. Then Brad wobbled heavily to the left and I saw a tiny gap open up on his right. I got out of my saddle and pushed myself through the little crack, and back on to the front. I was picking up the pace again and looked across and back towards Brad. His top lip was curled up in a wince of pain that I hadn't seen before. Ever.

Shit. Brad was done; he was spent. And I knew Cobo was in front, going for it.

What were the choices?

I didn't wait. Brad hadn't got it in him any more and the race was up the road already. I needed to go now. No words passed between us. I just looked at Brad again and we knew what I had to do. Staying with him wouldn't make him go any faster. It was every man for himself now, even if it would be seen as insubordination later.

I went. Wouter and Menchov tagged along.

I was pulling these guys now and they smelled opportunity. They hung back and waited as I pulled for the last 2 or 3 kilometres, before it flattened out on top all the way to the line.

I watched the TV footage later. With a kilometre to go, Cobo was 1 minute 10 seconds in front. That fallen motorbike meant there was just one surviving TV camera, focused on Cobo. There were no sightings of the red jersey group.

Then suddenly on screen I saw myself, Menchov and Wouter come out of the mist, riding like three bats out of hell. Menchov and Wouter came round me on the sprint and I finished 4th on the stage. Brad was 33 seconds behind us.

Crucially, coming 4th meant missing out on a time bonus. Cobo had taken 40 seconds in finish-line time bonuses that day: he'd had a 1st, a 2nd and a 3rd. Team Sky, meanwhile, had no bonuses. Menchov pipping me to 3rd place on the summit robbed me of an 8-second bonus.

That 40 seconds gave Cobo the red jersey. I was 20 seconds behind him at number two on GC. Brad was 3rd, 46 seconds behind Cobo.

At the finish I wasn't apprehensive like I was when I beat Brad in the time trial. I had worked the whole climb with Brad on my wheel and I hadn't gone out and attacked him. He couldn't hold the wheel; he had cracked. A few weeks ago he had a broken collarbone and he was human. I didn't feel I had stepped out of line.

At the finish Brad came and put his arm round me and said, 'Well done, you go for it now.' He acknowledged the reality: I had done the work and he hadn't managed to stay on my wheel. He was saying that basically now it was my opportunity.

Wow. How did we get to this?

That evening my world had shifted. From tomorrow the word was that the team would be riding for me. It was an amazing feeling to have got to this point. I spent half the night looking at every stage profile trying to figure out where I could steal back 20 seconds from Cobo.

I felt released, in a luminous dream which no accountants or corporate suits would ever know.

Tomorrow was another rest day. For a soul who likes suffering I was getting to relish these dawdling days.

Stage Sixteen: Badlands

The day was flat and long and I came 3rd on an intermediate sprint, gaining just 2 seconds. However, I was told later that I had actually come 4th and had to give the 2 seconds back. I had now finished 2 seconds behind Cobo, which meant I was 22 seconds behind him in the GC.

'Still, tomorrow, amigos,' I thought, 'we ride Peña Cabarga. On Peña Cabarga we would live or die. *Olé*.'

Stage Seventeen: *The Legend of Peña Cabarga*

The mountain where the day's stage would finish is close to La Pesa, the home town of Juanjo Cobo. He is known for some reason as the Bison of La Pesa, and so it was that busloads of his neighbours, many of them dressed as bison, had been transported up the mountain to support him. I have seen a lot of wildlife, kept some pythons and have even been chased by a hippo, but I haven't seen anything like the mountain bison of Peña Cabarga.

I had cased the joint. Today seemed to me the best chance of a heist that would net me 22 seconds. There were more mountains after this stage but no mountaintop finishes and I liked the look of this route from Faustino V to the mountaintop. It was 211 kilometres long with a short but very sharp jaunt up the peak at the end. Towards the top the gradient reached nineteen per cent, which after a long day with multiple climbs would grind and pestle us. There would be wheat near that summit and somewhere below on the mountain the chaff would be blowing.

On days like these other riders are able to do a lot more than me at the beginning but their output is a line that slopes down sharply on the graph. I don't start high but I decline very gently. The longer the stage and the more it eats into people, the better it suits me.

The peloton was particularly jumpy that day with lots of one-off attacks; this was the sting in the tail of the race.

Cobo had some good guys working for him: Carlos Sastre and Denis Menchov were his main henchmen all day but David de la Fuente and David Blanco rode strongly too. They got Cobo through the climbs with no problems.

It had been a blistering pace on to the lower slopes of Peña Cabarga and Cobo's men had done an impressive job making the race uncomfortably hard. I liked that. The explosiveness would be long gone from the more punchy riders, and I stayed as close to the front as possible without taking too much wind. It was perfect.

With about 5 kilometres to go, the phoney wars became real. Dan Martin of Garmin, who had ridden a good Vuelta, attacked on the lower slopes of the final climb and immediately I thought to myself that this was way too early. Yes, there had been a bit of a lull, but there was a long way to go and too many riders left in the group. Now was not the time to attack and I knew we would be seeing Dan later. Still, three riders chased off after him.

They were still out ahead when the Belgian Jurgen Van den Broek threw himself after them at a crazy pace. He caught them and overtook them. We were getting to the endgame now though. Van den Broek had mistimed everything and the pace had decimated the peloton. Now I was in a group of four with Brad, Cobo and Mikel Nieve, another Spaniard. Nieve took on the dog work as we approached 2 kilometres to go.

As we passed the 2-kilometre marker we were steaming past Van den Broek.

Then the crazy Belgian attacked again, even when he should have been dead. The pace was up once more and I felt myself go with him;

the pain was pure, exquisite and sublime. My lungs were burning and every muscle in my body howled for oxygen.

I got past and soon Van den Broek was history. We pushed on. I knew there were riders on my wheel or just off it, but the grind took all my concentration. Cobo was closest now and I pulled onwards for a few hundred metres. I wasn't thinking about the riders we had dropped. My focus was on Cobo entirely.

Then Cobo took over. We were on a steep part of the course and he actually started setting the pace himself. I had been expecting him to wait for other people to attack and this was a surprise. I followed him through a few switchbacks and under the *flamme rouge*. One kilometre to go. Everything had gone quiet behind me. I turned round and realized it was only the two of us left there to duel under the high and pitiless sun.

Just Cobo and me on the mountain. And the entire village of La Pesa, I would think. They had painted his name again and again on the road with a pair of horns protruding upwards from the first o in Cobo.

Just Cobo and me now, which suited him. If I got 1st place I would get a time bonus but if he got 2nd place he still got only a slightly diminished time bonus. I could do with having a teammate here to get in between the two of us.

Cobo had chipped this hefty shard of effort into the pot and now he too looked around to see where everyone was. He must have thought that he would either be alone or that the group behind would still be chasing. Instead, all he saw was me, which shook him. He didn't want to be pulling me up the mountain and I felt him ease off the pace a small amount. He hadn't got rid of me and I was feeling really good.

The road tilted up again ahead of us. I was just to his right now and he almost boxed me in. So I cut across to the side of the road a little but he was there too. He knew the game now and so did I. I was boxed in for a good 10 seconds and there were lots of spectators. He had me up against them, and they were hysterically excited. At one point a big ox of a man was running up in the road right in front of us. It was a wild scene. I really wanted to get out in front before

Cobo had time to recover from his pull. I wanted to attack and make this my one move; give it everything I had to put him in difficulty. But the big ox in front of me was in the way and the Bison of La Pesa knew this was useful.

Every second he blocked us was a second more for Cobo to recover.

In the end I got a little impatient. I dashed past Cobo on the inside and pushed up beside the ox. Placing a hand on his beefy shoulder, I shoved him out of the way.

I had a text message on my mind, which I had received from my old friend Matt Beckett that morning. He said, '*Just go. Don't go a little bit and then look around and then go again. Go once and make it count. Just put your head down. Don't hesitate. Don't wait for Brad. Don't do anything other than pedal your arse off. Make your move and make it count.*'

He was right. I was only going to attack once and I was going to make it count. All in. Everything on the line. Do or die. This was where I could win the Vuelta or lose it.

I was out of the saddle sprinting. I counted the seconds in my mind. One, two, three . . . until I had been sprinting for just over a minute on one of the steepest parts of the climb. Cobo immediately got on to my wheel again – he had the tenacity of a honey badger. He stayed there for maybe 30 seconds and then drifted off a bit. Even in all the hysteria I could feel that his presence now was gone. I looked down underneath my arms and saw that he was no longer there.

'Right,' I thought, 'I'm clear. I'm absolutely clear. This could be it. I could be on my way to winning the whole Vuelta here. Now.'

Stop thinking that, STOP, my brain was telling my body. *Keep your head down. Keep going. Block out the pain.*

But I can't block it: I've done a huge effort and sprinted for a minute – pain is all there is, replied my body.

Love the pain then, live the pain, argued my brain. There was probably just over 500 metres left to go now. I would have to dig really deep; I had to keep this advantage. Had to drive on. Had to. Had to.

Meanwhile my body was saying, *Go ahead, sunshine. There's nothing left. Less than nothing. Dig away.*

My brother Jonathan had also come to Spain to support me. He had told me that morning he was going to be standing just after the 'I kilometre to go' sign and that I was to look out for him. We didn't know the circumstances I'd be in when we arranged that, Jono! He sent me a text to say he would be wearing Team Sky kit. And lo and behold, there he was, waving a Kenyan flag so I wouldn't miss him. A policeman was holding him back as he was just as excited as the bison – a herd of them. He was screaming: 'Go on, Chris!'

'Well, indeed,' I thought. 'Can't stop now, bro.'

I went on. Passing Jono, I realized what a fantastic position I was in: I had dropped the leader. I got back into my saddle again and tried to keep my legs turning.

There was a guy running alongside me now. He said in very bad English, right into my ear, 'If you win, we kill you! If you win, we kill you!'

What an arse. I wanted to tell him that I was undeterred; I wanted to give him some stiff upper lip. But I didn't; I rode on. I needed to keep every little bit of energy now to get me to the end. I needed to sustain this pace and not to die on the bike. Not here. I could feel the lactate brewing up like a storm in my legs. Had I gone too deep?

I had attacked way too hard just there because I wanted to get rid of Cobo. But what if I had only put him on the ropes and winded him? Maybe I hadn't got the big punch in. He could have dropped off, letting me blow myself out while he sucked in the oxygen. What if he had paced it perfectly? What if he had sensed I was going too fast for him? For myself! He could have eased off my wheel and gathered himself while I was biting at the air and turning my pedals through treacle.

What if . . . ?

I could keep going, though; I could keep doing this. The road was starting to flatten out. It was not exactly flat, but not as steep as it had been with perhaps a reduced three to four per cent gradient, although it was picking up again ahead.

I could see the 400- and 300-metre markers in front, but they might as well have been a mile apart from each other.

'Where are you, where are you?' I thought. I still couldn't see the finish line. And then there it was: a long last straight followed by a left at the top – the finish line was just round the corner. *Ride. Shit. Shit. Shit.* He was back on. I sensed him from the noise of the crowd and didn't need to see him; I knew he was there. He caught me and he surged past me.

Unbelievable, *incroyable, increíble* – a babble of shouted commentaries sounded in my head.

He was a hard bastard. I was dropped and there was a gap already. For maybe 20 metres I wasn't even on his wheel. Hard. Hard. Hard.

I had to get up and sprint to control the damage – I couldn't let him take any more time on me. So I sprinted on legs of jelly, turning myself inside out until I got back to his wheel. I could sense that he thought he had already dropped me for the last time.

As we approached the final left-hand corner he was leading me. He had maybe 15 metres to the line, but I was on his wheel again. Surveying the corner, he must have heard the thunder of victory and seen the headlines already: the Bison was to win on his own mountain. But I would bet the farm that he hadn't realized I was here now.

The quickest path to take to the finish was the inside line, hugging the barrier. Cobo made a mistake: he drifted out on the corner. His mistake was only a yard wide, maybe less, but my handlebars would definitely make it through the gap.

My body and my brain skipped all formalities. The last kick I was capable of delivered no questions and expected no answers. I don't know where it came from but I ripped through the slender gap dizzy with adrenaline and aggression.

This wasn't the Vuelta any more. It wasn't the contract or the General Classifications either. It wasn't about the team and it definitely wasn't about the prize money. It was just about two boys on a sunlit mountain saying, 'See that summit, I'll race you to it.' It was 'I win you lose' racing. It was a high that nothing else can give you. Nothing.

There was no gap. And then, a second later, there was a gap. I was standing on the pedals ripping in as he tried to close his mistake. Too late, my friend. I was through. Our handlebars brushed together ever so slightly, and so fast that there was almost a crackle of electricity as I passed.

The line was 10 metres away and I was still out of my saddle. Cobo's head dropped. His shirt was wide open. Seconds later my arms were out. I was over the line.

I hadn't won the Vuelta, but I had won a stage in a Grand Tour – my first win as a professional. Everything would be all right from now on but that didn't matter to me then. I had just been in the greatest mountaintop finish I am ever likely to experience. Just to have been part of it – blow by blow – had been to know the best of our beautiful sport. I had won and he had won.

A few yards away Cobo bent his head over his handlebars as he stopped. People around him held him up but his head wouldn't be lifted. I, meanwhile, sat with my back against a barrier – dirt on my face, water in my hand. People were leaning down to me. We had turned each other inside out, Cobo and me, pushing each other to the limits and then pushing some more. Right now we were two voids on the top of a mountain.

This was special. People will tell me it was the single most exciting mountain race they had seen in years – belittled only by the reality that Cobo and I were not lead actors in the movie that was pro cycling.

I will tell grandchildren about this day sometime. Many times.

Still sitting by the barrier, the voices around me said I had won the stage by 1 second. Taking into account my time bonus, and Cobo's bonus, he was now 13 seconds ahead on GC.

This tough, squat mountain was topped by a huge camera obscurely placed in a tall white tower. An image was made with the light that was taken in through the lenses at the top of the tower. In a large circular room down below they projected the images on to the walls to make a 360-degree panorama picture of the world outside: mountains, plains, sea, everything.

It was beautiful, but it was an image on a wall. Just an image. Down below, Cobo and I were spent. We were two scraped-out shells sucking at air and water. We were unable to stand without agony.

We were real.

★

It ended there really. The stage after Peña Cabarga had mountains but a finish on the plains, although Cobo still eyed me all day. The next day was a sprint stage into Bilbao. I had stayed right at the front looking for any gaps to open up in the final kilometre of the sprint. I had taken a few risks to be further forward than the normal GC rider, mixing it with sprinters where I shouldn't have been. But Cobo was just as eager. He followed me around the peloton so that everywhere I went, he would go too. If I moved, he would be on my wheel. He wouldn't even let my teammates stay on my wheel. It was very strange having a second shadow.

He was odd. I tried to have a few words with him, as I thought we were tied together in some way after what we had been through. He had no interest in speaking, but he continued to fascinate me. He never wore glasses when he rode and never even wore gloves – he seemed a little set in his ways. Most of all, I knew he was nervous about me during those last few days. Whenever I pulled off to stop for a wee, he would do the same.

There were no obvious places to take back the 13 seconds, but I thought of the intermediate sprints as Cobo's lead was built on those bonuses. I would have no guilt about winning the Vuelta with bonuses of my own.

We set the whole team up like a train coming up to the sprints, but every time we did, Cobo was also there, magnetically drawn to my wheel. I tried on the flat but the team went too hard and too early when we were leading out and we fluffed it up. Did I mention that I'm not a sprinter?

Later in the stage we were to go over a climb and on the plateau at the top there was to be another sprint. As we went along a lake shore on the approach, the team said to me over the radio, 'Look out, Chris, the sprint intermediate is coming up soon.' I caught a glimpse as we went round the corner. The road went round the lake but 300 or 400 metres ahead I saw a banner. I thought that it was a sneaky place to put an intermediate sprint, just as we turned and lost sight of the banner again. But I also thought, 'Wow, maybe I can catch Cobo off guard.' We went round a couple of corners and, yes, I was right, I had glimpsed the banner a moment ago.

Right. This was my chance. He was unaware and not expecting me to dash off. I went as hard as I could. Even if he was coming after me, he wouldn't get me for these 10 seconds. I went through the banner, and although he came after me pretty quickly, I managed to get through first. I sat up with a huge grin.

But there was no excitement from the radio. No, 'Go on, Froomey, this is it.' There was nothing.

Gotcha! Cobo shook his head. No! No! No!

He pointed ahead. There was another banner. What? The radio crackled.

'Froomey? You know that was a banner saying "Intermediate Sprint 1 kilometre ahead"?'

The final day would be a criterium in Madrid and nothing would change there. So I gave it one last go on the day before. The team took over the pacemaking to try to make it hard in the climbs and we ended up with Brad and I having changed roles. He was going to do for me what I had been doing for him.

On the bus in the pre-race meeting I had said to the guys that the only card we had left was to make the stage as hard as possible for everyone and to hope that Cobo had a bad day. If that happened, I would attack in the last kilometre or two of the climb.

Thomas did a great job that day, a really big pull that exploded the peloton quite a bit. He handed over to Brad but it felt like Brad didn't continue that hard pace. It was more like Brad was trying to survive and get over the line in the group, instead of trying to fragment it even more. I tried to encourage him along, saying, 'Great, great, let's go.' But I didn't feel I could ask him to empty himself, even though we needed to make this harder.

I wanted him to bury himself, to die for me. But he was more conservative. I think he wanted to preserve his podium finish; he wasn't going to surrender that now. Maybe he thought it was all hopeless.

About a kilometre and a half from the top I went past Brad. I would try to do Peña Cabarga again: sprint and see if I could lose Cobo. But he was straight on to me. I went up with about a kilometre to go, dipped down for a few hundred metres, then down, around and back up again on a fast, sweeping right-hand bend. I was pedalling so quickly on the downhill, trying to keep the pressure on, that I almost didn't make it round the corner. I just managed to angle my bike to stay on course, pedalling at the same time to keep the pace up and to make it difficult to follow. I think he struggled following that – I was taking risks to squeeze on, to create a gap.

I eked out a small gap but riders who had attacked earlier in the day were now on the road in front of me. The crowds were going mad and had almost formed a barrier. I was coming really fast up a climb, when a French rider from Team AG2R and the fans blocked the road in front of me. I didn't really brake but I slowed down and had to force my way round them, half pushing the crowd and half pushing the rider to let me squeeze through and get past. That allowed Cobo to get back to me.

I carried on pushing all the way up but Cobo was comfortable. It was just the two of us over the top. We had started the descent when I spoke on the radio: 'I've gone as hard as I can but I haven't got anywhere. He's on my wheel. No point driving it down the other side.'

Stalemate. Over.

Cobo's Vuelta. Myself and Brad, 2nd and 3rd.

Still, the future was so bright I needed my Oakley shades.

20

One day I was a character actor getting bit parts; three weeks later I was getting my choice of the scripts. Well, almost.

First they wouldn't take my calls; now they were calling to ask what they could do for me — anything, just say, anything. Well, almost.

Life changed after the 2011 Vuelta a España. With the soft click of a switch my big future was ahead of me again and not behind me. I could have been a contender and then I was a contender.

Second place in a Grand Tour brings a cloudburst of UCI World Tour points and in my case a major re-evaluation. The performance was worth even more because inside the sport the result wasn't deemed suspicious. Credibility is currency in modern cycling. Despite all the toxic currents flowing through social media, the managers of rival teams believe Sky are clean. Riders and staff talk to rival teams and soon enough the information filters through. When I rode well in the Vuelta, I became someone they wanted. Just like that.

Of course, people had been expecting that I might wilt in the final week of the race but I actually got stronger. Suddenly there was a 'Wanted' poster with my name on it.

In terms of salary, I knew I'd jump a few levels, which was good news for me; but when wages increase, negotiations take longer. Re-signing for Sky was not straightforward.

After we crossed the finish line on Madrid's Plaza de Cibeles on the final day there were interviews and then the podium. I don't know how this happened but when Cobo, Brad and I got on the podium, I was on the wrong step. I finished 2nd but ended up on the lowest step.

It was my first time on a podium in a Grand Tour, and my first time finishing ahead of Brad in such a big race, but on the podium I was still below him. 'Well done, Chris,' I said to myself. I'm not sure if it was Brad or me who messed it up but right there and then I thought, 'This is not a photo I will be keeping.'

Before the Vuelta I would have settled for any extension of my existing contract but as the race progressed and I stayed in contention, my value was going up. Dave Brailsford still wanted the Vuelta to play out before talking turkey. Or talking to the turkey. I doubt that Dave expected me to hold it together for the three weeks. Wait for Froomey to have his bad day, then re-sign him for less. Maybe I would have done the same in his position. Business is business.

But the bad day never came, and when we got to the poker game I had some pretty good cards in my hands.

A few days before the race reached Madrid, Dave brought up the subject. 'Now that it's basically over, Froomey, we'll be giving Alex a formal offer.' That weekend the team offered us a deal.

There was a fanfare of trumpets. Uplifting choral music. Hallelujah!

But Alex was not impressed. He impressed upon me that I wasn't to be impressed either.

'Chris, this is not an option. This is well below your value. From the UCI World Tour points you've now got, you are worth considerably more.'

It was as if hemp had become suddenly fashionable; as if cycling-obsessed bald guys were what women suddenly wanted. There had been some tectonic shift in the market.

Team Saxo boss, Bjarne Riis, had been at the Vuelta and messaged me after he got my number from Alex: 'Chris, I would really like to make you an offer. You would be a great rider with our team.' He suggested a meeting in Madrid the night the race ended.

Noz had been at the Vuelta and we met most mornings. Normally the team got to the start of a race a good hour before start time. There was then a meeting on the bus and after that the riders changed and went to sign on. To make time for Noz I changed into my race kit as we drove from the hotel so that when the meeting ended, I was off to see him. I got him a pass for the corporate village and inevitably we would find some covered spot there for a chat.

Towards the end of the race, Noz and I talked more and more

about my future. What should I do? Which teams had been in touch with Alex? How much was being offered? Was I prepared to leave Sky? What team was right for me?

Unless I was genuinely prepared to leave Sky, my bargaining position was seriously weakened. Sky were gambling on me not being prepared to do that.

One morning Riis saw us as we were heading to the village. He stopped us, and said again how impressed he'd been with how I was riding. At that point I was Sky's leader in the race.

He then had a sly stab at Brad, hinting that he'd been slowing me down.

'You enjoying the freedom now?'

He also mentioned how impressed Alberto Contador, Saxo's leader, had been with my performance.

That last Sunday evening, Dave and most of the Sky riders and staff left Madrid. Keen to spend a couple of days in a great city with Noz, I stayed on. We hooked up with the Sky guys who were still in the hotel and we all had a great dinner together at a restaurant specializing in serving massive steaks.

The Movistar team were dining in the same restaurant that night. At one point during the evening their boss, Eusebio Unzué, came to our table, offered his congratulations and discreetly said that he would be speaking with Alex about the future.

All this was good – more suitors equalled more options. Although I wanted to stay with Sky (they had guessed my preference correctly), they had to deliver on two points: I wanted a salary that reflected my value and I wanted the opportunity to ride for the yellow jersey in the following year's Tour de France.

There would be no more bit parts.

After leaving the restaurant, Noz and I went back to the hotel. It had been a good evening but we were ready to turn in. The taxi ride took half an hour and we'd only just got back when Bjarne Riis sent a text. He was at a nightclub close to the restaurant where we'd just eaten and he wanted me to come and join him. I was curious, and so was Noz, so we jumped into another taxi and gave the driver the name of the nightclub.

Now, I am not a nightclub kind of guy. Noz is probably a few hundred years' worth of evolution away from being a nightclub kind of guy. He and I were riding in a taxi to a Madrid nightclub to meet a man who was once known within the peloton as Mr Sixty Per Cent due to an alleged hematocrit level enhanced by taking EPO. He confessed later to using EPO, recounting the scene in his hotel room when the Festina police raids were going on: 'I didn't have a choice. My vials of doping products had to disappear quickly. In just a few minutes I gathered all my doses of EPO and threw them down the toilet.'

The club was underground, which might not have been a bad place to meet a man with Bjarne's shady past. There were flashing lights everywhere and loud music thumping away steadily; it was hardly the perfect venue to conduct contract negotiations and Noz and I felt anything but at home.

To catch what Bjarne was saying, I had to stand really close to him while poor Noz didn't know what to do with himself. I felt foolish. Surely if Bjarne was really interested he would have come to us? But there we were, the business equivalent of love in an alleyway.

He used his lead rider, Contador, as the love arrow in the charm offensive.

'Alberto would love to have you on the team. If you came to us you could be Alberto's last man in the mountains for the Tour de France. Then you can choose the Giro or the Vuelta for yourself.'

He believed that this was what I wished to hear but he didn't really have any idea what I wanted. I was thinking, 'Hang on, Bjarne, it's the Tour I really want to go for.' He wasn't offering me what I wanted but he presumed I'd want to be in his team.

'Chris, this is how it will work when you join.'

One of the reasons I was keen to speak with other teams was that Team Sky had been delaying for so long over the contract that it would be a good thing if they got a bit nervous about my leaving. Another big reason for considering alternatives was my fear that if I stayed I would always be Brad's lieutenant. This was one of the things Bjarne didn't get; that penny never dropped. Why would I leave Sky because of the Brad situation to go and ride for Contador in the

Tour? Bjarne didn't ask these questions and couldn't get his head close to the idea that I didn't want to be anyone's lieutenant in the Tour de France.

But then again, we were having this discussion in a nightclub.

With the length of the stages, the climbs, the heat and the longer time trials, the Tour is the race that plays to my strengths. I didn't want a future that involved sacrificing my chance to help someone else win. There are enough teams out there with so few riders who can realistically compete for the Tour de France podium that I shouldn't be held back. Bjarne Riis and I were not singing from the same hymn sheet.

And I wasn't as in love with his team as he imagined I would be. He didn't mention Contador's positive test for clenbuterol at the previous year's Tour de France and for sure this wasn't the place to have the discussion. But it was on my mind, as was Bjarne's own reputation and the fact of that admission he had made about his own use of EPO.

As he was selling the team to me, I was looking around at where we were, and who I was with. I was thinking that to join him would be going a little to the dark side.

Very early in the conversation I should have just said, 'Thank you, Bjarne, I will consider it.' But that isn't me.

A few weeks later I would have dinner with Richie Porte in Monaco. We had gotten to know each other as he was coming to the end of his time with Bjarne's team and was about to join Sky. Based on his experience, Richie advised me against going to Saxo. He felt he'd been completely over-raced and that, as a young rider, he hadn't been that well looked after. He also felt the team was built around Contador and the few Spanish guys he surrounded himself with. This all seemed to confirm my misgivings. Still, I knew that plenty of other teams were keen to talk to me.

Noz and I met up with Giuseppe Martinelli, boss of the Astana team, the night after the Vuelta. Alex had warned me he was coming with a proper offer and that I should at least sit down and speak with him. Astana's headquarters are in Nice, close to where I am based in Monaco, so that was a plus. Alex thought Astana might work for me as, with Alexandre Vinokourov on the way out, they were looking for a new leader.

Alex came with us to Martinelli's hotel room in Madrid, where we discussed the offer. He spoke in Italian and the time I'd spent learning the language never seemed more valuable. I translated parts of the conversation for Noz. Martinelli said Astana would pay me more than double the annual salary Sky had offered.

From a business perspective, Alex hadn't been wrong: Sky had no idea what my market value had become.

What I liked about Astana was that they wanted me as leader – no ifs or buts. They would pay me a leader's salary and I would have to justify it, but I was cool with that.

There were minuses too. Astana were a Kazakh-backed team and though I'd overheard some dinner conversations, I couldn't tell whether they spoke Kazakh or Russian. Either way, I didn't fancy my chances if I had to spend a year or two with words in Cyrillic script stuck to my handlebars. A switch to Astana was obviously going to be a challenge for me. Vinokourov was central to the team and, like Riis, he too had a past. Also, Lance Armstrong had ridden for them in 2010 and, though we were still a year away from the 2012 USADA revelations, I didn't see the Lance association as a plus.

Still, I appreciated their offer and it showed me that Alex's reservations about Sky's offer were justified.

Alex then spoke with Garmin-Cervélo. They were interested but they had already spent most of their budget for 2012 and they offered a deal whereby I would get one figure for the first year and a significantly improved sum for years two and three. Jonathan Vaughters called me a few times and said all the right things. He wanted a new leader and would build the team around me. This was the single thing I most wanted to hear: a chance to be leader with a team built to support me. But their first offer was so far below Astana's that it was hard to seriously consider it. Alex went back to them and they said, 'Okay, what we're offering Chris in year one, we will triple for years two and three.'

From Madrid, I sent Dave a text: '*I love the team because it has the right approach and I want to stay. But you have to meet these other offers.*'

Money wasn't the only issue.

I also wanted Dave to agree that I would have the chance to win the Tour de France, or at least not to be stuck in a system where I couldn't. Finishing 2nd in Spain after doing so much work for Brad had given me confidence. Then when other teams proposed contracts that showed they wanted me as their leader, that made me think: why shouldn't I go for the Tour de France?

Dave listened and said that this worked perfectly for Sky because the team wanted to go to the race with two riders going for GC. It was too much of a risk with just one, he said. Look what had happened with Brad at this year's Tour, and then at the Vuelta. He said how good it was for the team that when Brad cracked, I was there to pick it up. Dave was enthusiastic and convincing and, though I wanted reassurance, I also wanted to stay with the team.

What I remember him saying was this: 'If you stay with us, we will basically guarantee to you that you go to the Tour and ride for GC.'

In hindsight I can see that Dave was being clever. I thought what he told me meant that I could go to the Tour de France and have my chance to win it. But he didn't actually say this. Instead he spoke of two guys riding for GC, with one being the designated leader and the other riding as his back-up. If anything happened to the leader, the second guy would take over.

Dave's approach was rather like a character's in *Through the Looking Glass*: 'When *I* use a word, it means just what I choose it to mean – neither more nor less.'

My understanding was that I would go to the Tour as a protected rider but the details were never teased out. Dave's words would actually mean just what he chose them to mean.

We talked about the salary and by now he was aware that other teams had offered far more. He wanted to know if I would accept a five-year contract. From his point of view, Sky were increasing my salary and giving me the security of a five-year deal. From my point of view, they were offering much less than other teams and I wanted a contract that reflected being a leader, rather than a domestique. It was getting stressful and I sent Dave a long and quite strong message saying there would be no more going back and forth. I also said that if that was the final offer, I was going elsewhere.

He called me soon after that, wanting to know which teams had made offers and for how much.

'Dave, it doesn't work like that. I'm not going to tell you which teams so you can just undercut them, knowing I want to stay with you. You need to tell me what you are prepared to give me to stay. If that isn't good enough, I will leave. The ball is in your court.'

To help him understand the seriousness of the situation I sent him a message saying there had been an offer of more than double for three years. We both knew I wanted to stay with the team and, to do that, I was prepared to accept less than was available elsewhere. So in that message I told him I would meet him halfway.

'This doesn't need to be difficult. You need to just tell me, "yes" or "no". I'm not looking for a five-year contract. I'm looking for three years with these numbers. You accept or you don't.'

Seconds later the phone rang. It was Dave. There was emotion in his voice, a tone that suggested he'd been upset by my message. In his eyes I'd given him what amounted to an ultimatum.

'Are you telling me that if we don't pay you that, you are going to leave?'

He sounded stern. I'd had enough though.

'Yes. Quite simply, yes. It doesn't have to be personal, Dave. You know what I'm looking for. Take it or leave it.'

'Okay. Okay then.'

And he hung up.

That could be the end of it, I thought. I'd pushed him too far. Maybe I'd overestimated my value. Still, other teams thought I was worth it. In my message to Dave I'd said he had forty-eight hours to decide because at that point I was signing a piece of paper – either their piece of paper or somebody else's.

Throughout those days in Madrid Noz was great and a calming influence. I didn't know why Dave had stopped negotiating through Alex, but by dealing directly with me, he made it my issue. I'd never been in this situation and had no experience of negotiating a contract. I was playing for very high stakes. What was clear, however, was that teams were prepared to pay a lot of money for General Classification riders that did not have dodgy pasts. Luckily for me, there weren't too many riders out there.

So that was it. Forty-eight hours to decide.

I quietly hoped Dave would come back and say my terms were okay. But while we waited, Noz and I went through the alternatives. Sitting in a Japanese restaurant with a writing pad, we made two columns – pros and cons. With the Astana money, I could create my own little world inside the team. I could probably get Bobby Julich on board, ask them to hire a couple of riders I knew, maybe even guys I'd already worked with, to create a group around me. It was definitely the harder option but it could be an interesting project.

It was easier to get my head round joining Garmin. There I would have the team's full backing, with English speakers all around me, and guys who seemed to get along well. Saxo wasn't as attractive. Part of me thought that Contador had become the Lance Armstrong of the new era – the main man but also under a cloud as the UCI and WADA (World Anti-Doping Agency) were appealing the decision of the Spanish authorities to exonerate him following the clenbuterol positive.

As it happened, Bobby was in England and from what I could tell Sky had convened a summit involving the team's top people to decide whether or not to keep me. Dave would be presiding, that was for sure, with Tim Kerrison, probably Rod Ellingworth, Carsten Jeppesen and Fran Millar. Bobby called me and I sensed that he had been asked by Dave to find out what I was thinking and whether or not I might actually leave to join another team.

I was non-committal.

'There isn't much to say, Bobby. I have given them my demands – they either want me or they don't want me.'

He pushed me a bit on which other team I might think of going to but I didn't want to get into that. Bobby was in a tough place because we had worked together and got on well, and when Dave told him he was increasing my salary, Bobby had thought that was a good deal for me. It was good but not the best.

Dave had asked him if he thought I was worth more and Bobby told him honestly that he didn't think I was. Bobby knew the team needed to invest more in coaching and development and believed the difference between what I had been offered and what I was demanding could be put to better use.

Bobby had no idea about the alternatives and I couldn't tell him at that point because he also had a duty to the team, so I wound up the conversation.

'Listen, Bobby, we'll catch up and have a coffee when you are back from the UK. The way I left it was that Dave knows what I want and I'm waiting to hear back.'

'Okay, Froomey. I hope you know what you're doing.'

After those couple of days in Madrid with Noz, I travelled back to Monaco and was out training when Dave called.

'We are going to accept your offer, so let's get this contract done.'

I was pleased and relieved. I immediately called up Robbie Nilsen in South Africa and told him Sky had agreed to give me what I'd asked for and that I would like him to help me draw up the contract.

Robbie knew what I wanted: I had to be guaranteed freedom to ride for General Classification in the Tour. They were the words I used. This would become quite a discussion point. We took the team's first draft of the contract and as it was just a standard contract we amended it to include a clause that would formally recognize my right to fight for the yellow jersey in the Tour.

To an outsider, unfamiliar with how teams work in cycling, it probably seems bizarre that a rider would have to persuade his team to allow him to try to win the biggest race in the sport. Isn't that supposed to be the whole idea of competition? That you try to win?

If only it were so simple. From Dave's point of view, the team's chances of winning any stage race, and especially one as tough as the Tour de France, are better if there is one designated leader that everyone else supports.

And he had Brad to consider.

Endless toing and froing between Robbie and Sky's people concluded with a clause that stated the team would support me in my ambitions in the Tour de France. In my eyes, that was strong enough: my ambition was to win the Tour and the team had officially agreed I would be supported in that aim.

I couldn't be too insistent with Dave because I knew I had to prove I could back up the Vuelta performance with a similar effort in the Tour. They still saw inconsistency riding in my slipstream. Never at any point in the negotiations did I say to the team that I could win the 2012 Tour, which would have been presumptuous. But I was saying I needed the freedom to try.

When Noz and I spoke about it I told him I thought I could make it to the top five in the Tour. The opposition was going to be much stronger than the Vuelta, but with the backing of the team, a top-five placing was attainable. Uppermost in my mind was the fact that I'd lost the Vuelta by seconds to Cobo after losing minutes working for Brad. That was one Grand Tour I had lost because I'd had to ride for someone else and I didn't want a second.

When I compared myself to Brad I knew that even though I'd beaten him in the Vuelta time trial I couldn't be guaranteed to do the same in the Tour; I couldn't count on it. In the mountains I would have the upper hand, but would I gain more in the mountains than I would lose in the time trials? Who knew? It was simply a question of having the right to find out.

After the Vuelta, we went to Copenhagen for the World Championships. On a circuit made for sprinters the GB team performed really well to control the race. Our aim was to give Mark Cavendish the chance to win the rainbow jersey. He didn't let us down. I would spend a year with Cav on Team Sky and never really get to know him, but I would come to understand that when the team worked for him that was when he was most likely to win.

A couple of days after the Worlds had ended Brad decided to speak publicly about his determination to win the following year's Tour de France. I was out training when I heard, and shortly afterwards I got a phone call from my brother Jono.

'What's Bradley Wiggins going on about? I thought Brailsford agreed you would go to the Tour and have your chance? Brad's talking like he's the only Sky rider for the Tour.'

Jono was pissed, and so was I. Brad had spoken as if he were the Team Sky leader for the Tour. I called up Dave.

'This isn't what we talked about. We said I would be allowed to go for the Tour.'

'Yeah, yeah, this won't stop you at all. Like I explained, we need two riders going for the GC. We will go there with Plan A and Plan B.'

At that point we didn't even know the route for the race, so we didn't know how many mountaintop finishes or how many time trials there would be. For all we knew, it might be a route that suited me far more than it suited Brad, but Brad wasn't waiting to find out. He was already proclaiming that he was going to win next year's Tour.

He had probably heard about my contract negotiations and my insistence upon a clause about next year's Tour. I saw this as Brad putting a stake in the ground to mark his territory.

What he had avoided saying was that the team now had two guys who could go for GC in the Tour.

I'd had so many conversations about this with my friend and lawyer, Robbie Nilsen. We had wanted the word 'guaranteed' in the contract but they had wanted something less binding, and in the end it was agreed that the team would 'support me in my ambitions in the Tour de France'.

By going public at the time he did, Brad created the impression that the team had only one guy with the ambition to win. I felt like I was being told to lie down, chill out, enjoy your new contract and forget about riding GC in the Tour.

I hadn't really analysed what Dave meant by Plan A and Plan B. Instead, I had a vague sense that Brad would have his chance to take time on everyone in the time trials while I would be allowed to go for it in the mountains. And the stronger guy would end up as team leader.

Before any discussion of how the team would use us, I felt we first needed to know how many mountaintop finishes there would be. If there were several, the Tour would be a difficult one for Brad. If there were not so many, but there were two long individual time trials, that would tilt the balance in his favour. With two or three mountaintop finishes, and the team's support, I believed I could aim for the podium in Paris.

With the team's support? That was a big question. Even then, at a time when I was getting a very big salary increase, I wasn't sure the team saw me as someone to lead the Tour de France charge. They knew that with a little more support I probably could have won the Vuelta but I would still have to prove to them that it was more than a one-off.

In the back of my mind there lurked a hazy fear which I didn't properly recognize at the time: might the team have been thinking that they needed to keep me because if they let me go to another team I could be the guy that would beat Brad?

After the season ended we had a team get-together in Milan. Mark Cavendish and Bernie Eisel, who had both recently come on board, were there. We had a few meetings over the two days and on the last evening we all went out for a night on the town. Brad was in Milan too and though we hadn't been close before, there was a new tension there which hadn't previously existed.

Now we had a reason to feel we were against each other.

The ink on the new contract was hardly dry and already I was unsure of my position. Salary-wise, I had been given a great deal, but I had the sense the team thought this should keep me happy. You can go for anything you want, Froomey, so long as Brad doesn't want it.

The tough conversations that needed to take place never happened. This wasn't the team's fault but mine. On the bike I can fight. Off the bike I am paralysed by passivity and politeness. I'm not confident enough, not assertive enough.

Blessed are the meek for they shall continue to ride for Brad.

PART THREE
The Tour de France

21

I am in my room at the Hotel Van Der Valk in Verviers, a Belgian city halfway between Liège and the German border. It's the last day of June 2012 and, man, I feel ready. Tomorrow is Le Grand Départ of my second Tour de France and though I don't often swear, let me just say that I feel very fucking ready.

This journey back to the Tour, four years after the first, well, there are tortoises in the Masai Mara that could have got here quicker. That's okay because I know how much progress there's been. That first Tour came a few weeks after my mother died. I prepared on a mountain bike while home for Mum's funeral in Nairobi. Back then, I knew so little about what was involved.

Now I'm part of Team Sky, the world's best team, and I'm coming back to the Tour understanding the race in a new way. Once I wasn't certain I could do anything in a race as competitive as the Tour. Now I know I can compete – I'm just not sure if the team will allow me to. It's not that they don't like me but Brad Wiggins is the Big Kahuna here. The team directory has no listing for Kahuna Number Two or Deputy Big Kahuna.

If I don't keep that thought on a tight leash, it will drive me crazy.

I want Dave Brailsford and the team to know that after a difficult first half to the season, I feel in the best form of my career. More than that, I want them to know that not only can I be the last man in the mountains with Brad but that I can stay with him every day. When there's an opportunity, I'd like to have the freedom to see what I can do.

Does that make me a bad person? This is meant to be a sport, correct? If you're good enough, you get the chance to win. However, I'm not sure the team wants to have this debate. Definitely not on the eve of the Tour de France.

Brad has ridden very well through the first half of the season and shown that he's capable of winning the Tour. He is Team Sky's leader and what the team likes more than anything is clarity: one leader supported by every other rider. They know I can be one of Brad's lieutenants, but I know I can be more than that.

Better to not think about it too much and enjoy the Hotel Van Der Valk, which isn't really your typical Tour de France hotel. It's too nice. It has four stars, big bedrooms, a modern lobby and a feel that borders on luxurious. It's a good place to spend our last night of freedom; from tomorrow we become prisoners of the road.

Right now I'm in the bedroom and my legs are inside the lower part of the skinsuit I will use in tomorrow's 6.4-kilometre prologue time trial around Liège. I've deliberately turned the skinsuit back to front and, using my legs to keep the upper section taut, I try to pin number 105 on to the lower back.

Richie Porte, my teammate, room-mate and all-round mate, is close by doing the same. Over the last six months we have become good friends. At first I wasn't sure about Richie but I'm like that with everyone; I give myself time to work them out. It didn't take long with Richie. He's chippy and what you see is what you get: there aren't many thoughts that start in Richie's mind and don't end up coming out of his mouth. I like that.

Pinning the number on to the skinsuit isn't as straightforward as you'd imagine. It takes time. As well as stretching it upwards, you've also got to get it hip-width. I like the pinheads on the inside so they don't catch the wind. Sure, they'll scrape my skin but that's better than seconds lost because of a fractionally higher drag coefficient. Richie has that smirk on his face.

'Nice performance plan?' he says, and then smiles. I know what he means.

Sean Yates, Sky's directeur sportif for the Tour, has come up with our battle plan. It details how Brad can win. It's a good plan, and tactically it's well thought out; Sean knows the ropes. Dave and Tim like it, but when I read it my heart sank. Brad is Plan A. There is no Plan B. Sean sees my role solely as one of Brad's lieutenants in the mountains.

Richie instinctively knows how I'm feeling. He smiles to let me know he's on my side and that, come what may, he understands my predicament.

I can't let Sean lower my enthusiasm for the race. I'm in really good form and though I'll support Brad and ride for the team, there will be opportunities. I keep telling myself Brad deserves to be team leader while another voice says, 'Yeah, but the team promised you'd be able to ride for GC.'

First things first. I need a good ride in tomorrow's prologue. To show them I am ready.

Next morning I speak with Gary Blem, who has prepared my time-trial bike. Gary talks me through the changes and they all seem good. At the bus I've got an hour and a half till my start time. I've planned this to the last detail so I don't end up waiting at the start line, which is almost as bad as running late.

I put on my skinsuit bottoms for the warm-up but don't pull the upper section over my torso. That would make me too hot on the turbo trainer. I wear an undervest for collecting sweat, then a light mountain jersey with a pocket for my iPhone. During the warm-up I will turn on my music and shut out everything else.

I check my time-trial helmet, fastening the strap to the right length so I won't have to adjust it later. I lay it on my seat. Holding the visor up to the light, I look for any marks that need to be cleaned. Then I fiddle with the magnets to make sure they are where they should be to hold the visor in place. Gloves are placed on my seat. Shoe covers ready.

I then soak two small pieces of cotton wool in Olbas Oil, stuff them up my nostrils, draw air through my nose and wait for the oil to start clearing my airways. A quick espresso and I'm ready for the turbo trainer. The team has set up the trainer on a specially built platform beside the bus; uneven ground can ruin a warm-up.

This warm-up; I could do it in my sleep. To do it right demands concentration. Think, get it right. I start with 3 minutes of easy pedalling. Then an 8-minute progression to threshold. At threshold I'm producing a power I can sustain for up to an hour – over 400 watts. I dance to the numbers coming up on the display fixed to the handlebars.

Two minutes of recovery are followed by a quicker 4-minute progression. As I start at 200 watts and need to get above 400, I increase my power output by 60 watts a minute until I hit 440.

I begin another 3 minutes' recovery, then I do three accelerations, which are almost sprints: two in the saddle, one out. Each lasts 10 seconds and is followed by 50 seconds of recovery. I then keep my legs turning for another 3 or 4 minutes. At 25 minutes I stop; warm-up complete. It is 10 minutes until I roll down the start ramp.

Back on the bus I take off the top and the undershirt; I have a small towel ready to mop up the sweat. A soigneur will help get my torso into the skinsuit, making sure not to rip my race number. If it is pulled too high, the pins will snap; this is an art.

I gulp down a hydromax gel, the one that tastes of pineapple juice, then I pick up my gloves and helmet. I'm ready.

The starter counts me down: *trois, deux, un, allez*. Just 6.4 kilometres – too short for tactics but I still don't want to set off too fast. Robbie Nilsen, from back in the day, has indoctrinated me: first ten per cent of a TT at ninety per cent capacity. I take one quick look at the SRM: 520 watts. That's good but not crazy. I'm going fast and breathing really hard. Another glance at the SRM: my heart rate is up to 170, which is as high as mine goes. I can hear myself breathing.

I don't know why it's so loud because I feel I'm going okay. Short, flat time trials don't suit me but this is not too bad. I keep pushing.

Right line into corners; nothing stupid. Fast and smooth; a kilometre to go. Empty it all now.

I zip through the finish where Szrekkie is waiting for me. I'm gasping for breath, struggling, but I can't think why. As I try to breathe deeply I feel like I've gone anaerobic; my body has seized up. I've never been so wasted. So helpless.

'Hey, boy,' Szrekkie says, 'take the cotton wool from your nose.'

Oh shit!

I'd forgotten to take out the nose plugs before the start. I'd raced the whole prologue with them in, blocking my breathing. Thirty per cent of your breathing is done through your nose. I feel embarrassed.

Really embarrassed. I've actually raced an okay prologue: 11th at 16 seconds down on Fabian Cancellara, a specialist in the short time trial. Brad is 2nd to Cancellara, 7 seconds down, and 9 seconds quicker than me.

But what has the blocked nose cost me? A few seconds, perhaps a little more. It definitely hasn't helped. Brad's 2nd place means the team is happy. No one makes much of a fuss about my mistake. Except the boys at the dinner table.

I'm one of the later ones to arrive for the meal. Bernie Eisel is sitting there with two paper napkins plugged into his nostrils. Funny. Genuinely funny. He looks at me.

'What's wrong?' he asks, all innocent, as if he's unaware he's got two tissues up his nose.

Brilliant, I think, just brilliant. 'Okay, guys, laugh it off . . .' My Tour de France has got off to the start I didn't want.

I was treated differently after finishing 2nd in the Vuelta. My opinion was sought. 'Froomey, what do you think about this?' The *kijana* was moving up in the world. The team had a system of rider representatives and I was asked to liaise with and speak on behalf of the British guys in the team.

This never really worked but at the time I was quite pleased with the new status. Perceptions changed on the outside too. People noticed the performance in Spain and towards the end of October 2011 I had run into Adam Blythe again. Adam is a British rider and someone whose company I enjoyed. He was about to the join the BMC team.

There was a junket to Langkawi in Malaysia and Adam was due to go with his teammate Philippe Gilbert, the Belgian star who'd won more big races than any rider in 2011. Late in the day Philippe wasn't able to make it and Adam asked if I wanted to go in his place. He saw the look of surprise on my face.

'Froomey, you were second in the Vuelta. They'd be delighted if you went. It's basically an all-expenses-paid holiday. You do one little appearance for them and they'll give you an attendance fee, as well as paying for everything.'

This wasn't a difficult decision. Between the beaches of Langkawi and time in Kuala Lumpur, we were away for ten days. It was a good trip and after returning to Monaco, where winter was kicking in, I was looking forward to a couple of months of the Johannesburg summer where I could begin my training for 2012.

However, in Langkawi, the rash that had started in the Vuelta had progressively gotten worse. My face was bloated, especially under the eyes, and it was very uncomfortable. In the middle of the night I would wake up and realize I had been itching the sores and making them worse. Then I wouldn't be able to get back to sleep.

Worried about using a medication that could produce a positive test, I was scared to do anything about it in Langkawi. I applied Nivea cream to the affected areas. If anything, it made things worse: the rash sapped my energy and disturbed my sleep.

Back in South Africa, I saw a dermatologist. Eczema, he said. Hydrocortisone creams were prescribed. They calmed the inflammation but after the next training ride, the symptoms returned. Bigger tubs of stronger cortisone-based cream brought more temporary relief but the underlying problem remained.

I'm not one for agonizing over how I look but at this time I could have done without the disfigured face. This was my time to impress Michelle Cound, a Welsh-born, South African-raised girl who I'd known for a few years and with whom I'd been friends in a long-distance sort of way.

She took photographs at races I'd ridden in South Africa and it was Daryl Impey who initially introduced us. We hit it off and once in a while I'd send her a text, she'd reply and we'd be mildly flirtatious. With 8,000 kilometres separating Europe and Johannesburg, nothing much happened other than the infrequent texts.

Towards the end of my second year with Barloworld, when the team had neither the money nor the enthusiasm to send us to a lot of races, I went down to Johannesburg on a short visit and asked Michelle out. We both lived in Midrand: me still with Noz and Jen, while Michelle had her own house. Though we were coming from the same suburb, we travelled in separate cars to Sandton, near the centre of Johannesburg.

We'd planned to see a film but instead went to Baglios Italian restaurant in Nelson Mandela Square at Sandton City. Knowing I would be riding with Sky the following season meant I was full of enthusiasm and confident about the future. Michelle was a bit further on in her career as an IT systems developer and was working for an insurance company called Momentum.

She drove an Audi S3, a car I really liked but only now, after joining Sky and moving on to a better salary, could I consider buying. Well, maybe I slightly exaggerated my interest in the car because I was hoping to kiss Michelle goodnight.

'Could I walk you to your car? I'd like to see the S3.'

'Why not?' Michelle said.

I checked over the car and thought about kissing Michelle goodnight. I thought about it and let the moment pass. 'My car is in the other car park. Would you mind dropping me round to it?' Inside her car, I'd be braver. As we said goodnight, Michelle gave me a hug. Like I was her brother.

Two years passed. I'd been involved in a relationship that didn't work out and a few months before I was due back in South Africa, Michelle and I set up a date for when I returned. It was not the time to get a horrible rash. But that didn't stop me and soon after I'd landed in Johannesburg we met for lunch at News Cafe, which was just down the road. For dessert, I invited her to come house-hunting that afternoon.

My new contract with Team Sky had also made buying a house possible, and as I'd been using Johannesburg as my out-of-season training base, it made sense to look there. Noz's conference business was growing and there were always people floating around at his place; I needed somewhere quieter. The roads around Midrand were becoming busier and busier too and more dangerous to train on.

I rented a cottage that my friend Matt Beckett's parents owned, and though that was better than my dad's in terms of access to training routes I still wanted my own space. Jono agreed to loan me what I needed until my new salary kicked in and I could pay him back.

Michelle didn't realize what she was getting into. That afternoon we looked at a house in Parkhurst, a northern suburb that has retained a village-like feel. Its 4th Avenue has cafes and restaurants that people walk to, and because I went to school not far from Parkhurst I knew I could head west or south and, after about half an hour of busy roads, I'd be on routes that were good for training.

Parkhurst is an affluent area. Although that first place wasn't right I soon found one that was. It was a lovely house, with a separate flat that was ideal for renting or having a friend stay to keep an eye on the main house when I was in Europe. It was the kind of home I never imagined myself owning or living in.

That first day with Michelle started with lunch, spilt over into house-hunting and ended at Luca's Italian restaurant in Sunninghill that evening. We got on really well. Michelle didn't seem to mind the miniature volcanoes on my face and arms. And there wasn't anything about her that I didn't like. We had plenty to talk about.

Michelle now had her own IT consultancy but had just been recruited by the banking and wealth management company Investec to be a systems architect for their operation in Mauritius. She could do this out of their South African headquarters in Sandton and was hugely excited by the chance to work for a big and progressive company. I told her about my hopes for the coming season and how I believed I could do well in the Tour de France.

After that first day we wanted to see each other again, and pretty soon. For the following two months, we were close to inseparable. I'd stay at her house, and she'd stay at the new house in Parkhurst. It helped that Michelle knew cycling. She had cycled with an amateur club in Johannesburg and even did a few stints as a team manager for some of the small local teams (she could have come in handy in Salzburg in 2007). Michelle ended up travelling to a lot of races and taking a camera with her. Her photos soon caught the eye of the local cycling publications and in the end she enjoyed taking photographs more than riding races. Understandable.

The new house was unfurnished but, fortunately for me, Michelle had decided to take December off before starting with Investec in January. The cutlery, crockery, cooker, washing machine, curtains, furniture and light fittings all became her responsibility. I thought electric shutters on the windows would be nice but hadn't worked out how we'd hook up the shutters to our power. Michelle sorted that out, too.

All the time my skin problem ebbed and flowed. Hydrocortisone helped with the inflammation but the underlying problem persisted. We talked about it a lot and Michelle wondered if maybe it wasn't actually eczema. The rubber in my shorts, for instance, irritated my skin. We were using Adidas gear and their famous three-stripe logo produced a three-stripe rash on my legs. Wanting to know more about skin conditions, Michelle trawled the internet in search of information that might provide a clue to the precise nature of my problem.

I went to another dermatologist in Johannesburg and spoke on the telephone with the Sky doctor Richard Freeman but nothing changed until Michelle stumbled across a photograph on the internet of someone with welts on their arms that looked the same as I had. She discovered it wasn't eczema but hives and treatable with antihistamine medication. I began taking one tablet a day and suddenly the problem was more or less under control.

Bobby called me a lot, asking how I was and how training was going. It felt like he was checking up on me. I don't believe this was coming from Bobby but from concern being expressed within the team. They were probably wondering if being put on a big salary would change me. Then they hear I've got a new house, and a new girlfriend . . .

And they worried that I might not have the same hunger. So without anyone ever accusing me of slacking, Bobby was making more calls than normal. That was fine. I liked Bobby and knew that he realized what kind of person I was too. I was two years into the team at this point and it was interesting that people still didn't know me. That was probably as much down to me as them. Either way, I wasn't going to become less dedicated.

One of the reasons Michelle and I hit it off was the fact that she had so much going on in her life. She had a great career, was close to her family, had a lot of friends and, basically, she had her own independent existence. She wasn't at all needy and, given my love for being on the bike, that was important. The last thing Michelle wanted was for me to lose focus.

Returning to Europe in mid January for the beginning of our 2012 campaign, I knew what I had to do: start well in training, use the early-season races to sharpen up and then produce the form that would show everyone I was ready to ride GC in the Tour de France. Our first race was the Tour of the Algarve, where Richie, who was in really good shape, was allowed to lead the team.

There was a mountaintop finish that was going to be decisive. We made sure it was. Though we didn't have the leader's jersey, we rode like we did, which was the typical Team Sky approach: try to control the race from the start, make it hard for everyone and trust that, at the end, your leader will be stronger than everyone else's.

I rode well on that stage as did almost everyone on the team. Richie finished it off easily, and went on to win the race. It was a good start for the team, but in the end, not that brilliant for me. Next day was a harder, lumpy day and I woke feeling terrible. Without an appetite or any energy, the moment I got out of bed I knew it was going to be a struggle. So I did what I always did at these times, I kidded myself: 'Let me just get into the stage and I'll ride through it.'

I put on full leg warmers and the thickest jacket I could find. On the bus I shivered all the way to the start, and something definitely felt not quite right. I spoke with Nicolas Portal, assistant director sportif, telling him I wasn't good.

'Chris, just try to stay in the wheels. It'll be fast until the break goes, then you'll be okay.'

Twenty kilometres in, I felt even worse. The break hadn't gone, the speed stayed high and once we hit a climb, I was off the back. Soon I was being overtaken by the race cars and when our second team car drew alongside, I spoke with Nico. 'I'm sorry but I have to get in the car. I'm feeling terrible and I'm not going to be able to get to the finish. I'm really sorry I can't stay and help Richie but, feeling as I am, there's nothing I can do.'

Next morning I was worse again so I was packed on to a flight back to Nice. For the following five days, I felt more sick than I'd ever done in my life. On my own in a tiny studio apartment, this wasn't an especially joyous time. The team had me on antibiotics but through those first few days they made no difference. There were times when I was afraid I was going to die.

Bobby later told me that when I abandoned the race on that Saturday morning, Sean had ribbed him about it. 'Ah ha, what's wrong with your boy? I told you he'd take the money and that would be it.' Well, there I was back in Monaco, enjoying the good life.

Having to pull out of Algarve was just an occupational hazard. It shouldn't have been a big deal. But often that initial setback is the first domino to fall. I'd asked the team a few months before if I could skip Paris–Nice as Jeremy was getting married in Kenya on the weekend the race finished. They said no. 'If you're going to fit into the Tour team, you need to be there.' I felt they were telling me, politely, that I had to do whatever I was asked. I understood that.

But I'd already told Jeremy that I'd be able to get that weekend off. Jono and I were the 'best men' so I had to be there. I asked Jeremy if he could put the wedding back for a week and told him that if anyone had to incur any extra costs to change their flight or their hotel booking, I'd take care of it. Jeremy put the wedding back and thankfully there were no extra costs.

A week before Paris–Nice I went for a training ride with Richie, and Bobby came along too on a scooter. We were on a climb when Richie pushed on a bit, and I struggled to stay with him. I was coughing every 10 seconds, as if my lungs were being squeezed, and I couldn't stop. Bobby moved up alongside me and shook his head.

'Listen, I've got to make a call here, there's no chance of you riding Paris–Nice. You will only destroy yourself if you try.'

I couldn't argue. That bug had been a bad one; the dominoes were continuing to tumble. Bobby told me to take it easy for four or five days and by the time Paris–Nice began, I was only just getting back into training again. On the day Paris–Nice ended, I went for a long spin with Adam Blythe. Our plan was to do a long, steady ride but instead of coming back directly to Monaco, we would ride on to Nice and I would watch the final Col d'Eze time trial on the Team Sky bus while he met up with his BMC teammates.

Our ride took us over the border into Italy and after going through Ventimiglia on the Italian side, I suffered a Crash Froome relapse. A serious one.

We were coming towards a border crossing at Latte and an inviting stretch of clear road that led through a couple of tunnels. 'I need to do a bit of an effort here,' I told Adam. As I occasionally do, I had used my time-trial bike that day. I needed practice in the time-trial position.

Adam tucked in behind me and I increased the effort. We were coming towards the border and just as I began to ease up, the road got a little busier. There was a cafe/liquor store on the right, cars parked along the road, but nothing dangerous until an older man suddenly stepped out from behind one of the cars, directly into our line.

'Whoooaaaa!' I screamed.

My brain saw him stopping when he heard the scream. He was going to stay right there. I was going to veer left. Everyone was going to walk away from this unhurt. But he kept going, quickening his step if anything. He shifted straight into my line and I smashed into him, my helmet crashing into his head. Down he went.

I carried on flying, but without the bike under me. I landed half on the island running down the middle of the road and half on the road itself. I rolled over. I had to get on to the island, out of the road. I needed to catch my breath. People gathered. Some came to where I was, others were around the man, who might have been in his late sixties, early seventies.

I had to know how the man was, but he wasn't moving; no movement at all. I sat up to take a look but that was met with instant disapproval from those around me. 'You mustn't move. Lie down. Keep your head still. You have a bad cut on your chin.' My helmet had been shattered. They were thinking *head injury*.

Adam had reacted to my scream by locking on his brakes and then veering round us. He was okay. All I could think about was the man lying there motionless. I felt sick, nauseous and dizzy. I kept trying to look over to where he was. I saw the brown paper bag he'd been carrying. It was on the road, brown turning to claret. His bottle of red had been another casualty. People were talking to me. 'You're going to need some stitches. Don't move until your head's been examined.'

'Please,' I said, 'can you check on that man. See if he's okay.'

Five minutes later someone came back.

'It's not good. It's really not good. There's a lot of blood coming from his head. It looks like he's dead. Someone felt for a pulse but there wasn't one. Just all this blood.'

I sat up again to look. Their voices were still telling me to lie down, but I had to see. A blanket or sheet had been put over the man. From where I was looking, it seemed it was over his entire body. 'I have killed this guy,' I thought. 'With my helmet, I have killed him.' It was the most horrible feeling I've ever had in my life.

I lay back down and thought, 'Christ. How can I ever come back from this? This is more than an accident. This is a situation where a man has died.'

I didn't feel at any point that it had been my fault. He had stepped on to the road in front of me, leaving me with no time to avoid him. I hadn't been reckless. No, this was an accident. But I didn't know what to do. I had my phone, and Adam was standing beside me. People asked if they could help but the damage was done.

Some amateur cyclists stopped and took photographs. I thought that these could be on Twitter and Facebook in the next few minutes. I thought of Noz, Jono, Jeremy, Michelle – I didn't want them to see them, not knowing if I was okay. I called Michelle, still lying there flat on my back. Someone whispered that I should ask to be taken to a French hospital as I'd be seen to quicker there than in Italy.

We were still in Italy though, so it was an Italian ambulance that arrived. Paramedics came towards me, then went straight to the old man. I strained to see. They took off whatever had been covering him, loaded him on to a stretcher and into the ambulance.

And I saw him move. He was still alive!

'This is so fantastic,' I thought, 'the best thing that's happened for a long, long time.'

They took him to Bordighera Hospital, on the far side of Ventimiglia. Another ambulance would come for me.

I'd lost quite a bit of skin from my legs and arms, but nothing major. I had a gash on my chin, but that wasn't too bad either. Then they discussed what to do with my bike. A man who'd been in the cafe offered to mind it until I was ready to collect it. Adam said he was riding back to Monaco to get his car and he could take it then. The police shook their heads and said it was part of the evidence. They were going to impound it.

We'd been given some new handlebars for our time-trial bikes and not everyone on the team had them. I'd got one of the last pairs and I was thinking, 'If they take the bike I lose the handlebars and I really don't want to do that.' I asked to keep the bike, but the police said no, the bike would be taken to the police compound in Ventimiglia. Then I remembered the old man on his way to hospital and the handlebars seemed less important.

While I waited for the ambulance I photographed the line of cars parked on the road beside the cafe/liquor store. All of those cars were on a no-parking line and if anyone was going to say this was my fault, I wanted evidence, just in case, to show that those cars shouldn't have been there.

At the hospital I had to sign forms I could barely read, before they took me for an MRI scan and then stitched up my chin. But mostly they left me on a surgical bed in a corridor staring at the ceiling.

From there I called Bobby. 'Listen, I'm not coming to the finish of Paris–Nice this afternoon. I've had an accident and hit an old man. I'm here at the hospital with him, waiting to see how he is and when I'm going to be discharged.'

The police said they needed a urine sample to check my alcohol level. Standard procedure. When the nurses came I asked about the man and was eventually told he'd fractured his skull. It was serious but he would be okay. More relief.

Adam returned in the car and had to hang around for a few hours before they allowed me home. It was a long, long day. But the man recovered.

In the aftermath of the accident I went to Ventimiglia police station close to ten times, and actually got to know the guys working there – two in particular were keen cyclists. They told me I had to pay a small fine for hitting a pedestrian, explaining that Italian law considers seniors in the same way it regards children and I would be held responsible.

Getting the bike back took for ever, but eventually I did.

The day after the accident I flew home to Kenya for Jeremy's wedding. Shaken up by the experience more than the fall, I was glad to have those days with the family. The service was held on the veranda of the Tamarind Hotel restaurant overlooking Tudor Creek on the coast just north of Mombasa.

It was a light-hearted service with a beautiful backdrop. During the ceremony they played a song that I hadn't heard for years but it was something my mother had always listened too, often when just she and I were together in the house. It made me feel very teary and, after that, I was choking back the emotion. It was just so sad that she couldn't be with us on this day. She would have been in her element.

The reception was on two traditional sailboats about a kilometre out on the Indian Ocean. The boats were roped together and linked by a bridge. We ate barbecued lobster, prawns, crab and lots of fresh fish.

Jeremy brought a mountain bike I'd left at his place in Kenya to Mombasa and the next day I got up early so I could do three or four hours of training before the sun got too hot. On the way home I stopped off at Dr Charles Chunge's practice in Nairobi. Charles had discovered my bilharzia and I was keen for him to check if it was still in my system and what level it was at. I'd also been having stomach problems and wanted him to examine that as well.

'The level's gone down since we first found it but you've still got it,' he said. The numbers were now in the three hundreds as opposed to the five hundreds they had been at the beginning. Still, it was time for another round of Biltricide. Dr Chunge gave me six big tablets, advised me to take them all at once and warned me it would be a few days before I felt one hundred per cent again.

His tests on my stomach found typhoid, another fairly common problem in Africa, and he gave me medication for that too. Soon, my stomach was feeling a lot better.

Michelle had a week's holiday. Women can seldom resist a man with parasites, a skin rash and typhoid. Michelle was no exception. She came to Europe to see me race at the two-day Critérium International. Girlfriends aren't typically welcomed at races, but Bobby Julich had convinced the team that I was in desperate need of some motivation. After being sick at Algarve, followed by slow recovery, followed by a bad crash, then a week in Kenya, I suddenly had a bit of catching up to do.

The Critérium International confirmed that. I wasn't good.

Michelle came back with me to Monaco, saw my little apartment and silently despaired. She thought about the days I'd spent here alone feeling sick as a dog after Algarve. It wasn't an easy decision for her to give up her job with Investec. I'd loved her for her independence, yet it was the one thing I was asking her to give up. She went home and, after a few weeks of deliberation, resigned.

The Critérium International had shown me that I was off the pace. At the Tour de Romandie I made a start at reparation. By then the Tour team was taking shape. Brad had won Paris–Nice and the question was who would be supporting him in the mountains. Mick Rogers and Richie were ahead of me. On the hard stages in Romandie, I was pulling fourth last. I was doing the work on the middle climbs too, but always trying to pull for longer than my body wanted.

I remember doing one long pull, thinking, 'I'm only going to be able to do another five hundred metres,' and somehow managing to get over the top of that specific climb before again counting in five hundreds up the next climb. Just a little further.

Mick was very experienced and I think he saw himself as the natural road captain and Brad's main man. He was riding well at the time.

Romandie brought me on a lot and at the Dauphiné a month later I felt like I was close to being back to my highest level. On the penultimate stage Richie and I were pulling at the front on the Col de Joux Plane, with Brad and Mick in behind us. The Joux Plane is hard but Richie and I felt good and pushed it. Or at least we did until Mick started telling us to ease up: 'Easy boys, easy.' Hearing that was good for our morale.

That Dauphiné ended in Châtel and we stayed on in the Alps for a fortnight to do a recce on some of the climbs we would ride in the Tour and a final block of training. Feeling good after the Dauphiné, I felt I moved on to another level during this last training camp. I'd been riding with Richie all year and he had generally been stronger than me in the mountains. Over these few days that changed. In the best form of my life, I would go to the Tour de France.

2012: *The Tour de France*

Stage One: Sunday 1 July, Liège to Seraing, 198 kilometres

At a team meeting on the bus Sean Yates outlined how things would work.

Brad and Cav were the protected riders. If one punctured, team-mates would wait and pull them back up to the peloton. I wondered what about me? Apart from Richie, no one would have guessed I might have been thinking along these lines. After all, what had I done this year? Fourth in the Dauphiné was my best result. Set against Brad's victories in Paris–Nice, Tour de Romandie and the Dauphiné, that 4th place was nothing. I kept telling myself that in the mountains there would be opportunities. There had to be.

The first stage was through the rolling countryside of the Ardennes but the climbs were too short to get rid of all the sprinters. Ten kilometres from the finish is generally where the jostling for places towards the front of the peloton begins. It's a fight you can't avoid and I had got into a good position; I was in the front third of the pack. Then I punctured.

Richie saw it. I didn't ask him to wait, and the team definitely didn't ask him to wait. But he did. Richie had every chance of finishing high up on GC in this Tour but on the first stage, he sacrificed that for me. That was an incredible thing to do.

We were on a long straight road that ran by the river, and a cross-wind was hitting us from the right. If there was one place on the entire stage you didn't want to puncture, this was it. Richie did a really long pull for me until we could see the peloton ahead of us, but with the crosswinds, it was so hard to make contact again.

Soon the crosswinds split the peloton and that meant we were never going to get back to the front group. The groups we caught were also struggling. Then the front group disappeared from view. It was out of sight. Gone.

We picked up our teammate Christian Knees, who'd done a lot of work for Brad but was spent and unable to do any more pulling at that pace. If it hadn't been for Richie, I would have been on my own.

I lost 1 minute 25 seconds because of the puncture, which was hard to stomach. All the talk I'd had with Dave about my riding for GC at the Tour now seemed like it was just that. Talk.

The race had hardly begun and already I was behind. It was a big blow. It also didn't help that, apart from Richie, hardly anyone noticed.

22

2012: *The Tour de France, continued*

Stage Seven: Saturday 7 July, Tomblaine to La Planche des Belles Filles, 199 kilometres

The Algarve sickness, missing Paris–Nice, *that* collision with the old guy in Latte, the Tour plan that saw me as nothing more than one of Brad's lieutenants and then the puncture on the first stage; most of what could have gone wrong, did go wrong. But I was riding well, and had what was probably the best form of my career. The first mountain stage of the race was to the summit of La Planche des Belles Filles in the Vosges.

I knew this would be interesting. We had been to recce the stage, and the climb at the end was going to be hard: it is steep at the bottom and never eases. It isn't extremely long – just 5.9 kilometres – but it is enough.

To get there we would have to go over a category-three climb and a lumpy approach through a bit of a forest. None of it was easy.

Ten kilometres before the start of the final climb, everyone was fighting for position. I was last in the Sky train, with Mick Rogers in front of me, and Brad in front of him. We were on the right-hand side of the road and were at the front of the peloton.

If you watch a bunch sweeping up a third-category climb on television it all looks pretty ordered: people swap positions, a line of four or five riders moves up through the pack, a guy peels off the front and someone takes his place. It seems like everyone knows what they're doing. But this isn't how it is.

Right now, to make a stressful situation worse, Greg Henderson had re-entered my life. For some reason he thought it was his right to be on Mick Rogers's wheel; Greg was now riding for Lotto, a

Belgian team, and he was a lead-out man for the sprinter André Greipel. But it was a hilltop finish – what was Greg doing at the front on a day like this?

I tried shoving him aside.

'Sorry, Greg, can you just let me in here? Climbers' day?'

Greg turned towards me and got aggressive. 'Why should I? You're always in the middle of my train when it comes to the sprints.'

I'd apparently caught Greg on a bad day; I never mix it with pure sprinters. Next thing I knew it felt like he was pulling right into me. I slammed on the brakes, just in time, but the deceleration cost me about fifteen places. It was the last thing I needed.

It took a huge effort to move back up to my teammates. I could only pass one rider at a time, leapfrogging from one to another, then waiting for an opening and accelerating through it. We got over the top of the category three and I was still chasing, braking late on the corners on the descent, taking risks.

If I didn't get to them before the start of the climb, it would be a disaster. I took some more risks and finally I reached them. Phew.

When Greg was in our team, I had listened to his harmonica-playing without complaint. I had defended him; told the lads he wasn't a bad guy. For him to do this now?

As soon as I got into our room later that evening, I would say to Richie, 'Fucking Greg, now I see why you guys didn't think that much of him.'

Back in the race, there was the team plan for La Planche des Belles Filles. Then there was my plan, which took the team plan and added a little bit extra.

The first part of the team plan was to make sure that Brad was well positioned when we hit the final climb. We did that. Then we controlled things all the way to the top. Eddie, Mick and Richie did the work in the early stages. I had never seen Eddie so lean and strong. Mick and then Richie did good turns at the front. I sit behind Richie, encouraging him to pull that extra few hundred metres further. The hurt is on; riders are dropping fast.

My job was to stay with Brad, and to take him to the last kilometre.

If I could take him inside that last kilometre, there was a 200-metre stretch that was really steep at the end. I couldn't help Brad go any faster up that little ramp. It will be every man for himself and that can be my launchpad to go for the stage. So I try to keep the pace as high as possible until I get there. If I'm working, I want the guys behind me to feel the same load on their legs. This is the bit that's not in the plan.

Richie did a good pull but we were still slightly too far out. Then, at probably 4 kilometres from the finish, I thought, 'Okay, I'll take it on.' It had been hard up until then and other guys had to be feeling it; Mick and Richie had burned off quite a few. This was how I liked it: not too many riders sitting on each other's wheels, waiting for somebody to do something. We've done a good job of this so far.

It was too fast for anyone to attack and when Richie handed over to me, my legs felt great. Riding on the front, I had one aim: no recovery for anyone behind me. So I kept the pace pretty uncomfortable. I still feel like I'm riding within myself.

Just before the top, the climb flattened out through a car park before kicking up to the 200 metres of twenty per cent gradient. I didn't want anyone to recover on the flat, so I shifted down a few gears and sped through the car park. Then we had a right-hand bend on to the really steep section. As we hit the corner, Cadel Evans surged past me.

He knew I'd been on the front for more than 10 minutes and must have presumed that I would be too tired to react. I'd done my job for Brad. He also knew that Brad wasn't going to like the steep ramp ahead. Once Cadel went by, I got a few seconds of recovery time, as if I were being pulled by him through the corner.

Fantastic, I thought, he's going for it. He was pushing on. Brad was behind me, then Nibali and then the Estonian Rein Taaramäe. Just five of us. Cadal's attack was perfect; he was giving me a lead out. Brad came up my right to keep tabs on Cadel, and got on his wheel, but he was blocking me in for a second. He didn't understand how I was feeling, and that I might still have something left.

I slowed a little, to allow Brad to go past me, and then I swung round him so that now I had some space on the right. Head down. Go! From the right side of the road I looked across at Cadel, wanting to see what he was going to do next. Would he try to get on my wheel? Was he going to come after me again? Then I caught it: he looked across at me and his head dropped ever so slightly.

This was exactly what I wanted to see. He came after me but he didn't have the legs to get back to my rear wheel. I won, 2 seconds ahead of Cadel and Brad. It was a special moment because I knew I had also done my job for Brad. I saw him at the finish and he came and put his arm round me – he surprised me a bit with that.

Brad got the yellow jersey and had to do lots of interviews. I heard him say something like, 'A fantastic day for the team. Chris winning the stage; I'm in the yellow jersey. Great.' Then he added, 'Now he's got his stage win, he's going to be an integral part of helping me to try to win the Tour.' I thought it was such an arrogant thing to say: Chris has had his little moment, now he can concentrate on his real job.

> WINNER: CHRIS FROOME
> OVERALL GC   1: BRADLEY WIGGINS
>   9: CHRIS FROOME +1 MIN 32 SEC

We rolled on. The waters would get muddier and the hills would become steeper. At the same time the cycling media began questioning the team's employment of Geert Leinders, the doctor who had been employed on a contract basis the previous year. Allegations about his past were hissing out like air from a punctured inner tube. Within the team, the mood wasn't as good as it should have been: Brad wasn't always happy, I wasn't happy and Cav wasn't happy. It should have been better than this.

One day on the bus Cav slipped me a note. He just leaned back and gave it to me, like we were in school.

Be not afraid of greatness. Some are born great, some achieve greatness, and others have greatness thrust upon them.

Shakespeare, Cav? Underneath, there was another quote, this time from Ralph Waldo Emerson.

No great man ever complains of want of opportunity.

I'm not sure what Cav reads between stages, or if the note had been given to him and then he had passed it on to me. It made a deep impression though and I still have the piece of paper.

There was something interesting to be said about people having greatness thrust upon them within the context of the team. Cav was unhappy about the peripheral consideration given to sprinting. He definitely gave me the impression he thought Brad was being given everything as the golden boy of the team. In fairness to Cav, and to Brad, I think we would all have felt that this was a role that Brad was being shoehorned into. The team's obsession with The Big Plan was making character actors out of all of us.

The quote from Emerson was more stirring. At that point I hadn't complained to anybody or expressed what was going through my head, but Cav was perceptive in seeing that down the road complaining would be a poor substitute for seizing the day.

I felt Cav was saying, 'Don't get to the end and say you didn't have the opportunity.' This was powerful; tough but powerful. I wasn't going to dandle grandchildren on my knee in years to come and explain that, 'Yeah, I had the chance to win a Tour de France but I passed it up for a quiet life on the team bus.'

Stage Nine: Monday 9 July, Arc-et-Senans to Besançon, 41.5 kilometres

Brad and I finished 1st and 2nd on the individual time trial to Besançon; the work with Bobby J and with Tim on the art of time trialling was starting to pay off. When the starter said '*Allez*' I also went, as I always did, with a bit of Robbie Nilson inside my head. The time trial left me in 3rd place on GC, 16 seconds behind Cadel Evans.

It continued to bug me that the 1 minute 25 seconds I had loss right at the beginning of the Tour had been so unnecessary. It just shouldn't have been there. As much as anything else, I was driven by the need to take that time back. Whatever I would achieve on this Tour I wanted it to be an honest and accurate reflection of where I was at.

I felt by now that the team didn't understand or weren't prepared to recognize that I was a potential winner of this Tour and if I wasn't allowed to try, accepting that would involve a very significant sacrifice on my part; they hadn't treated me in the way that had been promised.

I was in 3rd place now and I had my reservations as to how Brad was going to cope when we got to the real mountains, the real crucible of the race. If he popped in the mountains and I got to the stage where I had pulled and pulled and he was just dropping, maybe I would have to push on. Maybe then the team would have to go with me in the final week, as they did in the previous year's Vuelta.

That was hard but this was also pro sport. It is a hard world. I was not going to rule anything out at that moment.

I needed to be as close to Brad as possible in case I had to take over as our main GC competitor. That didn't mean that I had a rifle pointed at Brad's head. It meant that in terms of my own ambitions, and in terms of what had been promised, I was taking a bullet for the team but still doing my job.

Stage Eleven: Thursday 12 July, Albertville to La Toussuire–Les Sybelles, 148 kilometres

This was short, sharp and shocking: 148 kilometres of drama. We would race up La Toussuire to the line; the stage was made for me. In a different way, it was also made for Brad. One arrow he doesn't have in his quiver is the ability to accelerate away at the top of a climb and take a stage like that. He has the ability though to beat out a steady time-trial tempo and he had a team around him who would pull him up the mountain to a point where he would be safe on GC.

The plan was to scorch the earth again, just as we had done a few days ago on La Planche des Belles Filles to put Bradley in yellow. Still thinking of the 1 minute 25 seconds I wanted to get back, I suggested that maybe it might be possible for me to attack towards the end of the stage, after I had shepherded Brad almost to the top.

The response was a frown and a slight unease that the question had been asked. I was used to this hypersensitivity towards Brad's feelings but Brad was basically 2 minutes ahead on GC. Today was a day when we could kill off Evans and Nibali for him and take another stage for the team.

I wasn't putting my hand up and asking if I could help myself to Brad's Tour or have a weekend away with his wife. I was asking could I go for a stage win, and get myself in a slightly better position? I had ridden in Brad's service, as I was employed to do in the Vuelta the year before, and had sacrificed an outstanding chance to win a Grand Tour myself for the good of the team. I accepted that.

But my status in the team changed after that. I saw myself as a GC rider now and the team had agreed that this was how I would be seen by them too. Here I was still riding in Brad's service and I accepted my unchanged role, but I thought allowances would be made, and there would be some recognition of my personal ambitions.

The day unspooled oddly. Cadel Evans surprised everybody by launching an attack on the Col du Glandon with nearly 60 kilometres still to race. It was both an attack and a suicide mission. Cadel didn't believe he could win, otherwise he wouldn't have gone from so far out. Upon seeing Cadel take off up the road, I turned to Richie, no longer able to contain my excitement. 'Today, I'm going to rip his legs off in the final!' We worked well and we controlled well. There was no panic. We pulled him back on Croix de Fer and from there onwards his chance of winning the Tour was more or less over.

Richie led us into the climb of La Toussuire. Our group had thirteen riders in it, full of colourful fish, but the only fin sticking out of the water was Nibali. Twelve kilometres from the top, Nibali made his move.

As if shot from a gun he was up the road before we even heard the gunfire.

I looked at Brad. Richie looked at Brad. Richie looked at me.

'Froomey, you need to go. I'm done.'

This was a game for GC riders now. I was feeling good; better than good. Again there was no panic and I brought Nibali back with about 10 kilometres to go. Brad clamped on to my wheel. All was well; all was calm.

Nibali is pesky though. Always. He went again. Tsk tsk, Vincenzo. Now I could either put the foot down to go after him again. Or I could play smart.

I knew the climb was going to get even harder quite soon and I wanted Cadel Evans to expose himself. Maybe even attack again. He was hanging on the back. Was he recovering, saving up for another attack, or was he on life support after his effort earlier?

So I began displaying a few signs of weakness.

Look, Cadel, here, I'm struggling a little. My head is rolling, I'm flapping a bit, lurching off a straight line. This is hurting.

I wanted Cadel and Frank Schleck, who had also been having a free ride up the mountain, to think they had me on the ropes. Let them think they could get rid of me.

In my mind, the second they had made their move I was going to drive back on to the front. It was a case of control, control, control. Let them waste their energy and then burn the picture of me going past them on to their brains.

If I just kept riding at the front, they would have another free ride back to Nibali.

Now we started going downhill for a bit.

Okay, Cadel, how dead do I need to look? I really needed him to take the bait.

Please, Cadel. Come on. Attack. Take me. Let me see your jersey streaking past me. Look at my shoulders. I'm dying here. I'm swaying. Show me no mercy.

He didn't bite. Mainly because he had no teeth left, but I didn't know that yet.

Aw, look Cadel. I'm almost done. Stick a fork in me, man.

Hmmm. Nothing.

This was getting silly. I dropped back to get a good look at Cadel. I wanted to look as if I was struggling and at the same to time see if he was struggling too. I put on my best grimace.

Brad was at the front now and he wasn't panicking. He wasn't going super deep but setting a steady tempo. When I dropped to the back I got the car on the radio just to reassure them.

'I'm okay, I'm okay, I'm good.'

They would pass that on to Brad. When the climb ramped up again in about half a kilometre he could expect me to be there again. For now we were on a fairly gentle stretch and I was still taking Cadel's pulse.

But there was no pulse. He wasn't pedalling well and unless he was a better actor than I was, his body language was screaming out that his day was done. It was time to go and bring Brad back up to Nibali. I was enjoying this now.

Nibali was now the last threat, about 15 seconds up the road. There was plenty of road left to catch him and break him; it would be job done.

I rejoined Brad and went past, assuming he had latched on. I could hear him though. He was saying to me, 'Easy, easy, go easy.'

And I was saying, 'C'mon, Brad, we're almost up to Nibali.'

I could see Nibali just 20 or 30 metres ahead; he couldn't have much left.

'We're almost there. Then you can relax. Stay on my wheel.'

When I looked back at Brad though I could see he was suffering. Shit. If he could just hold on till we caught Nibali it would get easier from there. Once Nibali surrendered, the train would slow down.

Evans was already gone and now Frank Schleck fell back down the mountain. One minute he was clinging on, the next minute he was a tiny figure receding into the road behind.

This road was steep now. It was hard work but we almost had Nibali.

'Hang on, Brad. We have him.'

Nibali had latched on to a couple of guys ahead of him, Thibaut Pinot and Jurgen Van den Broek. This was good as they weren't going anywhere and there were five of us now.

Me – feeling good.

Nibali – spent.

Pinot – spent.

Van den Broek – spent.

Brad – spent but with a teammate to pull him along.

We were coming to a tiny village, Le Corbier. I said to Brad, 'Okay, get on to those wheels and just stay on them.'

Nibali was pulling the group at this moment. I would let him. He had made two attacks already and we had dealt with both. He was in trouble.

Brad wasn't saying anything at this point.

I decided to go, right then and there. I swung left and pushed past Nibali. *Okay, Vincenzo. What have you got now?*

The road was getting steeper. We rode from out of a shadow,

round a bend back into sunshine. The crowds on the climb were spilling on to the road. It felt electric; pure racing.

Brad could sit on their wheels while they chased me. I'll be damned if they're going to catch me, though! Brad and I were going to be 1 and 2 on GC tonight. Behind me, though, Brad had been dropped by Nibali straight away. Either Nibali had more left than I had thought or Brad had less.

Sean Yates was in my ear on the radio.

'Froomey, Froomey, Froomey. I'm hoping you've got the okay from Bradley for that?'

He was telling me that unless Brad explicitly said I could go, I would be having a spell in the naughty corner. I kept pushing. Then I heard Brad's voice on the radio.

'NOOOO, NOOOO, NOOOO.'

He sounded like a man who had just dropped his oxygen tank near the top of Everest.

I could hear that he was in trouble; my plan hadn't worked. I slowed immediately. Brad was panicking; I could hear his desperation.

This was all wrong. He was folding physically and mentally, and quicker than I had thought possible. I got the feeling that he would literally just get off his bike were I to carry on pushing. What was a simple and perfect plan to me seemed to translate for Brad into a public humiliation.

This was an extraordinary moment for the team. We were the people of marginal gains. We controlled the controllables. But where was the margin now? Where was the gain? Where was the control?

This was sport. This was life. It was as hard as it gets, and if it breaks you, there was no shame. You get knocked down, you get back up again.

These were the questions these mountains and this race were supposed to ask. This was the moment when the team decided. Stick with the plan? Seize the day? Big moment, Chris.

I slowed and waited for Brad, who had almost sat up by now. Two minutes ago we were riding at a faster pace and Brad was fine. He hadn't just cracked; I think he felt betrayed. By the time he was back in touch with me, Pinot had gone again and Nibali and Van den

Broek were dawdling, waiting for the free ride they'd get when Brad docked once more with the mother ship.

Brad perked up a little when he was back on the wheel. I was pulling again and the climb had eased off so it was quite a lot easier to stay on the wheel. I pulled faster. We could at least get Pinot back at this rate.

We hauled Pinot back in, along with a couple of other stragglers too. I had time to think as we rode. All around us the crowds were jostling and cheering, but not much of the internal drama was known to them at this point.

How would this play out? I had made an attack that the team didn't think was a good idea. I then called it off. All the same, I knew that by nightfall I would be in the stockades.

The history of cycling is littered with instances like this. In some cases, the guy who was stronger than his team leader said, 'Fuck it, this may never come around for me again.' Stephen Roche attacking Roberto Visentini in the 1987 Giro d'Italia is probably the great modern-day example. Over time many people have forgotten Roche went against team orders, remembering only that he won the race.

I'm the guy who turned back with the blue light flashing.

I pulled them to the end and when we rounded the last bend, with 50 metres of road left, I put my head down. Pinot and myself sprinted for the line but he edged me out. Surviving from an earlier breakaway, Pierre Rolland won the stage with Pinot 2nd and me 3rd. As a reflex, I looked behind to check on Brad as I crossed the line. He had lost a couple of seconds but Nibali was with him. Job done. Now for the bloody postmortem.

WINNER: PIERRE ROLLAND
OVERALL GC   1: BRADLEY WIGGINS
                 2: CHRIS FROOME + 2 MIN 05 SEC

23

Case for the Defence: By nature, m'Lord, Mr Froome is incredibly stubborn. He had a plan in his head; he felt it was a good plan. He was going to see it through. When the plan succeeded, all would see the beauty of his thinking.

Case for the Prosecution: Mr Wiggins or the agents thereof had retained the services of Mr Froome to do a specific job of adventuring. At a time when he could not be sure of Mr Wiggins's good health or spirits, Mr Froome chose to continue the adventure on his own thus causing physical and psychological damage to Mr Wiggins and spoiling everything.

Moreover Mr Froome had with some impertinence told Mr Wiggins what to do. Mr Wiggins had subsequently been brought 'close to the edge'.

I could see the point. Brad was a cycling track star who had been absorbed into road racing at a high level. He had never really been given orders in the way a domestique gets given orders. He was officer class, not enlisted.

His experience was that he just said 'faster' or 'slower' and the world around him went faster or slower.

Even in team meetings he would never pipe up and say, 'Okay, guys, this is what we are going to do today.' That job would be done for him. On the road he would supervise the implementation. Faster. Slower.

I knew there would be a reaction. Everybody had seen me go and what I had hoped would happen behind me hadn't happened.

After crossing the line, the inquisition began. I was mobbed by a swarm of journalists.

'Could you have won today?'

'What happened out there?'

'Were you pulled back there by the team?'

I gave my explanation.

I had thought I would try to gain some time back today. I thought Bradley was in a good place. He obviously wasn't. As soon as I heard that, I waited for him and brought him all the way to the finish.

The good lieutenant. No big deal.

A couple of journalists really pushed the point.

'But you could have won today, couldn't you?'

'You could have taken the leader's jersey today, how do you feel about that?'

I just responded along the party line. 'I know I'm here to do a job for Brad and he's the leader and I'm here to do a job, end of story.'

I never tried to say that wanting to win should not be such a bad thing.

Brad, though, was clearly rattled. He told journalists it was just a mix-up: Sean had said, 'Slow, slow, slow,' but because of crowd noise Chris thought he said, 'Go, go, go.' One of those things.

Sean Yates wasn't in the loop. He said I had pissed him off.

Going back to the hotel I knew there would be more to come.

The hotel was right by the finish; I could have done with a bus journey. When I got back some of the guys were finishing their warm-downs in an abandoned room on the ground floor.

Mario Pafundi came across and spoke a few words to me. Typical Mario. 'No problems, no problems. All good.'

No one came over and said, 'Christ, what the hell were you doing out there, Froomey?'

I warmed down as normal, went upstairs and showered. I then waited for Richie to finish on the massage table and made a few calls. I wondered if clouds were gathering.

My mind rewound the tape to the point where I had suggested before the stage that I might be allowed to attack. Sean Yates had made a point of saying, 'Uh, listen, Froomey, we know you want to attack but . . .'

We had agreed that Brad would be taken to the last kilometre or so. I had asked what was the difference if Brad was safe with 5 kilometres to go: 'If the opportunity presents itself, can I not go with

5 or 6 kilometres to go when the road is still hard, before it flattens out?'

In my mind was the fact that if I could only go with 500 metres left I could only reclaim a fraction of my lost minute and 25 seconds. Attacking that late was basically not attacking at all.

Sean had come back at me saying, 'Well, no, we're here to do this job. No, you're not going to attack far out.'

I went to Sean again about it and made the point again. 'I really want to attack today. I'm feeling fresh and I can definitely get back some of the time that I've lost. I need to get a good buffer over Cadel and Nibali so that if something does happen to Brad, I can take over with no problems.'

A little while later, Dave had called me to the back of the bus.

'Froomey, come in here a minute.'

Dave was disturbed. The tone in his voice was agitated. When he is worried his eyes get bigger than normal. They were like two planets now.

'Froomey, all this talk of attacking is beginning to unsettle people now and we're going to fall off track if we're not careful . . .' He made a gesture with his hands to suggest this sort of togetherness of the team. He was like an upset vicar. He was almost shaking at this point.

Okay, I said to myself, he's bothered now. Brad must be upset. That makes Sean upset.

I said to him, 'Dave, this isn't what we talked about. I was told I was going to have freedom in this Tour to go for it on the climbs. These are not the conditions under which I stayed at Sky.'

I'd called Michelle earlier that morning and said, 'Please go through my contract and just check exactly what the wording says. I'm going to need to remind Dave of that today. I'm going to tell him that I have every right to attack on this climb at the end of the stage. I feel fresh. I can do this.'

Dave just said, 'Look, this is causing a lot of agitation. A lot. Brad is up there stressing. Sean is just, well, he doesn't know what you're going to do. We need you to say you're going to go along with this.'

I said, 'Listen, I'm not going to do anything stupid, but I want to go for it today without jeopardizing this Tour. I'm not going to throw it away but if there's an opportunity and Brad is on the wheels and he's safe, then there's no reason why I shouldn't go for it.'

Dave immediately said, 'Well, what if he punctures when you've already gone?'

'Seriously, what are the chances? In any case, he has almost two minutes' advantage.'

'No, no, no, Froomey. That's too much chance, that's too much risk.'

We had a silly, worst-case-scenario discussion but it was settled in my head that they felt my desire to get that minute and 25 seconds back might put me in a position where it threatened Brad. Then I might turn rogue. They would have to control the uncontrollable. This scenario had never been in any of the PowerPoint planning presentations.

I had got my stuff for the stage and left for the start line. We were into the stage and I remember all day just feeling so at ease on the wheels, thinking that I was really fresh, and felt really good. Why not?

Anyway, that was in the morning. This was now. Aftermath time.

When I got to massage, David Rozman, our soigneur, looked at me and smiled – he was half pleased and half disapproving. I knew what he was thinking: you did the first part, but not the second part. By the time I got to dinner the guys had finished eating. I sat down at the table on my own.

Sean came along and sat down next to me. He gave a little laugh and just said, 'Eh, Froomey, what are we going to do with you?'

'What, Sean? I did exactly what was asked.'

'Well, no you didn't. You attacked, didn't you?'

'I did, but look at how the race unfolded. It was playing into our hands perfectly: Nibali had attacked twice, he was tired and I got Brad back to Nibali. I brought Nibali back twice, and I'd dropped Cadel. We were in a perfect position. I really thought Brad would have been able to stay with his group without any issues. As soon as I heard that he hadn't, I waited. So what's the problem, Sean?'

I said all this without aggression, more as if I were asking the question from a position of ignorance and innocence.

Sean conceded that he could see where I was coming from but

insisted that I had still disobeyed the orders that I'd been given on the bus. But I'd never fully bought into what we said on the bus and he knew that because I had challenged it. There was nothing really left to say.

Then Sean added, 'I think Dave wants to have a chat with you.'

I also explained to Sean that there were probably things he didn't know about, in the sense that Dave had promised me certain things; that I could go for this Tour and ride for myself. Or at least try to ride GC without being held back. I told him that those were the conditions under which I stayed at this team, things which had been written into my contract. I was just filling him in. We weren't being aggressive. He had been testing the waters; I was explaining the tides.

The tides were choppy on Twitter around then too. Cath Wiggins had tweeted a note of warm praise to Mick Rogers and Richie for their 'selfless effort' and 'true professionalism'. It wasn't the character limit on Twitter that prevented her adding the words 'Chris Froome'.

Michelle had fired back more economically with one word: 'Typical.' Then she had come back with an expansion about being 'beyond disappointed'. 'If you want loyalty, get a Froome dog – a quality I value although being taken advantage of by others.'

Later, Dave dropped me a message: 'Come up to my room.'

When I got there, Dave and Tim Kerrison were waiting.

'Okay, Froomey, tell us what's going on. What's happening, what's troubling you?'

It was funny. He had called the meeting. He obviously had something he wanted to say, but I went straight into my side of things.

'Listen, Dave, this is not what we had agreed at the end of last year . . .'

I went over all that I thought had been agreed and asked what had changed and why.

Dave said exactly what Sean had been saying. Brad was now in yellow. We only had one mountaintop finish to go and one time trial from today onwards. At the moment, standing right where we were in GC, Brad had the better chance of winning. So now we were all going to go one hundred per cent behind that.

My argument was just as blunt. What happens if – as we all remember seeing on the last two Grand Tours that Brad has done – he fades in the last week, or he crashes or something goes wrong? What if one of those things happens and I'm still too far off Nibali to be able to catch up again?

Dave, the man with a plan for all occasions, said that it was wrong to speak now in 'what ifs'. These were the facts. We had to work with the facts.

So we talked facts. Day one, I punctured. No contingency plan. Fact.

Dave immediately apologized for that oversight. It was a mistake. He was sincere but the point was made. There had been promises made and yet from the puncture to the special lightweight wheels and skewers, which Brad was using exclusively, all had been geared towards Brad. I had thought this was the team that didn't do oversights.

Dave said to me, 'Brad wants to go home, he's ready to pack his bags and leave the race altogether.'

I remember thinking, so it's okay for him to leave and not give anybody else a hand? If he leaves, will I have to carry his bags? My point was that we were at the Tour. How many chances was I going to get in my career? I just wanted what was agreed upon. I wasn't staging a coup; I was riding a race.

We talked for probably half an hour about where the team was and how it basically came down to the point that right here, right now, I was nowhere near being in as strong a position as Brad.

I had to accept that.

We talked through the different scenarios. If I were to attack, and Nibali came with me, and we both got to the line together, I would be in the yellow jersey. But if, in that position, I then punctured with 2 kilometres to go, or if something else were to happen to me in the last couple of kilometres, I'd lose time to Nibali, then Brad and I would both have lost the yellow jersey.

That was a whole pile of 'what ifs' from Dave, but I could see it from his point of view. I saw the big picture but I still felt let down about the promises I had been made.

The next morning, we got on to the bus and we all went to the back section and closed the frosted-glass doors. There was Brad, Sean Yates, Dave and myself. Tim too, I think.

I felt quite betrayed by Sean Yates. He took the much harder line and basically began reprimanding me for what had happened the day before.

'You went against the plan; you've rocked the boat, and you can't do that again. This is where we are in the race; you're not to jeopardize that.'

When we had spoken the night before he wasn't at all like this. I felt like he'd almost been given orders to perform a punishment shooting in front of Brad.

I turned straight to Brad and said to him, 'Listen, if you've got a problem with me, come straight to me, don't go round to other people and make the problem worse. Come speak to me and we can sort it out. But it doesn't help if you go telling Sean, telling Dave, telling everyone else what problem you've got or why you're unhappy. Speak to me about it.'

He sort of nodded and muttered a few words. I suspected that this may have been Sean and Dave's way of placating Brad. Brad would never do it himself. It was not in his nature. You didn't really expect to have a conversation with him, especially at the Tour where he was under all the pressure and the stress. We rode around him and his moods like he was a traffic island.

I went back to the team area on the bus feeling that whatever there had been between myself and Sean was gone and that I wasn't going to be able to go for a mountaintop finish, even though Brad was always going to secure his victory in the time trial on the second-to-last day. But I liked Sean, regardless of that. I've got a lot of respect for him as a bike rider, and as a director I think he did a really good job. It was just on a personal level that I felt a bit disappointed. I thought he was bigger than acting out that little performance.

That day, as the media inflated the whole La Toussuire episode into 'Shoot-out at the OK Corral' we rode a long, dullish stage. We rode that day still thinking about the day before. I hardly remember a thing about the stage.

The people closest to me were all saying the same thing: don't let this pull you down. Well done, keep plugging away at it. They would have been disappointed in the way that I had been held back but they knew that I wasn't the type of person to throw in the towel.

We had four stages to ride between La Toussuire and the second rest day of the Tour at Pau. I slept very little, on those days or on the rest day. I would lie awake for hours. I'd hear Richie nod off and I'd just be lying there thinking about all the different things going on in my mind. How could I ride differently? How could I stand up for myself without jeopardizing the position that Brad was in? I began wondering if I'd been bought off, if I had just been signed by the team in order to neutralize me. If I was riding for Garmin in this Tour and threatening Brad, questions would have been asked.

I wondered what options I had. Every single 'what if' ran through my mind.

If we got to Paris and Brad won, did that lay an even stronger claim for him to come back and defend the title next year? Was I just fooling myself here? How did this work? Where was I going to fit in in the long term?

These guys were really not taking me seriously. Not only might I not get the chance to win the Tour in 2013, I might not get the opportunity to even try.

I wanted to know what my potential was. I wanted to go as hard as I could in the mountains until I blew! I wanted to expend all my energy and have to crawl to the finish line one day. I wanted days when, instead of standing, I would have to sit down in the shower. I wanted to know how far I could go. That is a fundamental of sport, mining the talent, loving the raw ability to go *mano-a-mano* against somebody doing the same.

I worried about how the team were reacting. The guys picked up on everything. Did they think I was the baddie here? I got a lot of reassurance from Richie. He was the same with me all the way through, saying, 'Just do what you need to do.' He didn't need to say any more.

Those nights I would be awake until 4.00 a.m., usually texting Michelle. Texting. Texting. Texting.

At midnight she'd say, 'Okay, go to sleep now, you've got a race tomorrow.'

An hour or so later I'd send a message: 'I really can't sleep, I'm just lying here, are you still up?' And she'd get up and keep me company. We'd try to talk about other things but always we came back to the race and what was going on behind the scenes.

I'd go down to breakfast with a yearning for coffee, but I didn't allow myself coffee on the mornings of stage races. I don't think it's really healthy to have a stimulant in the morning. It dehydrates you and it's acidic so it starts your stomach on an acidic kick from the morning on. And it definitely brings you down again at a later point if you don't top it up.

The mornings were hard. I'd hear the alarm go off and know that I'd been lying there until the early hours texting or brooding. Once I was up and going though I was okay.

Those were flat days. Not just for me but for the team. We were winning the Tour but joylessly.

On the second rest day of the Tour my brother Jono and Noz came over to the team hotel. It was good to have them around.

The team had held a press conference out on the hotel lawn, and afterwards I probably had the best part of twenty minutes with Noz and Jono in the lounge area. We were sitting there talking when a few people came over, journalists wanting one-on-ones. I remember Jono trying to be polite, saying, 'Listen, guys, not now. We're just catching up and we're only here for a few minutes, we haven't seen him, now's not the time.'

Some hope!

During the day, Alex Carera, who was still my agent, had spoken to Dave. As a result of coming 2nd, my bonus was bumped up.

It was only money but at least there was the acknowledgement that I was giving something up. The team had recognized what I was talking about. I would happily have forgone the bonus for the chance to race for the win; money wasn't the issue. But it was a gesture.

We went for the usual rest-day ride as a team. It was an odd atmosphere. There was no giddiness, no sense of what we were achieving.

But at one point Brad and I were riding next to each other. He turned to me and said, 'Listen, Froomey, don't worry about this, your time will definitely come, and we'll be right back here next year, and we'll be riding for you.'

I glanced at him. He seemed to be saying that he didn't want to go through all of this again. If he won, that would be it for him. He'd focus on something else, but he'd come back here to help me. I appreciated those words greatly; they weren't typical of Brad.

I felt okay; this was Brad's time. Good luck to him. I knew I had to suck this up for now, but there was recognition here, even from Brad, that I would be a leader in the future and he would be there to help me next time around.

We were in a better place now.

Next day it was business as usual. Cav crashed in the feed zone, then Richie got a feed bag caught in his handlebars and crashed too. Nibali made a break down Peyresourde in the Pyrenees. We chased him down. I pulled. Brad pulled. We worked together and gave the media nothing to speak about.

The last three big contenders on GC (if I could include myself with Brad and Nibali) all came in together. Nothing more to be said.

On to the last mountaintop finish: Peyragudes.

Stage Seventeen: Thursday 19 July, Bagnères-de-Luchon to Peyragudes, 143.5 kilometres

I woke up on the morning of Peyragudes feeling fantastic, like I'd had a rest day the day before. Just walking to breakfast, I was bouncing along. I felt fresh; I felt really good. My legs were like the devil on my shoulder: *Hey, Chris! Pssst! Mountaintop finish? Feeling good, eh?*

I'd spoken to Sean the evening before.

'Listen, if we get to the point where it's just the three of us coming to the last kilometre, can I then go for the stage win? If Bradley is safe or if we can even get rid of Nibali, can I try and go for the stage?'

His response was 'yes', on the condition that Bradley was safe. And that Bradley gave his consent.

I didn't check if the consent had to be in writing. I floated away. I might have the chance to go for a stage. Just might. If a breakaway went that didn't threaten us, we would let it go. If Brad needed company, I would stay with Brad. There were a lot of Dave's 'what ifs' back in the equation.

We rode over Col de Menté, Col des Ares and so on until there were eight of us in the yellow jersey group. Brad and I, Nibali, of course, Van den Broek, Pinot, Van Garderen, Rolland and Chris Horner. Somewhere up the road, Valverde was making a solo run for glory. Good luck, Alejandro.

It was a grippy day. Even on the second to last climb, the Peyresourde, I remember thinking that there were going to be some struggles after this one; it had been a hard day of racing in the heat.

It was a stage of attrition. Everybody was hurting. Going up over the top I drifted back just a little bit so that I could have a look at everyone; see who was there, who was pedalling seriously, who looked like they were up for the last battle.

The radio said Valverde wasn't too far ahead; we could soon be at the front of the race. Guys in the breakaway were dropping; they'd been out there all day. I had hope.

Before descending Peyresourde, and heading on to the last climb, Peyragudes, I leaned across to Brad and asked for his consent. I said to him that Nibali was on his knees, looking terrible. When I had drifted back for a look, he was really struggling. You could see he was taking the strain; there was no fluency.

I said to Brad, 'Listen, Nibali's absolutely finished. Can I go on the last climb? You've got no more contenders left. Can I go for the stage? Valverde is within reach.'

He muttered something along the lines of, 'He's too far away, the breakaway is too far away.'

The 2012 Olympics, London. I won bronze in the time trial, which was an amazing feeling. Afterwards, in a funny way, it felt much better than the Tour podium. It really felt like a privilege just to be standing up there when I got my medal. [Photo credit: Michelle Cound]

Time-trial training with my mate and Sky teammate Richie Porte.

Mont Ventoux reconnaissance during 2013.

The Team Sky support car follows me during a huge block of training in the Suikerbosrand nature reserve in South Africa.

left: Resting during the final camp in 2013, pre-Tour de France. *right*: Putting in the final hours off-road.

[All photographs credit: Michelle Cound]

'The Giant of Provence': Mont Ventoux, stage sixteen, 2013. [Photo credit: Sonoko Tanaka]

'The biggest win of my career' – a great feeling, but afterwards I needed oxygen on Mont Ventoux. [Photo credit: Getty Images]

Earlier on stage eleven, winning the 33-kilometre time trial from Avranches to Mont-Saint-Michel. From this point on, I wondered if the race could be mine to lose. [Photo credit: Sonoko Tanaka]

Top: A night to remember – on the podium in Paris, being crowned the winner of the 100th Tour de France, 2013. [Photo credit: Sonoko Tanaka] *Bottom*: 'This is one yellow jersey that will stand the test of time' – I was so nervous before I gave my speech.

JE VOUDRAIX REMERCIE TOUT LE MONDE QUI AIT VENU SUPPORTER CETTE CENTIEME EDITION DU TDF. C'ETAIT VRAIMENT UN TOUR EXCEPTIONELLE ET UN COMBAT PERMANENT JUSQUE A LA FIN.

THIS WIN IS DEDICATED TO MY LATE MOM. WITHOUT HER ENCOURAGEMENT TO FOLLOW MY DREAMS I WOULD PROBABLY BE AT HOME WATCHING THIS EVENT ON TV. ITS A GREAT SHAME SHE NEVER GOT TO SEE ME COMPETE IN THE TDF BUT I'M SURE SHE WOULD BE EXTREMELY PROUD HERE TODAY.

THIS AMAZING JOURNEY WOULD NOT BE POSSIBLE WITHOUT THE SUPPORT I'VE RECEIVED ON & OFF THE BIKE. I'D LIKE TO THANK MY TEAM MATES WHO HAVE BURIED THEMSELVES DAY IN DAY OUT TO KEEP THIS YELLOW JERSEY ON MY SHOULDERS, & THE TEAM SKY MNGMT FOR BELIEVING IN MY ABILITY & BUILDING THIS TEAM AROUND ME. THANK YOU TO ALL THE PEOPLE WHO HAVE TAKEN THEIR TIME TO TEACH & MENTOR ME OVER THE YEARS TO GET ME INTO THIS PRIVILEGED POSITION.

FINALLY I'D LIKE TO THANK MY CLOSE FRIENDS & FAMILY. WHO HAVE BEEN THERE FOR ME EVERY STEP OF THE WAY, ESPECIALLY MY FIANCE, MICHELLE.

THIS IS A GREAT COUNTRY WITH THE FINEST ANNUAL SPORTING EVENT ON THE PLANET. TO WIN THE 100TH EDITION IS AN HONOUR BEYOND ANY I DREAMED. THIS IS ONE YELLOW JERSEY THAT WILL STAND THE TEST OF TIME.

Made in Kenya – my brother Jeremy and I.
[Photo credit: Michelle Cound]

We did it. Me with my African mentors, Robbie Nilsen and David Kinjah.
[Photo credit: Michelle Cound]

'Smile, Simbaz!' – me with local kids at Kinjah's place in Mai-a-Ihii [Photo credit: Michelle Cound]

'Attack' – taking advice from a real expert.
[Photo credit: Michelle Cound]

I can jump higher than you . . . unless you're a Masai.
[Photo credit: Michelle Cound]

My fiancée, Michelle Cound, and I, relaxing on safari in Kenya after the Tour.

'This is yours'– giving Kinjah a well-deserved thank you present. [Photo credit: Michelle Cound]

Just after he'd said that Sean's voice came on the radio and said that we were just within a minute from them. I turned back to Brad to see if he'd say anything else but he just looked down at the road.

I was floating. Feeling good. The words on Cav's note were buzzing in my head; those two quotes. It felt like everything was going my way today, if only Bradley would just give me the nod.

He hadn't, so instead I would try to get us on to the last climb. I would set a good pace on the front, make sure Bradley was on my wheel and then I would try to pull him up to the breakaway with me. We would see if we could lose the others. I would be ready to do all of the work on the front here, but seeing as I couldn't attack, this was my next best option now. I felt really good; it would be a waste not to spend it.

Tomorrow was a flat day anyway.

From our group of eight, gaps opened and a couple of guys dropped off. It looked as if everybody was in trouble, except for Brad and myself. Brad looked good – I thought he was still pretty solid.

We got to the front of our little group and when I started pulling, he was on my wheel. It wasn't long at all until it was just the two of us left. I kept on looking under my arm or around my shoulder, just to double-check he was there. I think he had realized, also, that everyone else had dropped off. He was safe. He wasn't worried about the stage.

I started saying to him, and gesturing to him, 'Come on, let's go! Let's go! We can get the breakaway.'

They were just a couple of corners ahead of us at this point. After the first 2 kilometres of the climb they were under 40 seconds ahead. I felt so up for it, I was like a kid tugging on his dad's sleeve saying, 'C'mon, c'mon.'

Only Dad wasn't bothered. On the radio Sean was saying, 'Just stay together, guys, stay together. Keep together all the way to the top.'

I wasn't thinking about attacking at this stage but I was trying to motivate Brad, to get some life into him. He was winning the Tour de France at this very moment. This was where the whole race was being won. Time for a little panache.

I'd get him on to the wheel and start pulling, gradually trying to increase it to speed up, and then he'd be off and I'd have to ease up again. He wasn't telling me when he was dropping off so I needed to keep checking the whole time. I was looking round, just checking, checking, checking, trying to pull at the right kind of pace for him. But we seemed to be yo-yoing the whole time.

With about a kilometre and a half to go it flattened out. I thought, 'Yes, right here I can absolutely empty it, I can go as hard as I can because it's flatter so there'll be a bigger slipstream effect. He can sit on my wheel quite a bit more comfortably.'

At one stage I let my hand dangle down to my side like Sugar Ray Leonard goading an opponent into a punch. Nothing. I flicked the hand: come on, come through, pick it up. Nothing. Now I was the dad. I felt like the lad wanted to be carried.

For Brad the race was won and the long struggle was over. I was a poor companion for him to have at this particular moment in his life.

Now I was just looking forward to getting home, getting out of this uncomfortable situation between us. We crossed the finish line up at the top and were swamped by two different groups of journalists.

I don't know what Brad was being asked. My questions were variations on 'What are you doing? You could be winning the race yourself.'

On the climb Michelle had tweeted, 'Damn it, gooooo.'

The guys had got hold of that one pretty quickly.

'Why didn't you just "gooooo"? Don't you want to attack?'

I gave the party line. 'Brad's in optimum position to win the race, and at the moment he's poised to win so . . . we're on track. And no, I'm not going to be attacking or anything like that.'

I realized, at last, that everything had been geared towards this. It was never going to be any different. The story was completed long before we got to France. Bradley wins. The book is written. The documentary is made. The promise is fulfilled.

We had just been acting it out. There was plenty worthwhile in that, and a lot to be learned.

24

We keep on keeping on.

As soon as the Tour was finished we already seemed to be ten steps ahead. Brad had won the race and Cav had won the final stage but our heads were already on the next thing. What do I need for the podium? What do I need for the flight? The Olympics are days away. What do I need for them? We didn't really have time to soak up the fact that we'd won a stage, let alone the whole Tour.

Three weeks of riding in the Tour and at the end we had a very brief sort of cocktail event in a fancy hotel. It felt formal and forced. I had one glass of champagne and a few snacks before a bunch of us left straight away for a plane flying straight to the UK.

It was a relief to get out of there and to see Michelle again and to spend time with her. I was excited about the Olympics. I'd never been to one, and this being a home Games had a special feel to it.

I remember getting to the room. All our bags were there. All of the kit for the Olympics. Everything all laid out and ready.

I did feel a little bit deflated that we weren't staying in the athletes' village. Instead, we were staying away from the other athletes at a plush hotel called Foxhills that had two golf courses. It was a breath of fresh air but not the Olympic experience I had expected. It almost felt like it could have been another race. Hotel. Sleep. Eat. Train. Repeat for five days. Then race. What was nice was that we had our partners with us for that week before the Olympics. That definitely made it a lot more comfortable.

We warmed up for the event mentally as well as physically. We got some amazing bikes to ride. They had come from the track. With the help of a wind tunnel and some clever minds they had been converted to our needs. I was very impressed; I was stunned at how the mechanics had set this thing up without me trying it or without me being there and yet it was a perfect fit.

I could imagine Rod behind the scenes pulling all the strings to make that happen.

My last ride for Kenya was at the All Africa Games in Algeria in 2007.

It was quite an experience. Maybe it isn't fair to compare it to London 2012 but that should be done by anybody who wants to understand the differences between the world of African sport and the privileges we enjoy here in Europe.

I don't want to sound like the spoilt *mzungu* recoiling in horror at what he found. That's not me. I just want to explain that this is world sport; this is just how it is over there.

The athletes' village in Algeria was very much like a big compound; it was almost like a staff quarters. All the toilets were simply holes in the floor and there weren't enough beds and mattresses. There were no pillows, no covers and no plug sockets. There was just one light bulb hanging from the ceiling in each room, and the corridors were dark. There was also a bit of a pungent smell.

We were told we couldn't travel outside the village because of bomb threats and terrorists. Not long before the Games, a huge bomb had gone off in Algiers, killing a lot of people. For a while things were in the balance, and the All Africa Games were almost called off. But of course they eventually went ahead. Life goes on. This was Africa.

The journey from the airport to the village was colourful. It lasted about an hour on a big motorway where everybody seemed to have competing interpretations of the rules of the road. I remember wondering if there were any rules for driving here. There were no lines painted on the roads, although the width of them allowed for three or four lanes across. The fast lane could have been on the right or on the left – it was anybody's guess. There were cars weaving everywhere but the minibus driver seemed to be quite relaxed. He was smoking and humming along to music, and driving very fast in between different lanes, not to mention getting very close to other vehicles. He didn't seem at all fazed by it.

I'll never forget our first meal in the village. Try this, Gordon Ramsay. There was rice and there was meat stew but there was very little in the way of plates and cutlery, and not nearly enough for everyone. At first people would wait for others to finish eating so that they could grab their plates and cutlery to give them a quick rinse and then re-use them, which was fine. But the queue got bigger and bigger and eventually the system imploded. Soon everybody was using one hand to dip into the large metal pots to grab fistfuls of rice. With the other paw, we would scoop up a handful of lukewarm stew and carry it to our table. There we would put everything into a little mound on our tablecloth and commence eating with our fingers. If we didn't do this we weren't going to be eating that night.

Of course, there was a vegetarian option: two handfuls of rice, no stew.

At breakfast the next morning I went along early. I helped myself to a few bananas and brought them back to my room to keep me going. This hardly mattered though because we couldn't train anyway: there were no turbo trainers and we still couldn't leave the village. There was a path around the perimeter but it was thick with runners. So we were all kitted up with no place to go.

I got a silver medal for the time trial. I made a mess of the final climb in the road race.

Afterwards, there would be a reward for my silver. It was substantial for me at the time, huge for a lot of other riders. As much as a couple of thousand euros. But I never saw the money. Despite travelling to the Games at my own expense, when I got back to Kenya it had disappeared. Some people had passed it on; other people never saw it. Nobody knew where it had vanished to.

The Olympic Road Race

After the Tour we had five days to get ready for the 2012 Olympic road race. We tapered our training off for this, doing two or three hours a day to keep things ticking over. One day was longer, when we went to see the circuit, but the rest was mostly just freshening up.

The road race route involved climbing Box Hill nine times. It wasn't exactly Ventoux, but stack it up nine times and it becomes very wearing both mentally and physically. We were there to support Cav, who was the favourite to take the gold.

Looking back, I do think it was realistic that Cav could win. What wasn't realistic was to expect that we could do it all on our own as Team GB. I think we'd banked on at least one or two other nations with the same kind of plan who would see the benefit of having the race end in a bunch sprint: Germany with Greipel, or Australia with Matt Goss. We expected someone else to come along at some point, late in the race, and say, 'We also want that breakaway to come back because our sprinter is here and feeling good.'

On the day, it felt very much like everyone really was racing just to beat us, as opposed to actually winning the race themselves. It was a tough day for us. We were a team of five, which was a lot of work for the four riding for Cav. When we started weakening, the race really started kicking off. Instead of other teams helping us, they sent riders into the breakaway. That's racing.

The last time up Box Hill, guys were attacking and going across to the breakaway. Cav said he had the legs to go. I think it was David Millar who turned round to him and said, 'No, no, don't worry, we'll bring it back.'

We went down the other side though and we didn't get it back at all. I hadn't gone that far into the red through the whole Tour de France. I had never got to the point where I was actually blowing up like I was now. I was absolutely flat, flat, flat. After going down the other side of Box Hill for the final time we were on a flat road. I thought, 'Okay, I can just sit on for a few seconds to recover and then I'll be able to get back on the front again to keep pulling.'

But I couldn't get back to the front. I went back to the car and got bottles instead, thinking, 'Right, I'll do one more effort, get bottles to all the guys, and then I'll pull off.'

I got up to our train again, I reached forward and gave Cav a bottle, and that was it. I was so far in the red that I couldn't actually go any further to give the rest of the team their bottles. We'd been on the front from kilometre 20 to kilometre 200. And now we weren't going to be able to deliver Cav a gold on The Mall. We had let him down.

Brad was strong. While I was struggling to get the bottles to the guys, he was still pulling at the front.

I rolled through the last 20 or 30 kilometres, to get to the finish, being slowly lifted by the crowds. For the first time there was an Olympic feeling, riding along the big open roads where thousands of spectators lined the sides, cheering.

As I rode towards the finish I wondered if Cav was up ahead about to win gold. We'd get to the finish and there'd be a huge celebration . . .

It was quite a disappointment when I got back to the small tent at the finish to see everyone crestfallen. We had been talked up so much. The Kazakh, Alexandre Vinokourov, had the gold we had hoped to help Cav win.

The day hurt. Afterwards I saw a lot of negative comments on social media. People thought I was just saving my legs for the time trial and was not really interested in the road race. I thought, 'Ah, if only you guys knew that I actually hadn't gone this hard in all of the Tour. Today I went much deeper than that!'

Hard times. And four days till the time trial.

When I left the Kenyan cycling world there was both the sadness of farewell and the lightness of feeling I was doing the right thing.

Mum and my brothers, but especially Mum, had strong reservations.

For Mum, the decision was tied to emotion – she felt truly Kenyan. I think she had even traded in her British passport for a Kenyan one so that she could work properly without having to apply for visas. She definitely had a Kenyan ID in her purse and Kenyan identity in her heart.

Mum always said to me, 'No, don't change from being Kenyan, you're Kenyan, you were born here.' She was very proud of me representing Kenya and she wanted me to keep riding for the country I grew up in.

I wish it had been that simple.

I remember explaining to her time and time again, 'Mum, it's just not that easy.'

I knew that by keeping my Kenyan passport I was causing more harm than good for Kinjah and the rest of the guys who were trying to make it from a more difficult starting point in life than I had; I was being used as a political weapon against them. The Kenyan Cycling Federation stopped giving Kinjah and the rest of the riders around him a licence to race in 2006.

As long as I was performing under a Kenyan licence it was making the Kenyan Federation and Julius Mwangi look like they were active. They could pretend they were doing something to develop riders in the sport. They weren't. For me to be their poster boy was basically hurting the riders, the guys like Kinjah who weren't getting any kind of support.

I knew too that compared to every other Kenyan that I'd raced with I'd had a very different journey. I'd had a much more privileged upbringing than they'd had. I grew up in a home that had running water and electricity. I loved every minute I spent with Kinjah and the guys. We ate the same food, slept in the same room, did the same things and rode the same bikes. I was one of them and it was a great, great thing in my life, but the difference which I was always conscious of was that I was staying with them; they were actually living there. In that sense, I didn't feel that I was really a Kenyan cyclist.

The road out for me was just a cycle home to Karen. The road out for Kinjah and my friends was a long, hard climb. When the time came I went to a good school in South Africa and I could afford better bikes. I could access different information and I could get myself to Salzburg. Kinjah and my old riding partners had none of those things.

They deserved opportunities and I didn't think it was fair that I was taking up one of the spots on Kenyan teams. I might as well have sat in Kinjah's hut every day and eaten all the food.

I talked to Kinjah about the switch and he was actually quite happy. In terms of career progression, he felt that it was going to be the best thing I could do. And in terms of helping his cause it was the best thing also because the Federation had started pointing to me saying, 'Chris is doing this. Chris is doing that. Chris is one of the guys we've developed.'

I had always been self-conscious and quietly guilty about that bit of comparative privilege in my upbringing; I had it easier than my fellow Simbaz did. It was unspoken among us but we all knew it. Deep down it sat poorly with me to take the easy road out and to represent Kenya. In doing so, as well as eating up resources I was going along with the pretence that cycling was being carefully cultivated.

I love Kenya but sometimes the best you can do for somebody you love is to leave them be and let them grow. Nobody will be prouder than me when a true Kenyan rider wins a stage on the Tour or stands on a World Championship podium with the anthem playing. Then Kenyan cycling will have travelled the road that Kinjah and the guys carved and paved. Whatever I can do for them to make that day come quicker, I will do, in gratitude for all I was given.

I think once Mum understood those elements of my choice she was better with it but I know she did feel sad that I wasn't representing Kenya any more. She'd been really proud of that and she didn't think that I would ever really feature within the British system.

She never got to see me ride the Tour de France. And here I was, four years later, at the Olympic Games in London, riding for Team GB. Bad days and good.

Olympic Time Trial

I'd had two decent time trials in the past month on the Tour, coming second to Brad on both of them. I thought I was obviously in good shape, but I couldn't expect to be anywhere near the likes of Fabian Cancellara or Tony Martin; I would be riding for 4th place.

Brad and I were the only two riders who had stayed on for the time trial – Mod Father and Tintin in the same story again.

We had the same sort of build-up to the time trial that we'd had for the road race: everything was done properly and we fell into our old pattern. Only one difference: I was using my standard team-issue TT bike. Brad was on a custom bike commissioned by UK Sport. When our paths crossed we swapped cordial hellos. We ate in near silence. We did our own thing.

After the Tour, I realized that Brad had never really said thank you. He'd never actually shaken my hand and said, 'Listen, Chris, thanks for all you did in the Tour, the sacrifices you made and everything.' I almost thought that in those few days in Foxhills it was coming. I kept on expecting it, thinking, 'Okay, maybe tomorrow morning he'll say it,' or, 'He'll have reflected a little bit on the Tour by now.' I found it really strange that it just never came.

I started the time trial thinking, 'Right, I'm feeling good here. I'm pushing on, pushing on.' It was a flat course and I began at quite a good pace. I held on to it. I can remember getting closer and closer to the end, and just when I was feeling as if I were running out of steam, I heard Rod on the radio saying how I was up on Cancellara, and I was sitting in 3rd place . . . I wasn't far off Tony Martin.

That news blew me away. It had gone pretty well and if I could keep pushing on there was even a chance that I could beat Tony. My legs were feeling completely full of lactate, and were so spent, but I thought to myself, 'The only thing I can do now is just stare at the SRM box; stare at the box and use that to motivate me. Get the numbers up to where I want to be. Ignore those legs.'

I got to the low to mid 400s; got that wattage out. I kept staring at the box and counting down the kilometres towards the finish. Whenever there was a corner, and every time there was a bit of a bend in the road, I'd steal as much recovery as possible. Two seconds of not pedalling, through the corner – bliss!

And then I would punish myself. 'Okay, now you've had your break, you can carry on pushing those 400s again. I don't want to see that number below 400 again.'

I hovered between 400 and 440. Those figures indexed my mood: the higher the number, the happier I felt. The lower it went, the more I fought with myself.

Close to 400ish, where I was not so happy, I'd think, 'At least it's not a long way off; at least I can hold it here. This is sustainable.'

In one breath I was thinking, 'Fantastic, I'm looking like I'm gonna get a podium here.' In the next breath I was thinking, 'I could make a silver if I catch Tony Martin.' So I tried to focus on Tony; I pictured myself closing in on him. Maybe he'd started fast and as I got closer to the end I'd hear the time gaps coming down; maybe he was struggling a bit.

It never happened.

Bronze.

For a short while I'd dreamed of silver, but before the race I'd almost written off being on the podium at all. It took a while now to absorb the achievement: this was different to 3rd in any other race. This was the Olympics. It was an amazing feeling.

In a funny way it felt much better than the Tour podium. The Tour podium felt staged and very false to me for some reason. At the Olympics, on the other hand, it really felt like a privilege just to be standing up there. Even though Brad and I had our differences, or whatever, I did feel an unusual amount of pride that we were there, the two of us, 1st and 3rd, both on the podium, in front of a home crowd.

It was a big deal; a good and happy ending.

The Tour gave way to the Olympics which quickly gave way to the Vuelta, which meant three weeks in the Spanish heat. We hadn't done any proper recces of the key stages but it was a course that looked inviting, with eight mountain stages and a lot of mountaintop finishes. I didn't know what was left in my tank but I was getting my chance to be the team leader at a Grand Tour.

The race was likely to be dominated by home headliners: Juanjo Cobo was going for back-to-back home wins, Alberto Contador was back in the peloton of a Grand Tour after his ban, and Alejandro Valverde and Joaquim Rodríguez were also in the mix.

Significant chunks of those days were spent in their company. On stage three, for instance, Valverde, Rodríguez and I chased Contador down half a dozen times on a single mountain.

It was an interesting race but I could feel my energy slipping away early on. There was a mountaintop finish in Andorra where we had taken the race on and put all the riders in the team on the front. Richie, Sergio Henao and Rigoberto Uràn had made a strong pace on the final climb as this was the day I planned to ride away from the three main Spanish riders.

With 4 or 5 kilometres left, I hit the front and tried to go. I went but Contador stayed on my wheel. After pulling for a few minutes I signalled for him to come through and give me a hand. He wasn't interested; he just looked down and shook his head.

We almost came to a standstill, and Rodríguez and Valverde came back to us. I thought to myself that these guys were a lot more punchy than me on the climbs. It would be in my interest now to try to keep the pace relatively constant, and not to let them have too much recovery.

So, stupidly, I got on the front and carried on pulling at a good pace. In the last kilometre they all left me for dead and took 20 to 30 seconds out of me.

There was a time trial that I had ringed in red as important. I came 3rd, some 39 seconds back. Then, on another day in the mountains, Rodríguez took 2 minutes 40 seconds out of me. I was getting used to seeing the backs of the three Spaniards rolling away from me.

But I kept going. I know now that to do the Tour and the Vuelta you need a break in between and then maybe three weeks of clear, dedicated training for the Vuelta. Back then I just kept on going to the well every day.

I had come 2nd in the Tour, I had won a bronze medal at the Olympics and now I'd come 4th in the Vuelta. If I had been offered that at the beginning of the year I would have taken it, for sure.

Bobby said to me that what I had endured at the Vuelta impressed him more than anything I'd done at the Tour.

I was persuaded that it had been ideal preparation for the World Championships, and with my head still echoing with the excitement of the Olympics, I went. However, I rode about 120 kilometres and it wasn't to be. My legs retired of their own accord.

I longed for a few weeks off; days when I might take the bike out to ride for an hour and then meet somebody for coffee. But there were not many of those days and 2013 was already beckoning. I needed to recharge first though.

On the last weekend in October the team were to gather in London. Brad was staging something called a 'Yellow Ball' to mark his win in the Tour. Then the team were to meet for a debriefing session about the season.

I didn't get an invitation to the Yellow Ball. I would also be left out of a bonus payment from Brad to all the riders that had ridden for him as a token of his appreciation. These were small things but it seemed that Brad was brooding ever more darkly on the Tour and how he saw my role in it.

As for the debriefing, the whole atmosphere of celebration which it had seemed to promise was sucked away by a new undercurrent. The team was going to purge some staff members as part of their ongoing zero-tolerance policy towards doping.

Staff members were being asked to come clean on any past involvement with doping. Who was going to own up? What did it mean for the people who owned up?

I can remember Bobby coming into my room and talking to me. He had obviously made the decision to tell the truth about his own past. He said, 'I'm going to go in there and I'm going to tell them that what I did was take EPO . . .'

He said he felt it was his responsibility to tell the team, and that he didn't want any negative association to rebound on myself or Richie. We knew what he was saying: he was our coach and, because he had taken EPO, people would think that he might be advising us to do the same. He said this wasn't fair on us. He was going to tell the truth because he feared it would come out sooner or later and the damage would be bigger. He preferred for it to come from him.

It was very clear to Bobby that if he did own up it would be pretty much the end of him. He went into the room knowing that. Of course, knowing something will happen in advance doesn't stop you from being disappointed when it does.

To add insult to injury for Bobby, when we went out for a last evening, he lost his jacket and his wallet. He had no cash, no credit cards, no job.

When we worked together, Bobby had a great deal of passion for what he did and for dealing with people. This came through in the way that he'd volunteer to come and follow us training to watch the efforts that we were doing. Or the fact that I'd upload a training file and he'd be on the phone five minutes later talking about it, and we might talk for an hour, or even two.

As an end to a big year for Team Sky; and, for me personally, it all seemed oddly disappointing but understandable.

I went back to Africa to get rested up for 2013.

25

On one of those faraway, forever-ago Christmases with Mum and my brothers, this particular one at Kilifi, a coastal town 55 kilometres miles north of Mombasa, I was a seventeen-year-old cycling dreamer without his bike. So on Christmas morning, thinking about the food that would come my way later in the day, I decided on some pre-emptive exercise: a run on the beach, the sun on my face and the Indian Ocean for company.

I'd gone about 3 kilometres, bounding along and happy, when it seemed like I'd stubbed my foot. But it was not your normal stub moment; it was more like the ground had grabbed me and wasn't letting go. I looked down and saw that a pencil-sized harpoon arrow had gone into my foot.

The difficulty was that while the arrowhead of the harpoon had torpedoed into my flesh, the other end was buried deep in the hard sand. I was stuck. 'On the first day of Christmas my true love said to me . . . what in the name of the Lord are you going to do?' What was strange was the absence of any pain. I didn't feel the harpoon go in and now that it was there, it didn't hurt. So I sat down and tried to prise it free.

Moving it at the point where it had entered, I could see the tip of the harpoon shifting under my skin much further up, towards the ankle. It had gone four or five inches into my foot. This was quite serious.

A guy with dreadlocks came walking towards me.

'Merry Christmas,' were not my first words.

My eyes directed him to the situation.

He looked at the harpoon, at my foot, and then at me.

'Oh, you've got a bit of a problem there.'

I moved the harpoon to show him how it had gone into my foot.

'That's not good.'

He tried to pull my foot free but it was too painful – there was a barb near the sharp point that had wedged into my flesh; the weapon had been designed to enter but not exit. He then tried to get the other end of the harpoon out of the sand. By bending it this way and that he eventually snapped it off.

It was rusty and old. Part of the broken harpoon was still poking out of the sand, but four or five inches of it were still in my foot, with another three inches sticking out from between my toes. Putting my arm round the shoulder of my new dreadlocked friend, I hobbled up the beach to a nearby hotel.

From there I called the rented house my family were staying in. My mother and my cousin, Sarah, came for me in the car. The hotel receptionist said the options were the public hospital in Mombasa – more than an hour away – or a local clinic. Not fancying the one-hour drive, we turned up at the local clinic, a smallish tin establishment not dissimilar to Kinjah's place at Kikuyu, where we found a cheerful guy in his mid sixties, in a white doctor's coat.

He sat me on a wooden bench and he moved the embedded harpoon, gently at first. He then tried to yank it out, but it wasn't budging. My mother and he agreed that forcing it out could do a lot of damage, probably leaving rusty chips inside, and potentially leading to infection and further complications.

'We're going to have to open it up,' said the man who I was guessing was a doctor. 'I will take out the harpoon and clean up everything that's inside.'

He injected me with what I imagined was a local anaesthetic. The razor blade wasn't quite what I had expected but it sure sliced open the sole of my foot. I don't know that the anaesthetic had much effect because after he'd opened up my foot it became really painful.

The amount of blood shocked me. It gathered in a small puddle on the bench and then flowed like a red waterfall on to the floor. That was about the time my cousin Sarah retreated from the room. I noticed the doctor was shaking a little and sweating profusely. He seemed worried.

'I hope we haven't cut too many nerves here,' he said, which wasn't reassuring. My mum looked over his shoulder. With the foot now opened up, he was able to free the harpoon.

Taking it out was the easy bit. Sealing the wound was much harder. He didn't have any surgical suture and the needle kept bending as he pushed it through my skin. I think it was a standard sewing needle rather than a surgical one, and instead of suture he had to use fishing line.

This was far from suitable as every knot seemed to come undone and after taking only five or ten minutes to make the incision and take out the harpoon, he spent two hours putting in about twelve stitches. The spacing between the stitches was uneven and, all these years later, the scar is still impressive.

Before we left the tin hut, my mother had to pay. We'd taken up more than two hours of this man's time and on Christmas Day. I thought this was going to cost my mother.

'How much will that be?' she asked.

'Eight hundred shillings,' he said.

Wow. That was about six euros.

We returned home and had a good Christmas lunch that day. Sometimes pain is just what you choose it to be. When you climb a mountain till your legs are jelly, or when you time trial till your lower back aches with pain, you know that it will end. The harpoon barb won't hold you for ever. No climb, no effort, no diet, no pain is for ever.

Still, I thought, in future I should stick to cycling.

Training days often go like this.

I ride out of Monaco, deserting the odd huddled world of bespoke clothes, expensive apartments and fine cars where I live, and on up to La Turbie, where the Trophée des Alpes was built by the Romans when they conquered the mountains. It still looms massive above the humble steeple of an old church. The outcrop above me is called Tête de Chien (Dog's Head), a great name. On up to the narrow, lovely streets of La Peille and just time to steal some quick snapshot glances down the mountain at the rocky gorges and the river below.

The signs warn you of the *lacets* or bootlaces, which is what the locals call the tight hairpin bends which seem to just lie here as if dropped carelessly from the sky on to the sides of the mountains.

This is the old Route du Sel where the mules used to carry salt inland from the Camargue. When I feel bad my heart goes out to those poor mules. Nothing is straight-lined here. No such concept as how the crow flies. Even the long railway tunnel through the mountain from here to Sospel loops around and around in the darkness.

L'Escarène straddles the river itself and has a beautiful row of viaduct arches supporting the railway bridge. Ride on. Push harder. Off now towards the Col de Saint Roch with its 25 kilometres of mostly gentle climb. Two dips in the middle and then a decent haul to the top. I'm feeling ready now for what is next.

And what is next? You swing towards the Col de Turini with its crazy hairpin bends all the way up. If you have seen the Monte Carlo rally then you have seen those bends – the petrolheads love driving them. You look out for oncoming thrill-seekers. Keep pushing up with all the staccato rhythms taking it out of your legs.

We are about three or four hours into the ride now. We have done a few climbs on the way but Turini is a good 20-kilometre drag up to 2,000 feet. This is the meat of the day, the point where the trip is starting to get hard. We go round a hairpin and the road gets even steeper for the last 5 kilometres. If Richie is here we might start half-wheeling each other at this spot. If not, I push my hardest anyway.

One day Joe Dombrowski, a young American teammate, put Richie and me under pressure at this point. We knew then the kid could climb. A lot to learn still, but the talent was there.

We reach the heart of things now, looping round towards the Col de Braus. There sits the small tombstone of the beloved French rider René Vietto who, on stage sixteen with the race lead almost in his *poche*, sacrificed his chance to win the 1934 Tour and filtered back through the descending peloton traffic to give his bike to his team leader, Antonin Magne, who had mechanical problems. Magne won the Tour. Vietto became a hero but he did grumble: 'I'm not going to play the slave for ever.' Right on, René.

(The story goes that in later life when Vietto lost a toe to sepsis before the 1947 Tour – what was the weight advantage there? – he asked that his friend and super domestique Apo Lazaridès have one of his own toes removed to match. Lazaridès, unable to refuse a man who defined the nobility of the domestique, walked with a limp for the rest of his days. Are you getting all this down, Richie?)

We are in Italy now, riding towards the old port town of Ventimiglia, the first train stop on the other side of the border. The blue waters lap against the brown and grey buildings which have been here for ever. Then it is time to turn for home. Home, back along the coast road through Menton, or a switch up the right towards Col de la Madone.

Ah, the Madone and her ghosts. Another story.

I'm waiting for dinner to come at a Team Sky training camp in Tenerife.

It's been twenty minutes and my stomach won't shut up about it. Kosta doesn't help.

Kanstantsin Siutsou aka Kosta. He doesn't know it but I am watching him, studying him like he is in a nature documentary. This is because Kosta doesn't have a digestive system: he has a full-blown industrial plant, which extracts what it wants from a river of food and incinerates the rest. I know this and I hate him for it.

He eats more than the rest of us combined but still has the lowest body fat and skinfolds of the whole team. He simply doesn't do fat – he has never heard of it – and he thinks that we are crazy with our suffering and our abstinence.

I am watching Kosta digging into the bread basket now. His fingers are lingering on the warm, soft, fragrant bread which the waiter has just placed on our table – a whole basketful of it just to torment us.

Hardly looking at his work, Kosta finds the most delicious-looking roll in the basket and rips it apart absent-mindedly. A wedge goes into his mouth with one hand while the other hand and his eyes start a casual search for the butter. I watch that first mouthful in slow motion, even though Kosta takes no care – it is just a thick chunk of bread after all; warm-up bread. Now Kosta is chasing down another. This second wedge of loaf is more sinful – he has loaded it with a hefty serving of almond butter and some honey. Mmm. His face greets the taste like an old friend and he chews lovingly as I watch.

I am a sad and hungry food voyeur. I hate myself for it. Even more than I hate Kosta at this moment.

Kosta's eyes are darting about the table now. He has seen the pot of strawberry jam. Why is there even strawberry jam at our table? He reaches out for the jam but I can't watch any more. My stomach begs me to change channels – anything but watching Kosta eat. Anything.

I turn to talk to Richie. But he too is watching Kosta now, tracking the movement of the strawberry jam like a wolf watching a spring lamb.

In the old days on Grand Tours they used to say that it took the Italians the first three or four hours of riding each day just to digest the mountain of pasta they would eat for breakfast. Only then would they be ready to race, which would of course be followed by another mountain of pasta for dinner that evening.

When I smell bread or I see pasta I am conditioned to the sound of alarm bells in my head. Gluten is taboo. *We don't eat gluten*, my brain says. *We could try*, my stomach says, *a little wouldn't hurt*.

As far as I see it, gluten just complicates everything: it blocks the muscles, retains water and bloats you. Bread and pasta are Trojan horses filled with gluten. We try to stay away from glutens. We just watch Kosta eat them, and we hate him for his industrial plant.

I try to go very light in terms of diet. In the mornings I limit myself to just the one bowl of porridge, and normally a two-egg omelette, with no hint of extras on the side. No second helpings, no picking, nothing. If there is a big stage ahead that day I'll try a three-egg omelette, but warily, and I'll mix a small amount of white rice into the porridge.

Sometimes on the giant epic rides I think that I am under-fuelled but I can still summon up the Barloworld days and the feeling of heavy bloat I used to get after some of the good old pasta meals. I know it has to be this way.

On to the desserts, which no longer contain 'love' as I like to put it. Instead, I'll chew a few pieces of fruit or have a pot of yoghurt. I don't count calories or know the values of most things; I just let my instinct guide me as to what is the right amount to eat. My instinct always says that the right amount is less than I feel like eating. In a previous life I think my instinct lived in a remote monastery.

I can think of food, see things in terms of food and watch Kosta love his food. But I just can't eat food. Not like before. It's a fidelity thing.

End of argument.

The sweat *du jour*, or training efforts.

Today's house special is served in three portions, up there on the blackboard.

The starter is a 20-second sprint served at the bottom of a climb. All in. Balls out. Bang!

This is followed straight away by a portion of zone-three riding, which is 20 minutes at tempo pace. It is not at threshold but luke-warm; not on the edge but close. So we sprint, then ride at tempo.

It's about racing.

Why sprint at the bottom of a mountain? Usually just to get into position for the upcoming mountain.

Why so much pain? To teach the body to recover from a blow-out sprint by using tempo pace instead of freewheeling.

We take the pain now, hoping that others will suffer later.

The final course varies in texture. It involves a sprint of 30 seconds followed by the same 20 minutes of recovery at tempo. Then there is a 40-second sprint, followed by another 20 minutes at tempo. All this is accompanied with a side serving of mountain.

I decide to make alterations; I don't think Tim Kerrison minds, as long as I'm making the effort more challenging. He sends us all a menu of efforts for our session. Everybody uploads the data from their effort and sends it back to him. I sometimes send my data back to him with slightly different or extra information, along with an explanatory note saying that I felt I had to do more.

Once I feel my form progressing, Tim knows I will add a few touches to make it a little more painful, a little sauce to flavour the suffering. He'll tell me to stick to the plan, but I'll do it and explain later. As a rule, the plan changes from day to day anyway. I might stick to the day's plan when I see it again. Maybe not. But tomorrow's plan is always fair game for alteration.

So today instead of just one sprint per 20 minutes of tempo recovery I throw in an extra sprint of the same duration at the halfway point of 10 minutes for each of the three separate efforts.

So now the pattern is 20 seconds of sprint riding followed by 10 minutes of tempo riding. Then another 20 of sprinting followed by 10 minutes of tempo. I turn round, descend back down to the bottom of the climb and repeat with a 30-second sprint this time. It's the same method for the final effort but this time a 40-second sprint.

I've sliced the 'recovery' period in half in order to add a lactic-generating sprint in the middle. It doesn't make me feel good but thinking that I could have done more would make me feel worse.

I have to really struggle to recover from this, which is good. My body definitely remembers when I go really deep and it all gets coded in so that the muscles remember the feeling and become more attuned to it. They adapt.

Today I think there is benefit for me because the rhythm has been coarsely chopped. My body had 20 minutes to recover, then suddenly just 10 minutes. After more work there was another 10-minute break. And so on. These intervals are designed to teach the body how to dissipate the lactic acid in order to recover from the sprint at the beginning. In a race, the recovery periods won't come at such nice, regular intervals.

I pile on these extras like a glutton at the punishment buffet. I rack my brain for ideas on the days when we are instructed just to do some 'general cycling'. Nine times out of ten I will add my own intervals on top of these rides to reassure myself that I'm in control, and that I'm making the most of my training.

When it's time to train, I don't like being on the bike for no reason and general riding days aren't really a reason. I want to take something away from each and every ride, so every day I ask the same questions. What do I want to get out of this ride? How am I testing myself? How am I getting stronger?

I don't necessarily like pushing my body to the limits the way I do in training. I can feel today that all this isn't necessarily that healthy for me. I don't think it's good for my body to push it this hard, and this often. It can't be good in terms of health and longevity; I'm sure that the aggregate of all these marginal debts will have to be paid by the body sometime down the road.

I know for now though that this is what is going to make me stronger, fitter and tougher. It's what I need to do to be a racer, and what I need to do to be at the front of the next race.

On days like today I don't care about anything else.

Back in Monaco, the Col de la Madone de Gorbio is a fallen woman. Her name is tainted by the sins of her former lover. I live nearby and have to admit there is some dark attraction in her notoriety. Richie and I have spoken about it. The Col de la Madone had poor luck. That's the only way you can explain it when a mountain falls in with a bad crowd.

The Col de la Madone was Lance Armstrong's test mountain. He loved her so much he named a bike after her. He talked about her so much that riders still want to test themselves up her slopes. We know the Col is blameless and beautiful, and today we are at the bottom, Richie and I, ready to take her up on her challenge.

It wouldn't be true to say that we have never been here before. We have used the Col de la Madone a lot for doing the 20-minute efforts or 24-minute efforts which Tim Kerrison plans for us. We have ridden up and down it many a time on training rides. We have never respected the mountain properly though. We've never gone from bottom to top as fast as we could go. We are here to time trial Col de la Madone. I am riding my mountain time-trial bike.

Armstrong used to come here to see if he was 'ready' for the Tour. Yes, we know now that it was just one of the more natural measures of 'readiness' that he was obliged to take but we have to admit, this is a good one, a useful barometer. It's a nice climb, about 12 kilometres (11.89 kilometres my downloaded file says) from start to finish, with a good consistent gradient of around seven per cent, climbing 808 metres of vertical ascent. There are a few flat stretches for recovery.

We can't know where others started exactly, as obviously there is no official starting line for an effort up the Col de la Madone, but traditionally people flick the stopwatch at the bus stop on the left side of the road just past the first switchback in Les Castagnins, right at the bottom of the climb. Nothing grand, just a pole on the side of the road with a few bus numbers and routes on it. That's our starting point anyway, exactly where the road begins to go uphill.

Richie sets off before me.

Richie is an unusual man. He is someone whom I can train very well with. I look at the road and I see little stretches where I can test myself, really push it on, and Richie looks and he sees the same. Finish lines, visible only to us of course, pop up all over our training routes. He's a competitor. We have a little training rivalry and constant challenges. Race you over the next rise ahead of us?

When we are on the boring valley roads, we don't just ride side by side chatting. We start swapping off, 2 minutes each, with each of us trying to do a harder turn at the front than the other one did. Harder, longer, tougher.

It's human nature that riders often like to make things easier for each other. Richie and I go the opposite way. We make each other's lives as hard as possible but as an expression of friendship. This is good for us.

Occasionally the young Americans in the team moan that they think the training's too long, and too hard. We're not good shoulders for them to cry on. When Richie and I ride with them we push on, to see if we can get them out of their comfort zone. We include the steepest climb we can find. We're just making a point; it's fun in a perverse sort of way.

Today, we want to see where we're at form-wise. So the Madone becomes our mountain time trial. I set off 1 minute after Richie and Tim Kerrison follows me, alone in his car. Richie has flown off quick as a fish at the start. I know what he is thinking: *No way does Froomey give me a head start and then catch me.*

It is a strange ride. We will end up in a badlands of stringy roads and mountain goats but we begin where the surface is fine and for the bottom 5 kilometres we are pushing through residential areas, with houses and driveways branching off from the Col. There aren't any big hairpin bends but the road is always turning left and right as we sweep our way up the climb. The houses look so quiet and serene but we careen past them like we are handling a getaway car.

After about 6 kilometres we start hitting a couple of hairpins but if you look over the edge of the climb here you have got the city of Menton below and, beyond that, the ocean. Amazingly beautiful. Our heart rates are okay. The scenery is breath-taking but today we pay it no attention.

About 18 minutes in, and just over halfway, we get to a junction where you can turn off to the town of Sainte-Agnès. To carry on up the Route du Col de la Madone you look to the small maroon sign for instruction and then coast round a very sharp left that doubles back on itself. Next you sprint to get back up to speed again and carry on up. From this point it is about 5 kilometres to the summit. You go through a couple of tunnels before the road flattens out for maybe 500 metres, and then you pass an avenue of trees. Now it kicks up into the last third of the climb, where the road surface is very rough. It's quite normal to meet goats, which roam up here. Goats and goatherds. That is the most traffic you will find: tourists on bikes and goats.

The road is narrow. For two cars to pass one needs to stop or pull a little off the road for the other to get through. It becomes less scenic as you come closer to the top and you hit the back of the mountain where you can't see the ocean any more. Nature just narrows your focus anyway.

This effort is taking its toll on me. That fresh, zippy feeling I had at the bottom has long since left my legs. I squeeze on. I have to squeeze on. This is where it counts – that stopwatch can easily gather more seconds here if I lose concentration.

There is a left-hand bend with a deserted hut on it. This marks the spot from where you have 1 kilometre to go. When you get to the hut you know you can start emptying it. You dig it out now, out of the saddle, drive it home. Squeeze hard. Because you know it's not for ever.

Once you get to the top there is an abandoned settlement. At some stage people thought better about riding up the Madone just to get home every evening. No windows or doors survive and some roofs and walls are all that is left. More ghosts. To the left, some massive antennas.

There is an old monument at the top of the climb. It is made from stone and old artillery shells and it looks like the Madonna in the form of a bomb cradling a baby. The inscription says 'Combats de l'homme, éclats d'obus, désormais ne soyez plus que la Madone de la paix', which reads along the lines of: 'Battles of men, shards of shells, from now on you are no more than the Madonna of peace.'

Once you hit the top of the Madone you know it. It descends immediately. You just crest the hill and you drop; there is no flat area.

We lean forward, sucking in the air, both of us fiddling with our bikes, both of us having the same idea. I scroll through the SRM data from the ascent: Power, Time, Heart Rate, Speed.

I think a lot about my competitors when I'm training. I think about how they might be riding, and wonder if they are out with their teammates chatting for five hours. Especially if I'm out on my own that day, doing more focused efforts. I'm not just dawdling along. I like to think I'm doing more than the other guys, even when I don't know if this is the case or not.

Alberto Contador told me once that he had moved up to Switzerland, somewhere around Lugano. He needed to be close to Bjarne Riis, and the bonus was that another couple of Spanish riders on the team had moved there with him. They were going to be training partners.

I like to think of those three amigos out training, just having a gentle ride and a chat. Maybe a coffee stop. The more my legs ache when I train the more I hope they are enjoying themselves. If one of them is a bit below par today, maybe all three will pack it in. I hope so.

In my head I am sure Contador and Nibali and my other rivals are out there training just as hard as I am. So some days I add in intervals or do more specific training or more intensity and tell myself they'd never think to ride like this – this is where I'll get my advantage.

Richie and I both struggle when we are told to take it easy; we want to be out there training. Work gives us the reassurance we need. We don't want Contador thinking of us sipping cappuccinos and talking bull. We are no-pain-no-gain fundamentalists. A lot of the time Team Sky want us to be recovering. If we've done a big training block in Tenerife they might say, 'Okay, guys, take four days easy back at home now before you go to the next race.'

Richie and I become edgy at the prospect, Richie especially. You have to take his bike away if you want him not to be doing five-hour rides.

'God, four days? We're gonna get fat in four days! We're gonna put on a kilo. It's better if we train.'

We can't train though. Otherwise they'll see that we have been training. So, we have found a way to get past our power meters. If we are supposed to do an hour, we'll probably do an hour and a half on the power meter, then disable it so it switches off and only shows that we've done an hour and a half.

Meanwhile, the two of us will go on and do more training. We might carry on and do another four hours. Afterwards, we'll make sure that we have our stories straight when talking to Tim: 'Oh, today we only did a recovery coffee ride.'

For us it is important just to keep the body going. Sometimes we imagine that no one really understands this except for us. We worry about putting on weight, about accumulating fluid. We worry that our legs will just stop turning. Training longer gives us reassurance.

I know that sometimes we do run the risk of over-training, that we need to be backing off. And it's something I'm learning to deal with. Having Michelle in my life has made it a lot easier. I'm starting to say, 'Okay, well, Tim has said take a day off. I'll do something with Michelle.'

Does that sound bad? Sometimes a day with Michelle is better for me than a day of pain. But pain is still the friend that always tells me the truth. Training is still an addiction. For sure there are days when the pain is overwhelming, where I push into the red so far that I wonder if I will come back. And on those days I speak to my rivals in my head. *I can do this. What can you do? I can do this here on my own in training. And when I do it in a race it will be much easier. It will be enjoyable then. Can you do this?*

★

Training in Tenerife. I got to the 40-second sprint a while ago. Halfway through, at 20 seconds, I was feeling nailed and in deep trouble. When you are sprinting up the side of a mountain, and when the pain owns you instead of the other way round, 20 seconds is a life sentence.

But then again, it's not. I thought, 'It's 20 seconds. *Only* 20 seconds. You can actually count that. Why don't you do that? Come on.' And I started counting:

Eighteen, seventeen, sixteen . . . It gave me something to do, and something to focus on. A voice in my head to talk over the complaints coming from my legs.

Fifteen, fourteen, thirteen . . . After about 15 seconds my power started dipping a little, wanting to head towards 600 watts. 'Stop. I have done this before. Keep pushing a little bit more. Get it back up to 700. Yes.'

Twelve, eleven, ten . . . 'Spit the words out. When I get to the bottom of this countdown it will be finished. Done.'

Six, five, four . . . Then I can recover at tempo for 10 minutes, maybe 9.

Two, one, zero. The big zero. That's it. That's *it*. I imagine a fragmented peloton behind me on the mountain. How's that coffee, Alberto?

Maybe I have another sprint in me in a few minutes' time.

Today I am working on the interval session on Col d'Eze. It's perfect, consisting of about 10 kilometres of climb with a very steep section at the bottom to give me a tough start.

When I get to the top after the intervals I do a small loop and ride straight back down. And then back up again. And then down. And then back up again. I ride for close to three hours doing this with the same loop at the top each time.

Like at other points in my career, I often train like this on my own. Not many guys would be interested in riding up and down the same road for three hours.

I'll upload this session later and wait to see Tim's response. What will he read into it? He had advised me to do these efforts but I've tweaked them as usual, and turned pain into torture. I'm hoping he might say, 'That's quite a good idea, you're getting double compensation there on the climb, you're really trying to work those recovery systems in your legs.'

But he may come back and say, 'That's not necessary. It's too early in the year. You don't need to be doing that much. Just do the one.'

In which case I'll stash this morning's work in the bank of things that I can do, and when I get closer to the Tour I'll draw on it then, and ramp up the training.

I'll say to him, 'Remember I was doing these things a while back and you said "wait a bit"? Now can I do them?'

Tim is not one to shy away from pushing on, but there is still a time and a place for it.

I felt good all the way up the Col de la Madone today. The numbers can tell me just how good. I'm not sure even now if I want to write them down here. The power I managed to hold for that half an hour up the Col de la Madone was the highest I have ever done – 459 watts in a pretty flat line all the way up. The highest in my life.

There's definitely something a bit strange with my heart rate. Not only today, but always. It just doesn't go very high, even when I'm going as hard as I can.

The heart rate is normally one of the most visible readings on the head display. Sometimes we can be riding a decent tempo up a climb and I will look across and see another rider's figures hovering around the 180 beats per minute mark. They glance back at mine and see my rate is under 150.

In the morning when I've checked it, or when I'm resting, I've seen my heart rate down as low as 29. It is a little odd and I'm sure it could be reason for gossip. I mean, I'll often do my threshold efforts for example between 145 and 150. That's quite a hard workout, but it's funny sometimes because there have been a few occasions in a race, on a climb, when someone has looked across at my power meter and almost looked twice at me just to check that I was still breathing.

My time from the bus stop down below to the summit was 30 minutes 9 seconds. That's some 36 seconds into Armstrong's supposed fastest time up here. It's faster than Tom Danielson's 30 minutes

24 seconds. If it's a record though, it is one that a rider would be reluctant to claim. It brings to mind too many thoughts of Michele Ferrari and his clients examining their own stats after a day on the Madone.

Richie has posted a much faster split time up to the turn for Sainte-Agnès. He started running out of fuel a little towards the end. He did a great time though, about 15 seconds behind me.

It is a strange feeling we both have after doing it. We feel slightly guilty and a bit sheepish. We don't want to tell anybody that we have gone and beaten those times because we don't want to invoke the ghosts of the past.

I turn to Richie.

'We can't tell people about this.'

We don't want to go there. It's happened so many times that it stops hurting you and begins to bore you – 'Hey, you climbed that hill faster than Pantani. Therefore you must be guilty.'

No more idols.

We are in good shape but it suits us not to make too much of this, not to be blowing our trumpet before the race and not to be drawing snipers. We are happy. We know what we have done. No need to tell everybody about it. It is great for our morale, our confidence and our faith in clean riding.

Richie turns to me and says, 'We're ready for this, mate. We're ready.'

This was 23 June 2013. A Sunday. We would start the Tour six days later.

26

Since the 2011 Vuelta I had been talking the talk. Now 2013 was upon us and I would have to walk the walk.

Nobody else was quite as excited as I was. For the team, this year would be tricky. Everything had been built on Brad in 2012 – he had delivered a Tour de France and an Olympic gold medal and was now literally a knight of the road. This year Team Sky would have to be explaining why last year's domestique would be the leader in the Tour de France. And Brad would still need to feel fulfilled and challenged.

All I could do was take care of my own part. Any time the team wanted to check what condition I was in, they should be pleased and no alarm bells should sound.

Six months' hard labour lay ahead but that was okay; pain has always been both an enemy and an ally. I had found a soigneur in South Africa, a guy called Stefan Legavre, who had worked with the local pro teams. He was based in Cape Town so I flew him to Johannesburg and put him up in the apartment of the place I had bought in Parkhurst. Jaguar South Africa gave us a branded team car with all the Sky logos so Stefan could follow me on every ride, providing bottles and food and acting as a buffer between me and motorists. This was some change from the days of sneaking out of St John's at dawn.

I did huge blocks of training into the Suikerbosrand nature reserve. The longest climb in the reserve is only probably a little under 4 kilometres but very undulating. It tops out at about 1,900 metres. On one part you ride up on to a big plateau and stay up on the top and then drop down on the other side of the reserve. It was somewhere I really enjoyed training and I was always able to look out for animals as I rode along: eland, waterbuck, wildebeest, zebra. Occasionally a fat puffadder stretched across the warm tar. Mischievous baboons and jackals darting out on to the road.

Team training for the year began in Mallorca and I wanted to make a statement. I wanted to show the team that I was taking the challenge seriously; I wasn't going to pitch up overweight and unfit. So I worked harder than ever in South Africa.

Most days I rode on my own. When I didn't I would ride with some of the local cyclists. If I was doing specific efforts I would go out on my own with Stefan behind. If it was a general training day I'd seek out some company.

It sounds excessive, having a man in a Jaguar follow you as you train, but it helped. For instance, I could ride the time-trial bike as far as the nature reserve, switch to the road bike for a few hours and then ride the time-trial bike back home again. And there was the safety factor. On South African roads there is little respect for cyclists. In mid January Burry Stander, the mountain biker who had helped Kinjah and myself during the Commonwealth Games in Melbourne, was killed on the roads in South Africa.

One minute Burry was planning his season. The next minute he was gone.

A few hundred of us took part in the memorial ride for him in Johannesburg. The roads were closed and we did a 10- to 15-kilometre procession on bikes. Even Michelle and Stefan joined in. During the procession, we mounted and chained a ghost bike, a white-painted bike, in memory of Burry, to the top of the iconic Nelson Mandela Bridge.

I had one night in Monaco to stop and pick up my racing kit. The next morning I was off to Mallorca.

Things had changed with the team and there were fresh faces as there are every year. Mark Cavendish had moved on, looking for an environment more sympathetic to a sprinter's needs, and a couple of guys had retired. The cut, that invisible scalpel, had done its work over the winter and now we had new blood. David López and Vasil Kiryienka had joined us from Movistar, along with the two talented but inexperienced Americans Joe Dombrowski and Ian Boswell, and Josh Edmondson, the English neo-pro.

The younger guys had to deal with the culture shock. Joining

Team Sky is like going from a desk job to working in a coal mine. When I arrived they were telling horror stories about some of the training days they had done in my absence – apparently some of them in December had been like full-on race days. I smiled thinly and nodded, doing the old-soldier routine. It was quite funny.

Bobby J. was gone. The scalpel hadn't been quite so invisible when the team cut several key staff members as part of the zero-tolerance policy to doping. Those who love trolling about Dave Brailsford and all his Piety in the Sky-ety statements could manage nothing more than a pretty juvenile 'I told you so' when staff members came forward and confessed to having been involved in doping in the past.

Not many people understood that severing those connections on the day of the long knives hurt everybody. Guys like Bobby had made mistakes and now they were paying for them. But so was the team. It was a sacrifice to lose their cycling knowledge as well as their presence about the place. Their past didn't mean they didn't understand the mistakes or the wrong they had done to the sport and themselves. It didn't mean they had nothing to contribute to a cleaned-up cycling world. They were casualties not of hypocrisy but of the fact that cycling needs to rebuild itself and different people have different ideas on how best to do that.

That was the end with Bobby. I missed him and still do; we had worked well together. I was slightly disappointed in him and very disappointed for him, I suppose. Whatever he had achieved while doping could never mean the same to him as what he had achieved while clean, and that's quite a punishment for a man who loves the sport so much.

I would stay in touch on the phone occasionally to see how he was doing and what he was up to, but we had no more contact about training. It wasn't like it was before.

I was in more contact with Tim Kerrison now, who was Head of performance at Sky. Tim hadn't been a rider himself so he brought a more analytical and cerebral approach to the whole thing. I enjoyed that too though, and we would test and challenge each other. I would push on with my instinct that more work is always better, whereas

Tim would quietly insist that more work at certain times might be more effective than all the time.

Cycling has its own conventional wisdoms and Tim has been a beacon in the way he has challenged them. In South Africa I would sometimes meet up with a big group of riders and tag along with them for a while. However, I would still need to do my 15- or 20-minute intervals so I would ride off the front at pace, complete my intervals and then pull a U-turn, come back and continue riding with them. Nothing was ever said but while I was coming and going I noticed smirks on faces and heard comments back through friends. They were all amused by my antics. 'Doing intervals in January? What an idiot! This is the time for long steady miles. Always has been and always will be.'

The point is that the Sky team prepares for the season in its own way. I know that to a certain constituency, those hurt most by the Lance Armstrong business, there is no point explaining what makes Sky different. They say they have heard it all before and they won't get fooled again. That's fine. Certain riders and their teams treated the sport and its followers with such cynicism that those followers are entitled to their cynicism now.

I am not a student of Lance Armstrong or that period in cycling. He doesn't interest me and that era doesn't interest me. As such I am no expert on what was done and what wasn't done. I do know though that a range of cycling people, from South Africa to the seasoned pros in Europe, expressed surprise at how hard Sky went so early in the season. Also, at the time that we spent at training camps at altitude as a team. We came to events like the Tour of Oman prepared to race, and not to prepare for future races.

At first the peloton disapproved but then it adapted. Last time I was on a training camp in Tenerife the guy in the next room at the Hotel Parador on Mount Teide was a rival pro cyclist – Vincenzo Nibali.

Tim's approach has influenced things. I have had lots of lucky breaks along my journey through the people I have met, from Kinjah to Robbie to Bobby. Meeting Tim, who through science reached many of the same conclusions as I had through instinct, was another of those breaks.

In Mallorca I definitely felt that some of my teammates were trying to use me as the gauge for their own efforts. They would be outriding each other one day and then falling off the back of the group the next day with sore legs or wounded knees.

Tim took me aside to say, 'Listen, don't worry about the other guys, some of them are way out of their zones trying to match the efforts you are doing at the moment. Because you are the main guy in the team, people will compare themselves to you all the time. Just carry on doing what you are doing.'

That was good to hear. It was what I had hoped to achieve when I had been putting the work in down in South Africa.

Of course, some guys coped because they knew how to. You knew that old warriors like Danny Pate or Xabier Zandio had been doing the work. There was no trying to turn heads or show off their form, they just did their work. They were good, consistent guys.

We developed a rhythm to the days. Richie and I would go to the gym before breakfast, where we would often find Kosta and Kiri. Their cores are so good we wondered why they felt the need, and then, of course, we realized that it was exactly these early-morning gym sessions that helped to build and maintain their core strength. Within the team everybody had their own habits and their own ways.

Brad was in and out. He was at the camp during the week and he would fly home at weekends to be with his family. Once he and I sat down for a round-table discussion with journalists who wanted to talk about the season. Brad controlled the conversation and did most of the talking. He was very engaging and switched on, a side of him the team didn't always get to see. I felt like I was just adding in a few words here and there but that didn't bother me. Brad was more accustomed to that scene than I was. We spoke about the Tour in 2012, and what we had learned. Brad then talked about the Giro and how he intended to come and support me afterwards in the Tour de France. We toed the party line.

The journalists wrote afterwards that there didn't seem to be a lot of warmth between the two of us. Well, we were saying what we needed to say but neither of us felt comfortable sitting next to each other. I was nervous about what Brad might come out with, whether or not he would follow the pointers set out for us by the team in the one-page 'media messages' print-out.

Brad was to focus his comments on the Giro; I would focus mine on the Tour. As the season progressed we would see how things panned out. The idea was for Brad to come and help me at the 2013 Tour, and if any questions about 2012 were framed in a Brad-against-Chris way, we would play them down.

We were trying to portray an image of us working together and that was fine. Brad sounded very confident and genuine; it didn't have to be all warm and brotherly between us as long as we were singing from the same sheet. That day I didn't think there would be much of a problem. We just got on with it and I felt reassured about what was to come.

If there was pressure early in the season, it was subtle. The team wanted me to win one or two races in springtime in the hope that winning would build the confidence of the team around me; it was felt I needed to establish that I was the leader. This was expressed equally subtly. Tim might say to me after one of the harder training rides, 'Listen, Chris, your numbers are right up there – there is no reason why you shouldn't, oh, let's see, win Oman for example.'

Okay, Tim. I never saw a race I didn't want to win, so the guys were pushing at an open door.

Oman was the first race of the season. We won but it would be a more interesting week than the bald result suggested.

In the first couple of stages I had the feeling the race wasn't doing what it said on the tin. It was too easy to sit in the bunch between the critical parts of the race, which was going very slowly. I had expected a more action-packed race in the desert; I had imagined there would be more hills and lumps.

In terms of the big picture, this didn't seem like a very useful way to be spending a week. I had been training a lot harder and faster than this race was willing to be.

The event picked up gradually though and I went with it, stayed out of trouble and kept my head down till we got to the showpiece day on Green Mountain.

Again, even that stage wasn't quite what had been promised. The pace was painfully slow which meant that everybody would be fizzing on the climb. I prefer for it to be hard all day, a race of attrition. This day instead seemed set up for a guy like Contador, who is maybe more explosive than me.

It may have been called Green Mountain but it was not really a mountain. It was more of a sudden and eye-catching change in terrain, as if an interior designer had decided to make the desert interesting. At first glance I thought that if this was the Green Mountain then I was the Incredible Hulk, but as we climbed the air became cooler and thinner, losing the furnace fierceness of the desert. The views stole our breath away.

Long before we got up to those heights I had a look at the power meter. I needed to use it to stop myself going too far into the red early on the climb. With everybody so fresh it would be easy enough to get carried away.

As it happened, Contador and his Saxo Bank team set an unbelievable pace at the bottom. They lined it up and made it really hard for everyone else for the first kilometre. I found I was dropped from the front group of fifteen to twenty guys.

After about a kilometre of climb on Green Mountain the road dips for a few hundred metres before going up again. The front group had dropped me by about 50 metres at that point. I turned round and saw that the next group of guys were 20 to 30 metres behind me. I was in no-man's-land and on my own.

Richie was in the front group with Contador and Nibali and a couple of the other big players. He looked back and saw me on my own on that flattish, downhill section. Immediately he filtered back, hooked up with me and led me all the way back to the front of the race for the next section of climbing.

It was a very tactical climb, so there were attacks all around. There was Nibali, Contador attacking and Rodríguez following. I did a small attack of my own just to make it seem as if I were pushing as hard as I could but I didn't put too much effort into it. I didn't want to go that far out, as there were still 3 or 4 kilometres to go.

It was very cat and mouse, with lots of bluffing and lots of pawing. Nobody really wanted to bite. It got down to myself, Nibali, Contador and Rodríguez. The four of us were all looking at each other and trying to work out who was bluffing and who wasn't. There was one other guy with us, a small French rider, Kenny Elissonde. At some point in all this, Cadel Evans latched on to our group as a temporary distraction. Then he was gone again.

I was still bluffing most of the way, by making it look as if I were really struggling. I didn't want them to keep using me, working me only to attack me in the final stretch. So with about a kilometre to go Rodríguez accelerated. I looked at the other two and basically gave an expression which said, 'I can't follow that. Poor me.'

Inside I felt really good but I just spun off, dropping off their wheels and giving them 10 metres of space in front of me. They glanced back at me, amazed. *He has nothing left? Wow!*

Now it was Rodríguez, Contador and Nibali. And then me, toiling manfully a few metres back.

I can remember seeing the 500-metres sign and being absolutely shocked that we were at that point because I could see the road kept going right up into the hills.

I had miscalculated. Surely it went on further? I could see a road snaking up slopes higher than we were. The race *must* go on further, I thought.

But on the other hand, I didn't want to get it wrong, just in case this was the finish. If this was about establishing myself as the leader of the team, it wasn't going to work if I started by having to explain how I misjudged the finish.

Then again, wait. Could that sign have meant that there were 500 metres to go to the King of the Mountains hotspot? I couldn't risk it. There was nothing for it. I put my head down and went with everything I had left.

There was no doubt in my mind that Contador and Nibali wouldn't be able to follow me. I knew I was going a lot faster than them and I didn't expect them to be able to respond. Rodríguez was just out of my reach but I wasn't bothered by that as I knew he wasn't on GC.

In the end, he won the stage and I finished 5 or 10 seconds after him. However, in that 500 metres I had put a good 30 seconds into the others.

It was a good result but frustrating too; I thought I could have done more damage if I had only realized exactly where I was on the road. Still, I was in the leader's jersey and we had just two stages to go.

After giving some post-race interviews on Green Mountain I went to the bottom for the podium ceremony. After the presentation of the jerseys I thought I heard somebody behind the podium say something in Swahili. That was strange; really strange. Must have been my imagination.

A few minutes later somebody turned round to me.

'*Habari gani, Chris?*' (Hi, how is it going, Chris?)

I was shocked but I replied in the same manner.

'*Kila kito ni poa sana.*' (Things are really good.)

I then asked my new friend what he was doing here, such a long way from home. He said that, no, this was home, that he lived here. He went on to call some others over and they were all speaking fluent Swahili, just as you would hear it in East Africa.

I thought, 'What is this? Are they on holiday? On the run?' They didn't look like tourists.

It turns out that there are a lot of East Africans in the country, and many people in Oman speak Swahili because of the big influx of East Africans into the country.

That made my day. It was a really nice surprise, getting the leader's jersey and then being able to make some small talk in Swahili.

After we'd finished shooting the breeze, the team car was waiting to take me back to the hotel. This was the first thing I learned about life in a leader's jersey: you no longer took the bus and you were filed off from the team. Your colleagues had eaten and showered on the bus back to the hotel while you would be detained for other duties.

While your teammates were being massaged, you would still be winding your way back.

I had been finding it harder than usual to read Brad all week. On Green Mountain, for instance, he hadn't done much to help the team. The last 10 kilometres into the bottom of the climb involved the usual jostling, pushing and shoving and it was quite hectic. But I didn't see Brad there; he just stayed out of it, above it.

The plan had been for him to lead us into the bottom of that climb and to take us up on the first kilometre or so, but instead we were all over the place. I don't think there was anybody around me and this was disappointing after such a long, slow wind up.

Unfortunately the team meetings weren't going great either.

Nico Portal was moderating the discussions in the mornings and the tension was written all over the poor guy's face. These were no longer the usual open forums. It wasn't, 'Okay, guys, well, what are we going to do today?' Instead, the atmosphere was very tense and forced. We all enjoy working with Nico but you could see he was under pressure.

I felt that everybody was on eggshells around Brad and how he was feeling about not being top banana. I had hoped that all this would have been dealt with in Brad's head, and by Dave, who has some access to Brad's head, before we got there.

In the meetings Nico's voice would occasionally tremble as he spoke about the stage ahead. Every day was judgement day for Nico: Dave looking at him, Brad looking at him, all of us just looking at him. How would he describe Brad's role? And my role?

At the end of each meeting Dave would try to get round and speak to everybody to gee us up: 'Just enjoy it. Go out and have a good ride.'

Okay, Dave!

But the mood was way too tense. Nobody ever added anything to what Nico was saying, we were in too much of a hurry to get away.

One evening Brad was having physio or running late and didn't show for dinner. The atmosphere was completely different; it became light-hearted with the usual banter and nobody tiptoeing around the situation.

I said to Pete Kennaugh, 'Does this feel different to you?' He nearly exploded with relief.

'Fooking hell, I thought it was just me. It's not! I'm glad you said something. I'm afraid to open my mouth.'

It felt very unhealthy with everybody on edge; like a week working at a job poisoned by office politics. We were there because we were paid to be there, but the dynamics were off.

I had gone to Oman thinking that I had to race with these guys as often as possible, the ones I would be at the Tour with, and help to set the mood within the team for the season to come. Everybody should feel free to say what they'd like to say over dinner, and there should be no tensions. There was work to be done to get us on the right path.

The stage after Green Mountain caught us all off guard and was much harder than any of us had imagined. It went over the same climb, came back and went over again: three times in all and then to the finish.

We had gone over the climb once and Christian Knees and Joe Dombrowski had both done really decent pulls. Joe, in particular, had set a very good pace. When we got down to the U-turn and came up the climb for the second time I can remember being astounded that Brad was in the line. This was where we really needed him to take his turn and pull on the front and race hard. 'He's going to do it,' I thought. Then, suddenly, he seemed to remember a prior engagement. It literally looked as if he pulled the brakes. He swung out of the line and dropped off just as the second climb began. He hadn't done a pull or a turn on the front. Maybe he'd left the gas on at home?

It really felt to me that he wasn't interested, that he just didn't feel like suffering that day.

I don't know if it was that or if he didn't want to ride for me. I was coming to the conclusion that if you were riding out to battle through early-morning mists with your standards flying high, Sir Bradley

Wiggins was a man you would want at your side. Because after lunch he just might not be bothered.

I tried to keep the rest of the guys together in our formation. Halfway up the climb Saxo Bank took it up again with Contador and a couple of his henchmen pushing everybody hard. Very quickly I was left with Richie and it was just the two of us.

Richie did an incredible job. He pulled to the last kilometre of that second climb, getting back to Contador who had attacked off the front. Then Contador sat on the front and controlled the race all the way round and down the mountain, before doing the U-turn and leading us back up for the last time.

Saxo Bank came swarming around us quite early on the final climb. After a few hundred metres they were pulling really hard, trying to launch Contador off the front. Richie had already done quite a bit of tough work containing things and when Contador went, I could see Richie was close to being done.

I said to Richie, 'Relax, it's great, you are doing just fine, he's not getting away from us. Just keep working. You are doing a great job.'

Richie carried on pulling for a little bit longer and then turned to me. I could see he was spent.

Contador was about 15 seconds up the road so I accelerated from the group I was in towards him. Rodríguez hung on to my wheel and now we were both in pursuit. When we got to the top of the last climb Contador was probably only about 7 to 10 seconds in front of us.

There were a few more lumps and bumps and then the proper descent. On the little dip where it started going down I could see that Contador got up out of his saddle, sprinting to get on to the back of the camera motorbike. I was working hard behind in the headwind and was worried. If he managed to get the protection offered by the motorbike he would gain a few extra kilometres an hour right there. I was on the limit already so I really wanted him not to make the motorbike. I turned to Rodríguez and told him he needed to help me now. If he didn't, we would both lose.

He made his calculation. He did his share of the work. He came through. I was happy to have his help. Rodríguez is a rider

I respect – somehow his love for the bike and the sport has always seemed really pure to me. Once at the hotel in Tenerife when I was there with Team Sky, he was there on his own. No team, no minders, just a guy and his bike doing a lot of good work, and loving it. His nickname is Purito, which is actually Spanish for little cigar, but to me it seemed to reflect the purity of his character. 'Purito,' I thought, 'you're well named.'

We got Contador back on a little dip near the start of the descent, and we rode down the mountain eyeing each other. On one of the corners I felt like I had taken the wrong line and I was forced to pull my brakes a little harder than I should have done. A very small gap opened up to Contador, just a few metres more than he would have been expecting. He was as quick as a cobra to spot this and was up and ready to strike on the next corner.

I could see he was pushing harder than he would do normally because I had lost his wheel for that one second. It was a good lesson for me. If I gave this guy 10 centimetres he would take 10 metres. He looks for every chance to get one over.

The three of us more or less rolled on into the stretch. When we got to about a kilometre to go I knew that nobody wanted to do a turn. The two of them had pulled but that was over. I could see them looking at each other; alliances were shifting.

That was my cue to say, *Sorry, guys, I'm going to go for it. Now.* I don't think I stood up or sprinted. I just sat in my saddle and accelerated, trying to get a gap on them. They were on to it pretty quickly and within a few hundred metres they had me reeled me back.

With 500 metres to go now, the three of us were still looking at each other, and I was still on the front. A stand-off prevailed. There would be no more mutual interest; just three selfish cats.

Nobody wanted to lead it out and our brains had to be whirring as quickly as our wheels because we had to make the right call and go with it. I decided to take things into my own hands with about 300 metres to go and then lay down a sprint. They weren't going to take GC time on me today. That was the main thing; I had nothing to lose.

As so often happens, the wind determined the tactics. When I started the sprint I could feel that the breeze was coming from the front left. I was the furthest over on the right-hand side of the road against the barrier, and the road also curved round to the right.

Everything favoured the guy who started the sprint because anybody coming past him had to go the long way round to take the outside lane, thus doing more distance. They would be coming out to the left and into the wind as opposed to just coming round me on the right and getting the slipstream while coming past me.

I realized as I wound it up that I could win this stage.

And so it was. Contador made an effort to come round the long way on my left but I had enough in the tank to hold him off.

Defending the lead with a stage win was a good feeling.

The last day in Oman was more or less a criterium-type race. Again, Brad surprised me. We got out on to the circuit and it was a gunfight with lots of pushing and shoving, and sprint teams coming to the front. There was a small climb on the circuit and a section where you almost had to jump over the pavement to get on to a roundabout and double back. It was quite a tricky circuit in parts and wide open in other sections, which meant that riders could come round you easily. Brad did some massive pulls on the wide stretches. He'd get on the front and it would almost feel like he was riding a time trial and we were all sitting on his wheel.

I was impressed and bewildered. It crossed my mind that this incredibly strong ride on the front was part of his own training, rather than rolling up his sleeves and doing a job for either me or the team. I hope I'm not being unfair to him, but I just didn't know.

'This is Brad,' I thought. 'This is just how he is. One day he is fantastic but other days you can't rely on him. That's his personality. He was up for it today, but yesterday, it seemed, he wasn't. I am glad to have him when he is doing a good job. When he is up for it, he can be excellent. When he wants to engage with people, he can be charming.'

Listen, Brad looks like Paul Weller; I look like Tintin.

Maybe we're not created to appear in the same story.

27

The old story about burning the boats is a motivational cliché now. Alexander the Great had landed on the shores of Persia where his army was going to be vastly outnumbered. Some of his generals argued that the wisest course was to regroup and to come back another day with more men. One asked, fairly reasonably in the circumstances, about how everybody would get home after work. But Alexander, on hearing this, gave the order for his men to burn the boats. He turned to his soldiers and roared, 'We go home in Persian ships, or we die.' In other words, if your commitment is complete, defeat isn't an option at all.

In March we went to Italy for the Race of the Two Seas, or the Tirreno–Adriatico. Not a lot sticks in the memory except the mountaintop finish on stage four. I took it ahead of Contador, Nibali and Rodríguez. For me, that win after a 15-kilometre climb up the Prati di Tivo was confirmation that things were still on the right track. I was developing some consistency and the team were working well. On the climb that day my teammates controlled everything and left me to launch off to the summit with a kilometre to go. The stage win put me within 4 seconds of the lead with three stages left.

I was starting to settle into a leadership role that didn't come naturally to me. I had never seen myself standing on a beach ordering men to burn their boats. My inclination would be to suggest other travel options or get Michelle to go online and check out the work visa requirements in Persia. The idea of having a train of professional cyclists working for me was odd but we were establishing a pattern. In Italy I had the two Colombians Rigoberto Urán and Sergio Henao with me and they did a huge job on the mountain the day we won. Dario Cataldo did too.

I felt that following on from Oman we were settling into a method of winning mountaintop finishes. Rigoberto's story is one about the realities of professional life. The team seemed to realize early on that of the two Colombians we could afford to keep only one long term. It was rumoured they were both going to Quick-Step and rather than lose them both we had to choose the one we thought had the greater potential. Sergio fitted better into the Sky model, although Rigoberto was stronger. Sergio was young and willing to learn; he was the Moneyball choice. Rigoberto was more set in his ways.

On the climb up Prati di Tivo, Nibali and Contador had been attacking enthusiastically and flying up the road. I found I was preaching calm, a chip off the Kerrison block. 'No stress, guys. No problems. We'll carry on riding this high tempo and we'll get them in a minute. Trust me.' That was quite something. When we then won the stage it vindicated how we were going about things; I had fresher legs than Contador and Nibali in the last kilometre.

It was a style that had been developed by Tim for Brad: ride the stage in the manner of a time trial and see what happens. Now I brought to the table an ability to accelerate off a high tempo. This was the most efficient way to win a stage; let other teams waste energy making attacks. But I also had the sense after that mountain that we were being picked apart by other teams as they tried to find ways to beat us. On stage five I took the leader's jersey and there was some grumbling from Nibali about the style of our riding.

The penultimate day, stage six, was a very hilly ride around Porto Sant'Elpidio. The weather was miserable and we raced badly, tactically speaking, letting a very big breakaway go early. That put us under pressure to ride hard all day trying to get them back. Thirty riders had gone up the road and we had been slow to respond, debating among ourselves as to whether we were chasing or waiting. Back in the car our directeur sportif, Marcus, didn't really know what was going on. He asked us to chase and told us not to worry; we were in chaos and it was lousy weather. But by the time we settled on a plan we had to chase pretty hard.

The stage incorporated Muro di Sant'Elpidio, a short but brutal climb that we had to take three times. I would have said that morning that I had never met a climb I didn't fancy the look of but the weather here changed my mind.

I had lots of race food in my pockets, including gels and rice cakes, but the race itself was too full on and I had lost all feeling in my fingers from the cold, which meant that I couldn't even manage to lift my rain jacket over my pockets to get at the food. With the driving rain and strong crosswinds, there was never a chance to refuel properly. Also, I hadn't dressed for the weather. I had worn a short-sleeved rain jacket for most of the day and it was only when I was too cold to feel my extremities that I thought to ask for a long-sleeved one.

On the last ride up the climb Nibali went away with Peter Sagan and all I could do was turn my gears and get up the climb as best I could. It was that sort of day. Over fifty riders quit altogether and a large number, myself included, got their gearing wrong. My cadence dropped to fifty revolutions a minute, which felt like strength work, grinding just one stroke at a time. It was so wet that when you stood up to put pressure on the pedals your back wheel would simply slide as if the bike were on rollers; there was no traction. This meant we had to sit in our saddles, making it even harder. Normally when it gets that steep – up to gradients of twenty-seven per cent – all you want to do is stand up and use your weight on the pedals. It wasn't to be.

So I hung with the group I found myself with. I limited the losses but lost the jersey. The worst aspect was the feeling that I had let my teammates down. They had put me in the leader's jersey. When it came to the crunch in the bad weather they had buried themselves again. After the race I got on the bus cold and shivering and full of apologies: *Sorry. I couldn't follow Nibali. Thanks for all that you did.* The response from guy to guy was the same: *Don't worry, bro. That was a day from hell. Now let me jump into the shower.*

The week finished with a time trial in San Benedicto del Tronto. I was 34 seconds behind Nibali as I rolled down the ramp. The course was just 9.2 kilometres and not enough to take that 34 seconds back. End of story.

It was a disappointing defeat but it wasn't a lack of form that had caused the loss. I had been caught off guard and learned a lesson about the cold: overdress don't underdress. This was not so much a rookie error as an African error. As a team we had learned a bit about controlling the race more efficiently from the start. We would make sure in future that the only breakaways that got away in the morning were the ones that we were prepared to allow to let go.

Nibali threw a pinch of salt into the wounds with some comments about how we at Team Sky race by numbers and spend our days huddled over our SRM meters trying to work out our next move. Little did he know.

For a while Michelle had been eyeing up the trophy for winning the race, which was a lovely trident. I think she had a spot picked out for it! Now Nibali had the trident and thought I cared about being called an SRM slave.

I was enjoying the challenge of leading the team. That day on Prati di Tivo in Italy when we had watched the big guys riding off up the road and had the guts to say, 'It's fine, let them go,' only to reel them in later, gave us the rush you might get from playing high-stakes poker. We had to trust in the strength of our own hand.

After Tirreno, the two-day Critérium International had additional importance as it took place in Corsica where the Tour itself would be starting and staying for three stages. We went over early so that we could do a recce of the Tour stages before the start of the Critérium. I remember noting that the third stage was going to be quite tough. Winding and undulating, a crosswind could blow the field apart that early.

The Critérium itself started with a short 89-kilometre stage on Saturday morning where practically the entire field came home in a bunch sprint. The real racing commenced after lunch with a short time trial where Richie took the jersey a couple of seconds ahead of me. Richie was the leader overnight, continuing the amazing form he had shown in winning Paris–Nice a couple of weeks before.

The third and last stage took place on Sunday with a mountaintop finish on Col de l'Ospedale. Richie had the jersey so our plans changed. We had worked out our tactics before the race began. If I had a lead after the time trial Richie would attack towards the end of the next day's stage. If our rivals couldn't bring him back then he would win the stage and most likely the race. If they got up to him, that would set it up for me to counter-attack them in the last kilometre.

With Richie beating me in the time trial, the roles switched. Now I would attack 2 kilometres out and Richie would counter if they hauled me back. It worked pretty much perfectly.

Kosta and Josh Edmondson rode well to control the race for us, but with more than 30 kilometres left to go, Richie and I were left with only Kiryienka. Kiri took the challenge head-on. He sat on the floor for the next 20 kilometres, reeling back attacks and keeping the pace high a good way up to the climb. It was impressive to say the least. It was then my turn to pull and I pulled hard. Richie thought this was the point to let me go on.

I had gone on the front to pull but Richie sat off the wheel and let the gap open. He turned to the other riders and looked for a reaction. He got on to Tejay van Garderen's wheel as Tejay started chasing me.

It wasn't long before I got across to a few others who had broken away earlier. I could see straight off that they would be of no help so I attacked them and rode on my own to the finish.

Back down the road Richie saw that Tejay was labouring as the climb went on, so Richie attacked him. We ended up coming in 1st and 2nd.

I took the jersey off Richie. I felt a little apprehensive; it didn't give me any pleasure to take the jersey off my friend and teammate. But, typical of the man, there wasn't an ounce of resentment in his face.

'Hey' he said, 'we smashed them! They didn't know what to do!'

It was this moment, I think, which truly cemented our friendship. For the two of us it had been a day in the saddle when we didn't need words. I just looked round at him once that little gap had formed and he had sat off my wheel. He was in the leader's jersey but he was saying, 'Go, and keep going.' I also know I would have done the same for him. In a heartbeat.

I remember the two of us coming back home after that, knowing we were both on a really good path. We just needed to keep that competition between us in training and that bond between us in races.

In Tenerife I had amused myself by getting a small wearable action camera with special bike mounts. You can stick it on the front of the bike, or on the back; anywhere, really. I spent my time thinking of cool ways of filming the training we were doing. I hoped to put something together at the end of it to show people what we do, including all the exercises, the team time trials and the days where we go right to our limits, pushing ourselves even harder than in a race.

I particularly enjoyed the team time trials up the mountain, so I put the camera behind my saddle so that the lens was looking back at the guy behind me. I was able to film his facial expressions over a half-hour climb that got faster and faster as we approached the end of our team effort.

We would break the squad down into two or three teams and have a full-speed race trying to catch each other. On this particular day I was in a team with Pete Kennaugh, David López, Dario Cataldo and a couple of others. Pete was having it tough; he was behind me and not really ready for his close-up.

We premiered the video afterwards – you might call it a tragi-comedy. It was hilarious to see Pete's face as he tried to get back on the wheel at the end of his turn: wincing with pain trying to hang in there. We watched him get to the last kilometre and eventually just blow up. It was funny because we all knew the pain. Pete's face was all of our faces.

When we come home from Tenerife, and from the daily inflictions of Tim's imagination, we are generally all a kilo or two lighter and generating more power.

After Tenerife, time was shortening and the dates in the calendar were crowding together. The Tour de Romandie was at the end of April. Then back to Tenerife and then on to the Critérium du Dauphiné.

Romandie is a race which throws up a worthwhile story. We needed the story to have a happy and meaningful ending this time because we had just done Liège–Bastogne–Liège, complete with all the usual luck that I enjoy in that part of the world. I punctured early and was on the back foot all day. Sergio was our other leader in the race but he didn't have a good day either. In terms of La Doyenne, my coming home in 36th place was actually a personal triumph.

In Romandie there was a predominantly uphill prologue which I won, with Andrew Talansky, another young American on the scene, coming in 2nd. I kept the lead till the end of the race but, more importantly, we all rode well: no dramas, no crises.

The penultimate stage of the five days was a sentimental journey around some of the roads and slopes where I had trained when I went to the UCI school in Aigle as a naive young kid out of Africa. I had to remind myself that this was now; all that stuff was a long, long time ago.

I wrapped the race up on that fourth stage. The weather was so bad that the final ascent up the snow-capped Col de la Croix had to be abandoned in favour of something more rider-friendly. I had learned to cope with bad weather while the conditions had broken the peloton into pieces. The team rode heroically. Towards the end of the last climb the attacks came right, left and centre. You couldn't begin to cover every one of them; the only option was to counter.

Myself and Simon Špilak of Katusha ended up away from the field. When we crossed the line at Les Diablerets he had the stage and I had sown the guts of a minute into my GC rivals. The final day was a time trial. Job done.

We had worked hard for the week in Romandie, grinding out the result. Once I got back home my mind dawdled over the possibilities for the Tour.

The cast was shaping up. Pete Kennaugh, the star of the time-trial snuff movie, had looked a few kilos lighter the previous week; he is a guy who can keep his hands by his sides when the bread arrives. At Romandie he auditioned strongly for a role on the Tour. Geraint Thomas and Ian Stannard had been in my mind from the beginning of the season because of their tactical ability, as well as their riding; they are very good with positioning. If they've got the legs, you find them in the right place at the right time.

David López had been solid. Edvald Boasson Hagen was certain to be in the team, a good all-rounder who had been one of the strong men in the previous year's Tour. Kosta? It was too early to say as he was coming back gingerly from a broken leg and he had to ride the Giro; it would be a tall ask.

Ditto with Christian Knees; he was going to the Giro with Brad. Pulling that off and then riding the Tour would have been hard. In terms of the big guys, it was between Christian and Stannard. I had ridden more with Ian, and Christian was doing the Giro. I like a guy who understands crosswinds; a guy who has the physical arrogance to muscle his way into a place near the front and who then fights for it no matter what. Ian, I thought, was that guy. I thought Kiryienka would make it too although he had already had a long and tough season.

Brad going for the Giro meant diluting the team's strength and both of us would pay a price for this. He would have the Colombians pulling for him in the mountains but I would have Richie at my side in the Tour.

There was speculation that Brad was going to do the Giro and then the Tour. I wasn't sure. He could be the man to take us into the last climb and maybe halfway up it because he does have a big, big engine. He would also be a major asset for the team time trial. But, before that, we had to be sure that he and I could work together.

It was a recovery day. I had been out earlier on an easy ride after Romandie and was now back at my apartment going through emails when I started getting all kinds of alerts coming through on my email. Then text messages on my phone.

Uh oh. Something was happening in the world. People were asking what the story was with Brad. *What's going on with Brad? Have you seen this?*

Brad had done a press conference. The gist of his message was that he was thinking now about trying to do the double. If the Giro went well, then why not the Tour? He said he would come in as a joint leader, and after the first week we would see who was in the better position. As defending champion, many probably thought that what he said was reasonable.

Within the team, it was seen differently. He had just gone back on everything that had been agreed beforehand; things that had been said and understood for a long time. On the second rest day of the 2012 Tour he had taken me aside when we were out on a recovery ride near Pau. His words were: 'Listen, Froomey, don't worry, I'll be back here next year to help you.'

He had told me that my chance would come, and that he would be pulling as hard as he could for me. He'd confirmed that as recently as in Mallorca in January when he told the media he was focusing on the Giro but going to the Tour 'to help Chris'.

Now it all seemed pretty hollow. Brad had issued a gilt-edged invitation to the media. *Sir Bradley Wiggins cordially invites you to Wiggins vs Froome, a duel to the death to be staged under a July sun . . .*

There was a populist appeal to his argument. He was the Tour de France champion, the Olympic gold medallist, the mod god. A lot of people generally didn't understand why he couldn't just win another Tour de France as a matter of course.

I was confused; I didn't know where all this had come from. It hadn't been discussed with me and it hadn't been talked about within the team.

This stuff at the press conference wasn't glib. It wasn't a voluble man letting his mouth run away from his brain. Brad is bright, he's articulate. He doesn't often open his mouth just to make small talk.

In Pau that day in 2012 he asked me just to get him through that last week and he'd be here in 2013 to help me. It was very powerful to hear him say that; I knew it wasn't easy for him. For the rest of that last week I didn't leave his side. I believed him.

I tried to get hold of Dave. No luck. I got Chris Haynes, our head of media, on the line.

'Listen, Chris, what is going on there? Was this in the messaging plan that was given through the team?' Whenever we do a media day we get briefed beforehand on key messages, things that the team would like us to put forward.

Chris didn't see that anything was out of place.

'No, things went smoothly and it all went according to plan . . .'

He wasn't the man I needed to speak to. Either that or I was completely out of the loop and had been deluding myself all year. To fend off the media I issued a statement via email saying that as far as I was aware nothing had changed from the team's side; I was going to the Tour de France as leader.

I sent a copy to Dave's office adding a note that this message would be much stronger if it came from the team. The subtext was: *or is Brad now bigger than the team?*

I spoke to Dave the next day. He said he hadn't seen Brad's statement. He claimed that none of it had been discussed with him but he knew that Brad was under a lot of scrutiny. People couldn't understand why he wasn't defending his Tour title. He was just saving face.

I was confident in what Dave said. I believed that it wasn't a conspiracy within the team. I got ready for another two-week stint in Tenerife. It was 30 April. The bomb was defused but the clock kept ticking. Shortly afterwards, Dave issued a statement:

'Given Chris's step up in performances this year, our plan, as it has been since January, is to have him lead the Tour de France team.'

Hallelujah.

In Tenerife on top of our old volcano the internet seldom works. The rooms have small prison-cell TV sets that only trade in Spanish. There is nothing interesting to do and no distraction. We rely on each other for entertainment and, knowing just how entertaining we all are, we take the precaution of bringing box sets of television series.

For those two weeks we were all watching *Dexter*, a very dark comedy series about a serial killer. We thought it was a comedy anyway. The main character is basically a forensic analyst. He's the good guy in the programme, but there's a slight catch in that he moonlights as a serial killer. To his credit he only kills murderers and people who have slipped through the cracks in the pavement of the legal system . . .

We all enjoy _Dexter_. The thing was, Dexter himself looked very like . . . well, very much like Tim Kerrison. It just seemed too perfect that this guy was the sort of very dry laboratory analyst who lived his life through numbers and was really methodical about everything.

Poor Tim. By day he was coming up with tortures which he might inflict on us out on the mountain. Killing us softly with his stats. Then in the evening he was helping us bond by appearing to us in the guise of a fictional serial killer.

Apart from that we had little or no distraction. If it was somebody's birthday we had a small celebration. My own birthday is 20 May. Normally we would take the chance to go to a restaurant in Villaflor, a good half-hour drive down the mountain. We might run wild and sinful by allowing ourselves to eat something different. We might even have a few sips of wine. Decadence. But on 20 May we were flying home so there was no chance of an evening celebration. That morning, instead, we had a surprise. Knowing my weakness for pancakes, Michelle had contacted the soigneurs to see if they could get the kitchen staff to make some pancakes for breakfast. The waiters brought out a big platter of pancakes for us all. It was really nice and something different.

The last step before the Tour was the Critérium du Dauphiné starting on 2 June.

When we planned the season I knew that Brad would be at the Giro. But he had won the Dauphiné for the last two years and he would haunt us, although I didn't know how.

Brad had pulled out of the heavily touted Giro campaign after twelve days, laid low with a chest infection. He was also having a little trouble with his knee. A few days later he announced that he was in no condition to ride the Tour.

I knew the team hadn't just dodged a bullet; we had ducked a cannonball. No matter what was said or how much we had deferred to each other in public, the first weeks of the Tour would have been played as Froome against Wiggins. The gangly Kenyan-born Brit against loveably gruff mod geezer.

The media would have had fun and the Tour would have had its storyline, but the pressure could have cracked the team. Deciding where to sit at breakfast might have become a political decision.

Instead we went into the Dauphiné with a sense of relief. On a personal level it was a tough break for Brad and after the year he had enjoyed in 2012 the disintegration of 2013 seemed cruel. On a professional level it meant getting on with what had to be done. Life: it goes on.

The Dauphiné didn't have a mountaintop finish till stage five, which ended on the massive Valmorel. Everything came together for us that day. Contador attacked late but not convincingly after we had worked well all day pushing a high pace. He was reeled in and I accelerated away to take the stage win and the yellow jersey.

The next day we even got up early and did a recce of stage seventeen of the Tour, the time trial to Chorges. We had left another marker down on top of another mountain. There were three stages left, but the race was basically over. In the mist and rain to Risoul on the Sunday we applied the lessons we had learned in the spring and didn't respond instantly when Contador made his big attack. We upped our pace and waited for the race to come to us.

The Dauphiné finished with Richie and I on the top two steps of the podium. We had eight of the nine guys who would ride the Tour with us at the Dauphiné. Kosta was the exception.

We went to the French Alps for our final preparations. Our team. My team.

28

2013: The Tour de France

Stage One: Saturday 29 June, Porto-Vecchio to Bastia, 213 kilometres

Here we were.

I had caught a plane to Corsica on Wednesday. The ferry ride would have been more spectacular but it takes around three hours to get here from Nice. No romance – I was going to work.

The usual pre-tour hoopla began: a medical, followed by a press conference, followed by a presentation. The team rode to the latter in a motorboat, with all of us trying to give deep, meaningful looks like Vikings arriving to pillage a new land.

As usual the media attention felt odd. Every person in the press conference room seemed to have at least four cameras and we looked out into a wall of lenses, microphones and lights. If you scratched your nose, crinkled your face or looked up at the ceiling, the shutters whirred. So you looked blank and vacant. No Viking stuff here.

Nine of us would live and breathe together for the next three weeks: myself, Richie, Edvald Boasson Hagen (Eddie), Vasil Kiry-ienka (Kiri), Kanstantsin Siutsou (Kosta), David López, Ian Stannard (Yogi), Geraint 'G' Thomas and Pete Kennaugh.

From the Isle of Man to Belorussia, the Ngong Hills to Norway, Spain to Tasmania – some anthology of life stories for one team.

Over the next twenty-three days we would race twenty-one stages: two individual time trials, one team time trial, seven flat stages, five stages which were a bit hilly and six mountain stages. Four of the mountain stages would have summit finishes. For us, the Tour would probably be won or lost on those stages.

To paraphrase the golfers, 'we sprint for show, we climb for dough'. And stage one was mostly for show.

We were rolling out of Porto-Vecchio for Le Grand Départ; our heads full of dreams and plans.

The day began with a gentle ride through the neutral zone. I always give myself a little task each morning when we're rolling through the zone. Today I tried to get to the front of the race by the time we reached the official starting point, where race director Christian Prudhomme would wave the white flag.

I do this because I like to start at the front; I don't like the idea that I have to catch up before we've even started. I began roughly halfway back in the bunch, slowly moving up the sides. I could feel everyone was slightly more nervous than usual, but then again, this *was* the start of the Tour. I felt confident though; I had my teammates around me as we went up towards the front.

Richie was just in front of me with Yogi. The three of us were moving up together when we got to a left-hand turn, which sort of doubled back on itself and then dropped downhill. Now the speed started picking up.

It was a slightly tricky turn, but nothing crazy. And we were only going about twenty kilometres an hour. But as the turn looped back on itself, the width on the outer side of the road narrowed.

The barriers that had been placed in the road squeezed the space on the corner, making it tighter than expected. Well, much tighter than I expected.

Richie made it round the barriers but only just. I didn't. I couldn't brake in time.

Going towards them, I was thinking, 'Please let the barriers be plastic . . . if I hit them they're going to just move a few metres and I'll be able to unclip fast and carry on.'

Turns out they were concrete. I hit one and it didn't budge a millimetre. The bike stopped dead and I went from being on the saddle to being half over the wall. I didn't actually hit the ground, but draped myself there like a coat dropped on the back of a sofa.

For maximum indignity, one of my legs remained clipped into the bike. As it went down on to the ground, I dropped on to the wall and my other leg remained still attached to the left pedal.

I – a team leader in the Tour de France, on stage one, in the neutral zone, doing twenty kilometres an hour – had crashed into a concrete barrier.

I was dazed and grazed, and landed quite hard on the side of my leg and arm. There was a bit of blood, I'd got a dead leg and my pride was broken in about nine places. But if I had been shot full of bullet holes at that moment, I was still getting back on that bike.

This race wasn't going to ride away from me before it had even started.

I'd fallen on the right side of the bike, which had the derailleur, the gears and all the mechanisms. Froome's law. That *would* be the side I fell on. The derailleur had bent and I could see the damage straight away. So I called for a new bike on the radio and said I'd had a small crash.

There was silence on the line; then again, people make no noise when they roll their eyeballs.

Eventually Nico said, 'Okay, we're coming, Chris.'

Nico is pretty calm but I could pick up the concern in his voice. From an outside perspective I'm sure it would have looked like: FROOME CRASHES IN NEUTRALIZED ZONE! HOLD THE BACK PAGE . . .

Thankfully Gary Blem, our lead mechanic, was in the car and was on to it straight away. I got the spare bike.

The race also hadn't gone too far ahead. When I caught up, the guys were all at the back waiting. Except Richie, who had been told to stay with the bunch.

Seeing the team hanging back, waiting for their leader, did nothing to diminish the embarrassment.

I'm sure a lot of people, including some of my rivals, would have enjoyed this, thinking that I was a nervous wreck. Sky had gone from having all their eggs in Brad's basket to being led by a basket case: 'If he can't even make it through the neutral zone, he's not going to make it off this island without having lost ten minutes . . . He might drown when we hit the coast!' I felt there might be a Crash Froome Anecdote competition inaugurated in my memory: 'He hit a commissaire. He rode over an old man. He ended up in a garden.'

More than anything it was my pride which was damaged. I responded with frantic nonchalance. Ultimately, I still felt relaxed in myself, and I began to laugh at it. This was typical for me. Last year it was the nose plugs . . .

I steadily moved through the group again. There were a few comments as I moved up, with guys saying, 'Ah! Are you okay?' with big grins on their faces. I tried to joke it off: 'Yeah, yeah, yeah . . . just taken my stabilizers off . . . bit wobbly . . . still learning.'

However, when I thought about it later I got a sick feeling in my stomach. If I had been going a little bit faster, the spill could have been nasty; it really could have been the end of my Tour before it had begun. Who would trust me to lead again?

I was mightily thankful to have a bruise and a dead leg and nothing more.

Luckily the race laid on more embarrassment and controversy and by dinner time I was just a footnote. The Orica-GreenEdge team bus had got jammed under a gantry over the finish line. The organizers moved the finish forward by 3 kilometres and somebody eventually had to let the air out of the bus's tyres for it to be freed. The finish was moved back again and then there was a mass crash. Contador took a tumble, as did G Thomas, who was shot like a human cannonball over his handlebars. He came back to earth with a bang; he thought his pelvis was broken.

Marcel Kittel won the sprint; Cav lost his shot at yellow when he had a crash near the finish.

Making a show of myself on the opening stage soon became old news.

Welcome to the Tour.

WINNER: MARCEL KITTEL
2: ALEXANDER KRISTOFF
41: CHRIS FROOME
(ALL RIDERS AWARDED THE SAME TIME.)

Stage Two: Sunday 30 June, Bastia to Ajaccio, 156 kilometres

Corsica is drenched in history. A lot had been said about this, the one-hundredth staging of the Tour de France taking place entirely within the nation's borders. Even as we rode, people were worrying themselves about Corsican separatism, but I had no side to take in the discussion. I just knew it wouldn't really feel like the Tour until we got back to the mainland, and what felt like France. But with the rocky landscape of Corsica set dramatically against the perfect blue sea, I was hardly itching to get out of there.

That day was all set up for the sprinters. We rode down to Ajaccio, the birthplace of Napoleon Bonaparte. Everybody started but we were worried about the health of G Thomas.

There was a modest climb thrown into the stage just to keep us interested. I needed to take my body for a test drive so I took off and went over the top ahead of the bunch. The bonus was being able to come down the other side without worrying about more chaos in Corsica. One spill on the tricky downhill could have scattered a lot of us all over the hillside. For a man yet to master riding slowly around concrete barriers it was best to play safe.

Having tweeted birthday wishes to Michelle in the morning my attack prompted speculation that I was attempting to win the stage as a romantic gesture. Alas, it wasn't to be.

RadioShack-Leopard's Jan Bakelants won the stage ahead of Peter Sagan. I trundled home safe and happy in the peloton.

WINNER: JAN BAKELANTS
OVERALL GC   1: JAN BAKELANTS
                    2: PETER SAGAN +1SEC
                    18: CHRIS FROOME +1SEC

Stage Three: Monday 1 July, Ajaccio to Calvi, 145.5 kilometres

Up the west coast to Calvi. A mildly lumpy ride.

We didn't have a good day and G was in agony. If he were a

racehorse we would have him put down. He was Welsh though. He was surviving that too.

Two-thirds of the way along the road he appeared out of the blue beside myself and Richie at the front of the peloton.

'Not dead yet, G?' we asked.

'Goooo on, boys,' he roared and let us be. My old friend Daryl Impey performed a fine lead out to set the stage up for Simon Gerrans. A South African, setting up an Aussie, in Corsica. Who would have thought?

After the day's stage, a lot of the guys in our team felt frustrated. We went over the last climb with only two or three in a front group of about ninety. They felt they needed to step it up; they hadn't been in the right places when they needed to be. There was no sense of despair though; no self-doubt. Just an itch to get started properly – we had something to prove.

At the end of the day I was still on course. And so was Richie. We hadn't been great, but we had been strong enough to keep everyone's hope alive. If anything, Corsica – especially that day – was just a bit of a wake-up call. We were not sailing through this race; sacrifice and suffering were all that lay ahead.

WINNER: SIMON GERRANS
OVERALL GC   1: JAN BAKELANTS
    2: JULIEN SIMON +1SEC
    15: CHRIS FROOME +1SEC

Stage Four: Tuesday 2 July, Nice Team Time Trial, 25 kilometres

Team. Time. Trial. These days are a long shredding of the nerves. One screw-up and the whole peloton is laughing at you. Go well, and you make a statement.

Richie and I got changed into our time-trial skins and put our helmets on in the hotel room. We took a few goofy selfies to take some of the pressure off, then we got to work.

Team. Time. Trial.

Everyone was in one long line pumping as hard as they could. We

were individual parts of the same machine; just one of us feeling
bad could have a chain reaction. When you're racing in one frantic
line, it's quite hard to make calls to the guy on the front. Should he
be going faster? Or slower? On the other side of the coin, when
things go well, it's smooth and it's beautiful and no one needs to say a
thing.

But you never really know what's going to happen.

Geraint was the limping question mark today. There was a crack in
his pelvis; on the X-ray, it looked like a river. For normal people, this
would mean ceasing all activity. For G it meant somebody had to
give him a hand getting his leg over the saddle.

We couldn't put him anywhere else other than on the back. If he
was going to lose the wheel in front of him, he couldn't take the guys
with him. If we lost him, we couldn't wait. We all knew his difficulty
would be hanging on through the first few kilometres, when his
body would be trying to bully him into submission.

The plan had been to keep it smooth but fast through the initial
few corners until we got out on to the big promenade, where it was
open and wide. We would leave G on the back, and if he felt good
enough to contribute at any point it would be a bonus.

We settled: we each did a turn, filtered back, and then got in line
just in front of G. Nico was on the radio calling the shots.

'Okay, Kosta, you're coming back now, you need to slip in behind
G or . . . oh no, behind Yogi. Or Eddie.'

He did that for almost every rider coming through. We also had
hand signals. If you had spent a little too much energy and were
going to slow it down for everybody, you dropped off and when you
got to the back, or just in front of G, you gave a thumbs-down sign.
This told Nico that you needed some extra recovery time and you
would skip a turn. So then the next one coming back would pull in,
just in front of you.

'Okay, guys, López is now skipping a turn on the back. Yogi, you
need to come in behind Kiri.'

When you were ready to go again you gave the thumbs-up sign
and Nico did the rest.

'Okay, fall in behind López now, he's coming back into the line.'

After about 5 or 6 kilometres riding on the big open promenade, Geraint started moving up through the line. He came and did a turn; he sustained our high speed.

What a lift.

He filtered back through the line, roaring in his Welsh accent. 'Let's have it! Gooo on! We're gooonna do this.'

Eight of us were now grinning and grimacing at the same moment. There was a buzz.

'G's really committed today. He just had to hang on but . . . he's actually managed to squeeze a few more seconds out of his perform-ance to get everyone a little bit faster. He's left us with no excuses. We're gonna really pull today.'

I tried to do more time on the front than most of the other guys as time trialling is one of my strengths; I hoped I could contribute here.

We have a rule. We look at the speed that we've been given by the man in front of us and try to hold it there for maybe a 30- or 40-second turn, but only on the condition that the speed doesn't drop. If we see the number dip we pull off straight away. On the other hand, if we feel really good there is no point in pushing the number from say 56 kilometres per hour up to 60 kilometres per hour, as it will hurt down the line.

We didn't fall apart; our complex little machine worked.

The Orica-GreenEdge team were fastest and Simon Gerrans was in yellow. Omega Pharma Quick-Step finished 0.75 seconds behind. At Sky we were 3rd, just 3 seconds off the lead. Not bad for a team carrying a broken pelvis. We were happy and there was a good energy between us all again.

Team. Time. Trial.

I loved it.

Today.

WINNER: ORICA-GREENEDGE

OVERALL GC   1: SIMON GERRANS

                     2: DARYL IMPEY (SAME TIME)

                     7: CHRIS FROOME +3SEC

*Stage Five: Wednesday 3 July, Cagnes-sur-Mer
to Marseille, 228.5 kilometres*

These dull flat stages were a torture mentally.

I was just following my front wheel, which was following the wheel in front of it.

I was also getting into a pattern in the evenings now. I liked to be in bed before 11.00 p.m., if possible, and most evenings I would put something on to watch to switch off from the day. I was still on *Dexter* and I would watch ten minutes or so, just enough to get me into the story and stop me replaying the events of the day as I went to sleep, or thinking about the next day.

As for Richie, usually he conked out first and I could hear his breathing change. His breaths get very deep and it isn't long before he's snoring. He can really snore; he's not a big guy but he snores like an ogre.

Sometimes I listened for a few minutes, then fell into the same kind of breathing rhythm and drifted off. Even for getting to sleep, he's my pilot fish.

If our hotel room overlooked the car park, close to where our team's trucks were, we knew the mechanics would be washing the bikes early in the morning and loading up their equipment and suitcases, so I would probably put earplugs in to block it out.

Mario Pafundi, our head soigneur, says that one of his jobs is to try to make sure the riders are kept away from the noise when assigning rooms. We tease him. '*Really*, Mario? We didn't know that was even on your radar. We thought the biggest part of your work was making sure the soigneurs had the best rooms.'

On dull days like today we would often only find out about the closing sprint when we were on the bus or back at the hotel. Today was slightly different.

Cav, who had bronchitis all week, took the win. Our man Eddie Boasson Hagen was in the shake-up, and got 2nd, beating Greipel, Sagan and Kristoff.

Eddie would probably do better with more support but our policy is that the strong riders in the team don't spend energy leading out sprints. That leaves Eddie free to sprint but without back-up. I understand the thinking, and I benefit from the strategy but, still, it's tough for Eddie.

As the stage finished, Simon Gerrans ended up with the yellow jersey after more selfless riding from Daryl. I was happy for them.

Winner: Mark Cavendish
Overall GC   1: Simon Gerrans
                    2: Daryl Impey (same time)
                    7: Chris Froome +3sec

Stage Six: Thursday 4 July, Aix-en-Provence
to Montpellier, 176.5 kilometres

Today wasn't thrilling but it finished on a high.

Simon Gerrans led out Daryl in the last kilometre and Daryl finished 13th, which was enough to put him in the yellow jersey. For me, this was the noblest moment of the race so far. Daryl had done so much himself to get Simon into the jersey, and had then done even more to keep him there. You can say it was his job, but wearing the *maillot jaune* isn't like putting on overalls or a pinstripe suit.

Simon owed Daryl.

Today he repaid him.

It was very good to see. Daryl was an ex-teammate, and an ex . . . I'd like to say sort of South African brother, who had been there with me from the early days and who had introduced me to Michelle. Seeing him now wearing the yellow jersey was a thrill; the first African to get that jersey.

Daryl is from a South African cycling family. His dad had been a pro and later owned a bike shop. Daryl was always in the thick of it, and although I came in as more of an outsider, he made me feel like I belonged. We had ridden together and against each other back in Johannesburg; he had shared his room with me in Salzburg; we had sat side by side in the broom wagon at Paris–Roubaix. Now, I went to find him to congratulate him.

He's not unlike Richie. He grinned and said, 'Hahaha, I've got it before you.'

He laughed. We hugged. Same old Daryl.

'Ah, no, thanks a lot,' he said. 'This is really special.'

It was. Back in the hotel, I tweeted: 'An incredible day for African cycling, a Saffa in yellow!'

I hoped the whole country, the whole continent, appreciated what he had done today and would get behind him.

Winner: André Greipel
Overall GC   1: Daryl Impey
                        2: Edvald Boasson Hagen +3sec
                        7: Chris Froome +8sec

Stage Seven: Friday 5 July, Montpellier
to Albi, 205.5 kilometres

Team Cannondale decided to make it very hard about two-thirds into the race today. We still had about 50 or 60 kilometres to go when they got on the front.

They took a lot of people by surprise as the stage was expected to finish in a bunch sprint. There was a small climb that shouldn't have been a factor, but they made it extremely fast for the duration of the climb. Peter Sagan had yet to win a stage. Their plan was to get rid of the pure sprinters, such as Cav and Greipel, who rolled into Albi nearly a quarter of an hour after the stage had been decided.

Cannondale shook us all out of the pattern of the previous few days, and for that I think they deserved to win the stage. They set up Sagan perfectly and he did the rest. It was very impressive.

Daryl stayed in yellow; he is quick but he can get over the climbs too. Eddie was 2nd on GC for the second day. He survived the climb but didn't get it together in the sprint. He finished 5th on the stage which was frustrating for him as we headed into the mountains; his own chance of wearing yellow was gone for another year.

WINNER: PETER SAGAN
OVERALL GC　　1: DARYL IMPEY
　　　　　　　　2: EDVALD BOASSON HAGEN +3SEC
　　　　　　　　7: CHRIS FROOME +8SEC

*Stage Eight: Saturday 6 July, Castres
to Ax-3 Domaines, 195 kilometres*

So far, a lot could have gone wrong. Today, we planned for a lot to go right.

We would know after today. This was the first true day of business in terms of GC; it was the first day when we would see if Contador had stepped up from the Dauphiné; if Rodríguez, if Valverde, if any or all of them had more than we anticipated. And there was Quintana, who had come back from a long training stint in Colombia. How good was he going to be?

In the races leading up to the Tour there had been a vibe coming from the Contador camp: *He isn't at his best, but you ain't seen nothing yet.* In the Tour, he would be the old Contador; irresistible in the mountains.

For a long time I had been determined to attack on this stage; I wanted to reach that final climb and cause a real GC shake-up. The team kept saying softly that I needed to be careful, and not to go too early. As if.

Our plan was to ride hard to make the race as tough as possible, then to let it fall to the GC guys to scrap it out over the last few Ks.

On the valley road building up to the last two climbs you could feel the volts of tension shooting through the pack. Twenty kilometres to go before the climb and it was already kicking off: a war of pushing and shoving started as everybody was frantic for a position close to the front. There was big pressure: this was the race for the Tour de France yellow jersey.

All the domestiques were helping their leaders to be at the front, the sprinters were pulling for the climbers and, as we were getting closer to the climb, it was just getting faster and faster.

Eddie gave a really big pull in that valley, as did Yogi and Kiri, who were all swapping off. Geraint was just surviving at that point. We got a good position early on, and the rest of the battle was holding on to it.

Climbs. There were two mountains close together at the end of today's stage: Pailhères, which is very difficult, and Ax-3 Domaines, which is shorter and less difficult, but because the race was finishing at its summit, it was where the battle would be.

On Pailhères, Nairo Quintana attacked. So this was it. This young and very talented Colombian climber had been sent on a mission: go early, make the others chase, make them spend a lot of energy and create the opportunity for your leader, Alejandro Valverde. This felt like a tiny victory to me; Quintana was the unknown, the one who could be the dangerous dark horse. Valverde, I knew. I didn't fear him.

A few years before, I would have pushed all of my chips to the centre of the table and gone with Quintana. All or nothing. Today, my face was as expressionless as a corpse. Kiryienka did a good pull at the bottom of the climb, followed by Pete Kennaugh, who took over and did a huge pull. Over the top and down. He laid down such a ferocious pace that I began to wonder whether I was actually in the shape I thought I was in. He took us to the bottom of Ax. This was hard. Really hard.

Pete took us a little bit further, then handed over to Richie.

At home, Quintana might ride up a lot of mountains all day long, but he didn't seem to have done many hairpins: he was giving up seconds every time he took the wrong line round a corner.

In his ear the Movistar directeur sportif must have been telling him that Richie Porte was coming for him. Richie was leading a disparate gang which consisted of me, Contador, Valverde and Roman Kreuziger, a teammate of Contador.

The good news was that there was no sign of some of the other big GC favourites. There was no Cadel Evans, no Joaquim Rodríguez, no Andy Schleck. And where was Tejay van Garderen?

The pace that Richie was setting was causing chaos behind us. By the time we caught Quintana, we had dropped everyone. This lifted my spirits.

Then I couldn't wait any longer. With just under 5 kilometres to go, I made my move. It was slightly earlier than planned but . . .

I passed Quintana. I knew he had nothing and that he had gone too early; I had been that guy. As he saw me go by he must have been wondering about Valverde. Why wasn't he here?

I was alone in the lead. It was painful but joyful. I told myself that every second I gained could be the second that won the Tour.

I crossed the line. My mate from Tasmania rolled over in 2nd spot, 51 seconds behind me, having attacked Quintana.

We had sown time into the field. I had the yellow jersey. Richie was with me. Perfect.

There is one other lovely memory. We were speeding towards the start of the climb to Ax-3-Domaines when Daryl pulled alongside me in his yellow jersey.

'Make sure you bloody well get this jersey, bru. You'd better be wearing it tonight.'

That hit home in the best sense. Daryl knew he wasn't going to keep it, and that it was going to be with a climber this evening. But he had the generosity to say he wanted it to be on my shoulders. A lot of people die a little when a friend succeeds. Not Daryl. That's the measure of the man.

WINNER: CHRIS FROOME

OVERALL GC 1: CHRIS FROOME

2: RICHIE PORTE +51SEC

Stage Nine: Sunday 7 July, Saint-Girons to
Bagnères-de-Bigorre, 169.5 kilometres

House of cards.

On the bus we made our plans. We had the yellow jersey, yesterday we had bullied the peloton, and this morning the papers were saying that the Tour was already over: finished after just one mountain stage.

That yellow jersey colours everything around it, so we planned to ride in as controlled a way as possible. We were only interested now in the big dogs. If a breakaway had no big GC names in it, we would let it go. Anything else we would chase down like collies bringing sheep back to the fold.

That was our first mistake of the day.

On the bus, feeling all-powerful and with the happy yellow bleeding into our thoughts, we didn't specify what we meant by this. We didn't pause to think that with Richie and me in the first two spots in the GC the rest of the peloton would be feeling bruised and aggressive.

The attacks started straight away. The first climb, a category-two hors d'oeuvre, was still 30 kilometres down the road, but the peloton was popping and fidgety. Attack. Attack. Attack. With yellow now in our brains we chased down just about everything; if a piece of paper had blown up the road, we would have gone after it. And the peloton saw what we were doing and knew they had a chance to break us. Like schoolkids sensing weakness in a student teacher, they went after us.

Garmin-Sharp declared jihad from the start. They launched an insane barrage of attacks on the way to that first climb, the Col de Portet d'Aspet.

Dan Martin of Garmin and Igor Antón of Euskaltel were the two breakaways that had us in a quandary. They were borderline cases: a few minutes down on GC but if they got away maybe they would be a problem later. They could both climb.

Nico was on the radio urging us to go. We were trigger happy, so we went.

We should have said our goodbyes. 'See you later, guys.' As the yellow jersey team, we should have worked slowly and methodically through the day at our own pace. Instead, we let everybody else set the agenda. It was my mistake. I should have called it. I should have let them go but I didn't have the experience to know.

I was coasting through the peloton, staying close to the front and keeping an eye on who was going away, but there were just so many attacks. The team were taking it in shifts to patrol the front of the peloton. Even by the first climb, when Dan and Igor attacked, you could see the toll it was taking on us. And so could the other teams.

Soon we were a man down. Pete Kennaugh swung out of our line towards the left of the road just as Ryder Hesjedal from Garmin came sprinting through from behind us to attack. Pete was knocked into the ditch like a skittle and rolled down for 4 or 5 metres. By the time he climbed back up and remounted, the race had gone.

We kept thinning out. After more chasing it was Richie, Kiri, Kosta and me now controlling things at the front. Other teams were using us. After we had done a tough stint at the front in pursuit of Dan and Igor, they would counter-attack and, one by one, our guys started popping and dropping.

In the valley after the first climb we were already beaten dockets. Now it was only Richie and me left.

It got worse on the second climb, the Col de Menté.

At this point, ironically, we found some sense. 'Okay,' we said, 'let's leave the breakaway alone. Let's just regroup, recover and reorganize. Let's work as a team.'

But more attacks came. Nicolas Roche went, who was Alberto Contador's teammate. Mick Rogers went too. Ditto. They were starting to gamble now on the basis that we would let them go, so we chased. Richie worked like a dog on the flat before the Menté.

We hit the climb and another wave of attacks began. Richie turned to me and said he was busted. I would have to go on my own.

I could see the big guys moving now. Alejandro Valverde had attacked, who wasn't a discretionary case. He and his teammate Quintana had to be covered, as did Contador.

Suddenly I was very alone: the only Sky rider in a group of twenty-five or thirty, which was under the control of Movistar. I sensed everything could go very wrong very quickly before this day was done.

When in doubt, act tough. I immediately went right to the front so everybody in the group could see that I was alive and well.

'I'm the sheriff. I'm restoring law and order. Calm down. Nothing to see here.'

I sat up to make it look like I was quite relaxed and strong and feeling no pressure.

They looked around. No Sky jerseys.

'Well, tough guy, if you're the sheriff, where's your deputy? Where's the posse? You just have a tin star pinned to you. That's really all, isn't it?'

Movistar figured out that this could be good for them. Between the guys already up the road and the group of twenty-five plus that I was part of, they had seven. It meant that as the stage developed, they would have a lot of cards to play.

Saxo had maybe three or four riders but enough to give them options. Between Movistar and Saxo, if they handled things well enough, they could use their numbers against me.

But if you're me, you're not panicked by being the outsider.

I went to Contador. I pointed out to him that there were a lot of Movistar guys around us and up the road in front of us – Quintana and Valverde plus five teammates – which made them dangerous. I told Contador what must have been obvious: he couldn't expect Sky to control these guys; Saxo would have to do it. Contador and Valverde are Spaniards and there's a natural rivalry between them. Each wants to be King of Spain. I just wanted to make sure they didn't form an alliance and use their big numbers against me.

I told him it was his race to lose as much as it was mine. This was not quite true. Today it was more mine to lose because of the colour of the jersey I was wearing – but Contador had to think he could also miss out if he sat back and watched me get dropped. I had to make that clear to him. Movistar would sting him like a scorpion. That was their nature. Contador would need to use his teammates to protect him (and me). The conversation was in English. Contador just said, 'Yeah, well, we'll see how things go today.'

I was happy enough that he was thinking about it. He knew that for me to lose the race today wouldn't be enough. He could lose serious time as well if he didn't play his own cards right. If he thought about this for long enough, I might just survive.

I started looking for small signs of encouragement. I had been able to go with the most dangerous attack of the day. I was here now. I had to think my way through the next couple of hours.

There was a largely harmless group up the road, maybe 25 seconds ahead of us. Tom Danielson, Ryder Hesjedal, Yuri Trofimov, Igor

Antón and some others were first over the second summit of the day while we eyed each other in the group behind.

My eyes were glued to Contador, Valverde and Quintana. This was where they would have to stay. I was letting these thoughts settle as I rode second or third from the front down through the valley.

Next thing, Valverde came from behind, attacking down the right-hand side of the road. He had a Movistar colleague with him. If we were doing 40 kilometres an hour, they were riding at 55 when they passed. They got a huge jump, just when I thought things had steadied.

This was very dangerous. It wasn't on a climb; it wasn't where I felt comfortable. I couldn't just accelerate knowing that everybody else would hurt worse. If I was left chasing here on a flat road I could get into trouble. I wouldn't sit on the front and tow Contador and company back to Valverde. I'd be spent. Contador, Valverde and Quintana would leave me behind like roadkill on the final climb and maybe take as much as 10 minutes on GC. So I shifted down two gears before they were 20 yards past me. I sprinted after Valverde, putting in a 40- or 50-second acceleration to get across to them. I would let the others in the group look around and make their plans; surprise was my only asset here. I surprised myself mainly. I was the only rider from the group who made it on to the back of Valverde. His back wheel was my lifeline.

Now I had the two Movistar riders with me for company. They were pulling and taking turns. Ahead were the few guys who had already attacked on the previous climb. They were being caught by Valverde and his mate with me hanging on. If they had made that bridge on their own, it would have been very dangerous, because some of the riders up the road were also from Movistar: they had two or three in that front ten. They would have spent the rest of the day pulling.

Behind was the group with Contador and the others. Their view on what was up the road had just changed.

I was still in bad trouble but I wasn't dead.

A couple of times Valverde and his mate looked over at me. They said, 'Come on, you have to help us.' I just shook my head. No way.

Why would I pull on the flat for no reason? They recognized that and didn't persist. They kept working and I stayed with them.

As soon as the Movistar boys and I looked like bridging the gap to the front group, Contador gathered his remaining teammates together, including Mick Rogers and Nicolas Roche, and they gradually closed the space between us. They were 30 or 40 seconds behind us through the valley and it took them the best part of 15 minutes to reel us in. It was quite a bit of chasing from their point of view, but they did it.

I added that work into my calculations in this new scenario. Whatever happened in the race from here on, at least everybody would get to the last climb pretty tired. The pace hadn't eased up all day.

Once we all regrouped at the bottom of Peyresourde, the whole race slowed down a little bit. Movistar took control and Saxo kept a watch. Again, I had survived the most imminent danger. Time for . . . oh shit . . . for the first time I figured out I would have to go back for bottles and gels. They wouldn't be coming to me. No room service today.

I put my hand up and thought, this must look strange: the yellow jersey putting his hand up to go back and feed. I went back to the car trusting that the unwritten rule as regards attacking when somebody is feeding or taking a leak would hold firm. It did.

It was good to chat with Nico when I got back to the car. Despite the relatively tricky situation we were in, he smiled and was full of encouragement, we would get through this together.

Back in the chain gang this was still a day of politics; it was very nervy. I went and positioned myself where, in my opinion, the best chance was: on the back of the Movistar train.

Movistar suddenly upped the tempo and were working really hard now. What had caused this? Suddenly it dawned on me. The news had come to me over the radio; it must have come to them too. They were working hard because Richie was coming up from behind with Kiri helping him.

I had spoken to Nico on the radio. Maybe the guys would be better off conserving their energy for tomorrow rather than killing themselves on a wild goose chase? We could regroup and learn from today.

Nico saw it differently. Richie and Kiri were closing in. Soon they would be just a minute behind.

Of course, Movistar's directeur sportif was listening to the Radio Tour, hearing reports of Richie's comeback, and of course he passed that on to Valverde and Quintana. Richie was 2nd on GC, and they wanted him out of the way. But that was the limit of their ambition now: to kill Richie.

They didn't want the words 'Team Sky, one and two on GC' being rubbed in their faces again. And that's why the tempo had so suddenly increased. Richie didn't get back, and I wasn't put through the torture of Quintana then Valverde attacking me in turn on the Peyresourde.

Poor Richie. He didn't know it but by trying so hard and so honestly to get back to the front to help me, he had done a great job.

It was quite a strange feeling sitting in a line of seven Movistar guys all riding as hard as they could. I wondered what I would have asked my teammates to do here if they were all riding at the front at this point. Eureka! I would have asked them to ride in much the same way as Movistar were riding. That gave me comfort.

Their guys were wearing different jerseys but they may as well have been wearing Sky jerseys; I was sitting in their train.

Today Movistar were my team and they were doing the job for me. It would be about legs and not tactics in the last shake-up, which suited me.

Movistar were fully aware of what they were doing. They knew they were riding Richie out of the race for GC and they probably took satisfaction from that, even though I was getting a free ride. I was for another day as far as they were concerned. Sometimes in life, there's not going to be another day like the one you've just had.

On the final climb Quintana had obviously been given the freedom to attack. Maybe they thought I'd stay with Valverde and Contador and it would be Quintana's opportunity to steal some time. But first it was Dan Martin and Jakob Fuglsang who attacked. I decided that this wasn't my battle. I stayed in the group but it wasn't long till Quintana started his own attack. Now it was different: each time he went, I reacted. I didn't get up out of the saddle to sprint after him like a crazy man; I just sat on the front and did a bit of a progression back to his wheel, then we would slow down for a few seconds and he would go again. I think that happened four times.

I was within myself. They were hard attacks but I had them under control. After each one I remember thinking, 'Okay, I've closed another one.' Each time I did, I looked around to my left and to my right.

Now it was surely going to be Valverde or Contador to be the next one to go. To my surprise, neither of them did anything, which was interesting. Quintana and Valverde didn't seem to be in tune with each other: they were two individuals. Either they hadn't got it in their legs or they didn't fancy the final descent on their own. Anyway, they never moved.

We got to a point about a kilometre from the top of the last climb where it just felt like stalemate. I was riding at the front and a number of guys from the group started riding next to me as if to say to Quintana and Valverde, 'Look, you had your chance, it's not going to happen. We are just riding now. No more attacks up here.' They made an unspoken truce.

I survived. Dan Martin had a famous stage win. Overall, it was one of the most complex, tactical and interesting days the Tour had seen.

I got over the finish line and almost immediately the France 2 TV reporter, who was always at the finish area doing the on-the-spot reports, had a microphone in my face. His first question had nothing to do with the race.

'A lot of people are questioning your performances here. What can you say about that?'

I felt so pissed off. Of all the questions he could have asked after that day of racing, this was it? It hadn't even occurred to me as I saw him coming that he would ask me about doping.

The dark side still blows clouds over, even on the brightest days.

WINNER: DAN MARTIN
OVERALL GC   1: CHRIS FROOME
                        2: ALEJANDRO VALVERDE +1 MIN 25 SEC

29

Monday 8 July, Rest Day

We could have surrendered the Tour yesterday. Instead, today was a new day. We had moved northwards, jumping from the Pyrenees to our hotel in Brittany.

When we went out for our rest day warm-down ride, Dave made a point of coming out with us. As we rode he spoke to each rider in turn, flitting around like a bumblebee gathering pollen.

The guys weren't happy. There had been bad luck and misunderstandings, for sure. G had crashed, Eddie wasn't sure of his role, Kosta had been over-raced and we'd lost Kiri. David López had ridden really well to make the Tour team but it seemed to us that he'd then relaxed. When he pitched up in Corsica it appeared that he'd gained a bit of weight and lost some form.

Dave took in all the stories and processed them.

Stage Ten: Tuesday 9 July, Saint-Gildas-des-Bois
to Saint-Malo, 197 kilometres

Dave sat us all down in the bus that morning and said, 'Okay, guys, here we are.' Dave loves to start his talks in that way. 'We have got what we have got.' 'It is what it is.' 'We do what we do.' 'We are at this fitness level and it won't change.' 'We can't bullshit each other.' 'Some of us are not going as well as we would have hoped.'

After identifying the issues – the guys who weren't performing and the guys who weren't happy with their roles – he outlined the solutions. Dave handled this mini-crisis well. I wasn't the only person to have learned from 2012.

I had gone to have a chat with Kiri before he left the hotel. He had worked so hard in the last race and had done such a big job trying to get Richie back, pulling along that long valley road that I had chased Valverde across. However, he hit the next climb and got dropped. Then he slipped back into the gruppetto, and then into the no-man's-land behind the gruppetto.

When the second team car was up ahead behind Richie, Kiri slipped through the net. He only got eliminated by a minute and a half, which I felt was quite a big mistake from our point of view. We should have had someone egging him on, telling him, 'Listen, you have a minute to make up, you can do it.'

The team had a huge feeling of regret about this.

Today's stage was another one for the sprinters. Our concern is to stay out of trouble during the hectic final 30 kilometres of these stages, so we will have a Sky train at or near the front and it can be pretty annoying when someone from another team tries to muscle his way into our train. If there is any one rider who sticks out for always wanting to push in, he'd go down as, well, we have the phrase Arsehole of the Day. There is always one. There is a Movistar rider who scoops the title regularly. He cuts into our train and brakes for whatever reason, which causes a gap between our front guys and our back guys. It is part of racing but it is irritating. When the stakes are higher it is very annoying. When you are ambling along with 150 kilometres to go it isn't a huge issue. The stress comes at the more crucial moments, coming into a climb or during the wind-up finish.

I didn't think he was deliberately trying to get under our skins; I got the sense he figured the best place to be was wherever we were. But he wasn't fully aware of what was happening around him or why we were all in a line.

Most of the time I bite my tongue in situations like this. Richie isn't so gentle.

'Hey, you think it's just a coincidence that we all showed up here wearing the same jerseys, and now we're all on each other's wheels?'

L'Arsehole du Jour was just on a different wavelength to us. I hoped that his understanding of English was just as poor, and that he didn't quite catch what Richie was saying.

WINNER: MARCEL KITTEL
OVERALL GC   1: CHRIS FROOME
                        2: ALEJANDRO VALVERDE +1 MIN 25 SEC

*Stage Eleven: Wednesday 10 July, Avranches
to Mont-Saint-Michel, 33 kilometres*

I woke up in the morning leading Alejandro Valverde by 1 minute 25 seconds and Bauke Mollema by 1 minute 44 seconds. I had 2 minutes on Alberto Contador. The stage was just 33 kilometres of time trial but this was where I hoped to buy myself some time and a cushion in case I had a bad day in the Alps towards the end of the Tour.

I had to empty myself to gain as much time as possible. Today was a day which had to count.

I see my time trialling as a godsend. I am extremely lucky to be able to time trial *and* climb. More often than not, people can do one or the other. Doing both very well is quite rare.

Today I had a very good ride. I finished 1 minute 10 seconds faster than Richie. People like Valverde and Contador were 2 minutes or more back. Quintana was the same. These were all excellent climbers but not as strong on the time trial.

The exciting thing for me was that I had set out at a good pace and had taken a few kilometres to ease into things. I felt I had ridden a good time without over-extending in the first half of the race. When I got to the time check I heard that I was around a second up on Tony Martin. That really motivated me and made me think – either Tony was having a terrible day or I was going very well. If that was the case it would be an excellent result.

Nico was in the car talking to me all the way.

On the second time check I was 2 seconds ahead of Tony. He went faster to the finish, gaining 14 seconds for the last stretch. But I could definitely live with that.

My lead was up to 3 minutes 25 seconds – could this race now be mine to lose?

★

The first race I did with Barloworld was in 2008 in South Africa, just five years before this Tour. We had done the training programme over in Italy in January and had come back to South Africa for the Intaka Tech World's View Challenge in March.

I was a bit nervous at the start but on the third day I got into the break on one of the hilly sections and then broke away on my own on a climb about 10 kilometres from the finish in Pietermaritzburg. Coming into the finishing straight I had everything going for me to win the stage. It was mine to lose.

All of a sudden, a guy on a motorbike at the front of the race said to me, 'You can relax, they are more than three minutes behind you.'

I thought, 'Super,' and so I relaxed, because there was no point in being stupid and wasting my energy.

I sat up, zipped up my jersey and set about looking prim and proper for the finish.

Luckily I hadn't quite raised my hands in the air for victory.

I heard the screeching of brakes and the crashing of metal. Guys flew past me in a bunch sprint, and some even crashed trying to get round me; I was a slow-moving obstacle they hadn't expected to see. There was a terrible pile-up and Daryl Impey came down.

The field had come past me at 60 kilometres per hour while I was cruising home happily at about 35 kilometres per hour.

I lunged back into race mode but it was too late; I could only come 7th in the bunch sprint.

I remember the absolute shame. All the press were there, including a TV camera, and even the lens seemed to be grinning. I felt so embarrassed.

That was the Intaka Tech World's View Challenge; it was mine to lose, and I lost.

I couldn't think like that any more.

I had a sense that maybe the riders in 2nd, 3rd and 4th, and even down to 5th, 6th and 7th, were looking at each other now, as opposed to looking at me and how they would take three and a half minutes out of my lead. I would let them race among themselves; let them focus on their private battles for podium places.

Winner: Tony Martin
Overall GC   1: Chris Froome
              2: Alejandro Valverde +3 min 25 sec

Stage Twelve: Thursday 11 July, Fougères to Tours, 218 kilometres

A dull day; another one for the sprinters.

In the mornings I would generally sit next to G at the table. Most of the time we discussed race-related stuff. Because today was going to be a sprint day, Cav's Omega Pharma team needed to contribute to controlling the race. I said to G that maybe he could have a word with Cav about this.

However, as it was, not a lot got said out on the road. There was a bit of swearing when the hammer went down in the final sprint, but that was it.

Kittel went past Cav for his third stage win of the Tour, which killed Cav's mood. It wasn't a great day for us either: we lost Eddie in a crash, which fractured his shoulder. That killed our mood.

I was also learning that for the race leader, the day didn't end when you thought it had. In between the podium ceremony and the doping control, I had the media. Usually I had Chris Haynes from Team Sky with me, as well as the former rider Dario Cioni.

Before the press conference I had to go to between ten and fifteen media outlets for one-on-one interviews. Dario said to each of them, 'Two questions, just two questions.' The first question was always, 'How was it today?' The second question was usually a very long sentence with five questions in it. Something like: 'Are the rest of the team holding up – if so, what do you think about tomorrow – and of course, what about your own knee after that fall – are you now in the position you expected to be – would it be good to have Bradley Wiggins with his experience in the team at this point – you look fresh but how is your physical state?'

Dario would catch my eye, and shake his head gravely. I would say, 'Yes,' and walk on to the next microphone. Two questions are not six questions.

The length of the journey in the team car back to the hotel could vary greatly depending on traffic and distance. Nine times out of ten I would tuck into a bowl of rice and tuna and have a protein drink. We would chat about which journalists had been especially irritating or pushy. Who had asked that same stupid question again? It was a very different routine from being with my teammates on the bus.

WINNER: MARCEL KITTEL
OVERALL GC   1: CHRIS FROOME
                          2: ALEJANDRO VALVERDE +3 MIN 25 SEC

Stage Thirteen: Friday 12 July, Tours to
Saint-Amand-Montrond, 173 kilometres

Buried within the stage today was an interesting story:

Valverde lost his Tour chance on the road to Saint-Amand-Montrond.

Something had been on everyone's minds from the start of the race; I imagine on every team bus the riders would have been talking about it, and each directeur sportif would have been telling his riders the same: 'You've got to stay at the front today, today's the day. We're expecting crosswinds. Big crosswinds.'

It was a nervous day, and once we set off, we hit the crosswinds relatively early on.

Valverde punctured at a bad moment. At the time the pace wasn't full on but it was decent and the crosswinds were blowing. We knew immediately that he would struggle to get back on; the race would almost have to wait for him.

I was sitting close to the front with Yogi, G and the rest of Sky. Then, just at the point when Valverde hit trouble, the Belkin team started swapping off on the front.

Belkin had something to gain. Valverde was still 2nd on GC and Belkin's riders, Mollema and Ten Dam, were 3rd and 4th. Without Valverde, they would move up to 2nd and 3rd.

It was an interesting move in terms of peloton etiquette. Were

Belkin entitled to take advantage of Valverde's bad luck? Did the unwritten law that protects the yellow jersey from this kind of attack apply to his closest challenger? A lot of people would have thought it did.

Valverde's Movistar teammates definitely thought it did. They were coming up and saying, 'Listen, what are you doing? Valverde has punctured. This isn't sporting.'

One of the Belkin guys responded in an amazing way.

'Oh, you're asking us to be sporting? This is the guy who's gone down for two years for his involvement in Operation Puerto. How sporting was that?'

Basically, they were saying, 'We're not waiting for him. Why should we?'

Obviously Belkin's motivation wasn't entirely to do with doping and Operation Puerto but I still thought it was a powerful thing to hear.

The race got strung out. Everyone at the front had reason to ride, and Valverde's race hopes were being killed by the General Classification teams and the sprinters' teams, who were riding to keep Kittel behind. No one actually took the race by the horns and ripped it to pieces until we got to about 40 kilometres to go. Then Contador gave the order and his Saxo Bank boys accelerated. Yogi turned back to me and just said, 'Go, Froomey!'

He was looking at me, as if to say, 'We've been caught out but now you need to get on to the back of Saxo Bank before any damage can happen.'

At that point we were probably sitting in about 30th position in the bunch, not that far back. But it was too late. They had accelerated and opened a gap of 20–30 metres. I got out of the saddle and sprinted to try to get on to them. Cav was 10 metres in front of me but his acceleration was a lot quicker than mine. He managed to make it on to the back of Saxo Bank. I didn't.

As soon as I found myself in no-man's-land I pulled over to the left-hand side of the road and cruised, waiting for the peloton to come back so I could find my teammates. I got everyone working. It took no longer than a minute or so, and then the Katusha team realized it was in their interests to help us and we got a decent chase going.

We felt the loss of Eddie and Kiri through those final 40 kilometres.

I was able to sit on the wheels until the final 2 kilometres when our chase began to flag. Then I went to the front and rode steadily to the finish. We were about a minute behind Contador's group and I didn't want it to get to a minute and a half.

I realized that here, in the middle of this stage, which to all intents and purposes was a bad, bad day, I was dialling for help and drawing on the lessons that Tim Kerrison, Rod Ellingworth, Bobby Julich and others had been driving into me for years. Their notes of caution worked. I trundled in safely 1 minute 9 seconds behind the Saxo group, but it could have been much worse; Valverde had fallen out of the top ten.

Elsewhere, Bauke Mollema and Contador closed the gap at the top of the GC and Cav came back into sprint glory. The day after tomorrow was the iconic Mont Ventoux, where we would settle some accounts. Roll on and don't look back.

> WINNER: MARK CAVENDISH
> OVERALL GC　1: CHRIS FROOME
> 　　　　　　　　2: BAUKE MOLLEMA +2 MIN 22 SEC

Stage Fourteen: Saturday 13 July,
Saint Pourçain-sur-Sioule to Lyon, 191 kilometres

Back at the Dauphiné, before the Tour, I had raised the issue of the food we get on the bus after a stage. For as long as anybody could remember, it had always been tuna and rice. I wasn't attacking this choice, but it would have been nice to have some variety every once and a while.

The team listened, and after the Dauphiné we started getting different post-race dishes. Søren, our Danish chef, looked after us well. One day we had couscous with strips of chicken and the next we had fish and potato. It was a small change but I think it worked, and it carried on into the Tour.

Usually I got to dinner later than the other riders. There was an understanding that you would eat when you could eat, you would get a massage only when your soigneur was free and you would fit into the Tour, not the other way round.

The norm in pro cycling is that riders sit at one table and the staff sit at another. This was private time to spend by ourselves, but I think it would have been more relaxed if we were all together. I understand the counter-argument, especially if the soigneurs experience long, stressful days on the Tour; they may need the space to unwind away from the riders. But I would still prefer a system where we all just go and sit down wherever is free.

Another argument is that because the riders are fed with Soren's healthier and more nutritious food, it's better to seat us at a separate table. The rest of the team eat hotel food, and although our food was 'better' for us, theirs were covered in tasty sauces and gravies. A man could crack.

Today's stage was settled by a break. It was a break of guys enjoying their day in the sun, and not a GC day; the peloton and the overall challengers rolled in 7 minutes later.

Mont Ventoux was on my mind.

I told myself that it was better to coast to the finish today. Yes, I had lost a minute yesterday but I knew that the mountains were beckoning once more. This was where I was going to need all my energy.

WINNER: MATTEO TRENTIN
OVERALL GC   1: CHRIS FROOME
                          2: BAUKE MOLLEMA +2 MIN 28 SEC

Stage Fifteen: Sunday 14 July, Givors to
Mont Ventoux, 242.5 kilometres

The 'Giant of Provence'. The 'Bald Mountain'. One of the Tour de France's most famous climbs.

Before the Tour, I spoke to Contador about Ventoux. I'd watched a video of him racing up it, against Andy Schleck. I said to him: 'It's going to be a big day for us in the Tour.'

He nodded, and had a little think.

'Yeah, yeah, it's a tough climb, but in the final [section] it's always headwind and it's difficult to make a selection. [It's] because you're riding into a headwind. So you can't . . .'

In a headwind it's very hard to get away from another rider. You're pushing against a huge amount of wind, and in turn you're making a fine slipstream for anybody behind you. They just stick to your wheel as you suffer.

That conversation lodged in my brain until I was two-thirds of the way up Ventoux on stage fifteen.

Alberto, I don't want you having that pleasure if we get round Chalet Reynard, and there you are looking for my slipstream.

But here we were, nearing the end of this punishing but iconic 242.5-kilometre stage. Richie had done the work and had laid it all out. I could launch myself now to the top of Ventoux.

It was the perfect ambush, as Contador hadn't expected anything here. The road flattened just before Chalet Reynard, which was 6 kilometres from the finish. This was recovery territory before the last skirmish. I had to be smart; I didn't want to get up out of the saddle and sprint; I didn't want to look hell-for-leather desperate, splurging all my energy with such a long way to go. If I got out of the saddle here, he would let me go and surely later pass my empty husk on the road up ahead.

I took over the pace, but stayed low in my saddle, spinning my gears.

I sowed more confusion than I had hoped for. I hadn't actually been able to change gear fast enough because the road had been flat and I was accelerating. I was spinning very fast; far faster than it was efficient to spin. I was actually in the wrong gear. But this now was my attack.

Come after me, Alberto. If you want to be with me to the top, you're going to have to forget any recovery time. Accelerate now. If not, we might not see each other again till the podium. What's it to be?

I couldn't resist any more. About 30 seconds into my acceleration

I turned to check on him. He wasn't there; he's wasn't on my wheel any more.

One down.

My focus shifted to Quintana, who was 30 metres in front of me, but coming back. 'Not too quick now, Nairo,' I thought. I needed some recovery time myself.

I wasn't going to race up to him all puppy-dog keen, *Hey, I'm back!* When it came to taking him I wanted to go straight past him; I wanted to be a couple of bike lengths in front before his brain had registered me at all.

I got to him. I attacked immediately. Too soon. He followed me very easily, or so it seemed.

Okay, this isn't going to be easy. This can't become a poker game where we ponder our hands till Alberto and the boys catch up on us.

I was looking for the headwinds but there weren't any. Not today; nothing. I rode steadily for a bit, mulling this over. I asked Quintana to come through. He declined.

One more shot at dropping him.

I got up and accelerated again; another good hard acceleration. But I went nowhere. He closed me down, again.

Okay, that's fine. I'm basically going to have to put winning the stage out of my mind, and I'm going to have to ride to the top with you, Nairo. You are going to let me do most of the pulling and you'll have the legs over me in the last few hundred metres. You'll win the stage and take a few seconds from me. But I can live with that. I have to.

I settled in, ready to do the lion's share of the work. Any time he came through, he pulled at a slower rate.

Listen, don't play games with me here. I've stopped attacking you. I'm not going to keep attacking. Just pull! Pull with me. Because you can move up on GC too, you're 5th, or whatever, right now. Just do some work.

I was telling him this in my broken Spanish with a splash of Italian. It might as well have been Swahili. I assumed he was just thinking about the final showdown. How he would weaken me. How he would 'kill' me.

A kilometre to go. I had worked out where the Tom Simpson memorial was, even though it wasn't visible with so many people on

the mountain. It was a stark reminder of the mountain's merciless-
ness; the British rider had tragically died there on 13 July 1967.

Quintana would be sucking in the air now, getting ready for
the end.

I rode with my head down most of the time. It meant that I could
see down between my legs, and behind my seat post. I could see
where Quintana's front wheel should be, and if he was on my wheel.

I glimpsed down.

He wasn't there! Not where he should have been.

I didn't have much left. I wasn't going to get up out of my saddle
and attack right here, and take the chance that he would close me
down again. So I pushed on a little bit harder. If he really was on the
limit, this would be it. If he wasn't, his wheel would reappear.

I upped the pace by 30 watts or so; I looked down. There was
nothing but road . . .

It took me a few minutes to ride the last kilometre. I was light now
though. One moment I had been surrendering the stage tactically;
now I was winning it. With every pedal stroke I was taking more and
more time from my rivals. It wasn't because I was going that fast but
because Quintana had run out of fuel.

I was in yellow riding to a stage win on the hardest climb there
would be in the Tour this year. It was an amazing feeling. Now I was
going up that last bend. Photographers were swarming the outside of
the corner, with the towering meteorological station above them at
the top of Ventoux.

I was riding to the finish line now.

This was the day. The biggest win of my life. Say it again. This was
the biggest win of my life.

I was 29 seconds clear at the summit.

In the yellow jersey.

On Ventoux! It was dreamtime.

Michelle was here. I went through the crowd and around the barrier. We wrapped ourselves around each other. I couldn't speak; I
didn't know if she could either. All the rides, all the years, all the
pain, was for this. Pain and joy, inextricably linked.

I could hardly breathe. I began coughing and couldn't stop. Somebody led me to a camper van and a race doctor planted an oxygen mask on my face. A few minutes later the euphoria returned.

At the team hotel in Orange that night we forgot about being Team Sky for a while, and did something spontaneous. Dave ordered champagne and made a short speech; the mechanics Igor and Richard poured the bubbly.

We had a couple of toasts and a bash at our low guttural victory chant before the food came. 'OoooooOOOOOOOOOOOOHHH-HHHHH!' Everybody joined in. Michelle had made a massive milk tart, a South African pudding, for the team. Tomorrow was a rest day and we were relaxed, happy and loose.

I was just putting a fork into my starter when there was a tap on my shoulder.

Sorry. Anti-dopage.

I scoffed some food while the man watched and then I headed off to give a blood and urine sample; the same thing I had done this morning before the race. I had also given another urine sample after the stage end.

Three tests in one day. If this is the price we pay to restore our damaged sport, it is a small one.

My early cycling idols tended to test positive and die in my affections. I never want any kid to look at Ventoux today and wonder if it was all an illusion created by chemicals and cheating.

WINNER: CHRIS FROOME
OVERALL GC   1: CHRIS FROOME
                    2: BAUKE MOLLEMA +4 MIN 14 SEC

Monday 15 July, Rest Day

Jeremy and three old friends, the Jethwa brothers – Kiran, Sam and Jaimin – were all here. They turned up today at the team hotel in Orange and I had no idea they were coming. They had travelled from

Kenya, on a marathon journey that began for Jeremy with a flight from the Nandi Hills to Nairobi, from there to Abu Dhabi, then Paris, a TGV to Marseilles and, now, a camper van to Orange.

Greater love hath no man than this . . .

Jeremy was wearing a Kenyan rugby jersey. My bike had a little Kenyan sticker placed discreetly on its frame. I am Chris Froome (GB), I have always felt British and I live in Monaco. But today, with Jeremy and the guys here, home seemed both closer and further away.

30

Before Robert de Niro and Christopher Walken go to war in *The Deer Hunter* we see the people they are and the bonds they have. There is a wedding; Walken flirts. There is the scene high in the mountains. De Niro loves to hunt. With the clouds at shoulder height and the guys done teasing each other, they are at one with the world around them. They don't need words.

I have days like that on my bike. Richie and other friends might be there with me or I might be on my own, high on some summit. I can't describe the feeling of getting up there under my own steam. Knowing the path that is behind me, feeling the ease in my legs as the mountain plateaus. Getting ready to hurtle down the far side like a carefree boy, the wind in my face.

Cycling is my job but it also feels spiritual and connected and it's all I ever wanted to do. Somehow – through genetics, through meeting a line of people, starting with Kinjah, who have helped me enormously – I have been given a great gift.

Millions of people end up spending lives as the wrong person in the wrong job with the wrong boss. I know how fortunate I am, how blessed. My heart is in those high mountains.

Sometimes I wonder, why me?

There are two tales of Ventoux. We toasted one last night; this is the other one.

The morning had begun with an early knock on the door. It could only be one thing: the testers were here. Richie and I looked at each other.

'Well, here we go again, bro.'

We had a long stage ahead of us before climbing Ventoux. It was early and now the testers were here. They were going to take my blood and my urine, which was fine. They were going to take an hour of our sleep too, that's the price.

From the moment the tester knocks they are obliged to chaperone you. So you go to the door, open it, walk back in and the tester follows so he can stand and watch.

You put on a pair of tracksuit bottoms, throw on a top and you go with them. You don't shower or wash. You do not pass go. You do not pass water. You go straight to control.

Usually they have set up in a conference room or somewhere like that. They are decent people, doing a hard job that has to be done. There is no point in resenting them. I save that for the heroes who tested positive.

In the mornings they generally want blood. Ironically, in the morning urine is seldom a problem – the testers just aren't in the market for it.

Once you reach the testing room there is a rule that you have to be seated for ten minutes before you can give a sample. During that time you fill out the forms.

Have you been to altitude recently?

In the last two weeks have you had a blood transfusion?

In the last two weeks have you lost a lot of blood?

Are you on any medications . . . ?

And so on. Eight or nine questions give you the chance to explain anything that might affect your blood values.

We are young and fit and lean so they find a vein easily.

One person handles the documentation while a second looks after the blood, needles, phials and other such paraphernalia. You seal and number the bottles in front of them, then you sign. Our team doctor Alan Farrell is there from beginning to end.

Some mornings they want the entire team for testing, sometimes just me, sometimes me and Richie. We decide the order of who gets the needle first by means of who is the most awake.

So we get it done, go to breakfast, go back up to our room, have a wash, pack our stuff and get on the bus. It's just a part of life, part of our routine. We understand why it has to be this way.

So far on this Tour I have been spat at maybe a dozen times and I know there will be more. A guy has squirted something over me. I took it to be beer or urine although I didn't have it tested.

Some days I don't get spat at all while other days it happens three or four times. Sometimes out of pure consideration they aim their spit at my jersey though mostly it comes at my face. If I'm lucky my shoulder or my helmet gets it. Most of the time I'm not lucky. I am riding up a mountain a few feet away from spectators who are leaning into my path, when I hear the sound of spit being launched. Even through the general noise I am attuned to that noise. Then I feel a warm, globby clump hit my face. It's hard to be lucky when they are spitting from two feet away.

It is horrible.

Usually I take my glasses off and wipe them on my jersey, then use the back of my glove like a rag to wipe my face.

You know, I haven't actually done anything wrong. I am left with no way to prove that except to be the person that I am and to let time and the push of technology prove that I am clean.

This is a sport for people's pleasure and entertainment. To dope is to abuse that, but to spit in a rider's face does the same. Don't talk to me about the lost integrity of our sport and then spit at me.

Picture this: I have a huge wad of spit on my face. Nicolas Roche and Alberto Contador are on my wheel. They have seen the launch and they have seen the landing. Now they can see me defaced with this beery saliva. I am pawing blindly at myself with the back of my glove.

I handle the moment as well as I can, mainly by ignoring it. I might have turned round and sworn at the guy or pegged a bottle at him but that is not my battle on this Tour.

Nicolas comes up and puts his hand on my shoulder. He says, 'Even Alberto is disgusted at what happened there. That shouldn't be happening. You don't deserve it.'

I know Nicolas and I know Contador well enough to appreciate the sincerity of what was conveyed: here was my biggest rival reaching out with a few words. I didn't understand it though. Nicolas wasn't targeted. Alberto, with his achievements and his history, wasn't targeted.

When I crossed the finish line yesterday I know there was booing. I didn't hear it then – maybe out of excitement, or exhaustion – but I did notice it on the way up Ventoux. There was one moment when I was pulling Quintana along and it started getting really steep towards the top. I wasn't going very fast and there were people standing almost in the middle of the road, just baying and booing at me. They would stand there right until the last second, daring me to ride straight into them. You never know which one could be the lunatic who doesn't duck out of the way.

Yesterday was a great day on Ventoux. If you had dreamed my dreams, if you had given the thousands of hours I have given to this sport, you would know that. Nothing could really knock me off that high. I had a stage win and the yellow jersey, and I was leading the race in the best position possible after one of the hardest days possible.

When I went into the rest day press conference this morning the questions about doping came down like balls of spit from the hills. I felt the pressure of having to justify myself, to prove that cycling is clean, to take responsibility for the past and to defend myself for the present and the future.

I'm clean. To be honest, I struggle to see how I could be any cleaner. I want a clean sport, I want us to be open and honest about what has happened in the past and I want the technology that proves I am clean.

I don't know where we are going with all the spitting and the finger-pointing and the innuendo. Sometimes I'd just like to be able to talk about the race, about spiked efforts, about training my body to conquer its own weaknesses. Ask me. But the doping discussion is circular. You think I'm guilty. Can you prove it? *No.* I know I'm clean. Can I prove it? *No.* You heard it all before from Lance Armstrong. Well, I'm not Lance Armstrong. You won't get fooled again. Not by me you won't, ever.

All I could tell the press conference in the Park Inn Hotel was that sin isn't contagious. We have inherited the wreckage of cycling's past but not the habits of cyclists past.

Lance cheated; I'm not cheating. That should be the end of it, but of course it's not.

Finally Dave offers to hand over performance data to the World Anti-Doping Agency for an independent – and this is important – expert assessment.

When David Rozman, our soigneur, did me the great honour of naming his son after me, I told him that I hoped it was because of the person I am, not the rider I can be. Here in France, my brothers and old friends are coming together. Mum is on my shoulder. In Nairobi, Kinjah and the boys are gathering in that little shack that once felt like home to me. Michelle is in the crowds.

I owe them all. And I owe my sport. I owe it to them to be the best person I can be. First, second or also-ran doesn't matter if I can give them that. I owe it to them to be honest to myself and to them and to this dream they helped me achieve.

Spit in my face. Stand in my way. Boo me. Hiss at me. Troll your accusations. You don't know my blood. You don't know my heart.

The people who matter to me do and for now that is enough.

Stage Sixteen: Tuesday 16 July, Vaison-la-Romaine to Gap, 168 kilometres

All the action went down on a mountain behind Gap, the Col de Manse. Contador and his teammate Roman Kreuziger tried to scorch the earth for Saxo. As we approached the summit, they went up like fireworks. Richie and I chased and caught them. Kreuziger burst free next. And Contador again. Bang. Bang. Left and right to the jaw each time. They took it in turns to attack us again and again. Richie must have pulled them back five times.

In the last kilometre Richie finally turned to me and said, 'Okay, I'm done now, you need to follow them yourself.'

Contador noticed that Richie was gone and attacked again. I chased him down.

It wasn't long until Contador, Kreuziger and I were going down that final descent.

Contador tried to accelerate a couple of times, looking to distance me. They had a plan: Contador in front, then Kreuziger, then me third in the line. As he was going into a corner, Contador accelerated,

Kreuziger decelerated and I had to brake. While I was forced to slow, Contador was surging.

I didn't mind chasing but when you've got someone in front of you blocking when you're trying to go round the corners it can be difficult. It seemed like very negative racing tactics to me.

And this was the famous descent where Joseba Beloki had his crash in 2003 and where his career ended. Lance Armstrong did a bit of off-road riding here and came back on to the hairpin. Beloki's career ended there.

It was a place of nerves and we were jumpy, and Contador and Kreuziger chose this downhill to play their games. I wasn't impressed.

Richie rejoined us, tagging on the back. Rui Costa arrived with him.

In the circumstances it was probably not clever of me to react to every Contador acceleration but I couldn't allow him to gain from this bullshit. I could have just given him 30 seconds and taken no chances but I didn't want to encourage this behaviour.

They wanted to know if I had the balls. Good for them.

They wanted to know what I would do for the yellow jersey. I'd show them.

Finally I made a decision. It was game up. *Kreuziger, I'm not letting you sit on Contador any more. I'm going to do that instead.* I drove into a gap past Kreuziger and got on to Contador's wheel.

He knew now he was going to be followed down every inch of road. If he was to gain anything he was going to have to take bigger risks.

He went through one corner extremely quickly and I let him get a little distance on me. I didn't want to be on top of him if he came off. Now it was me asking him if he had the rocks. Sure enough, at the next corner he overcooked it and ended up on the road.

The couple of bike lengths I'd been giving him into the corners saved me. There he was now in my line but to avoid him I had go to the left and a little off-road. Luckily there was no drop or ditch so I was fine.

I wasn't hurt but I had to unclip the pedals and lift the bike back on to the road. By the time I had recovered, the chasing group of six or seven had gone past. Richie eased off the back to help me yet again.

Contador caught up with me by the next corner.

His hand was hurt and his knee was bleeding; his tail was between his legs. He went past me and said he was sorry, what had happened back there was his fault. As a gesture he moved forward to help get us back to the front of the race.

He caught me in a rare moment of anger. My feathers were ruffled. If I had ridden over him I could have broken a collarbone or worse.

'No. You are not leading us any further down this hill, you're staying on my wheel now. Otherwise we'll crash again.'

He had pushed it too far. Richie pulled us both back to the rest of them.

Rui Costa stole the stage by 42 seconds for Movistar.

WINNER: RUI COSTA
OVERALL GC 1: CHRIS FROOME
2: BAUKE MOLLEMA +4 MIN 14 SEC

Stage Seventeen: Wednesday 17 July, Embrun to Chorges, 32 kilometres

Sometimes it's not where you're at, it's where you're going.

Today was a time trial that started on top of a mountain, took us down the mountain and then up the mountain next door, along a plateau and down the next descent. I was drooling.

There was a lot of discussion about what bike to use. My time-trial bike? Or my road bike for the mountains? And which wheels would go with what bike? Every rider had a different opinion. I had a plan: use both bikes.

For the climb I needed the lightest bike possible with the lightest wheels known to mankind. Aerodynamics don't count for anything when you're slogging uphill at 15 kilometres an hour. I also knew that the first descent was pretty technical in terms of twists and turns. To me it made sense to use the road bike until I got to the flat plateau and then switch to the time-trial bike and go all out across the plateau, down the second descent and across 3 flat kilometres to the line.

It would either work or I would look like a fool.

We've never done a bike change in a time trial before. We did a dummy run with Nico in the car and we practised it again this morning. The plan was that I would give a hand signal near the top of the final climb and indicate 5, 4, 3, 2, 1 to tell the car that I was ready. The car would come along beside me and I would leap high into the air and land on the time-trial bike, which was being steered along the road from within the car. Crash Froome is dead. Say hello to Evel Knievel Froome.

No, actually, I would lean my bike at the front of the car while Gary Blem got the time-trial bike off the roof. While I was clipping my feet into the time-trial bike, Gary would give me the biggest push he could give a friend and off I would go.

It made sense to me. The last bit of road was so fast that being in that aerodynamic position would help me gain a lot of time. After this stage we would hit three hard days in the Alps and I figured I needed to go into the red – to hurt myself but do no damage. There were bigger sufferings ahead.

Coming into the final time check, having done the bike switch, I was 10 seconds down on Contador. Doh. I wasn't sure I could take that back.

It wasn't too efficient to change bikes under pressure but I reckoned it was more efficient than having a bad body position on the road bike down the hill and across the flat. If you are out of the saddle and pushing on a road bike, your upper body is stealing seconds from your legs. On the time-trial bike the handlebars are set in an aggressive, more aerodynamic position, low down. Contador had opted to ride his road bike for the whole trial.

The gamble paid off. I won by 9 seconds. Now I was four and a half minutes ahead going into the Alps.

I still couldn't feel that I had the race in my grasp though. One bad day during the next three and I could lose all that time on a single climb. So, yes, it might be fair to say that the race is now mine to lose. It's just something I didn't want to say.

WINNER: CHRIS FROOME
OVERALL GC   1: CHRIS FROOME
            2: ALBERTO CONTADOR +4 MIN 34 SEC

*Stage Eighteen, Thursday 18 July, Gap to Alpe
d'Huez 172.5 kilometres*

In the evenings I shower before I go down to get a massage. There is just enough time to get clean.

The shower measures the toil of the day. I turn the shower on, grab the shampoo and shower gel and, if it has been a brutal day, I just sit down. I sit with my knees pulled up to my chin, the posture of the small boy in the front row of a class photo back in primary school.

That's when I know it has been a really tough day – I can't stand up for an extra five minutes on my legs. I sit down so I can wash myself without feeling like I am about to topple over.

This evening I sat for a long time with the water just powering down on me. I sat there and thought, postponing the effort of standing up again.

I get those days in training sometimes as well. Today, this was how my legs told me this was hard, maybe too hard.

Today we rode up Alpe d'Huez twice. If you grew up in France or Italy or Belgium, some place that wasn't Nairobi, twice up the Alpe is a lot of snow-capped myth. I just looked on it as two category-one mountains in the final 50 kilometres of a stage. Two 45-minute climbs at the end of a long day.

After climbing Alpe d'Huez once we would be about 122 kilometres through the stage. Things would get a bit flatter, then we'd dip down and then start a gentle climb up the Col de Sarenne. Over 13 kilometres the road rises about 954 metres. Then there is a sharper hill to the summit, 3 kilometres long, before a hair-raising descent.

Then we are facing up Alpe d'Huez again.

If I was looking to challenge someone for GC this would be where

I would launch the ambush. You've got that whole 3 kilometres to the top of the Sarenne to get a gap and then a dangerous descent. It's as steep as an elevator shaft, with a bad surface and no guard rails. Tony Martin in particular has been very critical of the state of the descent. One misjudgement and you could be falling down the side of the mountain.

There had even been some talk of abandoning the second ascent of Alpe d'Huez in order to eliminate the descent from the Sarenne. But the Tour has a public, especially the public served by television, and a brutal descent can sometimes be great television. So it was decided that unless the weather got really bad, the dangerous descent stayed.

I told any team that came up to us on the climb today not to worry about the descent. We wouldn't be racing it. 'Nice and easy, guys,' I said, 'nothing crazy.' I spoke to Valverde and he said, 'Don't worry, Chris, we're not going to be lunatics either.' I got the feeling that not everyone saw it quite that way but the people I spoke to agreed with me.

Contador was the worry. Losing the time trial yesterday would have gotten under his skin. I think they had a look at the possibilities because they sent two riders up the road in front of the peloton at one stage. I presumed they were dispatched to be there for Alberto for after he'd made his move. He would attack on the Sarenne, hook up with his teammates and then throw himself down the descent, risking life and limb to get some time back.

I saw the two of them go and I sent instruction to my guys to close them down. We had to make sure Contador had nobody to get across to.

He did try on the descent anyway; about a third of the way down he managed to slip through us and rode away. I said clearly to the team that there was no need to stress. If he wanted to take the risk, that was on him. He had about 15 kilometres to go down the hill and through the valley after the descent. Then back up the Alpe.

If this was his big move of the day he would have to ride that 15 kilometres on his own, taking all that wind. We knew from the radio there was a headwind in the valley. I knew no credible GC rider would do that knowing they had to climb Alpe d'Huez all over again. Even if he committed a hundred per cent and it worked, he wouldn't take back more than a minute.

At the same time I knew the race was on. We needed to close this down. As it happened we got down the mountain nice and safe and it wasn't long before we found Contador off his bike. He'd pulled off the side of the road and was doing a bike change. It seemed a bit pointless to go on the offensive only to then sit up and change his bike.

I don't know what the issue was, but we were told soon after that the race had announced they were going to control our bikes at the finish. Rumours went around, of course. Had he switched from a bike that was under the allowed 6.8 kg weight? There was gossip, too, about a special lube that worked wonders by reducing fiction. I'm sure he just had bike problems.

Movistar started bearing the load. They rode a really good tempo leading up into Alpe d'Huez. Our guys had done a good job pulling back Contador's two teammates. David López was proving his worth. He had done a really good job ascending l'Alpe d'Huez and taken us over the Col de Sarenne.

Pete Kennaugh was riding heroically too. At one point about 5 kilometres from the second climb up the Alpe I asked him to go back to the car for gels. All was good but we were empty. Three of us were sitting behind Movistar and Pete peeled out into the wind to go back.

As he went, I spoke into the radio mouthpiece: 'Nico, Pete is coming back for the gels – please can we have some pineapple.'

Pineapple gels don't contain caffeine. I find the ones that contain caffeine make me feel flustered and generally not very good. All I'm looking for is some readily available sugar, electrolytes and carbohydrates to go straight into the system.

I didn't hear anything back. A few minutes later Pete returned and told us the car wasn't there. That was odd – one of the perks for the team in yellow is that the car gets to ride first in the convoy.

I got on the radio again.

'Nico, Nico. Can you hear me? We need some gels. Can you come to the front please?'

Pete was empty. I was empty. Richie had one caffeine gel, which he offered to me. Caffeine? At least it's got some sugar in it.

I didn't want to make a bigger deal of this than it needed to be. The climb was coming up and we had to focus.*

If I am close to a rider who I am on good terms with, I can ask them for a gel and nine times out of ten that would be fine. But this was a relatively select group of contenders just 5 kilometres off the last climb. I needed to hold my position. It wouldn't do to look desperate and show weakness. If I asked the wrong person the word would be out: *He's low. Let's make it hard for him.* We had zero options.

We said farewell to Pete at the bottom of the Alpe. He needed to save his legs for the next day. I sat behind Richie and we let Movistar work; they had the numbers. They took us about 3 or 4 kilometres up. The group was stringing out. I remember turning to Richie and saying, 'Okay, now.'

He looked back at me.

I nodded, as in, 'Let's go.'

People were on their limits. I didn't feel great myself. Richie picked up the pace and we dropped a number of riders and then I rode over the top of him and kept on pushing for a minute or so.

It was not a huge attack but it was an early attack. There were 10 kilometres of mountain stacked above us but with people on their limits it was time to push on. No free rides.

---

* There has been much speculation over the use of the painkiller Tramadol in Team Sky. I do not take any painkillers or stimulants while training or racing. People have described 'finish bottles' containing crushed-up painkillers and stimulants. I do have a finish bottle on occasion, but it contains nothing more than a double espresso. I fully support the introduction of TUEs for Tramadol and any other medication which may be viewed as performance enhancing that is being used without a valid medical reason. I believe the peloton would be a safer place without the use of Tramadol. I did not need or use Tramadol to win the Tour de France and I hope that this serves as an example to others that it is not something that is necessary to compete at the top end of our sport.

Myself, Rodríguez and Quintana were now out in front. I was not prepared to pull all the way up, so we shared the workload but not wholeheartedly. No one really wanted to commit to it. With so far still to go, I could understand that.

I calculated it would take the best part of 30 minutes to do this last 10 kilometres. Richie had dropped back, fallen in with Contador and the others, seen they were wasted and ridden away from them. He rejoined us and it was pretty impressive to see him again. This gave me a tremendous boost.

Not long after, I said to him, 'You know I'm not good, I'm fairly spent.'

The four of us rode on for another 2 or 3 kilometres. I couldn't contribute at all to the work at this stage, I felt hollowed out. I asked Richie to pull just enough to keep me in the group.

I was worried about a big loss. Thankfully, Contador was struggling, and Quintana and Rodríguez, who stood to gain most from my weakness, were around 7 minutes down on GC.

With about 4 kilometres to go, I heard Nico back on the radio.

'Okay, I'm back at the front now with you again, guys.'

I shot my hand up to say I needed something from the car. Richie asked me what I wanted. The man was unbelievable.

'Gels, please, I need sugar.'

He said, 'Okay, you stay here, I'll go back for them.'

It didn't even occur to me that there was a rule against feeding in the last 5 kilometres of a stage. Nico was there, so surely there was no reason why I couldn't get a gel?

But I'd given the game away.

When I put my hand up to signal I needed something from the car, Quintana looked around and recognized that I needed help. A few moments later he accelerated off the front.

I thought to myself, 'Chris, you know what he's just done. This goes into the memory bank.' For all Quintana knew, I had a flat tyre. Anyway, for now he was gone.

That attack was not something I was going to forget. Two days ago Contador and I had got into trouble on the descent and Quintana had been the one to push on. There was a pattern here and I was going to have to keep an eye on it. It could be inexperience or naivety, but I would keep it in mind all the same.

Richie came back with the gels and I took two immediately. Rodríguez had latched on to Quintana, so they were 50 metres up the road now. Richie just settled into work in front of me. He was going well.

There were times when I had to call to him to say I was losing contact. It was horrible, not having the energy. I had a damp blanket of weakness over me and the higher we went the heavier it got.

Whoa. Focus. My head was all over the place. There was less and less power in my legs, just jelly. I had nothing. It was quite humbling to have my friend's back wheel as my only goal. Richie was doing the job. I just really needed to concentrate on that now. I had no idea how many guys were in front of us at this point. I assumed Rodríguez and Quintana had caught the earlier breakaway by now and were fighting for the stage win. (As it turned out they hadn't. Christophe Riblon of France was away and would stay away.)

As we approached the finish Richie pulled aside to let me go over first. I demurred. That wouldn't be right. He deserved to go before me and take a place on that stage. As he pulled off I pushed him to make sure he stayed in front.

He turned and thanked me!

I didn't have the energy to explain that all the debt and gratitude were mine.

We were blessed. I finished a bad day by increasing my lead on Contador who had a worse day.

I had mixed emotions at the finish. This was the one day I had worried about having a blow-up in the mountains. Now it had happened but I'd come out of it okay. I'd settle for that.

Nico was apologetic about the car. A cool box had leaked and destroyed the electronics. The car had shut down. I knew the feeling. Stuff happened.

Nico started talking technicalities. He was expecting that I would get a time penalty for taking the gels on board in the last 5 kilometres. There was a brief discussion about legalities.

But it seemed like bad karma and sharp practice when I got to think about it. We shouldn't appeal. I'd had a bad day and I'd survived in front. I would take the 20-second penalty.

If the worst days were only this bad, we could handle them.

Later on I went for a massage with David Rozman. Richie was still there being worked on when I got down so I used the 5 or 10 minutes to myself to make a few phone calls and put out a tweet.

Most of the time a daily plan goes up to say that dinner is at 8.00. Sometimes I only get on the massage table at 7.15 and I know Rozman will take an hour and a half to take the mountains out of my muscles.

He starts on the back, which not many soigneurs do. His thinking is that once the back is released then we can work on the legs and it makes a more logical progression. If you have a tight back it limits your legs. After that he starts on the back of my legs, getting into my hamstrings and glutes.

What I like about his massage is that he hasn't got a by-the-numbers system of three rubs here and three rubs there, now press here, now press there. Rozman can feel for himself where something is tighter than it should be. He knows the spots where I have trouble with different muscle groups and he takes longer on those points, stretching them, coaxing them to relax.

Some days I am exhausted and we don't say much at all. A muttered greeting might be all we manage. Other days we talk about life, the universe, everything: time away, his family, his wife, Manja, and small child, Kris.

I remember when he told me what he had named his son, my surprise almost spoiled the moment. 'No way! C'mon, really, what is his name? You wouldn't call him Chris. Seriously, what's his name?'

'No, no, Chris. After you. But with a K. Not with a Ch because in Slovenia we don't use Ch.'

Whatever that meant to Rozman I believe he'll never know what that meant to me. I remember the feeling that this guy from Slovenia, whose path had intersected with my path coming from Kenya, this guy believed in me. He had connected with me as a person, not as a bike rider. It was a lovely thing to do and I was moved and humbled.

I still am. I just hope he didn't get into trouble for bringing home his work like that.

On brutal days, like the one on Alpe d'Huez, we don't speak much. But Rozman always gives me a very clear view of things.

I lay on the table and said, 'I can't believe this has happened today. And . . . I'm not sure about tomorrow.'

Rozman just said, 'It's simple. It's a bicycle race. It goes uphill, so you pedal uphill. Why think so much? Just go.'

And that stays in my mind when I am racing. *Just go.* What would Rozman do? Wait till 2 kilometres from the top, the hardest point. *And just go, Chris! Just go!*

Simple.

He stopped me running through all five hundred different scenarios that I had thought of for the next day. I switched off. His final formulation was straightforward.

'You are strong enough to win this on your own, but you aren't on your own, so it will be fine, Chris.'

31

Stage Nineteen: Friday 19 July, Bourg-d'Oisans to
Le Grand-Bornand, 204.5 kilometres

A big sprawl of a day: over 200 kilometres in length with a large amount of climbing. The stage didn't finish on top of a mountain but on a descent, so at least it shouldn't be the same GC battle as yesterday was with Alpe d'Huez. Still, it had the Col du Glandon and the Col de la Madeleine. We couldn't be sure.

We rode out preparing ourselves for the worst. Helpfully, the Glandon and Madeleine came early in the stage and everybody who was left from the team (minus Eddie and Kiri now) all pushed over as a unit.

The team rode so well. As G and Yogi were pulling up the climbs I was thinking, 'One of them has a fractured pelvis and the other weighs over 80 kilos.'

Throughout the tour we had talked about these final three big days as being decisive. Today, before the race began, I had even wondered if we would have the manpower to ride at the front for such a huge stage.

Pete, for instance, was really tired by now; he was the youngest on the team. So I was so relieved when we got over these two big climbs and we still had everyone with us.

Then Saxo came to the front and almost relieved us of our duties.

I couldn't work that out. I asked Nico on the radio what was going on. Had they decided to work with us to control the race? He figured out that they were riding for the team competition. This was an unexpected bonus for us.

As we approached the last climb the weather turned for the worse: very heavy rain and a thunderstorm. López was still with me, along with Richie.

I said to López at this point that Saxo were controlling things now and he didn't need to ride up here at a ridiculous pace. He was doing good work at this stage but he could afford to save his legs.

On that final climb, going up in the storm, I knew there would be attacks towards the top from Contador and Quintana and possibly Rodríguez. They would figure that it would be quicker to take the descent on their own and steal a few seconds. So I followed those attacks when they came and I was conscious that Contador was likely to take crazy risks in the wet. He started the descent very fast but it wasn't long before the rest of us had pushed on and kept him to roughly within 20 metres.

He saw that we weren't going to surrender and then he turned to us and gave us a look that said, 'I'm not going to keep pushing you on the wet corners. I'll back off.'

So no drama, really. In the end, Movistar's Rui Costa won the stage. All the GC riders rolled across the line 9 minutes later. Everything stayed the same.

I got on the massage table and Rozman said to me: 'Well, how are you? How was your day?'

Most days I would say, 'Fine, how was your day?' but today I felt different.

'Rozman, I'm actually feeling quite tired.'

I expected him to say, 'Okay, my friend, just relax. I'll go a bit easy here.'

Instead, he just buckled over and started laughing at me heartily. I looked at him with a question mark instead of a face. *What?*

He turned to me.

'You're amazing, you know that? You don't need to say anything else. Just shut up now. For the past eighteen days I asked how are you and every day you've said, "I'm good, how about you?" Well, it's about time you're tired. I'm glad to hear that you finally admit you're tired. I am a hundred per cent sure that each one of your rivals has been saying they are tired every evening for the last two weeks. So to hear you saying you're tired now? Well, lucky you! You've got nothing to complain about. Just relax and enjoy.'

I got it. I genuinely did feel the fatigue after the stage today. The Tour is tough and it takes its toll every day being in yellow. I just needed to get to the end now.

Tomorrow would hopefully be a short gift of a stage. In my mind it was just a 3-hour ride. I almost didn't need to pack any rice cakes into my pockets because it was so short. I would just bring along some gels. They are normally just a finishing product that I use closer towards the end of a stage, but tomorrow's race was only 125 kilometres. I would start eating at 50 kilometres so that would leave me with 75 remaining kilometres, which I could pretty much do on the gels alone. It was quite a nice feeling not to have another 200-kilometre stage. What was happening to me? Was I becoming obsessed with food and rest?

> Winner: Rui Costa
> Overall GC   1: Chris Froome
>   2: Alberto Contador +5 min 11 sec

Stage Twenty: Saturday 20 July, Annecy to Annecy-Semnoz, 125 kilometres

A short, hard day.

No puncture and no crash, but it was a day to survive. I felt I couldn't relax until it was over.

Once we had got on to the final climb I half admitted to myself that at this point it was going to be very difficult for me to lose the Tour.

Rodríguez and Quintana were among the first to attack on the early slopes and I had let them go; I knew that this was now the race for the podium. I looked back at Contador to see what his response was. He just looked down at the ground as if to say, 'I don't have anything today, I can't go after them. It's beyond me.'

At that point I felt well enough to make up my own mind: I was going after them myself. I released a lot of tension out of that acceleration and then I was off to the front. I hoped that this wouldn't be the end for me.

I did get a little carried away and went straight past Quintana and Rodríguez. I thought, 'Right, I'm going to keep going!'

After a minute or two it began to hurt. My energy levels dropped and the pedals got heavier. Quintana and Rodríguez came back and latched on to my wheel.

I made the attack after about 3 or 4 kilometres of the 10-kilometre final climb. After that, Rodríguez did the lion's share of the pulling. He asked me to come through and help him and I did once or twice but I could feel I was only slowing him down. I also thought to myself, 'I have the yellow jersey. What am I doing? I don't need to be pulling.' I started to feel rough at that moment but I wanted to try to stay on the back of those two guys. It was one of the hardest climbs I had experienced in the Tour, in the sense that I wasn't feeling great. I really regretted that cocky acceleration.

With 1 kilometre to go, Rodríguez eased the pace up on the front; the race for the stage had started. We looked at each other. I really didn't have anything left in the tank but I thought there might be a chance if I attacked. These two were so busy marking each other there was a chance I might slip through and ride away.

I made a very sluggish attack: I got out of my seat and the bike lurched forward slightly, but it wasn't long until Quintana had gone straight past me. Oh well.

Towards the final 20 kilometres or so I got on the radio to everyone in the team. Movistar had been working hard and our responsibilities once again had fortunately been taken over by another team. This was a bit of a relief but I said to the guys, 'We have 20 kilometres to go. We are going to finish this off properly. When we start dragging up towards the last climb we're going to put everyone on the front and let's ride as hard as we can into the bottom of the climb.'

In my eyes this was partially a safety measure, for the team to go as hard as they could in one long line. But it was also for ourselves; we needed to do it.

Closer and closer we got to the finish. I told the guys to get ready for it. 'We're going to move to the front in 1 kilometre – start lining up now. The finish line is just at the bottom of this climb and then we're done pulling in this Tour.'

They did a fantastic job. All of them. They lined out the race and made it extremely hard for everyone else building up into the climb.

A great way to knock off duty.

There was a story I was thinking of. Around ten years earlier I had gone down to a place called Howick in South Africa, which is where Nelson Mandela was arrested before he was tried.

All week I'd gone out training on my own, putting the big miles down.

There aren't many roads to choose from around Howick – it has a strange geography – so I had been riding a circuit which was about 200 kilometres long. It was one big loop of tarmac road around the whole area.

This day I had got through 150 kilometres of my loop. I was coming into the last hour or so, and was on the home run, when I hit a long, straight piece of road where I could see for a long way ahead of me and behind me. Up the road there was a group of young guys walking in my direction. They were around my own age, and there were six or seven of them on the left-hand side of the road.

As far as the eye could see there was just them and there was just me. As I got closer they fanned out and made a straight line across the road; a human barrier. I knew I was in trouble.

I was still 200 metres away and there wasn't a car in sight. We were in the middle of nowhere, just a crop farm on the right side of the road. I did the calculation: 'Okay, they'll take the bike. And I have a phone. They'll take that too, along with my glasses.' I had nothing else but they were certainly going to mug me.

I slowed down for a second, thinking through my options, although I think I already knew which one I was going to take. I could have rung for help. I could have gone backwards and ridden the whole loop I had just done, but there were no shortcuts linking one side of the route to the other – just farmland and a lake in the centre. It would take another five hours to get home.

I could have ridden for a distance back down the road and hung around there, come back in an hour and hope they would be gone. But this was Africa. People walk for ever.

My other option was to go forward.

I got my head low. I flicked down a couple of gears and I got out of the saddle. I started sprinting hard. My hands were gripping the dropped handlebars for dear life. Hard. Harder.

I picked out the two guys in the centre of the road. I aimed at the small gap between them. I got to within 10 metres and I roared like a beast.

'Aaaaarrrrrrrrrrrghhhhhhhhh!'

They did the calculations now. They would have to stop me with their bodies; I clearly wasn't going to slow down myself. On either side of them the guys on the flanks saw what was happening and started to close in. They were too late. In the last couple of metres I aimed myself at one of the two guys. Then, just at the final second, and just before impact, I went to his side. He flinched enough to open the gap a little more.

I made it straight through them. As I went past I felt their hands on me briefly but they came off just as quickly as they made contact. They had needed to get a hold of my handlebars, and although the guys coming in from the side had tried clawing at the bike, I had the momentum.

I stopped pedalling when I was a couple of hundred metres up the road. Coasting, I could feel the adrenaline racing through me. My heart was pumping in my throat and my stomach felt like I was just falling through space. I looked back at them and they looked at me. It was over. They weren't going to catch me.

I remember that day because in terms of common sense, in terms of the way the world runs, I had taken the least sensible course of action. However, I knew somehow even before I started thinking of my options that this was the option I would take.

Sometimes you have to live that way. Forget common sense, grab the handlebars, dip the head, push the legs and ride hard for the gap.

Tomorrow I would win the Tour de France. Most people, I hoped, would have enjoyed the race and not wondered how I had got to be there at all. The people who knew me would know that I had received a lot of help along the way and that I would always love those who were there for me. And they would also know that quiet grain of madness that runs through me. Some people who have never known me may tell each other that I cheated. Some of them may tell their readers the same.

I think back to that day in Howick. I know I am here today because I have that madness in me. I could have been the quiet guy who told you at the office party that he liked cycling on the weekends. I could have ridden the big loop of life doing the safe thing.

But I gave up everything, put my head down and rode hard for the gap. Tomorrow, credit me for that, at least.

WINNER: NAIRO QUINTANA

OVERALL GC   1: CHRIS FROOME

               2: NAIRO QUINTANA +5 MIN 03 SEC

*Stage Twenty-one: Sunday 21 July, Versailles to
Paris Champs-Élysées, 133.5 kilometres*

Last night the mechanics were still working on the bikes when we all went outside to join them and Dave B. served them the champagne.

It was a good touch, and really nice to be able to have a glass with everyone, just to say, 'We made it, guys.' The mechanics were still working as they did every night but we all knew Paris would just be a procession.

There was a small element I couldn't quite get my head around.

Hold off the champagne, Chris. At heart you are still Crash Froome. You might have got to this point but you haven't won the Tour yet. The cobbles on the Champs-Élysées are made for you to take a tumble on. It's very easy to have a mechanical there and the race doesn't exactly wait for you. All those traffic islands and photographers asking you to stop for photos coming into Paris with your arm around this person or that person? It's made for you to screw up. You'll run into someone holding a flag pointing you where to go, or the flower bed from Romandie will pop up on a road somewhere! They have old men on the streets of Paris, you know.

As an added bonus it was also the first time in Tour de France history that there would be a night-time finish on the Champs-Élysées.

I wasn't completely at ease that evening.

That morning at the hotel, before we flew up to Paris for the start in Versailles, Jeremy had come through to say congratulations. We had about twenty minutes together before the buses were to leave so we sat and talked.

There was a bit of a crowd forming outside in the hotel lobby, made up of people who wanted photos and autographs. For a bit of fun, and because everyone had seen me walk down from my room in my team tracksuit, cap and glasses, we decided to dress Jeremy up in my clothes and let him walk to the bus.

It was hilarious. He went out there and made a few scribbles on a few pieces of paper and people went along with it. I stood by, taking photos of him signing 'my' autographs.

Then he felt so guilty he had to come back in. Little kids were happily gazing up at him, tugging his sleeve to have a photo taken with him. We both felt guilty now, so we went back out there and brought each of them back in, where I give them all a proper autograph and picture.

Still, we had a few photos taken for posterity of me wearing Jeremy's clothes and Jeremy wearing my tracksuit. Afterwards, I thought more about how Jeremy and I are quite similar in some ways but there was one question that stuck to me, even on the day I was winning the Tour de France. Jeremy is seven years older than me. Was I really ageing that fast?

At the start of the stage, just after we left the Palace of Versailles, Joaquim 'Purito' Rodríguez pulled out some Cuban cigars as we were riding. He handed one to Quintana, one to myself and one to Peter Sagan – the winners of the Polka Dot (King of the Mountains), White (Best Young Rider), Yellow (GC) and Green (Points Leader) jerseys respectively. We didn't light them or anything but he just wanted a few photos of us with them.

Meanwhile, I was wearing some new yellow shoes that SIDI had provided for me for the final stage. They hadn't been worn in and they pinched a little. There was always something!

Before the race began – it was a late start – there had been a lot of waiting around because the organizers wanted us to arrive in the evening, when the sun had gone down. In the afternoon I sat on the bus, thinking about what I was going to say on the podium that evening. It was quite daunting thinking that somebody was going to hand me a microphone without asking any questions. They were just going to let me speak.

I decided I would begin my short speech in French, knowing the majority of the people on the sides of the streets would be French. I wanted to thank everyone who had supported the race, and I remember asking Nico along the way if what I hoped to say sounded right.

He said it was fine.

'I'm sure the people will be very happy that you're at least making an effort to say something in French. Quit worrying!'

I took his advice.

It is always a big deal who the first rider is on to the Champs-Élysées to begin the final circuits and I wanted that to be Richie because he had been there for me in the race when I most needed him. As we approached the famous Parisian avenue, I rode alongside Richie and said, 'Come on, let's go.' I went to the front with him glued to my wheel.

As we swung out of Place de la Concorde, I looked at Richie. 'Now you go.' He led us on to the Champs-Élysées. It was perfect and I could feel myself welling up; I felt so pleased for the whole team. I pointed out the planes trailing the French Tricolour over the Arc de Triomphe to Richie, holding back the tears. It really was a strong moment. We'd put so much into the last three weeks and this was finally it. Every guy had delivered some moments of heroism. This was the end, and seeing it nearly broke me.

Cycling around the Place Charles de Gaulle, I tried to soak up the carnival atmosphere as British flags mingled with French, Spanish and Colombian colours. But the finishing circuit was by no means easy. The section of the Champs-Élysées from the finish line to the Arc de Triomphe was on a gradual, painful incline, and each lap got quicker as the lead-out trains for the sprinters jostled for position. A brave breakaway attempt led by David Millar and Juan Antonio Flecha was up to 35 seconds ahead at one point, but they were eventually reeled in.

Kittel beat Cav in the final sprint. A few moments later, comfortably in the bunch as twilight replaced the golden sunset, all seven of us in Sky pulled alongside each other and linked arms. Together we crossed the line. We had done it.

At the line I had four schoolfriends from South Africa who had flown over especially: Matt Beckett, Simon Gaganakis, who was part of the St John's cycling club, Ricky Reynolds, also from St John's, and Anthony Holdcroft, or Anto as we called him, who I used to sit beside in maths, memorizing the sayings written on our classroom walls, instead of listening to our teacher.

Anto chose the moment to make a complete monkey of himself, live on television. He had given an interview to Orla Chennaoui from Sky Sports, who had asked them to introduce themselves and recall a few memories of times spent with me. Anto immediately went into a recital of the old saying we had learned off the wall: 'He who knows not, and knows not that he knows not is a fool, shun him. He who knows not and knows that he knows not is a child, teach him. He who knows and knows not he knows is asleep, wake him. He who knows and knows that he knows is wise, follow him.'*

Well, he attempted it, but made a mess of it after about ten seconds and then heard a voice saying, 'We'll need to cut this!'

Poor man. But we were all in tears at the line. It was so special to have them there.

I was standing on the podium. The Arc de Triomphe was illuminated behind me in glowing yellow with the historic numbers '100'

---

* Anto, if you ever read this, I wrote this quote without looking it up!

projected majestically on to its surface. In between its arches the giant Tricolore blew lightly in the wind.

On the podium I wanted to talk about Mum, to express my sadness that she couldn't be with us. I knew she would have been so happy to see me standing there.

'*It's a great shame she never got to come see the Tour, but I'm sure she'd be extremely proud if she were here tonight. Without her encouragement to follow my dreams, I'd probably be at home watching this event on TV.*'

I dedicated my victory to her.

The next thing was to thank everyone. There were so many people who had helped me along the way and so many people who had given me chances. The list went on and on, from Kinjah to Team Sky. I couldn't stand there and rattle off a phone directory of names. And what if I left somebody out? So I just summed it up by saying a massive thanks to everyone who had helped me along the road from Karen to Paris.

'*I would like to thank my teammates who buried themselves day-in, day-out, to keep this yellow jersey on my shoulders and the Team Sky management for believing in me and building this team around me. Thank you to all the people who have taken the time to teach me over the years. Finally, I'd like to thank my close friends and family for being there for me every step of the way . . .*'

One thing I expressed – though maybe not enough – was my feeling for the team.

Michelle, of course, deserved special mention. A year ago when I came 2nd she was back at the team bus, not allowed to come close to the podium. She had given up her job and life, and dedicated herself to helping me achieve my goals and dreams. She had supported me, protected me and defended me as only she could and I wanted to thank her. When I saw her run on to the Champs-Élysées, straight after I crossed the line, it was a moment that I will never forget; we had both given so much to get to this point.

I wanted to finish with a reference to the past and to the future. This was the one-hundredth staging of the Tour de France. It was the first staging after the final act of the dark Lance Armstrong era. It was a surreal moment, standing there in the spotlights, surrounded by close to complete darkness, the Arc de Triomphe lit up behind me.

'This is a beautiful country and it hosts the biggest annual sporting event on the planet. To win the 100th edition is an honour . . . this is one yellow jersey that will stand the test of time.'

Those twelve final words meant the most. After one hundred races, the Tour starts anew. We begin making fresh history. No footnotes. No asterisks. Days that will stand the test of time.

Asante sana.

WINNER: MARCEL KITTEL
FINAL GC   1: CHRIS FROOME
           2: NAIRO QUINTANA +4 min 20 sec

Glossary

Swahili

asante sana – thank you
askari – night watchman
bakkie – pickup truck
boda boda – bicycle taxi
bwana – Sir
kijana – youngster
manyatta – village
matatu – colourfully painted taxi
murungaru – gangly kid
mzungu – someone of European descent
panga – machete
posho – powdered maize
shamba – garden
shúkà – traditional red dress of the Masai
sukuma wiki – leafy green vegetable stew
ugali – maize-flour porridge

Cycling Terms

aero bars – handlebars, often used in time trial races, to reduce a cyclist's wind resistance. A cyclist places his or her forearms in a pair of bars in the centre of the handlebars.

aero helmet – a streamlined helmet designed to reduce wind drag. Often used in time trials.

broom wagon – the vehicle that follows at the back of a road race behind the peloton and the team cars. Picks up struggling riders who are unable to make it to the finish.

cadence – the rate at which a cyclist pedals, measured in revolutions per minute.

categorized climb – most climbs in cycling are designated from category one (hardest) to category four (easiest), based on both steepness and length.

chainring – the large cog carrying the chain on a bike, which transfers energy to the wheel. A chainring consists of one or more sprockets – profiled wheels with teeth or cogs that engage with the links of the bike's chain. These are in turn driven by the crank arms and pedals.

classics – one-day professional cycling road races. The Five Monuments of Cycling are generally considered to be the oldest and the most prestigious classics: Milan–San Remo, the Tour of Flanders, Paris–Roubaix, Liège–Bastogne–Liège and the Giro di Lombardia.

commissaire – a cycling race official.

compact gearing – compact cranks and chainrings are normally smaller in size than traditional gearing set-ups, offering a lower low gear. This can help when climbing.

criterium – a multiple-lap race around a short distance course.

deep section wheel – a wheel with a deep rim which is more aerodynamic, and which is subject to less drag. Commonly used in time trials.

derailleur – a mechanism that changes gears by lifting the chain from one sprocket to the next.

directeur sportif – team manager, or the person who directs a professional cycling team during a road-racing stage.

domestique – a rider who works for and supports other riders in their team.

dossard – the number on the back of a cyclist's jersey.

EPO – a performance-enhancing drug. Erythropoietin (EPO) is a naturally occurring glycoprotein hormone which can also be manufactured. When injected under the skin it can stimulate red blood cell production to increase athletic endurance.

equipiér – a team member.

flamme rouge – a red banner that marks 1 kilometre to the finish line.

General Classification (GC) – the overall classification during a stage race. The winner of the race is the rider with the best overall time after all stages.

gruppetto – the group of riders behind the peloton.

Grand Tour – the three major European stage races are referred to as Grand Tours: the Tour de France, the Giro d'Italia and the Vuelta a España.

hematocrit level – the percentage of red blood cells in blood.

maillot à pois rouges (polka dot jersey) – worn by the leader of the mountains qualification in a stage race. In the Tour de France, this is also known as the King of the Mountains classification.

maillot blanc (white jersey) – worn by the best-placed rider under 26 years of age at the Tour de France, and other stage races.

maillot jaune (yellow jersey) – worn by the overall leader on GC in the Tour de France, and other stage races.

maglia rosa (pink jersey) – worn by the overall leader on GC in the Giro d'Italia.

maillot verte (green jersey) – worn by the leader in the points competition in the Tour de France and other stage races. Normally contended by sprinters.

neo-pro – a cyclist in their first year as a professional.

out-of-category climb – any climb that is harder than category one is designated as out-of-category or *hors catégorie* ('beyond categorization').

OVL – overlapped.

DNF – did not finish.

palmarès – a pro cyclist's list of achievements, showing their key race results.

pavé – paved road surface, often known as 'cobbles'.

peloton – the main group of riders in a cycling race. Also known as the pack or bunch.

skewer – the rod mechanism that attaches a wheel to a bike.

soigneur – a person who assists the riders in a team. Jobs include massage, support during races and training, transportation, and the organization of accommodation, equipment, food and other supplies.

SRM power meter – a device fitted to a bike to measure the power output of a rider.

TUE – therapeutic use exemption.

turbo trainer – equipment used to warm up before a race or to train indoors on a stationary bike. Some trainers consist of a clamp to secure the bike, a roller that presses up against the rear wheel and a mechanism that offers resistance to pedal against.

UCI – the International Cycling Union.

Acknowledgements

Thank you to David Walsh, for taking the time to get to know me and for writing a book that truly reflects my character. I've enjoyed sharing my life with you and appreciate the friendship and guidance that you've given me over the last few months. Thank you for believing in me.

Thank you to my wife to be, Michelle, for your dedication in seeing this project through. Without your commitment this book would not have happened, at least not in the next ten years. You have been instrumental in the development of my career over the last few years, and I would not be where I am today without you.

Thank you to everyone who wants to read my story and to get to know me beyond what they see at the Tour de France in July. This book is for you. I hope you enjoy it!